CSS3

SIXTH EDITION

JASON CRANFORD TEAGUE

Peachpit Press

Visual QuickStart Guide
CSS3
Sixth Edition
Jason Cranford Teague

Peachpit Press
www.peachpit.com

Find us on the Web at www.peachpit.com
To report errors, please send a note to errata@peachpit.com
Peachpit Press is a division of Pearson Education

Project Editor: Nancy Peterson
Development Editor: Bob Lindstrom
Copyeditors: Liz Merfeld and Darren Meiss
Production Editor: Katerina Malone
Compositor: David Van Ness
Indexer: Jack Lewis
Cover Design: RHDG / Riezebos Holzbaur Design Group, Peachpit Press
Interior Design: Peachpit Press
Logo Design: MINE™ www.minesf.com

ISBN 13: 978-0-321-88893-8
ISBN10:   0-321-88893-6

9 8 7 6 5 4 3 2 1

Printed and bound in the United States of America

Dedication

For Jocelyn and Dashiel, the two most dynamic forces in my life.

http://960.gs {for grid template

Special Thanks to:

Tara, my soul mate and best critic.

Dad and **Nancy** who made me who I am.

Uncle Johnny, for his unwavering support.

Pat and **Red**, my two biggest fans.

Nancy P., who kept the project going.

Bob, Darren, and **Liz**, who dotted my i's and made sure that everything made sense.

Thomas, who was always there when I needed help.

Heather, who gave me a chance when I needed it most.

Judy, Boyd, Dr. G and teachers everywhere who care. Keep up the good work.

Charles Dodgson (aka Lewis Carroll), for writing *Alice's Adventures in Wonderland*.

John Tenniel & Arthur Rackham, for their incredible illustrations of *Alice's Adventures in Wonderland*.

Douglas Adams, H.P. Lovecraft, Neil Gaiman, Philip K. Dick, and **Carl Sagan** whose teachings and writings inspire me every day.

BBC 6 Music, The Craig Charles Funk and Soul Show, Rasputina, Electric Six, Cake, Client, Jonathan Coulton, Cracker, Nine Inch Nails, Bitter:Sweet, Metric, Captain Sensible, HIDE, Origa, Richard Hawley, the Pogues, New Model Army, Cocteau Twins, Dead Can Dance, the Sisters of Mercy, the Smiths, Mojo Nixon, Bauhaus, Lady Tron, David Bowie, Bad Religion, The Black Belles, T. Rex, Bad Religion, Dr. Rubberfunk, Smoove and Turell, Dury, The Kinks, This Mortal Coil, Rancid, Monty Python, the Dead Milkmen, New Order, Regina Spektor, The Sex Pistols, Beethoven, Bach, Brahms, Handel, Mozart, Liszt, Vivaldi, Holst, Synergy, and **Garrison Keillor** (for *The Writer's Almanac*) whose noise helped keep me from going insane while writing this book.

Contents at a Glance

Table of Contents

Introduction

These days, everyone is a Web designer. Whether you are adding a comment to a Facebook page, creating your own blog, or building a Fortune 50 Web site, you are involved in Web design.

As the Web expands, everyone from PTA presidents to presidents of multinational corporations is using this medium to get messages out to the world because the Web is the most effective way to communicate your message to the people around you and around the world.

Knowing how to design for the Web isn't always about designing complete Web sites. Many people are creating simple Web pages for auction sites, their own photo albums, or their blogs. So, whether you are planning to redesign your corporate Web site or place your kid's graduation pictures online, learning Cascading Style Sheets (CSS) is your next step into the larger world of Web design.

What Is This Book About?

HTML is how Web pages are structured. CSS is how Web pages are designed. This book deals primarily with how to use CSS to add a visual layer to the HTML structure of your Web pages.

CSS is a style sheet language; that is, it is *not* a programming language. Instead, it's code that tells a device (usually a Web browser) how the content in a file should be displayed. CSS is meant to be easily understood by anyone, not just "computer people." Its syntax is straightforward, basically consisting of rules that tell an element on the screen how it should appear.

This book also includes the most recent additions to the CSS language, commonly referred to as CSS3 (or CSS Level 3). CSS3 builds on and extends the previous version of CSS. For the time being, it's important to understand what is new in CSS3 because some browsers (most notably Internet Explorer) have incomplete support or no support for these new features.

CSS3 Visual QuickStart Guide has three parts:

- **CSS Introduction and Syntax (Chapters 1–4)**—This section lays the foundation you require to understand how to assemble basic style sheets and apply them to a Web page. It also gives you a crash course in HTML5.

- **CSS Properties (Chapters 5–12)**—This section contains all the styles and values that can be applied to the elements that make up your Web pages.

- **Working with CSS (Chapters 13–15)**—This section gives advice and explains best practices for creating Web pages and Web sites using CSS.

Who is this book for?

To understand this book, you need to be familiar with HTML (Hypertext Markup Language). You don't have to be an expert, but you should know the difference between a `<p>` element and a `<br>` tag. That said, the more knowledge of HTML you bring to this book, the more you'll get out of it.

Chapter 2 deals briefly with HTML5, bringing you up to date on the latest changes. If you are already familiar with HTML, this chapter has everything you will need to get going.

What tools do you need for this book?

The great thing about CSS is that, like HTML, it doesn't require any special or expensive software. Its code is just text, and you can edit it with programs as simple as TextEdit (Mac OS) or Notepad (Windows).

Why Standards (Still) Matter

The idea of a standard way to communicate over the Internet was the principle behind the creation of the World Wide Web: You should be able to transmit information to any computer anywhere in the world and display it in the way the author intended. In the beginning, only one form of HTML existed, and everyone on the Web used it. This situation didn't present any real problem because almost everyone used Mosaic, the first popular graphics-based browser, and Mosaic was the standard. That, as they say, was then.

Along came Netscape Navigator and the first HTML extensions were born. These extensions worked only in Netscape, however, and anyone who didn't use that browser was out of luck. Although the Netscape extensions defied the standards of the World Wide Web Consortium (W3C), most of them—or at least some version of them—eventually became part of those very standards. According to some people, the Web has gone downhill ever since.

The Web is a very public form of discourse, the likes of which has not existed since people lived in villages and sat around the campfire telling stories every night. The problem is that without standards, not everyone in the global village can make it to the Web campfire. You can use as many bleeding-edge techniques as you like. You can include Flash, JavaScript, QuickTime video, Ajax, HTML5, or CSS3, but if only a fraction of browsers can see your work, you're keeping a lot of fellow villagers out in the cold.

When coding for this book, I spent 35 to 45 percent of my time trying to get the code to run as smoothly as possible in Internet Explorer, Firefox (and related Mozilla browsers), Opera, Safari, and Chrome. This timeframe holds true for most of my Web projects; much of the coding time is spent on cross-browser inconsistencies. If the browsers stuck to the standards, this time would be reduced to almost nothing. Your safest bet as a designer, then, is to know the standards of the Web, try to use them as much as possible, and demand that the browser manufacturers use them as well.

Values and Units Used in This Book

Throughout this book, you'll need to enter various values to define properties. These values take various forms, depending on the needs of the property. Some values are straightforward—a number is a number—but others have special units associated with them.

Values in angle brackets (< >) represent one type of value (**Table i.1**) that you will need to choose, such as <length> (a length value like **12px**) or <color> (a color value). Words that appear in code font are literal values and should be typed exactly as shown, such as **normal**, *italic*, or **bold**.

Length values

Length values come in two varieties:

- **Relative values**, which vary depending on the computer being used (**Table i.2**).

- **Absolute values**, which remain constant regardless of the hardware and software being used (**Table i.3**).

I generally recommend using ems to describe font sizes for the greatest stability between operating systems and browsers.

TABLE i.1 Value Types

Value Type	What It Is	Example
<number>	A number	1, 2, 3
<length>	A measurement of distance or size	1in
<color>	A chromatic expression	red
<percentage>	A proportion	35%
<URL>	The absolute or relative path to a file on the Internet	http://www.mySite.net/images/01.jpg

TABLE i.2 Relative Length Values

Unit	Name	What It Is	Example
em	Em	Relative to the current font size (similar to percentage)	3em
ex	x-height	Relative to the height of lowercase letters in the font	5ex
px	Pixel	Relative to the monitor's resolution	125px

TABLE i.3 Absolute Length Values

Unit	Name	What It Is	Example
pt	Point	72pt = 1inch	12pt
pc	Picas	1pc = 12pt	3pc
mm	Millimeters	1mm = .24pc	25mm
cm	Centimeters	1cm = 10mm	5.1cm
in	Inches	1in = 2.54cm	8.25in

Color values

You can describe color on the screen in a variety of ways, but most of these descriptions are just different ways of telling the computer how much red, green, and blue are in a particular color.

Chapter 7 provides an extensive explanation of color values.

Percentages

Many of the properties in this book have a percentage as their values. The behavior of each percentage value depends on the property in use.

URLs

A Uniform Resource Locator (URL) is the unique address of something on the Web. This resource could be an HTML document, a graphic, a CSS file, a JavaScript file, a sound or video file, a CGI script, or any of a variety of other file types. URLs can be local—describing the location of the resource relative to the current document—or global—describing the absolute location of the resource on the Web and beginning with *http://*.

Reading This Book

For the most part, the text, tables, figures, code, and examples should be self-explanatory. But you need to know a few things in advance to understand this book.

CSS value tables

Each section that explains a CSS property includes a quick-reference table of the values that the property can use, as well as the browsers compatible with those values **A**. **Table i.4** lists the browser icons and abbreviations used in this book.

TABLE i.4 Browser Abbreviations

Icon	Abbreviation	Browser
@	IE	Microsoft Internet Explorer
😃	FF	Mozilla Firefox
🅾	Op	Opera
🔵	Sa	Apple Safari
🔵	Ch	Google Chrome

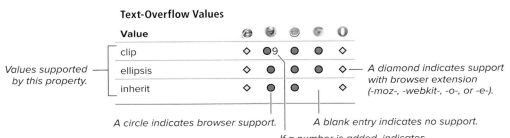

Text-Overflow Values

Value	@	😃	🔵	🔵	🅾
clip	◇	●9	●	●	◇
ellipsis	◇	●	●	●	◇
inherit	◇	●	●		◇

Values supported by this property.

A diamond indicates support with browser extension (-moz-, -webkit-, -o-, or -e-).

A circle indicates browser support.

A blank entry indicates no support.

If a number is added, indicates support is recent since that version.

A The property tables show you the values available with a property, the earliest browser version in which the value is available, and with which version of CSS the value was introduced.

The Code

For clarity and precision, this book uses several layout techniques to help you see the difference between the text of the book and the code.

Code looks like this:

```
<style type="text/css">
p { font-size: 12pt; }
</style>
```

All code in this book is presented in lowercase. In addition, quotes in the code always appear as straight quotes (" or '), not curly quotes (" or '). There is a good reason for this distinction. Curly quotes (also called smart quotes) will cause the code to fail.

When you type a line of code, the computer can run the line as long as needed; but in this book, lines of code have to be broken to make them fit on the page. When that happens, you'll see a gray arrow →, indicating that the line of code is continued from above, like this:

```
.title { font: bold 28pt/26pt times,
→ serif; color: #FFF; background
→ color: #000; background-image:
→ url(bg_title.gif); }
```

A numbered step often includes a line of code in red from the main code block:

```
p { color: red; }
```

This is a reference to help you pinpoint where that step applies in the larger code block that accompanies the task. This code will be highlighted in red in the code listing to help you more easily identify it.

Web Site for This Book

I hope you'll be using a lot of the code from this book in your Web pages, and you are free to use any code in this book without asking my permission (although a mention of the book is always appreciated). However, be careful—retyping information can lead to errors. Some books include a CD-ROM containing all the code from the book, and you can copy it from that disc. But guess who pays for that CD? You do. And CDs aren't cheap.

But if you bought this book, you already have access to the largest resource of knowledge that ever existed: the Web. And that's exactly where you can find the code from this book.

My support site for this Visual QuickStart Guide is at *www.jasonspeaking.com/css3vqs*.

This site includes all the code you see in the book, as well as quick-reference charts. You can download the code and any important updates and corrections from this site.

Understanding CSS3

Cascading Style Sheets, or CSS, is a language used to specify the visual appearance of a Web page—in contrast to HTML (HyperText Markup Language), which is a markup language that defines the structure of a document for distribution on the Web. HTML tells a Web browser how the content is organized on the page, whereas CSS tells the browser how it should look.

CSS3—an abbreviation for CSS Level 3—is the next generation of this style language that adds several new capabilities. CSS3 has taken its place alongside HTML5 at the forefront of all cutting-edge Web design.

In This Chapter

What Is a Style?

Word processors allow writers to change text appearance word-by-word or paragraph-by-paragraph, as well as in an entire document by means of *styles*.

Styles combine multiple properties—such as weight, font family, italicization, color, and size—that you want to apply to similar text types—titles, headers, captions, and so on—and they group these properties under a common name.

For example, suppose you want to format all the section titles in your document in bold, Georgia font, italic, orange, and 16 point. You could assign all those attributes to a style called Chapter Title 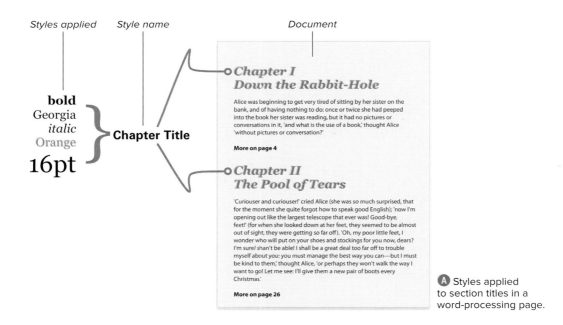.

Whenever you type a chapter title, you only need to use the Chapter Title style, and all those attributes are applied to the text in one fell swoop. Even better, if you later decide that you really want all of those titles in 18 point instead of 16 point, you can just change the definition of Section Title. The word processor automatically changes the appearance of all the text marked with that style throughout the document.

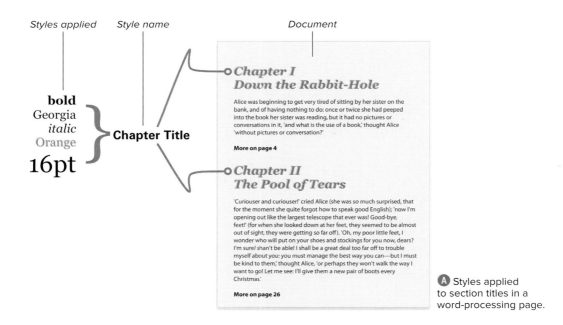

Styles applied   *Style name*   *Document*

bold
Georgia
italic
Orange
16pt

Chapter Title

Chapter I
Down the Rabbit-Hole

Alice was beginning to get very tired of sitting by her sister on the bank, and of having nothing to do: once or twice she had peeped into the book her sister was reading, but it had no pictures or conversations in it, 'and what is the use of a book,' thought Alice 'without pictures or conversation?'

More on page 4

Chapter II
The Pool of Tears

'Curiouser and curiouser!' cried Alice (she was so much surprised, that for the moment she quite forgot how to speak good English); 'now I'm opening out like the largest telescope that ever was! Good-bye, feet!' (for when she looked down at her feet, they seemed to be almost out of sight, they were getting so far off). 'Oh, my poor little feet, I wonder who will put on your shoes and stockings for you now, dears? I'm sure! shan't be able! I shall be a great deal too far off to trouble myself about you: you must manage the best way you can—but I must be kind to them,' thought Alice, 'or perhaps they won't walk the way I want to go! Let me see: I'll give them a new pair of boots every Christmas.'

More on page 26

A Styles applied to section titles in a word-processing page.

What Are Cascading Style Sheets?

Cascading Style Sheets bring the same style-setting convenience to the Web that you have in most word processors. You can set the CSS in one central location to affect the appearance of specific HTML tags, on a single Web page, or across an entire Web site.

Although CSS works with HTML, it is not HTML. Rather, CSS is a separate *style sheet language* that enhances the abilities of HTML (a *markup* language) by allowing you to redefine the way that existing tags display their contents.

For example, the level 1 header tag container, `<h1>...</h1>`, allows you to apply styles to a section of HTML text and turn it into a header. But the exact display of the header is determined by the viewer's browser, not by the HTML code.

Using CSS, you can change the nature of the header tag so that it is displayed as you want it to look—for example, bold, Times font, italic, orange and 36 pixels (px) **Ⓐ**. As when using word processor styles, you could choose to change the styling of the `<h1>` tag (for example, change the text size to 18 px) and automatically change the text size of all **h1** elements on the affected Web page.

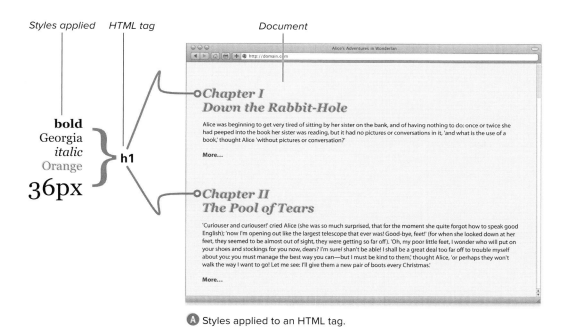

Ⓐ Styles applied to an HTML tag.

Table 1.1 shows some of the things you can do with CSS and where to find more information in this book.

How does CSS work?

When a visitor loads a Web page, either by typing in the URL address or clicking a link, the server (the computer that stores the Web page) sends the HTML file to the visitor's computer along with any files linked to or embedded in the HTML file. Regardless of where the CSS code is, the visitor's browser will interpret it and apply it to the HTML to render the Web page using that browser's particular *rendering engine*. Then the results are displayed in the browser window .

B The code used to create the Web page is downloaded, interpreted, and rendered by the browser to create the final display.

TABLE 1.1 CSS Properties

Property	What You Control	For More Info, See:
Background	Color or image behind the page or behind a single element on the page	Chapter 7
Box	Margins, padding, outline, borders, width, height	Chapter 10
Color	Text color	Chapter 7
Font	Letter form, size, boldface, italic	Chapter 5
Generated content	Counting and quotes	Chapter 9
Lists	Bullets and numbering	Chapter 8
Table	Table borders, margins, captions	Chapter 8
Text	Kerning, leading, alignment, case	Chapter 6
Transformations	Moving, rotating, skewing	Chapter 12
Transitions	Changing styles over time	Chapter 12
UI	Cursor	Chapter 9
Visual effect	Visibility, visible area, opacity	Chapter 11
Visual formatting	Position and placement	Chapter 11

C An HTML page using CSS to add an image in the background. Position the content down and to the right, and format the text.

D The same code displayed without the benefit of CSS. The page still displays but without the formatting shown in **C**.

The interpretation by the browser's rendering engine is where your headaches begin. The World Wide Web Consortium (W3C) has gone to great lengths to create specifications by which browser developers should render the Web code. Nonetheless, bugs, omissions, and misinterpretations still creep in. As a result, no two browsers render a Web page in exactly the same way. For the most part, these differences go unnoticed by most users, but occasionally the differences are glaring and require that you do some extra work to get the page to look right with the broadest range of browsers.

You always face the possibility that your page will be rendered *without* the CSS because of an error or because the software in use—such as many mobile device browsers—does not accommodate CSS. You should always consider how your page will look without the CSS styles, and make sure that the page will still make structural sense, as shown in **C** and **D**.

The Evolution of CSS

Over the years, CSS has evolved into its current form under the guidance of the W3C, but the process has often been slow. Although CSS is a standard—created by the W3C's CSS Working Group—it is up to each browser to interpret and implement that standard. This has led to uneven implementation, with some browsers more compliant than others 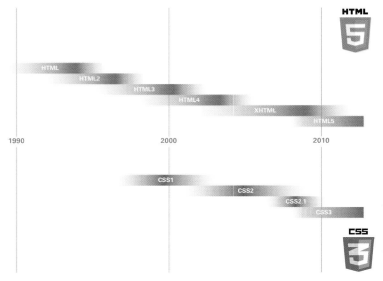.

Even more troublesome is that, although the standard strives to be as clear and specific as possible, different browsers will implement the specifications with slightly different quirks.

All modern browsers (Internet Explorer, Firefox, Safari, Opera) support the important capabilities of CSS3; but even after years of development, CSS3 remains a work in progress. Many features—such as transitions, transformations, and animation—are still not implemented or are underdeveloped in some browsers.

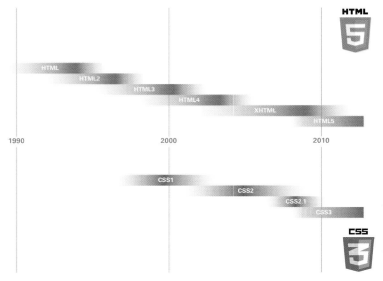

Ⓐ The evolutionary paths of HTML and CSS have not been particularly even or steady over the years. This timeline is not meant to be an exact historical chart, but does provide a general recount of when each version of the standard was in its prime.

CSS Level 1 (CSS1)

The W3C released the first official version of CSS in 1996. This early version included the core capabilities associated with CSS, such as the ability to format text, set fonts, and set margins. Netscape 4 and Internet Explorer 3 and 4 supported Level 1.

Web designers needed a way to position elements on the screen precisely. CSS1 was already released, and CSS Level 2 was still in the future, so the W3C released a stopgap solution: CSS-Positioning. This standard proposed that the parties concerned could debate the details for awhile before the CSS-P standard became official. Netscape and Microsoft jumped on these proposals, however, and included the preliminary ideas in version 4 of their browsers.

CSS Level 2 (CSS2)

The CSS2 spec came out in 1998 and is the most widely adopted by browser makers. Level 2 includes all the attributes of the previous two versions, plus an increased emphasis on international accessibility and the capability to specify media-specific CSS.

In 2006, the W3C published an updated version: CSS Level 2.1, that corrected some errors, clarified a few issues, and included specifications for features that were already implemented in some browsers. CSS2.1 effectively replaced CSS2.

CSS Level 3 (CSS3)

Unlike CSS1 and 2, a single, comprehensive CSS3 does not exist. Instead, rather than trying to release the entire specification at once, the CSS Working Group split the spec into a series of modules, each with its own developmental timeline. To read more about the ongoing work, check out *www.w3.org/Style/CSS/current-work*.

TIP While knowing the differences among the CSS versions may be interesting, it isn't necessary for using styles on the Web. However, you do need to know which styles are supported by the browsers you're designing for. Although all modern browsers support most of the CSS Level 2 specification, older browsers support combinations of older versions of CSS. See Appendix A for details on which CSS properties each browser supports.

CSS and HTML

When HTML was created, style properties were defined directly in the code. However, rather than just adding more and more tags and properties to HTML, the W3C introduced Cascading Style Sheets to fill the design void in straight HTML, allowing the Web to become semantic in structure. (See the sidebar "What Is the World Wide Web Consortium?")

Take the `<strong>` tag, for example. In HTML, this common tag does one thing and one thing only: It makes text "stronger," usually by displaying it in bolder font. However, using CSS, you can "redefine" the `<strong>` tag so that it not only makes text bolder, but also adds more emphasis by displaying text in all caps and in a specific font. You could even set the `<strong>` tag to not make text bold .

Although both HTML and CSS have evolved over the years, they have rarely evolved in tandem. Instead, each standard has pretty much followed its own path. It's a happy accident that both CSS3 and HTML5 have hit prime time at the same time, creating the new foundation and framework for modern Web sites.

The power of CSS comes from its ability to mix-and-match rules from multiple sources to tailor your Web pages' layouts to your exact needs. In some ways, it resembles computer programming—which is not too surprising, because a lot of this stuff was created by programmers, rather than Web designers. But once you get the hang of it, "speaking" CSS becomes as natural as putting together a sentence 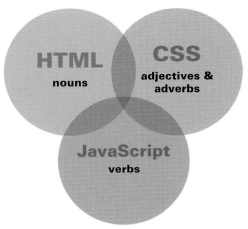.

A The HTML `<strong>` tag is used to make text stand out; but using CSS, you can style that text any way you see fit.

B The three core Web technologies—HTML, CSS, and JavaScript—work similarly to parts of speech. HTML provides the nouns, CSS the adjectives and adverbs, and JavaScript adds the verbs.

Types of CSS Rules

The best thing about Cascading Style Sheets is that they are amazingly simple to set up. They don't require plug-ins or fancy software—just text files with rules in them. A CSS rule defines what the HTML should look like and how it should behave in the browser window.

CSS rules come in four types, each with specific uses:

- **HTML selector:** The text portion of an HTML tag is called the selector. For example, **h1** is the selector for the **<h1>** tag. The HTML selector is used in a CSS rule to redefine how the tag displays. (See "(Re)Defining HTML Tags" in Chapter 3). For example:

  `h1 { color: red; }`

  will style:

  `<h1>...</h1>`

- **Class selector:** A class is a "free agent" rule that can be applied to any HTML tag at your discretion. You can name the class almost anything you want. Because a class can be applied to multiple HTML tags, it is the most versatile type of selector. (See "Defining Reusable Classes" in Chapter 3.) For example, the class:

  `.myClass { font: bold 1.25em times; }`

  will style the tag:

  `<h1 class="myClass">...</h1>`

continues on next page

- **ID selector:** Much like class selectors, ID rules can be applied to any HTML tag. ID selectors, however, should be applied only once to a particular HTML tag on a given page to create an object for use with a JavaScript function. For example, the ID:

```
#myObject1 { position: absolute;
→ top: 10px; }
```

will style the tag:

```
<h1 id="myObject1">...</h1>
```

- **Universal selector:** The universal selector is a stand-in selector represented by an asterisk (*) that is used when you want to apply a style regardless of the exact selector in use. This is especially helpful when you are using contextual styles and don't know the exact context. For example, the universal selector:

```
article * strong { position:
→ absolute; top: 10px; }
```

will style the strong tag in:

```
<article><p><strong>...</strong>
→ </p></article>
```

as well as in:

```
<article><blockquote><strong>...
→ </strong></blockquote></article>
```

What Is the World Wide Web Consortium?

The World Wide Web Consortium (www.w3.org) is an organization that sets many of the standards that browser developers will use to create their products, including HTML and CSS (with the notable exception of JavaScript).

Created in 1994, the W3C's mission is "to lead the World Wide Web to its full potential by developing protocols and guidelines that ensure the long-term growth of the Web."

The W3C comprises more than 350 member organizations around the world. These organizations include vendors of technology products and services, content providers, corporate users, research laboratories, standards bodies, and governments.

According to its Web site, the W3C has four goals:

- **Web for Everyone** —To make the Web accessible to all people by promoting technologies that take into account the vast differences in culture, education, ability, material resources, and physical limitations of users on all continents.
- **Web on Everything** —To allow all devices easy access to the Web. Although most access is still through desktop or laptop computers, an increasing array of devices can access the Web.
- **Knowledge Base**—To develop an environment that permits each user to make the best use of the resources available on the Web.
- **Trust and Confidence**—To guide the Web's development with careful consideration for the novel legal, commercial, and social issues raised by this technology.

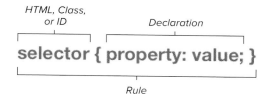

HTML, Class, or ID — selector

Declaration — { property: value; }

Rule

A The basic syntax of a CSS rule. You start with a selector (HTML, Class, or ID). Then add a property, a value for that property, and a semicolon, which together are called a *declaration*. You can add as many definitions as you need as long as they are separated by a semicolon.

The Parts of a CSS Rule

A CSS rule consists of properties and their values, which together are referred to as a *declaration* **A**. A single CSS rule can have multiple declarations, each separated by a semicolon (;). All rules, regardless of their locations or types, have the following structural elements:

- **Selectors** are the alphanumeric characters that identify a rule. A selector can be an HTML tag selector, a class selector, an ID selector, a universal selector (discussed in Chapter 3), or a combination of those basic selectors to create context-based styles (discussed in Chapter 4).

- **Properties** identify what is being defined. Several dozen properties are available. Each is responsible for an aspect of the page content's behavior and appearance.

- **Values** are assigned to a property to define its nature. A value can be a keyword such as "red," a number, or a percentage. The type of value used depends solely on the property to which it is assigned.

TIP Don't confuse the selector of an HTML tag with its attributes. In the following tag, for example:

`<img src="picture.gif">`

img is the selector, and src is a property.

TIP Although you don't have to include a semicolon with the last definition in a list, experience shows that adding this semicolon can prevent future headaches. For example, if you forgot to put in the required semicolon before the addition and you later decide to add a new definition to the rule, you may cause the rule to fail completely. What's worse, not only will that one definition fail, but all the definitions in the rule won't be applied.

CSS Browser Extensions

In addition to supporting the specified CSS properties set by the W3C, a browser developer will occasionally introduce browser-specific properties. This is often done for one of two reasons:

- A spec is still under development by the W3C but the browser developer wants to start using the style now.

- The browser developer wants to try a new idea but doesn't want to wait for the W3C to accept it and begin work on it, which can take years.

Sometimes the exact syntax of the official CSS specification will be slightly different from the "sandbox" version created for a specific browser.

To avoid confusion and ensure forward compatibility of CSS code, each rendering engine has adapted its own prefix to use with CSS properties that are extensions unique to that browser. The prefixes for each browser are shown in **Table 1.2**.

TABLE 1.2 CSS Browser Extensions

Extension	Rendering Engine	Browser(s)	Example
-webkit-	Webkit	Safari, Chrome	-webkit-transition
-moz-	Mozilla	Firefox	-moz-transition
-o-	Presto	Opera	-o-transition
-ms-	Trident	Internet Explorer	-ms-transition
TimeToText (time)	The text equivalent of the supplied time, for use with formulas involving text or text-oriented functions		

```
selector {    -moz-property: value;
              -wekit-property: value;
              -o-property: value;
              -ms-property: value;
              property: value; }
```

Ⓐ The browser CSS extensions can all be included to ensure a style is applied when available to a particular browser.

These CSS extensions sometimes overlap and conflict when different browsers promote their own solutions. The good news is that due to the nature of CSS, you can include versions of each of the properties for individual browsers, so that the browser will use whichever version suits it Ⓐ. Throughout the book, I include browser CSS extensions, when appropriate, so that you can ensure the widest interoperability of your styles.

TIP **Most browser manufacturers will drop an extension version of a style within two releases after they adopt the official version. This practice allows designers to catch up before their style sheets stop working.**

One Webkit to Rule Them All? No, Just Don't Be Lazy.

One disturbing trend in Web design is for developers to simply rely on Webkit browser extensions, and ignore other browsers. There is little doubt that Webkit has been the leader in many new innovations. As a result, designers who want to use cutting-edge technologies are not using *progressive enhancement* to ensure cross browser functionality, even where that functionality is available in those other browsers using their own browser extension.

For example, rather than include transition code for all browsers, some developers include it only for Webkit and leave other browsers out in the cold. This is a huge mistake, because neglecting Internet Explorer, Firefox, and even Opera alienates a sizable chunk of your audience.

To complicate matters, Microsoft, Firefox, and Opera have openly stated that they will begin to support the -webkit- extension, which defeats the purpose of having these extensions in the first place.

The problem, though, isn't with the browser developers—who just want to make sure people use their browsers—but with lazy Web developers who don't want to include a few extra lines of code to address cross-browser compatibility. But, you would never do that, right?

New in CSS3

This is a particularly exciting time to be a Web designer because we are about to get an entirely new box of tools. A lot of new CSS3 capabilities are ready for prime time and they will explode your creativity.

This slim volume covers the breadth of CSS3, much of which remains unchanged since CSS2/2.1. If you are an old hand at CSS, look for the "New in CSS3" mark  to quickly find the good, new stuff.

A The "New in CSS3" mark.

Here's a brief peak at what's new:

- **Animations**—Move objects without using JavaScript.

- **Borders**—Multiple border colors on a side, border images, and rounded corners can be applied.

- **Backgrounds**—Multiple backgrounds can be added to a single element, backgrounds can be more precisely positioned, backgrounds can be extended and clipped to the inside or outside of a border, and backgrounds can be resized.

- **Color**—Color opacity settings, gradients in backgrounds, and HSL color values are available.

- **Text**—Text shadows, text overflow, and word wrapping are available.

- **Transformations**—Scale, skew, move, and rotate an element in 2D or 3D space.

- **Transitions**—Use simple dynamic style transitions.

CSS4?

Believe it or not, the CSS Work Group has already started working on the next generation of CSS, appropriately named CSS4. While it is unlikely that it will be ready to affect your work for a couple of years, it's good to know that progress is being made.

The group is focusing on adding a variety of new selectors to better refine styling. One new selector that I am especially gratified to see is the `:local-link` pseudo-class. I've been lobbying for something like this for 15 years. The `:local-link` pseudo-class will finally give us the power to style links based on where you are within a Web site (current page or in a particular section) and differentiate between local and external links.

For more details, check out the working draft: www.w3.org/TR/2011/WD-selectors4-20110929/.

- **Box**—Add drop shadows, place user-resizable boxes, and set overflow separately in horizontal and vertical directions. Use outline offset to set the space between the outline and the border, and apply box model specifications to set how width and height are applied to a box.

- **Content**—Styles can add content to an element.

- **Opacity**—Elements can be transparent.

- **Media queries**—Style pages can be based on the viewport size, color, aspect ratio, resolution, and other important design considerations.

- **Web fonts**—These update and extend the ability to link to fonts for use in a design.

Not everything in the CSS3 specification is ready for use, though. When it would be "jumping the gun" to use new features right now, I've added a section near the end of some chapters called "Coming Soon!" that includes quick overviews of what to expect in the future.

2

HTML5 Primer

HTML is the coding language used to mark content types on the page and add structure using tags. Over the past 20 years or so, the language has changed—some tags were added, some removed, and some stayed exactly the same. HTML5 is the most recent version, adding tags to improve the ability to structure pages semantically, insert audio and video clips, and create more meaningful forms. Although mostly supported by all major Web browsers, there are still plenty of older browsers out there that do *not* support HTML5 at all. Fortunately, you can do something about that.

First, let's take a look at what markup languages are and how HTML5 fits into the new world order.

What Is HTML?

The HyperText Markup Language is a system of code *tags* that define *elements* on the page, which create the *structure* of a document for use on the Web. For example, you take a block of text Ⓐ and add HTML tags, as follows: Ⓑ

```
<h1>Alice's Adventures in
→ Wonderland</h1>
```

Here, you've used the `<h1>` tag to create a header element, which is the most important header for the page: the level 1 header. Different tags are used to tag different kinds of content, and tags can be *placed* within other tags. For example:

```
<p>I wonder if I shall fall right
→ <em>through</em> the earth!</p>
```

These tags tell the browser that the text is a paragraph, and the word "through" should be presented with emphasis, probably by displaying it in italics.

Ⓐ Plain text without any markup.

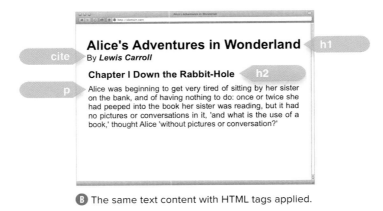

Ⓑ The same text content with HTML tags applied.

What Is a Markup Language?

HTML is used to mark up the structure of Web pages, but other markup languages are used by computers on the Web and beyond.

The Standard Generalized Markup Language (SGML) is the grandfather of most markup languages used for print and the Internet. SGML is the international standard used to define the structures and appearance of documents. Multiple SGMLs have been created for a variety of document types and for various specialties—such as physics, accounting, and chemistry. HTML and XHTML are the Web's primary version of SGML.

Basic HTML document structure

All HTML documents have similar basic structure, which includes the following elements:

- **Doctype** (**<!DOCTYPE>**) sets the type of markup language the document is using (**Table 2.4**). This is important to include so that the browser can quickly and accurately interpret the HTML code.

- **Head** (**<head>**) includes information *about* the page, such as the title and meta tags. You should also place links to external CSS and JavaScript files in this area. The head should not be confused with a page *header*. Nothing in the head of the page will be directly displayed in the Web page.

- **Body** (**<body>**) contains the elements you actually see in the Web browser page, such as navigation, headers, paragraphs, lists, tables, images, and much more.

HTML properties

HTML elements can be modified by placing HTML *properties* within the tag. Some properties are optional, some affect the performance of the element, and some are needed for an element to work properly. For example, the anchor tag (**<a>**) uses the **href** property to define where a link is pointing:

```
<a href="http://www.jasonspeaking.
  com">Jason</a>
```

Properties are also used to connect an HTML element to styles using the style, class, or id properties:

```
<p style="color: red;">Alice</a>

<p class="hilight char names">Alice
⤏ </a>

<p id="name01">Alice</a>
```

Every tag has one or more properties that can be applied to them. These become especially important when we start using CSS to style tags based on property values, as explained in Chapter 4.

Browser inherited styles

Most HTML tags have *browser inherited styles* associated with them. These default styles are actually defined by the Web browser developer. Because the browser developer has added them, you need to remember that they are there and will affect your design. For example, the `<em>` tag will italicize text on most browsers. No cosmic constant dictates that emphasized text is italicized; it's just that the guys and gals programming the browser software decided to do it that way. The good news is that you can use CSS to override the default browser styles.

For the most part, default styles are consistent from browser to browser, although some noticeable differences exist, especially with margins and font size. Many designers will start "from scratch" by resetting as many of the defaults as possible using a CSS reset (see Chapter 14).

What Is SVG?

The Scalable Vector Graphics (SVG) format is a method for creating vector graphics on the Web (see www.w3.org/graphics/svg). Like Flash, instead of plotting each point in a graphic, SVG data describes two points and then plots the path between them as a straight line or curve.

Although it still lags behind Flash in acceptance, SVG is natively supported in Firefox, Safari, Chrome, and Internet Explorer as of version 9. (Adobe does provide an IE plug-in at www.adobe.com/svg.)

Unlike Flash, which uses an editor to create files and hides much of its graphics code, SVG is a markup language that can be freely read.

ELEMENT	ELEMENT	ELEMENT

Ⓐ Inline elements flow horizontally using a soft line break when reaching the edge of their parent element.

Types of HTML Elements

HTML includes a large number of elements, each with its own specific tag and use for structuring documents. Elements can generally be sorted into two categories or display types:

- **Inline elements** have no line breaks associated with the element Ⓐ. **Table 2.1** lists the inline-tag selectors that CSS can use.

continues on next page

TABLE 2.1 HTML Selectors for Inline Elements

Selector	HTML Use	Selector	HTML Use
a	Anchored link	label	Label for form element
abbr	Abbreviation	legend	Title in fieldset
address	A physical address	link	Resource reference
area	Area in image map	mark*	Marked text
audio*	Sound content	meter*	Measurement range
b	Bold text	nav*	Navigation links
cite	Short citation	optgroup	Group of form options
code	Code text	option	An option in a drop-down list
del	Deleted text	q	Short quote
details*	Details of an element	select	Selectable list
dfn	Defined term	small	Small print
command*	Command button	source*	Media resource
datalist*	Drop-down list	span	Localized style formatting
em	Emphasis	strong	Strong emphasis
font	Font appearance	sub	Subscript
i	Italic	summary*	Details header
iframe	Inline sub-window	sup	Superscript
img	Image embedding	tbody	Table body
input	Input field	td	Table data
ins	Inserted text	time*	Date/time
keygen*	Generated key in form	var	Variable
kbd	Keyboard text		

* New in HTML5

- **Block-level elements** place a line break before and after the element . **Table 2.2** lists the block-level element selectors that CSS can use.

B Block-level elements stack vertically on top of each other.

TABLE 2.2 HTML Selectors for Block-level Elements

Selector	HTML Use	Selector	HTML Use
article*	Article content	header*	Section or page header
aside*	Aside content	hgroup*	Groups header information
blockquote	Long quotation	hr	Horizontal rule
body	Page body	li	List item
br	Line break	map	Image map
button	Push button	object	Object embedding
canvas*	Draw area	ol	Ordered list
caption	Table caption	output*	Form output
col	Table column	p	Paragraph
colgroup	Group of table columns	pre	Preformatted text
dd	Definition description	progress*	Displays progress of time-consuming task
div	Division	section*	Section in Web page
dl	Definition list	table	Table
dt	Definition term	tbody	Table body
embed	External content	textarea	Form text input area
fieldset	Fieldset label	tfoot	Table footer
figcaption*	Figure caption	th	Table header
figure*	Groups media content and caption	thead	Table header
footer*	Section or page footer	tr	Table row
form	Input form	ul	Unordered list
h1–6	Heading levels 1–6	video*	video player
head	Information about the page		

* New in HTML5

Not all CSS definitions can be applied to all HTML elements. Whether a particular CSS property can be applied (or not) depends on the nature of the element. For the most part, it's fairly obvious when a property can be applied.

For example, you wouldn't expect the text-indent property, which indents the first line of a paragraph, to apply to an inline tag such as `<strong>`. In fact, it can't be applied, unless you use CSS to change the display type.

When you do need help in this area, see Appendix A to determine the CSS properties that can be applied to specific HTML elements.

The Evolution of HTML5

HTML5 is the next step in Web markup and will take over from XHTML. Although XHTML2 was in development for almost eight years, it was laid to rest in 2009 in favor of HTML5.

To understand how this happened, let's take a little trip back to the halcyon days of the Web at the end of the twentieth century—1997, to be precise. It was still a Web 1.0 world, although we didn't yet know to call it that. The dotcom bubble was just starting to inflate, and everyone was surfing the Web with Netscape Navigator. Into that landscape the World Wide Web Consortium (W3C) introduced HTML 4.0 (HTML4).

HTML4 was a vast improvement, because for the first time it was created by a standards body that gave everyone a seat at the table and believed that Web pages should display the same across all available browsers.

And then came XHTML

XHTML1 (released in 2001) is a rewriting of the HTML 4.01 standard using XML, and was intended to bring the power of XML to Web page development. XHTML uses the XML Doctype. XHTML employs all the same tags as HTML, but the code will still work with a browser that does not understand XML.

Although XHTML2 was primarily meant to be a transitional technology to a brave new Web technology, from its very beginning, something went horribly wrong.

The problem with XHTML2

It was quickly realized that even XHTML1 was not enough to evolve the Web from its relatively static "page" nature into a truly interactive and universal environment of applications. XHTML2 was meant to change all of that. Starting in August 2002, the authors of the XHTML standard began crafting a new language that they hoped would completely retool Web markup for the twenty-first century, bringing about a golden age of semantic Web pages, interactivity, internationalization, device independence, and tapioca pudding for everyone! But they forgot one thing: XHTML2 was not written to be backward compatible with older Web markup languages. Existing browsers would not be able to run this whiz-bang new markup language. Web developers would have to develop one version of their site for older browsers and another for the XHTML2 standard.

And then there was HTML5

In June 2003, HTML5 started life as Web Applications 1.0 and was created by the Web HyperText Application Technology Working Group (WHATWG), an organization that was not associated with the W3C. Instead, this independent group, frustrated with the slow pace and errant direction that XHTML2 was taking, began working on an alternative standard that would be backward compatible, more suitable for writing applications *and* pages, and would also address many practical issues that Web developers faced.

For several years, both languages were developed simultaneously. But in 2007, seeing that Web Applications 1.0 was further along than XHTML2, the W3C adapted it as the starting point for a new HTML5 standard, publishing the "First Public Working Draft" of the specification on January 22, 2008. To focus attention on HTML5, the W3C did not renew the XHTML Working Group's charter and XHTML2 was no more.

Is it HTML5 or XHTML5?

Although XHTML2 has disappeared, the need to unify XML and HTML has not. Therefore, a parallel initiative exists to create XHTML5. To be clear, this is *not* a new or different markup language; it is simply HTML5 written using XML rules and is similar to XHTML.

If you know XHTML, then learning XHTML5 should not be difficult. They differ primarily in the ways they treat tags. Some of the most important differences are listed in **Table 2.3**.

Whether you choose to use HTML5 or XHTML5 is your call, but they will both work in modern browsers. For my part, I'm enjoying the more forgiving nature of HTML5, and it's what I use for the code in this book.

TABLE 2.3 HTML5 vs. XHTML5

	XHTML5	HTML5
Tag case	lowercase	upper or lowercase
Closing tags	required	optional
Self closing tags	required	optional
MIME type	application/xml *or* application/xhtml+xml	text/html
Well-formedness errors	fatal	not fatal

What's Not in HTML5?

HTML5 includes several changes. But if you want to start using it today, you also need to know what is *not* available anymore. The frame tags—**frameset**, **frame**, **noframes**—have been eliminated, but **iframe** is still available. Most presentation tags have been eliminated—such as **basefont**, **big**, **center**, **font**, **s**, **strike**, **tt**, **u**—and although **b** (bold) and **i** (italic) are still included, some debate continues over that decision.

What's New in HTML5?

HTML5 makes important structural changes to Web pages. For example, you can specify common elements such as headers, footers, articles, and asides. In addition, HTML5 introduces many features natively (that is, features built into the browser) that used to require plug-ins and/or scripting in the form of new elements and APIs:

- **The Canvas element** allows scriptable bitmap editing.

- **Document** editing permits users to edit content directly in Web pages.

- **Web forms** self validate and include more input types.

- **Drag-and-drop** allows the manipulation of elements without scripting.

- **Audio and Video Timed media playback** enables native control of media files without plug-ins.

- **New structural elements** remove the burden of using `<div>` tags with classes and IDs to create common elements such as headers and footers.

How Does HTML5 Structure Work?

One of the most significant changes in HTML5 is the addition of structural elements that will greatly enhance the semantic philosophy behind Web markup 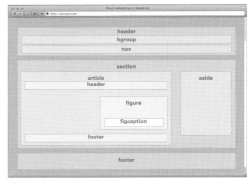. Most of the new structural tags are self-explanatory, but a few require some elaboration:

- **<header>** can be used for page headers, section headers, article headers, or an aside header.

- **<hgroup>** is used for a grouping of header elements (**h1**, **h2**, **h3**, and so on) that are related, generally as title and subtitle.

- **<nav>** can be included independently or as part of the header and/or footer.

- **<section>** defines the main parts of a page, generally one that includes articles.

- **<article>** is an individual blog entry or blog entry abstract.

- **<figure>** is used to contain images, audio, and video that are embedded in the page.

- **<figcaption>** contains a caption for the figure tag it is in.

- **<dialog>** replaces the **<dl>** element to contain conversation transcripts.

- **<aside>** is used for support content on a page, such as related links, secondary navigation, and of course, ads.

- **<footer>** is similar to the header and can be placed at the bottom of other elements.

Unfortunately, not all browsers are equipped to understand HTML5 without a little help.

A The wireframe of a typical HTML5 document.

Code 2.1 *HTML5page.html*—This shows a typical HTML5 page that is structured to use a header, navigation, article, aside, and footer for the layout grid.

```
<!DOCTYPE html>
<html dir="ltr" lang="en-US">
    <head>
        <meta charset="utf-8">
        <title>HTML5</title>
    </head>
    <body>
        <header>
            <hgroup></hgroup>
            <nav></nav>
        </header>
        <section>
            <article>
                <header></header>
                    <figure>
                        <figcaption></figcaption>
                    </figure>
                    <footer></footer>
            </article>
                <dialog><dialog>
        </section>
        <aside></aside>
        <footer></footer>
    </body>
</html>
```

Using HTML5 Structure Now

I'll let you in on a little secret: You can use the HTML5 syntax to structure your Web pages and combine it with CSS3 (or older versions of CSS). HTML5 is implemented on most current browsers (including Internet Explorer), and you should start using it now.

Although CSS can be applied to any version of HTML in use today—including XHTML1 and HTML 4.01—I'll be using HTML5 throughout this book. This book is by no means an exhaustive resource of HTML5. However, I want to show you how to set up the basic Web document that I'll reference in future chapters.

TABLE 2.4 Doctypes

Markup Language	Doctype Code
HTML 4.01 Loose	`<!DOCTYPE HTML PUBLIC "-//W3C//DTD HTML 4.01 Transitional//EN" "http://www.w3.org/TR/html4/loose.dtd">`
HTML 4.01 Strict	`<!DOCTYPE HTML PUBLIC "-//W3C//DTD HTML 4.01//EN" "http://www.w3.org/TR/html4/strict.dtd">`
HTML 4.01 Frameset	`<!DOCTYPE HTML PUBLIC "-//W3C//DTD HTML 4.01 Frameset//EN" "http://www.w3.org/TR/html4/frameset.dtd">`
XHTML1 Transitional	`<!DOCTYPE html PUBLIC "-//W3C//DTD XHTML 1.0 Transitional//EN" "http://www.w3.org/TR/xhtml1/DTD/xhtml1-transitional.dtd">`
XHTML1 Strict	`<!DOCTYPE html PUBLIC "-//W3C//DTD XHTML 1.0 Strict//EN" "http://www.w3.org/TR/xhtml1/DTD/xhtml1-strict.dtd">`
XHTML1 Frameset	`<!DOCTYPE html PUBLIC "-//W3C//DTD XHTML 1.0 Frameset//EN" "http://www.w3.org/TR/xhtml1/DTD/xhtml1-frameset.dtd">`
HTML5/XHTML5	`<!DOCTYPE html>`

Setting up a basic HTML5 document:

1. Add the HTML5 doctype (**Table 2.4**). Notice that the new !DOCTYPE for HTML5 is much simpler than the complex and hard-to-decipher HTML and XHTML doctypes in use today (**Code 2.1**). It simply tells the browser to use HTML.

```
<!DOCTYPE html>
```

2. Add the HTML tag, including the intended language and the language direction (generally **ltr** for left-to-right text).

```
<html dir="ltr" lang="en-US">...
→ </html>
```

3. Add the head to your document, which is where you will specify information about this document, including the title and the character set used by the text. I recommend using UTF-8 for best results.

```
<head>...</head>
```

4. Add the body to your document. This is where all the content to be displayed is added. I recommend giving every body element in your site at least one unique class name and others to identify its location in the site. By doing so, you can add styles on a per-page and per-section basis without including multiple CSS files.

```
<body class="section Name
→ pageName">...</body>
```

When Will HTML5 Be Ready?

It's important to note that many people are concerned that HTML5 is still a "Working Draft." The final "Proposed Recommendation" will not be finished until 2022. (Yes, that's a decade from now.) The skeptics throw up their hands and assume that it will be some time before HTML5 is relevant. But that date is really misleading.

All new browsers currently support the important HTML5 properties. The 2022 date is distant, but it is when *all* browsers will have adapted *all* the HTML5 properties.

Practically speaking, HTML5 is here now and will grow in use over the next few years until it becomes the main game in town.

HTML5 is ready for prime time, if you are ready to use it.

5. Add the header tag for your page. This is *not* the same as the head tag in step 3. This is where you put all the content that is displayed in your Web page's header. You can also include the navigation here or include it separately, depending on your design needs.

   `<header>...</header>`

6. Add the navigation tag, and include links to the top-level pages in your site.

   `<nav>...</nav>`

7. Add one or more article tags, which will contain the important content on this page. Many Web browsers and RSS newsreaders will now allow the user to focus on the articles to get to the main content of the page. Figures and sections fit well here.

   `<article>...</article>`

8. Add the aside tag, which is where supplemental content to the article is placed. This is also sometimes called a sidebar or rail, depending on who you talk to. It can include anything you want, but I like putting comments and dialogue over here.

   `<aside>...</aside>`

9. Finally, add a footer tag at the bottom of the page. This generally includes redundant top-level navigation, copyrights, and other small print.

   `<footer>...</footer>`

And that's it. You are ready to start using HTML5 tags. Go crazy. Oh, wait, that's right: it works in everything *but* Internet Explorer, which just happens to make up the majority of browsers in use today. So, what do you do?

Making HTML5 work in older versions of Internet Explorer

Although Internet Explorer does not know HTML5 tags, there is a partial fix (or kludge) that involves using JavaScript to create the HTML5 elements:

document.createElement('header');

Referred to as the "HTML5 Shiv," this will "teach" Internet Explorer 6 (and later versions) that these elements exist, and that they should be treated as HTML tags. You can add one of these lines of JavaScript for each of the HTML5 elements you need.

To make it simple to add these new tags, create an external JavaScript file (**Code 2.2**) and link to it from your HTML document using the IE conditional (**Code 2.3**), which you'll explore in greater detail in Chapter 13.

Code 2.2 *HTML5forIE.js*—This adds a blank HTML tag for each of the HTML5 tags that Internet Explorer is missing.

```
/*** CSS VQS - Chapter 2 - HTML5forIE.js ***/
document.createElement('abbr');
document.createElement('article');
document.createElement('aside');
document.createElement('audio');
document.createElement('bb');
document.createElement('canvas');
document.createElement('datagrid');
document.createElement('datalist');
document.createElement('details');
document.createElement('dialog');
document.createElement('eventsource');
document.createElement('figure');
document.createElement('footer');
document.createElement('header');
document.createElement('hgroup');
document.createElement('mark');
document.createElement('menu');
document.createElement('meter');
document.createElement('nav');
document.createElement('output');
document.createElement('progress');
document.createElement('section');
document.createElement('time');
document.createElement('video');
```

Why Use a Doctype?

If you do not use a doctype, modern browsers are forced into Quirks mode. That's a bad situation if you are creating new Web pages because it leaves the interpretation of the code solely to the discretion of the browsers, which can translate into a lot of display inconsistencies.

If you do not include the doctype in your Web page, newer browsers may not recognize all of your code.

Code 2.3 *HTML5page.html*—This includes a link to the JavaScript in Code 2.2.

```html
<!DOCTYPE html>
<html dir="ltr" lang="en-US">
    <head>
        <meta charset="utf-8">
        <title>HTML5</title>

    <!--[if IE ]>
        <script src="script/HTML5forIE.js"
        ↳ type="text/javascript"></script>
    <![endif]-->

    </head>
    <body class="pageName">
        <header></header>
        <nav></nav>
        <article>
            <figure></figure>
            <section></section>
        </article>
        <aside>
            <dialog></dialog>
        </aside>
        <footer></footer>
    </body>
</html>
```

Code 2.4 *HTML5forIE.js*—This does the same job as Code 2.2 but uses a JavaScript loop, making the code more compact.

```javascript
/*** CSS VQS - Chapter 2 - HTML5forIE.js ***/
(function(){if(!/*@cc_on!@*/0)return;var e =
↳ "abbr,article,aside,audio,bb,canvas,
↳ datagrid,datalist,details,dialog,
↳ eventsource,figure,footer,header,hgroup,
↳ mark,menu,meter,nav,output,progress,
↳ section,time,video".split(',');
↳ for(var i=0;i<e.length;i++)
↳ {document.createElement(e[i])}})()
```

If you want to get fancy, replace Code 2.2 with the JavaScript loop shown in **Code 2.4**. This has the same effect but is more compact.

TIP The document in this example has been structured to address my needs, but you needn't follow hard and fast rules for tag placement and nesting. You can place the navigation in the header, the footer, the article, or aside. Similarly, figures can go in the aside or the head. The preceding example is just a basic common Web page structure.

3

CSS Basics

CSS lets you control all the elements of your document's appearance—fonts, text, colors, backgrounds, sizes, borders, spacing, positioning, visual effects, tables, and lists. It even allows you to control the spatial and temporal styles of elements using transitions and transformations. However, the real power of using CSS for styles is that you can change the appearance of every page on your Web site by changing only a few lines of CSS code.

With savvy use of CSS, you can start with a plain web page, add visual design and interaction, and turn it into a webbed environment.

In This Chapter

The Basic CSS Selectors

CSS works by defining the styles of the elements on a Web page using *CSS rules*. Rules are applied using *selectors*, which come in four basic varieties: HTML selectors are used to reference a specific tag; class selectors are applied individually to elements; ID selectors are applied to a single element on the page; and universal selectors are applied to all elements on the page (**Table 3.1**). You will use these four basic selectors constantly, and they are the best place to start. In Chapter 4, you will learn about using other selectors for creating more selective styling.

TABLE 3.1 Basic Selectors

Format	Selector Name	What Elements Are Styled	@				O
a	HTML	All specified HTML tags	●	●	●	●	●
.myClass	Class	Any HTML tag where class is applied	●	●	●	●	●
a.myClass	Dependent class	Specified HTML tag where class is applied	●	●	●	●	●
#myID	ID	Any HTML tag where ID is applied	●	●	●	●	●
a#myID	Dependent ID	Specified HTML tag where ID is applied	●	●	●	●	●
*	Universal	All HTML tags	●	●	●	●	●

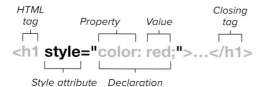

HTML tag · Property · Value · Closing tag

`<h1 style="color: red;">...</h1>`

Style attribute · Declaration

Ⓐ The general syntax for defining styles directly in an HTML tag.

Inline: Adding Styles to an HTML Tag

Although using CSS means you do not have to set the appearance of each tag individually, you still have the freedom to set a style within an individual tag, using an *inline* style Ⓐ.

This is useful when you've set styles for the page in the head or in an external style sheet, and you need to override those styles on a case-by-case basis. However, you should only do this as a last resort. Because inline styles have the highest priority in the cascade order, they are virtually impossible to override. (See "Why You Should Never, EVER Use Inline Styles in Your Final Web Site...Mostly.")

To set the style properties of individual HTML tags:

1. **Add the style property to the HTML tag.** Type **style=** in the HTML tag to which you want to apply styles (**Code 3.1**)

   ```
   <h1 style=
   ```

2. **Add your CSS declarations in a comma-separated list.** In quotes, type your style declarations in the format **property: value**, using a semicolon (**;**) and separating individual declarations. Be sure to close the declaration list with quotation marks.

   ```
   "color:red;"
   ```

Alice's Adventures In Wonderland

Chapter 1 Down the Rabbit-Hole

Alice was beginning to get very tired of sitting by her sister on the bank, and of having nothing to do: once or twice she had peeped into the book her sister was reading, but it had no pictures or conversations in it, "and what is the use of a book," thought Alice, "without pictures or conversations?"

Next: The Pool of Tears

B The results of **Code 3.1**. The header level 1 has been set to red, rather than the default black.

Code 3.1 An inline style is applied to the **h1** tag to define the color **B**.

```
<!-- HTML5 -->
<!DOCTYPE html>
<html lang="en">
<head>
<meta charset=UTF-8>
<title>Alice&#8217;s Adventures in Wonderland</title>
</head>
<body>
<h1 style="color:red;">Alice&#8217;s Adventures In Wonderland</h1>
<h1 id="ch01">Chapter 1 <span class="chaptertitle">Down the Rabbit-Hole</h1>
<p><strong>Alice was beginning to get very tired of sitting by her sister on the bank,</strong>
 → and of having nothing to do: once or twice she had peeped into the book her sister was reading,
 → but it had no pictures or conversations in it, "and what is the use of a book," thought Alice,
 → "without pictures or conversations?"</p>
</article>
<footer><nav> Next:
<a class="chaptertitle" href="AAIWL-ch02.html">The Pool of Tears</a>
</nav></footer>
</body>
</html>
```

Why You Should Never, EVER Use Inline Styles in Your Final Web Site…Mostly

Because inline styles are the last line of styling, you cannot override them using embedded or external style sheets. As a result, you either are stuck with this style permanently or have to change it manually, which may not always be possible. If you are working on a large-scale Web site, the HTML code is often set independently of the styles, and designers may not be able to access that code or easily change it.

I once spent three days trying to restyle a widget for a major Internet company, only to realize that the link style wouldn't change because the developer had used an inline style. Because I couldn't edit the HTML code, I was stuck. So don't use them. Ever!

Ok, there are a few exceptions:

- **Interfaces**: Often, when you are designing an interface, there are certain styles that if changed or removed will prevent the interface from working or appearing correctly. I will often use inline specific styles for that case.

- **Testing**: Inline styles can be useful for quickly testing styles. But to retain maximum flexibility, I recommend always placing your final styles into external style sheets, as discussed later in this chapter.

- **When you have to**: After you've been doing this stuff for a while, use your best judgment.

3. **Finish your HTML tag and add content.** After closing the tag, add the content to be styled. Then close the tag pair with the corresponding end tag.

```
>Alice&#8217;s Adventures In
 Wonderland</h1>
```

If you have conflicting styles applied to the same element, the cascade order determines which is applied, as explained in detail in "Determining the Cascade Order" in Chapter 5.

TIP You should *never* use inline styles in your final Web site. See the sidebar, "Why You Should Never, EVER Use Inline Styles in Your Final Web Site…Mostly" in this chapter.

TIP So as not to confuse the browser, it is best to use double quotation marks ("…") around the declaration list and single quotation marks ('…') around any values in the declaration list, such as font names with spaces.

TIP Font names made up of more than two words are placed in single quotes ('Font Name') when used with a style.

TIP When you are copying and pasting code from an application such as Microsoft Word into a Web-editing application such as Adobe Dreamweaver, make sure that you convert all smart quotes ("…") to straight quotes ("…").

TIP A common mistake is to confuse the equals sign (=) with the colon (:). Although the style attribute in the tag uses an equals sign, remember that CSS declarations always use a colon.

Embedded: Adding Styles to a Web Page

To add styles that apply to a single Web page—rather than just a single element (inline) or an entire Web site (external)—you *embed* the style rules in the Web page using the **<style>** tag, which in turn will hold all your style rules 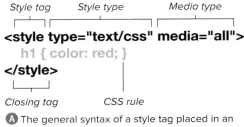.

Adding styles in this manner can look identical to adding styles directly to an HTML tag (as seen in the previous section). However, when you place styles in a common location—preferably in the **<head>**

A The general syntax of a style tag placed in an HTML document.

Code 3.2 Style rules are added within the **<style>** tag. A rule is added for the level 1 header to set its color, but it has no effect **B** because the **inline** style overrides it. That's why you should never use inline styles in your final code.

```
<!-- HTML5 -->
<!DOCTYPE html>
<html lang="en">
<head>
<meta charset="UTF-8">
<title>Alice&#8217;s Adventures in Wonderland</title>
<style type="text/css" media="all">
   h1 {
      color: orange;
      font-size: 3em;
      font-weight: normal; }
   h1 .chaptertitle {
      color: yellow;
      font-size: .5em; }
</style>
</head>
<body>
<h1 style="color:red;">Alice&#8217;s Adventures In Wonderland</h1>
<h1 id="ch01">Chapter 1 <span class="chaptertitle">Down the Rabbit-Hole</span></h1>
<p><strong>Alice was beginning to get very tired of sitting by her sister on the bank,</strong>
   →and of having nothing to do: once or twice she had peeped into the book her sister was reading,
   →but it had no pictures or conversations in it, "and what is the use of a book," thought Alice,
   →"without pictures or conversations?"</p>
</article>
<footer><nav> Next:
<a class="chaptertitle" href="AAIWL-ch02.html">The Pool of Tears</a>
</nav></footer>
</body>
</html>
```

Alice's Adventures In Wonderland

Chapter 1 Down the Rabbit-Hole

Alice was beginning to get very tired of sitting by her sister on the bank, and of having nothing to do: once or twice she had peeped into the book her sister was reading, but it had no pictures or conversations in it, "and what is the use of a book," thought Alice, "without pictures or conversations?"

Next: The Pool of Tears

B The results of **Code 3.2**. Notice that although the **h1** selector in the **<style>** tag specifies the color as orange, it does not override the inline style for the first **h1** tag, which remains stubbornly red.

of the document—you can easily change all the styles in a document. For example, rather than specifying the style of a single **<h1 id="ch01">** tag, you can specify the style of *all* the **<h1 id="ch01">** tags on the entire page, and then change the rule in one place to change the appearance of all level 1 headers on that page.

To set the style for tags in an HTML document:

1. Type the opening **style** tag in the head of your document (Code 3.2). Define the **type** attribute as **"text/css"**, which defines the styles that follow as CSS, not just any style. Also, define the **media** type using a value of **all**, which will apply the style sheet to the page regardless of the type of machine used to output it (see "Querying the Media" in Chapter 4). Then close the **style** tag.

    ```
    <style type="text/css"
     ⇥ media="all">...</style>
    ```

2. **Add your CSS rules.** Within the **style** container from Step 1, start a new rule by typing the selector to which you want to add styles, followed by opening and closing curly brackets (**{}**). (Basic selectors—HTML, class, IDs, and universal—are explained earlier in this chapter, and contextual selectors are explained in Chapter 4.)

    ```
    h1 {...}
    ```

    Within the brackets of your rule, type the declarations to be assigned to this rule—formatted as **property: value**—using a semicolon (**;**) and separating individual declarations in the list.

    continues on next page

3. **Add all the CSS rules you want to define.** Rules obey the cascade order (explained in detail in "Determining the Cascade Order" in Chapter 5). But generally, you can overrule a style by rewriting it lower in the list.

TIP To make a rule more easily readable, you can also add one or more line breaks, spaces, or tabs after a declaration without interfering with the code.

TIP Although you can place embedded styles anywhere in your HTML document, I highly recommend placing them at the top of your documents in the <head>; otherwise, the page will display without the styles at first and then blink as the page redisplays with the styles.

TIP However, I do not recommend placing embedded styles in your final Web page at all. Although they aren't as difficult to override as inline styles, embedded styles can confound you later when trying to redesign a page. It's always best to put all your styles in an external style sheet (explained in the next section) where site-wide changes are easy to make.

External: Adding Styles to a Web Site

A major benefit of CSS is that you can create a style sheet once and use it either in a single Web page or throughout your entire Web site. To do this, you create an *external* CSS file separate from the HTML document that contains only CSS code—no HTML, JavaScript, or any other code.

Establishing an external CSS file is a two-step process. First, you set up the CSS rules in a text file. Second, you link or import this file into an HTML document using the **<link>** tag or the **@import** rule Ⓐ.

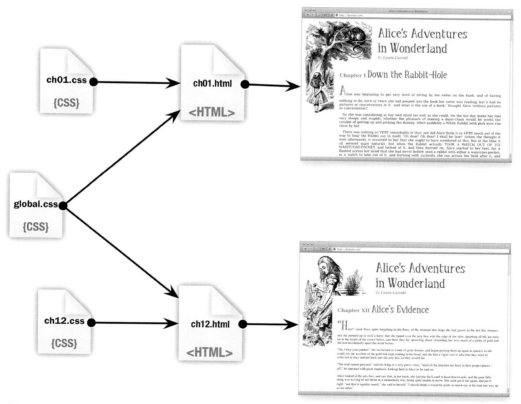

Ⓐ External CSS files can be used to style HTML pages directly by linking or importing them.

Creating an external style sheet

The first step in using an external style sheet globally on a Web site is to create the external file that contains all the CSS code. However, unlike adding embedded styles, you do *not* use **<style>** tags in an external CSS file. In fact, doing so would cause the external style sheet to fail.

In this example, I set up three CSS files: *global.css*, *ch01.css*, and *ch12.css*.

To set up an external CSS file:

1. **Create a new text file.** You can use a text editor or Web-editing software. Save the file using the .css extension. For example, *global.css*.

   Notepad or SimpleText will do, but you may want to use a specialized code editing software program such as Coda or BBEdit.

   Do *not* use Microsoft Word. It adds its own markup code that will interfere with your CSS code.

2. **Import CSS files.** This is optional, but you can create as many external style sheets as you want and import style sheets into each other to combine their styles (**Code 3.4** and **Code 3.5**). However, if an import rule is included in an external style sheet, it must be placed before all other CSS code. See "Importing a style sheet" in this chapter for more information.

   ```
   @import{global.css}
   ```

Code 3.3 *global.css*—All the basic styles for the Web site are contained in the default external style sheet.

```
body {
    padding: 220px 0 0 180px; }
h1 {
color: green;
font-size: 3em;
font-weight: bold; }
h1 .chaptertitle {
color: blue;
font-size: .5em;
font-weight: normal; }
p {
    color: violet;
    font-size: 1.5em;
    line-height: 2; }
```

Code 3.4 *ch01.css*—Adds a special background image for Chapter 1.

```
body { background: white
 ⇢ url('alice23a.gif') no-repeat 0 0; }
```

Code 3.5 *ch12.css*—Adds a specific image for Chapter 12.

```
body { background: white
 ⇢ url('alice40b.gif') no-repeat 0 0; }
```

3. **Add your CSS rules to the text file (Code 3.3).** Do *not* include any other code types—no HTML or JavaScript.

Start a new rule by typing the selector to which you want to add styles, followed by opening and closing curly brackets (**{}**). (Basic selectors—HTML, class, IDs, and universal—are explained in this chapter, and contextual selectors are explained in Chapter 4.)

```
h1 { color: green;
    font-size: 3em; font-weight:
→ bold; }
```

In the brackets of your rule, type the declarations to be assigned to this rule—formatted as **property: value**—using a semicolon (**;**) and separating individual declarations in the list. (You can also add comments as explained later in this chapter.)

You can now connect this file to your Web pages using one of the following two methods:

- **Link.** Use the **<link>** tag to connect external CSS files to an HTML file.

- **Import.** Use **@import** to connect external CSS files to an HTML file.

> **TIP** Although the external CSS file can have any name, it's a good idea to use a name that will remind you of the purpose of these styles. The name "navigation.css," for example, is probably a more helpful name than "657nm87gp.css."

> **TIP** A CSS file should not contain any HTML tags (especially not the **<style>** tag) or other content, with the exception of CSS comments and imported styles.

Linking to a style sheet

External style sheet files can be applied to any HTML file using the **<link>** tag ⓑ. Linking a CSS file affects the document in the same way as if the styles had been embedded directly in the head of the document; but, by placing it in a separate file, the code can be reused across multiple Web pages and changes made in the one central file will affect all of those pages.

To link to an external CSS file:

1. **Add a link tag to your HTML document.** Within the **<head>...</head>** of your HTML document (**Code 3.6**), open your **<link>** tag and type a space.

   ```
   <link
   ```

2. **Specify the link's relation to the document as a stylesheet.** This is important, since the link tag can be used to add other file types. Leaving this out will cause many browsers to not load the code.

   ```
   rel="stylesheet"
   ```

3. **Specify the location of the CSS file to be used, either global or local.** For example, *ch01.css*. This is the full path and name (including extension) of the external CSS document. In Chapter 15, you'll explore style sheet strategies for locating external style sheets in relation to your HTML documents.

   ```
   href="global.css"
   ```

4. **Specify the type of information that is being linked.** In this example, it's a text file containing CSS.

   ```
   type="text/css"
   ```

Link tag   Link relationship

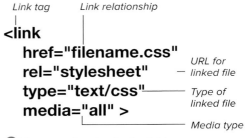

```
<link
   href="filename.css"          URL for
   rel="stylesheet"          — linked file
   type="text/css"              Type of
                                linked file
   media="all" >
                                Media type
```

ⓑ The general syntax for the link tag.

ⓒ The results of **Code 3.6**. Our page with all the default and Chapter 1 specific styles applied.

5. Specify the media type to which this style sheet should be applied. For more details, see "Quarrying the Media" in Chapter 4.

```
media="all">
```

TIP You can use the `<link>` tag to add as many style sheets to a page as you want.

TIP Keep in mind that the more style sheets you link to, the more server calls your Web page makes, and the slower it loads. Link as needed, but try to minimize links by combining files where possible.

Code 3.6 *ch01.html*—Imports the external style sheet ch01.css (**Code 3.4**) and global.css (**Code 3.3**).

```
<head>
<!-- HTML5 -->
<!DOCTYPE html>
<html lang="en">
<head>
<meta charset="UTF-8">
<title>Alice&#8217;s Adventures in Wonderland</title>
<link href='global.css' rel="stylesheet" type="text/css" media="all">
<link href='ch01.css' rel="stylesheet" type="text/css" media="all">
<style type="text/css" media="all">
    h1 {
        color: orange;
        font-size: 3em;
        font-weight: normal; }
    h1 .chaptertitle {
        color: yellow;
        font-size: .5em; }
</style>
</head>
<body>
<h1 style="color:red;">Alice&#8217;s Adventures In Wonderland</h1>
<h1 id="ch01">Chapter 1 <span class="chaptertitle">Down the Rabbit-Hole</span></h1>
<p><strong>Alice was beginning to get very tired of sitting by her sister on the bank,
→ </strong> and of having nothing to do: once or twice she had peeped into the book her
→ sister was reading, but it had no pictures or conversations in it, "and what is the use
→ of a book," thought Alice, "without pictures or conversations?"</p>
</article>
<footer><nav> Next:
<a class="chaptertitle" href="AAIWL-ch02.html">The Pool of Tears</a>
</nav></footer>
</body>
</html>
```

Importing a style sheet

Another way to bring external style sheets into a document is to use the **@import** rule **D**. The advantage of importing is that it can be used not only to put an external CSS file in an HTML document file, but also to import one external CSS file into another.

To import an external CSS file:

1. **Within the head of your HTML document, add a style element (Code 3.7).** This is the same as discussed earlier in this chapter.

   ```
   <style type="text/css"
   → media="all">...</style>
   ```

2. **Add your @import rule.** In the **<style>** tag, before any other CSS code you want to include, type **@import()**, and between the parentheses include the URL of the CSS document to be imported. The URL can be global, in which case it would start with **http://**, or it could be a local path pointing to another file in the same domain.

   ```
   @import url(global.css);
   ```

   You can include as many imports as you want, but all of them must be placed before any embedded CSS code in that **<style>** tag.

   You can also place **@import** directly into another external style sheet. This will import the CSS code from one style sheet to the other so that when the second style sheet is linked or imported into an HTML file, the styles from the first style sheet are also included.

URL for external file
|

@import url(filename.css);

D The general syntax for the @import rule.

E The results of **Code 3.7**. The page with all of the default and Chapter 12 specific styles applied.

3. Add the rest of your embedded CSS.
You can include additional embedded CSS rules here, if necessary. (See "Embedded: Adding Styles to a Web Page" in this chapter.)

TIP Using the `@import` in external style sheets is now widely discouraged due to the way in which browsers process them. In order to work, the browser has to stop rendering other style sheets until it finishes with a `@import` style sheets, slowing the site and preventing other important styles from appearing.

Code 3.7 *ch12.html*—Imports the external style sheet ch12.css (**Code 3.5**) and global.css (**Code 3.3**) **E**.

```
<!-- HTML5 -->
<!DOCTYPE html>
<html lang="en">
<head>
<meta charset="UTF-8">
<title>Alice&#8217;s Adventures in Wonderland</title>
<style type="text/css" media="all">
@import url('global.css');
   @import url('ch12.css');
   h1 {
      color: orange;
      font-size: 3em;
      font-weight: normal; }
   h1 .chaptertitle {
      color: yellow;
      font-size: .5em; }
</style>
</head>
<body>
<h1 style="color:red;">Alice&#8217;s Adventures In Wonderland</h1>
<h1 id="ch01">Chapter 1 <span class="chaptertitle">Down the Rabbit-Hole</span></h1>
<p><strong>Alice was beginning to get very tired of sitting by her sister on the bank,
 ⇥</strong> and of having nothing to do: once or twice she had peeped into the book her
 ⇥ sister was reading, but it had no pictures or conversations in it, "and what is the use
 ⇥ of a book," thought Alice, "without pictures or conversations?"</p>
</article>
<footer><nav> Next:
<a class="chaptertitle" href="AAIWL-ch02.html">The Pool of Tears</a>
</nav></footer>
</body>
</html>
```

(Re)Defining HTML Tags

Almost all HTML tags have default browser styles associated with them. Take the `<strong>` tag, for example: Its inherent style declaration is the equivalent of `font-weight: bold`.

By adding new CSS declarations to the **strong** HTML selector, you can change any element tagged as **strong** to look like anything you want 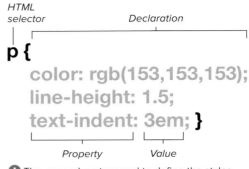. For example, you could make all italicized text bold or even set `font-weight: normal`, which would prevent the text from being bold.

To define an HTML selector:

1. **Start with the HTML selector whose properties you want to define.** Add a curly bracket (**{**) to open your rule (**Code 3.8**). Make sure you always close your declaration list with a curly bracket (**}**). If you forget this, it will ruin your day!

   h1 {...}

continues on page 52

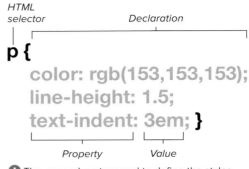
Ⓐ The general syntax used to define the styles for an HTML tag.

Ⓑ The results of **Code 3.8**. Paragraphs are indented and are no longer bright violet.

Code 3.8 *Ch01.html*—Styles the paragraph tag **B**.

```
<!-- HTML5 -->
<!DOCTYPE html>
<html lang="en">
<head>
<meta charset="UTF-8">
<title>Alice&#8217;s Adventures in Wonderland</title>
<link href="global.css" type="text/css" rel="stylesheet" media="all">
<link href="ch01.css" rel="stylesheet" type="text/css" media="all">
<style type="text/css" media="all">
    h1 {
        color: orange;
        font-size: 3em;
        font-weight: normal; }
    h1 .chaptertitle {
        color: yellow;
        font-size: .5em; }
    p {
        color: rgb(153,153,153);
        font-family: perpetua, georgia, serif;
        line-height: 1.5;
        text-indent: 3em; }
</style>
</head>
<body>
<h1 style="color:red;">Alice&#8217;s Adventures In Wonderland</h1>
<h1 id="ch01">Chapter 1 <span class="chaptertitle">Down the Rabbit-Hole</span></h1>
<p><strong>Alice was beginning to get very tired of sitting by her sister on the bank,
→ </strong> and of having nothing to do: once or twice she had peeped into the book her
→ sister was reading, but it had no pictures or conversations in it, "and what is the use
→ of a book," thought Alice, "without pictures or conversations?"</p>
</article>
<footer><nav> Next:
<a class="chaptertitle" href="AAIWL-ch02.html">The Pool of Tears</a>
</nav></footer>
</body>
</html>
```

CSS rules can be defined in the head of your document within the `<style>` tags or in an external CSS file that is imported or linked to the HTML document. (See "Embedded: Adding Styles to a Web Page" in this chapter.)

2. **Add declarations for styles.** Within the brackets, type the style declarations to be assigned to this HTML tag—formatted as **`property: value`**—using a semicolon (**`;`**) and separating individual declarations in the list. You can also add one or more line breaks, spaces, or tabs after a declaration without interfering with the code to make it more readable.

```
color: red;
```

Add as many declarations as you want, separated by semicolons:

```
font-size: 3em; font-weight:
→ normal;
```

TIP Be sure that the properties will work with the HTML tag in question. For example, you cannot use the `text-indent` property (which works only on block elements) to define the bold tag (which is an inline element). See Appendix A to verify the properties that can be assigned to specific selectors.

TIP Redefining a tag does not implicitly override that tag's preexisting properties. Thus, the `<strong>` tag still makes text bold unless you explicitly tell it not to with `font-weight: normal`.

TIP Although the body tag can also be redefined, it acts like a block-level tag. (See "Types of HTML Elements" in Chapter 2.) Any inherited properties will affect everything on the page. You can actually use this to your advantage to set default page styles, as explained in Chapter 4, "Inheriting Properties from Parents."

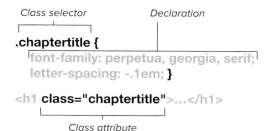

Class selector   *Declaration*

.chaptertitle {
font-family: perpetua, georgia, serif;
letter-spacing: -.1em; **}**

<h1 **class="chaptertitle"**>...</h1>

Class attribute

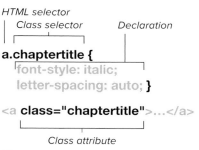 The general syntax of a CSS rule using a class selector, which can then be applied to any tag using the class value.

HTML selector
Class selector   *Declaration*

a.chaptertitle {
font-style: italic;
letter-spacing: auto; **}**

<a **class="chaptertitle"**>...</a>

Class attribute

B The general syntax of a dependent class selector rule, which can then be applied *only* to tags using that HTML selector.

Defining Reusable Classes

A *class* selector allows you to set up an independent style that you can apply to any HTML tag **A**. Unlike an HTML selector, which automatically targets a specific tag, a class selector is given a unique name that is then specified using the `style` attribute in the HTML tag or in any tags you want to use it. However, you can also specify styles to apply using a class applied to a specific HTML tag, making it a dependent class **B**.

To define a class selector:

1. **Give your class a name.** Type a period (**.**) and a class name you give it; then open and close your declaration block with curly brackets (**{}**) (**Code 3.9**).

   `.chaptertitle {...}`

   CSS classes can be defined in the head of your document within the **style** tags or in an external CSS file that is imported or linked to the HTML document.

   The class name can be anything you choose, with the following caveats:

   ▸ Use only letters and numbers. You can use hyphens and underscores, but not at the beginning of the name.

   ▸ The first character cannot be a number, underscore, or hyphen.

   ▸ Don't use spaces.

   author is an independent class, so you can use it with any HTML tag you want, with one stipulation: The properties set for the class must work with the type of tag you use it on.

continues on next page

2. **Add declarations to the rule.** Within the brackets, type the declarations to be assigned to this class—formatted as **property: value**—using a semicolon (;) and separating individual declarations in the list. You can also add one or more line breaks, spaces, or tabs after a declaration without interfering with the code to make it more readable.

```
font-family: perpetua, georgia,
 ›serif;

letter-spacing: .1em;
```

3. **Add dependent classes to your CSS.** You create dependent classes, which tie the declarations of the class to a particular HTML tag by placing an HTML selector in front of the class.

```
a.chaptertitle {...}
```

In the same document, you can create different versions of the dependent class (using the same name) for different tags and also have an independent class (applied to all tags with the class), as shown in Step 1.

continues on page 56

Alice's Adventures In Wonderland

Chapter 1 Down the Rabbit-Hole

Alice was beginning to get very tired of sitting by her sister on the bank, and of having nothing to do: once or twice she had peeped into the book her sister was reading, but it had no pictures or conversations in it, "and what is the use of a book," thought Alice, "without pictures or conversations?"

Next: *The Pool of Tears*

Ⓒ The results of **Code 3.9**. The chapter titles are styled differently in a hypertext link.

Code 3.9 *chapter01.html*—The **chaptertitle** class is used to style chapter titles where they appear .

```
<!-- HTML5 -->
<!DOCTYPE html>
<html lang="en">
<head>
<meta charset="UTF-8">
<title>Alice&#8217;s Adventures in Wonderland</title>
<link href="global.css" type="text/css" rel="stylesheet" media="all">
<link href="ch01.css" rel="stylesheet" type="text/css" media="all">
<style type="text/css" media="all">
    h1 {
        color: orange;
        font-size: 3em;
        font-weight: normal; }
    h1 .chaptertitle {
        color: yellow;
        font-size: .5em; }
    p {
        color: rgb(153,153,153);
        font-family: perpetua, georgia, serif;
        line-height: 1.5;
        text-indent: 3em; }
    .chaptertitle {
        font-family: perpetua, georgia, serif;
        letter-spacing: .1em;
    }
    a.chaptertitle {
        font-size: 2em;
        font-style: italic;
        letter-spacing: auto;
    }
</style>
</head>
<body>
<h1 style="color:red;">Alice&#8217;s Adventures In Wonderland</h1>
<h1 id="ch01">Chapter 1 <span class="chaptertitle">Down the Rabbit-Hole</span></h1>
<p><strong>Alice was beginning to get very tired of sitting by her sister on the bank,</strong>
→ and of having nothing to do: once or twice she had peeped into the book her sister was reading,
→ but it had no pictures or conversations in it, "and what is the use of a book," thought Alice,
→ "without pictures or conversations?"</p>
<footer><nav> Next: <a class="chaptertitle" href="AAIWL-ch02.html">The Pool of Tears</a>
</nav></footer>
</article>
</body>
</html>
```

4. **Add the class attribute to the HTML tag to which you want to apply it.**

```
<span class="chaptertitle">Down
→the Rabbit-Hole<span>
```

```
<a class="chaptertitle" href=
→"AAIWL-ch02.html">The Pool of
→Tears</a>
```

You can apply multiple classes to a single HTML tag by adding additional class names in a space separated list:

```
class="name1 name2 name3"
```

Notice that when you defined the class in the CSS, it began with a period (**.**). However, you do *not* use the period when referencing the class name in an HTML tag. Using a period here will cause the class to fail.

TIP You can mix a class with ID and/or inline rules within an HTML tag. (See "Inline: Adding Styles to an HTML Tag" and "Defining Unique IDs" in this chapter.)

TIP Because the `<div>` and `<span>` tags have no preexisting properties, you can use them to effectively create your own HTML tags by adding classes. However, use these sparingly because once they are associated, you are locked in to using those specific classes with those specific locations.

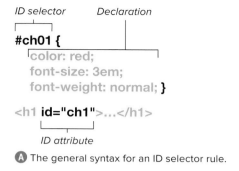

ID selector   Declaration

#ch01 {
  color: red;
  font-size: 3em;
  font-weight: normal; **}**

<h1 **id="ch1"**>...</h1>

ID attribute

A The general syntax for an ID selector rule.

Defining Unique IDs

Like the class selector, the ID selector can be used to create unique styles that are independent of any particular HTML tag **A**. Thus, they can be assigned to any HTML tag. IDs are used in HTML to help establish the structure of your page layout, identifying unique elements in the code, singling them out for special treatment, either for positioning with CSS or JavaScript.

To define an ID selector:

1. **Add the ID selector to your CSS.**
   ID rules always start with a number sign (**#**) followed by the name of the ID (**Code 3.10**).

   #ch01 {...}

   The name can be a word or any set of letters or numbers you choose, with the following caveats:

   ▸ Use only letters and numbers. You can use hyphens and underscores, but do so with caution. Some earlier browsers reject them.

   ▸ The first character cannot be a number, hyphen, or underscore.

   ▸ Don't use spaces.

   CSS rules can be defined in the head of your document within the **<style>** tags or in an external CSS file that is imported or linked to the HTML document.

   continues on next page

2. **Add declarations to your ID.** Within the curly brackets, type the style declarations to be assigned to this ID—formatted as **property: value**—using a semicolon (**;**) and separating individual declarations in the list. You can also add one or more line breaks, spaces, or tabs after a declaration without interfering with the code to make it more readable.

```
font-family: perpetua, georgia,
→ serif;

text-shadow: 4px 4px 6px
→ rgba(0,0,0,.5);
```

3. **Add the `id` attribute to the HTML tag of your choice, with the name of the ID as its value.**

```
<h1 id="ch01">...</h1>
```

Notice that although the number sign (**#**) is used to define an ID selector, it is *not* included for referencing the ID in the HTML tag. If you add it, the rule will fail.

B The results of **Code 3.10**. The chapter title is using perpetua with a drop shadow.

Code 3.10 *chapter01.html*—The ch01 ID styles the chapter title for chapter 1 **B**.

```
<!-- HTML5 -->
<!DOCTYPE html>
<html lang="en">
<head>
<meta charset="UTF-8">
<title>Alice&#8217;s Adventures in Wonderland</title>
<link href="global.css" type="text/css" rel="stylesheet" media="all">
<link href="ch01.css" rel="stylesheet" type="text/css" media="all">
<style type="text/css" media="all">
   h1 {
      color: orange;
      font-size: 3em;
      font-weight: normal; }
   h1 .chaptertitle {
      color: yellow;
      font-size: .5em; }
   p {
      color: rgb(153,153,153);
      font-family: perpetua, georgia, serif;
      line-height: 1.5;
      text-indent: 3em; }
   .chaptertitle {
      font-family: perpetua, georgia, serif;
      letter-spacing: .1em; }
   a.chaptertitle {
   font-size: 2em;
   font-style: italic;
   letter-spacing: auto; }
   #ch01 {
      font-family: perpetua, georgia, serif;
      text-shadow: 0 0 4px rgba(0,0,0,.75); }
</style>
</head>
<body>
<h1 style="color:red;">Alice&#8217;s Adventures In Wonderland</h1>
<h1 id="ch01">Chapter 1 <span class="chaptertitle">Down the Rabbit-Hole</span></h1>
<p><strong>Alice was beginning to get very tired of sitting by her sister on the bank,</strong>
→ and of having nothing to do: once or twice she had peeped into the book her sister was reading,
→ but it had no pictures or conversations in it, "and what is the use of a book," thought Alice,
→ "without pictures or conversations?"</p>
<footer><nav> Next: <a class="chaptertitle" href="AAIWL-ch02.html">The Pool of Tears</a>
</nav></footer>
</article>
</body>
</html>
```

TIP You can also create dependent IDs 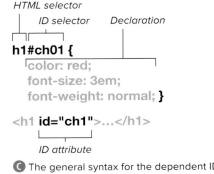, which use the declarations of the ID only when applied to a particular HTML tag. However, I never have a use for these because the point of IDs is that you use them only once per page.

TIP Although you can use the same name for both a class and ID, you should try to avoid this because it will inevitably lead to confusion.

TIP You can mix an ID with a class and/or inline rules within an HTML tag.

TIP IDs can give each screen element a unique name and identity. This is why an ID is used only once, for one element in a document, to make it an object that can be manipulated with JavaScript.

HTML selector

ID selector *Declaration*

```
h1#ch01 {
    color: red;
    font-size: 3em;
    font-weight: normal; }
```

`<h1 id="ch1">...</h1>`

ID attribute

C The general syntax for the dependent ID selector rule.

Asterisk
|
```
* {
    color: red;
    font-size: 3em;
    font-weight: normal; }
```
Declaration

Ⓐ The general syntax for the universal selector rule.

Defining Universal Styles

The universal selector is a wildcard character that works as a stand-in to represent any HTML type selector that can appear in that position in a contextual list Ⓐ.

Keep in mind, though, that the universal selector can be used in place of any HTML selector in any configuration, not just as a stand alone selector as shown in this section. The usefulness of this will become apparent in the next chapter when you use contextual styles.

To use the universal selector:

1. **Add the universal selector.** Type an asterisk (*****) and then the open curly bracket (**Code 3.11**). This selector is then a wildcard that can be any HTML tag.

   `*  {...}`

2. **Add declarations to your universal selector rule.** Within the curly brackets, type the style declarations to be assigned to this ID—formatted as **property: value**—using a semicolon (**;**) and separating individual declarations in the list. You can also add one or more line breaks, spaces, or tabs after a declaration without interfering with the code to make it more readable.

   `margin: 0; padding: 0;`

   In this format, the styles are applied to *every* element on the page.

Code 3.11 *chapter01.html*—The universal selector is used to reset the margin and padding of all elements to 0, overriding any browser default styles Ⓑ.

```
<!-- HTML5 -->
<!DOCTYPE html>
<html lang="en">
<head>
<meta charset="UTF-8">
<link href="global.css" type="text/css" rel="stylesheet" media="all">
<link href="ch01.css" rel="stylesheet" type="text/css" media="all">

<title>Alice&#8217;s Adventures in Wonderland</title>
<style type="text/css" media="all">
  * {
    margin: 0;
    padding: 0; }
  h1 {
    color: orange;
    font-size: 3em;
    font-weight: normal; }
  h1 .chaptertitle {
    color: yellow;
    font-size: .5em; }
  p {
    color: rgb(153,153,153);
    font-family: perpetua, georgia, serif;
    line-height: 1.5;
    text-indent: 3em; }
  .chaptertitle {
    font-family: perpetua, georgia, serif;
    letter-spacing: .1em; }
  a.chaptertitle {
    font-size: 2em;
    font-style: italic;
    letter-spacing: auto; }
  #ch01 {
    font-family: perpetua, georgia, serif;
    text-shadow: 0 0 4px rgba(0,0,0,.75); }
</style>
</head>
<body>
<h1 style="color:red;">Alice&#8217;s Adventures In Wonderland</h1>
<h1 id="ch01">Chapter 1 <span class="chaptertitle">Down the Rabbit-Hole</span></h1>
<p><strong>Alice was beginning to get very tired of sitting by her sister on the bank,</strong>
→ and of having nothing to do: once or twice she had peeped into the book her sister was reading,
→ but it had no pictures or conversations in it, "and what is the use of a book," thought Alice,
→ "without pictures or conversations?"</p>
<footer><nav> Next: <a class="chaptertitle" href="AAIWL-ch02.html">The Pool of Tears</a>
</nav></footer>
</article>
</body>
</html>
```

TIP Although you can also apply styles to the html or body element to have them cascade to their child elements, not all styles will be inherited by their children. Using the universal selector applies the styles directly to every element.

TIP Universal selectors provide an easy way to create a CSS reset, explained in Chapter 13.

TIP Universal selectors do *not* work in IE6.

B The results of **Code 3.11**. All the margins and padding are set to 0 on everything, giving you a clean slate for your designs.

Grouping: Defining Elements That Are Using the Same Styles

If you want two or more selectors to have the same declarations, group the selectors in a list separated by commas 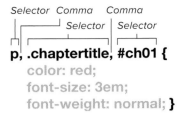. You can define common attributes in the declaration block and then add rules for each selector individually to refine them, if you like.

To group selectors:

1. **Add a grouping of selectors, separated by commas.** Type the list of selectors (HTML, class, or ID) separated by commas (**Code 3.12**). You can also add one or more line breaks, spaces, or tabs after a comma without interfering with the code to make it more readable.

   ```
   p, .chaptertitle, #ch01 {
   ```

   These selectors all receive the same declarations. CSS rules can be defined within the **style** tags in the head of your document or in an external CSS file that is imported or linked to the HTML document.

2. **Add common declarations for the selector grouping.** Within the curly brackets, type the style declarations to be assigned to all of the listed selectors—formatted as **property: value**—using a semicolon (**;**) and separating individual declarations in the list. You can also add one or more line breaks, spaces, or tabs after a declaration without interfering with the code to make it more readable.

   ```
   font-family: perpetua, georgia,
   → serif;
   ```

continues on page 66

```
Selector  Comma    Comma
                Selector  Selector
p, .chaptertitle, #ch01 {
    color: red;
    font-size: 3em;
    font-weight: normal; }
```

Ⓐ The general syntax for a list of selectors, all receiving the same declaration block.

Code 3.12 *chapter01.html*—Common styles for the level 1 headers, **chaptertitle** class, and ch01 ID are defined **B**. In reality, though, this code will look no different from code 3.11, since we haven't added any new styles, just moved a single style to be shared.

```
<!-- HTML5 -->
<!DOCTYPE html>
<html lang="en">
<head>
<meta charset="UTF-8">
<title>Alice&#8217;s Adventures in Wonderland</title>
<link href="global.css" type="text/css" rel="stylesheet" media="all">
<link href="ch01.css" rel="stylesheet" type="text/css" media="all">
<style type="text/css" media="all">
    * {
        margin: 0;
        padding: 0; }
    p, .chaptertitle, #ch01 {
        font-family: perpetua, georgia, serif; }
    h1 {
        color: orange;
        font-size: 3em;
        font-weight: normal; }
    h1 .chaptertitle {
        color: yellow;
        font-size: .5em; }
    p {
        color: rgb(153,153,153);
        line-height: 1.5;
        text-indent: 3em; }
    .chaptertitle {
        letter-spacing: .1em; }
    a.chaptertitle {
        font-size: 2em;
        font-style: italic;
        letter-spacing: auto; }
    #ch01 {
        font-family: perpetua, georgia, serif;
        text-shadow: 0 0 4px rgba(0,0,0,.75); }
</style>
</head>
<body>
<h1 style="color:red;">Alice&#8217;s Adventures In Wonderland</h1>
<h1 id="ch01">Chapter 1 <span class="chaptertitle">Down the Rabbit-Hole</span></h1>
<p><strong>Alice was beginning to get very tired of sitting by her sister on the bank,</strong>
→ and of having nothing to do: once or twice she had peeped into the book her sister was reading,
→ but it had no pictures or conversations in it, "and what is the use of a book," thought Alice,
→ "without pictures or conversations?"</p>
<footer><nav> Next: <a class="chaptertitle" href="AAIWL-ch02.html">The Pool of Tears</a>
</nav></footer>
</article>
</body>
</html>
```

3. Add refinements as needed. You can then individually add or change declarations for each selector to tailor it to your needs. If you are overriding a declaration set in the group rule, make sure that this rule is placed after the group rule in your CSS. (See "Determining the Cascade Order" in Chapter 4.)

TIP Grouping selectors like this can save a lot of time and repetition. But be careful. By changing the value of any of the properties in the combined declaration, you change that value for every selector in the list.

TIP Grouping selectors does not directly affect their cascade order (explained in Chapter 4); rather, the grouping is treated as if each selector had this rule assigned to it in the order the selectors are listed.

B The results of **Code 3.12**. The font family perpetua is applied to all of the common elements.

Slash ⊤⊤ *Asterisk*

/* Styles for Alice's Adventure in
Wonderland —
Uses neutral color palette and
Tenniel Illustrations in the
background. */

Asterisk ⊥⊥ *Slash*

Ⓐ The general syntax for CSS comments.

Adding Comments to CSS

Comments allow you to add important notes to your code, as a reminder to yourself or others. A comment does not affect code; comments only add notes or give guidance to those viewing your code. You can include comments in **\<style\>** tags or in an external CSS file.

To include comments in a style sheet:

1. **Add an opening comment mark.** To open a comment area in a style sheet (**Code 3.13**), type a slash (/) and an asterisk (*).

   /*

2. **Type your comments.** You can use any letters, numbers, symbols, or even line breaks by pressing the Return or Enter key.

   Styles for Alice's Adventure in
   → Wonderland

3. **Add a closing comment mark.** Close your comment by typing an asterisk (*) and a slash (/).

   */

TIP **Within the slash asterisk, you can add whatever text you want.**

TIP **You cannot nest comments.**

TIP **Comments are a great way to organize your code, allowing you to add "headers" that separate different parts of the code.**

TIP **I recommend placing constant values— like color values—at the top of your CSS code in comments for quick reference.**

Code 3.13 Comments in the CSS code have no effect on the final product. They are just there to add notes.

```html
<!-- HTML5 -->
<!DOCTYPE html>
<html lang="en">
<head>
<meta charset="UTF-8">
<title>Alice&#8217;s Adventures in Wonderland</title>
<link href="global.css" type="text/css" rel="stylesheet" media="all">
<link href="ch01.css" rel="stylesheet" type="text/css" media="all">
<style type="text/css" media="all">

/*   Styles for Alice's Adventure in Wonderland — Uses neutral color palette and Tenniel
 ↪Illustrations in the background. */

* {
    margin: 0;
    padding: 0; }
    p, .chaptertitle, #ch01 {
    font-family: perpetua, georgia, serif; }
  h1 {
    color: orange;
    font-size: 3em;
    font-weight: normal; }
  h1 .chaptertitle {
    color: yellow;
    font-size: .5em; }
  p {
    color: rgb(153,153,153);
    line-height: 1.5;
    text-indent: 3em; }
  .chaptertitle {
    letter-spacing: .1em; }
  a.chaptertitle {
    font-style: italic;
    letter-spacing: auto; }
  #ch01 {
    font-family: perpetua, georgia, serif;
    text-shadow: 0 0 4px rgba(0,0,0,.75); }
</style>
</head>
<body>
<h1 style="color:red;">Alice&#8217;s Adventures In Wonderland</h1>
<h1 id="ch01">Chapter 1 <span class="chaptertitle">Down the Rabbit-Hole</span></h1>
<p><strong>Alice was beginning to get very tired of sitting by her sister on the bank,</strong>
 → and of having nothing to do: once or twice she had peeped into the book her sister was reading,
 → but it had no pictures or conversations in it, "and what is the use of a book," thought Alice,
 → "without pictures or conversations?"</p>
<footer><nav> Next: <a class="chaptertitle" href="AAIWL-ch02.html">The Pool of Tears</a>
</nav></footer>
</article>
</body>
</html>
```

Selective Styling

It's not enough to style a Web page element. The art of CSS—and thus the art of Web design—is the ability to style elements based on their context. You must consider where an element is in the document; which elements surround it; its attributes, content, and dynamic state; and even the platform displaying the element (screen, handheld device, TV, and so on).

Selective styling is the closest that CSS gets to traditional computer programming, allowing you to style elements *if* they meet certain criteria. This level of styling can get increasingly complex, so it's important, at least in this chapter, to start out as simply as possible and build a firm foundation of understanding.

In This Chapter

The Element Family Tree

When a tag is surrounded by another tag—one inside another—the tags are *nested*.

```
<h2><strong>Chapter 2</strong> The
→ Pool of Tears<h2>
```

In a nested set, the outer element in this example (**<h2>**) is called the *parent*, and the inner element (**<strong>**) is the *child*. The child tag and any children of that child tag are the parents' *descendents*. Two tags in the same parent are called *siblings*, and two tags immediately next to each other are *adjacent siblings* .

- **Parent elements** contain other elements (children). Child elements will often inherit styles from a parent element.

- **Descendent elements** are any elements within another element.

- **Child elements** are first-generation descendent elements in relation to the parent. Second generation and higher elements are sometimes referred to as *grandchildren*.

- **Adjacent** or **preceding sibling elements** are child elements of the same generation that are immediately next to each other in the HTML code.

In Chapter 3, you learned ways to specify the styles of an individual element regardless of where it is placed in the HTML code. However, CSS also lets you specify the element's style depending on its context. Using *contextual selector*s, you can specify styles based on a tag's relationship to other tags, classes, or IDs on the page.

Parent   Descendent child

```
<article class="chaptertext">
    <p>
    <strong>Alice was</strong>
    beginning to get
    </em>very tired<em>...
    </p>
</article>
```

Preceding sibling   Adjacent sibling

A The article element is the parent to the elements created by the paragraph, strong, and emphasis tags, which are its descendents. Only the paragraph tag is a direct child. The elements created by the emphasis and strong tags are the children of the paragraph tag, and each other's siblings.

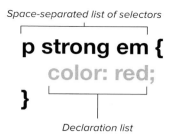

Space-separated list of selectors

p strong em {

color: red;

}

Declaration list

A The general syntax for the descendent selector.

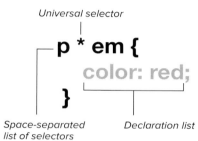

Universal selector

p * em {

color: red;

}

Space-separated list of selectors

Declaration list

B The general syntax for the descendent selector using the universal selector.

Defining Styles Based on Context

Contextual styles allow you to specify how a particular element should appear based on its parents and siblings. For example, you may want an emphasis tag to appear one way when it's in the main header of the page and differently when it appears in the sub-header. You may want still another appearance in a paragraph of text. These *combinatory* selectors (**Table 4.1**) are among the most used and useful in CSS.

Styling descendents

You can style individual descendent elements depending on their parent selector or selectors in a space-separated list. The last selector will receive the style if and only if it is the descendent of the preceding selectors **A**.

When you want to indicate that the exact selector does not matter at any given level, you can use the universal selector (*) described in Chapter 3 **B**.

TABLE 4.1 Combinatory Selectors

Format	Selector Name	Elements Are Styled If...					
a b c	Descendent	**c** descendent of **b** descendent of **a**	●	●	●	●	●
a * b	Universal	**b** within **a** regardless of **b**'s parents	●	●	●	●	●
a > b	Direct child	**b** direct child of **a**	●	●	●	●	●
a + b	Adjacent sibling	sibling **b** immediately after **a**	●	●	●	●	●
a ~ b	General sibling	sibling **b** anywhere after **a**	●	●	●	●	●

To style descendent elements:

1. **Set up a list of descendent selectors.**
   Type the HTML selector of the parent tag, followed by a space, and then the final child or another parent (**Code 4.1**).

   ```
   article.chaptertext p strong em
   → {...}
   ```

   You can type as many HTML selectors as you want for as many parents as the nested tag will have, *but the last selector in the list is the one that receives all the styles in the rule*.

2. **Styles will be used *only* if the pattern is matched.**

   ```
   <article class="chaptertext"><p>
   → <strong><em>...</em></strong>
   → </p></article>
   ```

   The style will be applied if and only if the final selector occurs as a descendent nested within the previous selectors. So, in this example, the emphasis tag (**em**) is styled only if it is in a paragraph (**strong**) that is within a paragraph tag (**p**), that is in an article tag using the class **chaptertext** (**article.chaptertext**).

   The emphasis tag would *not* be styled by the code in Step 1 in the following case, because it is not in a **strong** tag:

   ```
   <article class="chaptertext"><p>
   → <em>...</em></p></article>
   ```

   And emphasis will *not* be styled by the code in Step 1 in the following case because the article tag does not have the **chaptertext** class:

   ```
   <article><p><strong><em>...</em>
   → </strong></p></article>
   ```

   It is important to note, though, that although the selectors do not style the emphasis tag in these last two cases, it does *not* mean that styles from other declarations will not do so.

Code 4.1 The style is set for the emphasis tag if its parents are the **h1** tag and the article tag using the copy class **C**.

```html
<!DOCTYPE html>
<html lang="en">
<head>
<meta charset="UTF-8">
<title>Alice&#8217;s Adventures in Wonderland</title>
<style type="text/css" media="all">
    article.chaptertext p strong em {
        color: red;
        font-weight: normal;
        font-size: 2em;
        font-style: normal; }
</style>
</head>
<body>
<article class="chaptertext">
<p><strong>Alice was beginning to get <em>very tired</em> of sitting by her sister on the bank,
→ </strong> and of having nothing to do: <strong>once or twice</strong>  she had peeped into the
→ book her sister was reading, but it <em>had no pictures or conversations in it</em>, <q>and
→ <em>what</em> is the use of a book,</q> <strong>thought Alice</strong>, <q>without pictures or
→ conversations?</q></p>
</article>
</body>
</html>
```

Alice was beginning to get very tired of sitting
by her sister on the bank, and of having nothing to do:
once or twice she had peeped into the book her sister was
reading, but it *had no pictures or conversations in it*, "and
what is the use of a book," **thought Alice**, "without pictures
or conversations?"

C **The results of Code 4.1.** The only text that meets the selective criteria is in red, which is only the emphasis tag in the **h1**, in this example.

To style descendents universally:

1. **Set up a list of descendent selectors including a universal selector.** Type the HTML selector of the parent tag, followed by a space, and then an asterisk (*) or other selectors (**Code 4.2**).

   ```
   article.chaptertext p * em {...}
   ```

2. **Styles will be used *only* if the pattern is matched.** Generally, the universal selector is used at the end of a list of selectors so that the style is applied explicitly to all of a parent's direct descendents (children). However, the styles will not be directly applied to those children's descendents.

   In this example, the style is applied to the emphasis tag inside *any* parent tag (such as **strong**) in a paragraph, such as:

   ```
   <article class="chaptertext"><p>
   → <strong><em>...</em></strong>
   → </p></article>
   ```

   Or:

   ```
   <article class="chaptertext"><p>
   → <q><em>...</em></q></p></article>
   ```

   However, an emphasis tag that is *not* in another tag in the paragraph will *not* be styled.

   ```
   <article class="chaptertext"><p>
   → <em>...</em></p></article>
   ```

TIP Like grouped selectors, contextual selectors can include class selectors (dependent or independent), ID selectors in the list, and HTML selectors.

Code 4.2 The style is set for the emphasis tag with *any* parent that's in an article tag using the copy class **D**.

```
<!DOCTYPE html>
<html lang="en">
<head>
<meta charset="UTF-8">
<title>Alice&#8217;s Adventures in Wonderland</title>
<style type="text/css" media="all">
    article.chaptertext p * em {
        border: 1px double red;
        font-size: 2em;
        font-weight: normal; }
</style>
</head>
<body>
<article class="chaptertext">
<p><strong>Alice was beginning to get <em>very tired</em> of sitting by her sister on the bank,
→ </strong> and of having nothing to do: <strong>once or twice</strong>  she had peeped into the
→ book her sister was reading, but it <em>had no pictures or conversations in it</em>, <q>and
→ <em>what</em> is the use of a book,</q> <strong>thought Alice</strong>, <q>without pictures or
→ conversations?</q></p>
</article>
</body>
</html>
```

Alice was beginning to get *very tired* of sitting by her sister on the bank, and of having nothing to do: **once or twice** she had peeped into the book her sister was reading, but it *had no pictures or conversations in it*, "and *what* is the use of a book," **thought Alice**, "without pictures or conversations?"

D The results of Code 4.2. The text in red matches the selective criteria with the universal selector. In this case, all emphasis tags match.

Styling only the children

If you want to style only a parent's child elements (not a grandchild descendent), you must specify the parent selector and child selector, separated by a right angle bracket (>) 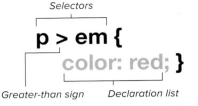.

To define child selectors:

1. **Set up a list of direct child selectors.** Type the selector for the parent element (HTML, class, or ID), followed by a right angle bracket (>) and the child selector (HTML, class, or ID).

   `article.chaptertext > p > em {...}`

   You can repeat this as many times as you want with the final selector being the target to which you apply the styles (**Code 4.3**). You can have *one* space between the selector and the greater-than sign or no spaces.

2. **Styles are used *only* if the pattern is matched.**

   `<article class="chaptertext"><p>`
   `→ <em>...</em></p></article>`

   The styles from Step 1 are applied if and only if the final selector is an immediate child element nested in the preceding element. Placing the tag within any other HTML tags will disrupt the pattern. In this example, the emphasis tag (**em**) is styled only if it is in a paragraph (**p**) within an article (**article**).

   However, any emphasis tag that is in another tag will *not* be styled:

   `<article class="chaptertext"><p>`
   `→ <q><em>...</em></q><p></article>`

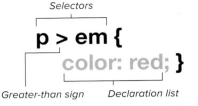

Selectors

p > em {
    color: red; **}**

Greater-than sign   *Declaration list*

E The general syntax of the direct child selector.

Code 4.3 The style is applied to the emphasis tag only if it is a child of a paragraph that is in turn the child of an article tag using the copy class **F**.

```html
<!DOCTYPE html>
<html lang="en">
<head>
<meta charset="UTF-8">
<title>Alice&#8217;s Adventures in Wonderland</title>
<style type="text/css" media="all">
    article.chaptertext > p > em {
        color: silver;
        background: red;
        font-size: 2em;
        font-weight: normal; }
</style>
</head>
<body>
<article class="chaptertext">
<p><strong>Alice was beginning to get <em>very tired</em> of sitting by her sister on the bank,
 </strong> and of having nothing to do: <strong>once or twice</strong>  she had peeped into the
 book her sister was reading, but it <em>had no pictures or conversations in it</em>, <q>and
 <em>what</em> is the use of a book,</q> <strong>thought Alice</strong>, <q>without pictures or
 conversations?</q></p>
</article>
</body>
</html>
```

Alice was beginning to get *very tired* of sitting by her sister on the bank, and of having nothing to do: once or twice she had peeped into the book her sister was reading, but it *had no pictures or conversations in it*, "and *what* is the use of a book," thought Alice, "without pictures or conversations?"

F **The results of Code 4.3**. The text in red matches the direct child criteria. In this case the emphasis tags match within the paragraphs but not within the headers.

Styling siblings

Siblings are elements that have the same parent. You can style a sibling that is immediately adjacent to another or occurs anywhere after that sibling .

To define adjacent sibling selectors:

1. **Set up a list of adjacent sibling selectors.** Type the selector for the first element (HTML, class, or ID), a plus sign (+), and then the selector (HTML, class, or ID) for the adjacent element to which you want the style applied (**Code 4.4**).

   ```
   strong + em {...}
   ```

2. **Styles will be used** *only* **if the pattern is matched.**

   ```
   <strong>...</strong>...<em>...</em>
   ```

   The styles will be applied to any sibling that occurs immediately after the preceding selector with no other selectors in the way. Placing any element between them (even a break tag) will disrupt the pattern. The following pattern will *not* work:

   ```
   <strong>...</strong>...<q>...</q>...
   ⟶ <em>...</em>
   ```

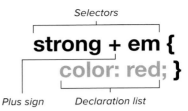

Selectors

Plus sign   *Declaration list*

G The general syntax for the adjacent sibling selector.

Selectors

Tilde   *Declaration list*

H The general syntax for the general sibling selector.

Code 4.4 The style is applied to the emphasis tag only if it is in a paragraph that is immediately after another paragraph ❶.

```
<!DOCTYPE html>
<html lang="en">
<head>
<meta charset="UTF-8">
<title>Alice&#8217;s Adventures in Wonderland</title>
<style type="text/css" media="all">
    strong + em {
        color: red;
        background: silver;
        font-size: 2em; }
</style>
</head>
<body>
<article class="chaptertext">
<p><strong>Alice was beginning to get <em>very tired</em> of sitting by her sister on the bank,
→ </strong> and of having nothing to do: <strong>once or twice</strong>  she had peeped into the
→ book her sister was reading, but it <em>had no pictures or conversations in it</em>, <q>and
→ <em>what</em> is the use of a book,</q> <strong>thought Alice</strong>, <q>without pictures or
→ conversations?</q></p>
</article>
</body>
</html>
```

Alice was beginning to get *very tired* of sitting by her sister on the bank, and of having nothing to do: **once or twice** she had peeped into the book her sister was reading,

but it *had no pictures or conversations in it*, "and *what* is the use of a book," **thought Alice**, "without pictures or conversations?"

❶ **The results of Code 4.4.** The text in red matches the adjacent sibling criteria—the emphasis tags within the second and third paragraphs in this case—but does not match the fourth paragraph because a block quote is in the way.

To define general sibling selectors:

1. **Set up a list of general sibling selectors.** Type the selector for the first sibling element (HTML, class, or ID), a tilde sign (~), and then another selector (HTML, class, or ID) (**Code 4.5**).

   ```
   strong ~ em {...}
   ```

   You can repeat this as many times as necessary, but the last selector in the list is the one you are targeting to be styled.

2. **Styles are used *only* if the pattern is matched.**

   ```
   <strong>...</strong>...<em>...</em>
   → ...<q>...</q>...<em>...</em>
   ```

   The styles are applied to *any* siblings that occur after the first sibling selector, not just the first one. Unlike the adjacent sibling, this is true even when other types of tags are located in between. In the case above, this includes both the second and third **strong** tags

> **TIP** Although the universal selector shown in this section is used with the combinatory selectors, it can be used with any selector type. Table 4.2 shows how you can apply it.

TABLE 4.2 Universal Selector Examples

Format	Elements Are Styled If...
a * b	**b** within **a** regardless of **b**'s parents
a > * > b	**b** is the direct child of any element that is the direct child of **a**
a + * + b	sibling **b** immediately after any element that is immediately after **a**
*:hover	mouse pointer over any element
*:disabled	any element that is disabled
*:first-child	first child of any element
*:lang()	any element using specified language code
*:not(s)	any element that is not the using indicated selectors
*::first-letter	any element's first letter

Code 4.5 The style is applied to the emphasis tag if it is in a paragraph with any preceding sibling that is a paragraph ⓙ.

```
<!DOCTYPE html>
<html lang="en">
<head>
<meta charset="UTF-8">
<title>Alice&#8217;s Adventures in Wonderland</title>
<style type="text/css" media="all">
    strong ~ em {
        color: red;
        background: gray;
        font-size: 2em; }
</style>
</head>
<body>
<article class="chaptertext">
<p><strong>Alice was beginning to get <em>very tired</em> of sitting by her sister on the bank,
 → </strong> and of having nothing to do: <strong>once or twice</strong>  she had peeped into the
 → book her sister was reading, but it <em>had no pictures or conversations in it</em>, <q>and
 → <em>what</em> is the use of a book,</q> <strong>thought Alice</strong>, <q>without pictures or
 → conversations?</q></p>
</article>
</body>
</html>
```

Alice was beginning to get *very tired* of sitting by her sister on the bank, and of having nothing to do: **once or twice** she had peeped into the book her sister was reading,

but it *had no pictures or conversations in it*, "and *what* is the use of a book," **thought Alice**, "without pictures or conversations?"

ⓙ **The results of Code 4.5.** The text in red matches the general sibling criteria—in this case the emphasis tags within the second, third, *and* fourth paragraphs.

★Working with Pseudo-Classes

Many HTML elements have special states or uses associated with them that can be styled independently. One prime example of this is the link tag, **<a>**, which has link (its normal state), a visited state (when the visitor has already been to the page represented by the link), hover (when the visitor has the mouse over the link), and active (when the visitor clicks the link). All four of these states can be styled separately.

A *pseudo-class* is a predefined state or use of an element that can be styled independently of the default state of the element 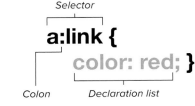.

- **Links (Table 4.3)**—Pseudo-classes are used to style not only the initial appearance of the anchor tag, but also how it appears after it has been visited, while the visitor hovers the mouse over it, and when visitors are clicking it.

- **Dynamic (Table 4.3)**—Pseudo-classes can be applied to any element to define how it is styled when the user hovers over it, clicks it, or selects it.

- **Structural (Table 4.4)**—Pseudo-classes are similar to the sibling combinatory selectors but allow you to specifically style elements based on an exact or computed numeric position.

- **Other (Table 4.4)**—Pseudo-classes are available to style elements based on language or based on what tag they are *not*.

A General syntax of a pseudo-class.

TABLE 4.3 Link and Dynamic Pseudo-Classes

Format	Selector Name	Elements Are Styled If...					
`:link`	Link	the value of href is not in history	●	●	●	●	●
`:visited`	Visited link	the value of href is in history	●	●	●	●	●
`:target`	Targeted link	a targeted anchor link	●	●	●	●	●
`:active`	Active	the element is clicked	●	●	●	●	●
`:hover`	Hover	the pointer is over the element	●	●	●	●	●
`:focus`	Focus	the element has screen focus	●	●	●	●	●

TABLE 4.4 Structural/Other Pseudo-Classes

Format	Selector Name	Elements Are Styled If...					
`:root`	Root	is the top level element in a document	●9	●	●	●	●
`:empty`	Empty	has no children	●9	●	●	●	●
`:only-child`	Only child	has no siblings	●9	●	●	●	●
`:only-of-type`	Only of type	has its unique selector among its siblings	●9	●	●	●	●
`:first-child`	First-child	is the first child of another element	●9	●	●	●	●
`:nth-of-type(n)`	Nth of type	is the nth element with that selector	●9	●	●	●	●
`:nth-last-of-type(n)`	Nth from last of type	is the nth element with that selector from the last element with that selector	●9	●	●	●	●
`:last-child`	Last child	is the last child in the parent element	●9	●	●	●	●
`:first-of-type`	First of type	is the first of its selector type in the parent element	●9	●	●	●	●
`:last-of-type`	Last of type	is the last of its selector type in the parent element	●9	●	●	●	●
`:lang()`	Language	has a specified language code defined	●8	●	●	●	●
`:not(s)`	Negation	is not using specific selectors	●9	●	●	●	●

Styling links

Although a link is a tag, its individual states are not. To set properties for these states, you must use the pseudo-classes associated with each state that a link can have (in this order):

- **:link** lets you declare the appearance of hypertext links that have not yet been selected.

- **:visited** lets you set the appearance of links that the visitor selected previously—that is, the URL of the **href** attribute in the tag that is part of the browser's history.

- **:hover** lets you set the appearance of the element when the visitor's pointer is over it.

- **:active** sets the style of the element when it is clicked or selected by the visitor.

For ideas on which styles to use with links, see the sidebar "Picking Link Styles."

To set contrasting link appearances:

1. Style the anchor tag.

   `a {...}`

   Although not required, it's best to first define the general anchor style (**Code 4.6**). This differs from setting the **:link** pseudo-class in that these styles are applied to all the link pseudo-classes. So, you want to declare any styles that will remain constant or are changed in only one of the states.

   continues on page 86

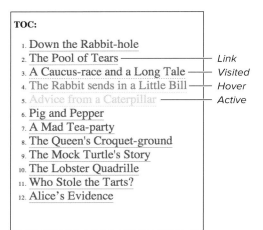

B The results of **Code 4.6** show the links styled for each state to help the user understand what's going on.

Code 4.6 The link styles are set for the default and then all four link states, creating color differentiation ⓑ. Notice also that I've turned off underlining with text decoration but added an underline effect using border bottom.

```html
<!DOCTYPE html>
<html lang="en">
<head>
<meta charset="UTF-8">
<title>Alice&#8217;s Adventures in Wonderland</title>
<style type="text/css" media="all">
   a {
      text-decoration: none;
      font-size: 2em; }
   a:link {
      color: darkred;
      border-bottom: 1px solid red; }
   a:visited {
      color: darkred;
      border-bottom: 1px dashed red; }
   a:hover {
      color: red;
      border-bottom: 1px solid pink; }
   a:active {
      color: pink;
      border-bottom: 1px solid pink; }
</style>
</head>
<body>
<nav>
<h2>TOC:</h2>
<ol>
<li><a href="AAIWL-ch01.html">Down the Rabbit-hole</a></li>
<li><a href="AAIWL-ch02.html">The Pool of Tears</a></li>
<li><a href="AAIWL-ch03.html">A Caucus-race and a Long Tale</a></li>
<li><a href="AAIWL-ch04.html">The Rabbit sends in a Little Bill</a></li>
<li><a href="AAIWL-ch05.html">Advice from a Caterpillar</a></li>
<li><a href="AAIWL-ch06.html">Pig and Pepper</a></li>
<li><a href="AAIWL-ch07.html">A Mad Tea-party</a></li>
<li><a href="AAIWL-ch08.html">The Queen's Croquet-ground</a></li>
<li><a href="AAIWL-ch09.html">The Mock Turtle's Story</a></li>
<li><a href="AAIWL-ch010.html">The Lobster Quadrille</a></li>
<li><a href="AAIWL-ch011.html">Who Stole the Tarts?</a></li>
<li><a href="AAIWL-ch012.html">Alice&#8217;s Evidence</a></li>
</ol>
</nav>
</body>
</html>
```

2. **Style the *default* link state.** Type the selector (anchor tag, class, or ID) of the element you want to style, followed by a colon (:), and then `link`.

```
a:link {...}
```

You can override styles set for the anchor tag, but this rule should always come before the `:visited` pseudo-class.

3. **Style the *visited* link style.** Type the selector (anchor, class, or ID) of the element you want to style, followed by a colon (:), and then `visited`.

```
a:visited {...}
```

4. **Style the *hover* link state.** Type the selector (anchor, class, or ID) of the element you want to style, followed by a colon (:), and then `hover`.

```
a:hover {...}
```

5. **Style the *active* link state.** Type the selector (anchor, class, or ID) of the element you want to style, followed by a colon (:), and then `active`.

```
a:active {...}
```

6. **Style is applied to the link state as needed.**

```
<a href="AAIWL-ch01.html">...</a>
```

All links on the page will obey the rules you lay down here when styling the various link states. You can—and should—use selective styling to differentiate link types.

In this example, the pseudo-classes are applied directly to the anchor tag, but any class or ID could have been used as long as it was then applied to an anchor tag.

Picking Link Styles

Most browsers default to blue for unvisited links and red or purple for visited links. The problem with using two different colors for visited and unvisited links is that visitors may not remember which color applies to which type of link. The colors you choose must distinguish links from other text on the screen and distinguish among the states (link, visited, hover, and active) without dominating the screen and becoming distracting.

I recommend using a color for unvisited links that contrasts with both the page's background color and the text color. Then, for visited links, use a darker or lighter version of the same color that contrasts with the background but is dimmer than the unvisited link color. Brighter not-followed links will then stand out dramatically from the dimmer followed links.

For example, on a page with a white background and black text, I might use bright red for links (rgb(255,0,0)) and pale red (rgb(255,153,153)) for visited links. The brighter version stands out; the paler version is less distinctive, but still obviously a link.

TIP You can apply the dynamic pseudo-classes `:hover`,`:active`, and `:focus` to any element, not just links.

TIP The general anchor link styles will be inherited by the different states and between states. The font you set for the `:link` appearance, for example, will be inherited by the `:active`, `:visited`, and `:hover` states.

TIP The Web is a hypertext medium, so it is important that users be able to distinguish among text, links, and visited links. Because users don't always have their Underline Links option turned on, it's a good idea to set the link appearance for every document.

TIP If you use too many colors, your visitors may not be able to tell which words are links and which are not.

TIP The link styles are set for the entire page in this example, but links can be used for a variety of purposes. For example, links might be used for global navigation, in a list of article titles, or even as a dynamic control. To that end, it's a good idea to style links depending on their usage:

```
nav a {...}
nav a:link {...}
nav a:visited {...}
```

TIP The preceding styles would be applied only to links in the navigation element.

Styling for interaction

Once loaded, Web pages are far from static. Users will start interacting with the page right away, moving their pointers across the screen and clicking hither and yon. The dynamic pseudo-classes allow you to style elements as the user interacts with them, providing visual feedback:

- **:hover**—Same as for links, but sets the appearance of the element when the pointer is hovering over it.

- **:focus**—Applied to elements that can receive focus, such as form text fields.

- **:active**—Same as for links, but sets the style of the element when it is clicked or selected.

To define a dynamic pseudo-class:

1. Style the *default* element.

   `input {...}`

   Although optional, it's generally a good idea to set the default, non-dynamic style for the elements receiving dynamic styles (**Code 4.7**).

2. Style the *hover* state of the element. Type the selector (HTML, class, or ID), a colon (**:**), and then **hover**.

   `input:hover {...}`

   As soon as the pointer enters the element's box (see Chapter 10 for details about the box model), the style change will occur.

Code 4.7 The input elements, with a special style for the button type, are set to change style when the user interacts with them by hovering, selecting (focus), or clicking (active) **C**.

```
<!DOCTYPE html>
<html lang="en">
<head>
<meta charset="UTF-8">
<title>Alice&#8217;s Adventures in
Wonderland</title>
<style type="text/css" media="all">
    input {
        border: 3px solid gray;
        background-color: silver;
        color: gray;
        padding: 0 5px;
        font-size: 1.5em; }
    input[type="button"] {
        border-radius: 1em;
        color: silver;
        background-color: gray; }
    input:hover {
        background-color: white;
        border-color: pink;
        color: silver; }
    input:focus {
        border-color: red;
        background-color: white;
        color: black;
        outline: none; }
    input:active {
        color: red;
        border-color: pink;
        background-color: silver; }
</style>
</head>
<body>
<footer>
    <label>Mailing List:</label>
    <input type="text" value="email"
    → placeholder="enter your eMail">
    <input type="button" class="active"
    → value="submit">
</footer>
</body>
</html>
```

Default

Hover

Active

Focus

Ⓒ **The results of Code 4.7.** This shows a simple form field in the four dynamic states. Providing this visual feedback can help users know which form field is ready for use or that they have clicked a button.

3. **Style the *focus* state of the element.**
   Type the selector (HTML, class, or ID), a colon (**:**), and then **focus**.

   ```
   input:focus {...}
   ```

   As soon as the element receives focus (is clicked or tabbed to), the style change occurs and then reverts to the hover or default style when the element loses focus (called *blur*).

4. **Style the *active* state of the element.**
   Type the selector (HTML, class, or ID), a colon (**:**), and then **active**.

   ```
   input:active {...}
   ```

   As soon as the user clicks within the element's box (explained in Chapter 10), the style change will occur and then revert to either the hover or default style when released.

5. **The styles are applied to the elements' states as necessary in reaction to the user.**

   ```
   <input type="button" value=
   → "Submit">
   ```

   All the tags using the specific selector will have their states styled.

TIP I recommend caution when changing some attributes for :hover. Changing typeface, font size, weight, and other properties may make the text grow larger or smaller than the space reserved for it in the layout and force the whole page to reflow its content, which can really annoy visitors.

TIP In this example, input is used to show the dynamic states. The input has one styling drawback in that all input types use the same tag. Later in this chapter, you will see how to use tag attributes to set styles, which will allow you to set different styles for text fields and buttons.

TIP The order in which you define your link and dynamic pseudo-classes makes a difference. For example, placing the :hover pseudo-class before the :visited pseudo-class keeps :hover from working after a link has been visited. For best results, define your styles in this order: link, visited, hover, focus, and active.

TIP One way to remember the pseudo-element order is the meme LoVe HAte: Link Visited Hover Active.

TIP You will want to always set :focus if you're setting :hover. Why? Hover is applied only to non-keyboard (mouse) interactions with the element. For keyboard-only Web users, :focus will apply.

★Styling specific children with pseudo-classes

Designers often want to apply a style to an element that is the first element to appear within another element, such as a parent's first child.

The first-child pseudo-element has been available since CSS2; however, CSS3 offers an assortment of new structural pseudo-elements for styling an element's child element exactly (**Table 4.4**):

- **:first-child**—Sets the appearance of the first instance of a selector type if it is the first child of its parent.

- **:first-of-type**—Sets the appearance of an element the first time its selector type appears within the parent.

- **:nth-child(#)**—Sets the appearance of the specific occurrence of the specified child element. For example, the third child element of a paragraph would be **p:nth-child(3)**.

- **:nth-of-type(#)**—Sets the appearance of the specific occurrence of a selector type within the parent. For example, the seventh paragraph would be **p:nth-of-type(7)**.

- **:nth-last-of-type(#)**—Sets the appearance of the specific occurrence of a selector type within the parent, but from the bottom. For example, the third paragraph from the bottom would be **p:nth-last-of-type(3)**.

- **:last-child**—Sets the appearance of the element of the indicated selector type if it is the last child of the parent.

- **:last-of-type**—Sets the appearance of the last instance of a particular selector type within its parent.

Text Decoration: To Underline or Not

Underlining is the standard way of indicating a hypertext link on the Web. However, the presence of many underlined links turns a page into an impenetrable mass of lines, and the text becomes difficult to read. In addition, if visitors have underlining turned off, they cannot see the links, especially if the link and text colors are the same.

CSS allows you to turn off underlining for links, overriding the visitor's preference. I recommend this practice and prefer to rely on clear color choices to highlight hypertext links or to rely on the alternative underlining method of border-bottom, which allows you better control over the style of the underline. See Chapter 14 for more information.

Code 4.8 The list has styles set based on the location within the list **D**.

```
<!DOCTYPE html>
<html lang="en">
<head>
<meta charset="UTF-8">
<title>Alice&#8217;s Adventures in
Wonderland</title>
<style type="text/css" media="all">
    li {
        font-size: 1.5em;
        margin: .25em; }
    li:first-child { color: red; }
    li:first-of-type { border-bottom: 1px
    → solid orange; }
    li:nth-child(2)  { color: yellow; }
    li:nth-of-type(6) { color: green; }
    li:nth-last-of-type(2) { color: blue; }
    li:last-of-type { border-bottom: 1px
    → solid indigo; }
    li:last-child { color: violet; }
</style>
</head>
<body>
<nav>
<ol>
    <li>Down the Rabbit-hole</li>
    <li>The Pool of Tears</li>
    <li>A Caucus-race and a Long Tale</li>
    <li>The Rabbit sends in a Little Bill
    → </li>
    <li>Advice from a Caterpillar</li>
    <li>Pig and Pepper</li>
    <li>The Queen's Croquet-ground</li>
    <li>The Mock Turtle's Story</li>
    <li>The Lobster Quadrille</li>
    <li>Who Stole the Tarts?</li>
    <li>Alice&#8217;s Evidence</li>
</ol>
</nav>
</body>
</html>
```

To style the children of an element:

1. **Style the children based on their positions in the parent.** Type the selector (HTML, class, or ID) of the element you want to style, a colon (**:**), and one of the structural pseudo-elements from **Table 4.4 (Code 4.8)**.

   `li:first-child {...}`

   `li:first-of-type {...}`

   `li:nth-of-type(3) {...}`

   `li:nth-last-of-type(2) {...}`

   `li:last-child {...}`

   `li:last-of-type {...}`

2. **Elements will be styled if they match the pattern.**

   `<li>...</li>`

   Set up your HTML with the selectors from Step 1 in mind.

1. Down the Rabbit-hole
2. The Pool of Tears
3. A Caucus-race and a Long Tale
4. The Rabbit sends in a Little Bill
5. Advice from a Caterpillar
6. Pig and Pepper
7. The Queen's Croquet-ground
8. The Mock Turtle's Story
9. The Lobster Quadrille
10. Who Stole the Tarts?
11. Alice's Evidence

D The results of Code 4.8 show the items in the list styled separately. In this case, the first child and first of type are the same element as the last element and last of type.

Styling for a particular language

The World Wide Web is just that—all around the world—which means that anyone, anywhere can see your pages. It also means that Web pages are created in many languages.

The `:lang()` pseudo-class lets you specify styles that depend on the language specified by the language property.

To set a style for a specific language:

1. **Style an element based on its language code.** Type the selector (HTML, class, or ID) of the element you want to style, a colon (`:`), `lang`, and enter the letter code for the language you are defining within parentheses (**Code 4.9**).

   ```
   p:lang(fr) {...}
   ```

2. **The element is styled if it has a matching language code.** Set up your tag in the HTML with the language attributes as necessary.

   ```
   <p lang="fr">...</p>
   ```

   If the indicated selector has its language attribute equal to the same value that you indicated in parentheses in Step 1, the style is applied.

   You can use any string as the language letter code, as long as it matches the value in the HTML. However, the W3C recommends using the codes from RFC 3066 or its successor. For more on language tags, visit www.w3.org/International/articles/language-tags.

TIP Language styles can go far beyond simple colors and fonts. Many languages have specific symbols for quotes and punctuation, which CSS can add. In Chapter 9, you will find information on how to style quotes for a particular language.

Code 4.9 Styles are set to turn paragraphs red if they are in French (fr) **Ⓔ**.

```
<!DOCTYPE html>
<html lang="en">
<head>
<meta charset="UTF-8">
<title>Alice&#8217;s Adventures in Wonderland</title>
<style type="text/css" media="all">
    q:lang(fr) {
        quotes: '«''»';
        color: red; }
</style>
</head>
<body>
<article class="chaptertext">
<p>Alice was beginning to get very tired of sitting by her sister on the bank, and of having
→ nothing to do: once or twice she had peeped into the book her sister was reading, but it had no
→ pictures or conversations in it, <q>and what is the use of a book,</q> thought Alice, <q>without
→ pictures or conversations?</q></p>
<p class="translation" lang="fr">Alice commençait à être très fatigué d'être assis par sa sœur sur
→ la rive, et de n'avoir rien à faire: une fois ou deux, elle avait regarda dans le livre de sa sœur
→ lisait, mais il n'avait pas d'images ni dialogues en elle, <q>et ce qui est l'utilisation d'un
→ livre,</q> pensait Alice, <q>sans images ni dialogues?</q></p>
</article>
</body>
</html>
```

Alice was beginning to get very tired of sitting by her sister on the bank, and of having nothing to do: once or twice she had peeped into the book her sister was reading, but it had no pictures or conversations in it, "and what is the use of a book," thought Alice, "without pictures or conversations?"

Alice commençait à être très fatigué d'être assis par sa sœur sur la rive, et de n'avoir rien à faire: une fois ou deux, elle avait regarda dans le livre de sa sœur lisait, mais il n'avait pas d'images ni dialogues en elle, «et ce qui est l'utilisation d'un livre,» pensait Alice, «sans images ni dialogues?»

Ⓔ The results of Code 4.9 show the paragraph in French rendered in red (with my apologies to French speakers).

★ *Not* styling an element

So far you've looked at ways to style a tag if it *is* something. The negation selector, **:not,** allows you to *not* style something for a particular selector.

To not set a style for a particular element:

1. **Style elements to exclude certain selectors.** Type the selector (HTML, class, or ID) of the element you want to style, a colon (**:**), **not**, and enter the selectors you want excluded from this rule in parentheses (**Code 4.10**).

   ```
   p:not(.dialog) {...}
   ```

2. **The element is not styled if it contains the indicated selector.**

   ```
   <p class='dialog'>...</p>
   → <p>...</p>
   ```

   The styles are applied to elements that match the initial selector but *not* the selector in parentheses.

Code 4.10 When the element is a paragraph that does not use the dialog class, it will be displayed in red and italics **F**.

```
<! DOCTYPE html>
<html lang="en">
<head>
<meta charset="UTF-8">
<title>Alice&#8217;s Adventures in Wonderland</title>
<style type="text/css" media="all">
    q:lang(fr) {
        quotes: '«''»'; }
    p:not(.translation) {
        color: red; }
</style>
</head>
<body>
<article class="chaptertext">
<p>Alice was beginning to get very tired of sitting by her sister on the bank, and of
→ having nothing to do: once or twice she had peeped into the book her sister was reading,
→ but it had no pictures or conversations in it, <q>and what is the use of a book,</q>
→ thought Alice, <q>without pictures or conversations?</q></p>
<p class="translation" lang="fr">Alice commençait à être très fatigué d'être assis par sa sœur
→ sur la rive, et de n'avoir rien à faire: une fois ou deux, elle avait regarda dans le livre de sa
→ sœur lisait, mais il n'avait pas d'images ni dialogues en elle, <q>et ce qui est l'utilisation d'un
→ livre,</q> pensait Alice, <q>sans images ni dialogues?</q></p>
</article>
</body>
</html>
```

Alice was beginning to get very tired of sitting by her sister on the bank, and of having nothing to do: once or twice she had peeped into the book her sister was reading, but it had no pictures or conversations in it, "and what is the use of a book," thought Alice, "without pictures or conversations?"

Alice commençait à être très fatigué d'être assis par sa sœur sur la rive, et de n'avoir rien à faire: une fois ou deux, elle avait regarda dans le livre de sa sœur lisait, mais il n'avait pas d'images ni dialogues en elle, «et ce qui est l'utilisation d'un livre,» pensait Alice, «sans images ni dialogues?»

F **The results of Code 4.10.** This shows that the paragraph that does use the dialog class does not receive the style.

Working with Pseudo-Elements

A *pseudo-element* is a specific, unique part of an element—such as the first letter or first line of a paragraph—that can be styled independently of the rest of the element. (For a list of other pseudo-elements, see **Table 4.5**.)

Working with first letters and lines

You can access the first letter of any block of text directly using the `:first-letter` pseudo-element. The first line of any block of text can be isolated for style treatment using the `:first-line` pseudo-element 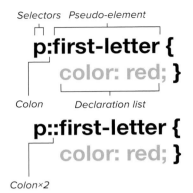.

To highlight the beginning of an article:

1. Style the default version of the element.

   ```
   article p {...}
   ```

   Although not required, it's generally a good idea to set the default style of the selector for which you will be styling the `:first-letter` pseudo-element (**Code 4.11**).

Selectors Pseudo-element

p:first-letter {
color: red; }

Colon Declaration list

p::first-letter {
color: red; }

Colon×2

A The general syntax for pseudo-elements. Pseudo-elements can have either a single or double colon, but use a single colon at present for increased browser compatibility.

Chapter I Down the Rabbit-Hole

Alice was beginning to get very tired of sitting by her sister on the bank, and of having nothing to do: once or twice she had peeped into the book her sister was reading, but it had no pictures or conversations in it, "and what is the use of a book," thought Alice, "without pictures or conversations?"

B The results of Code 4.11. A common typographic trick to draw the reader's eye to the beginning of a paragraph is to use a drop cap and to bold the first line of text, as shown here.

TABLE 4.5 Pseudo-Elements

Format	Selector Name	Elements Are Styled If...					
`:first-letter`, `::first-letter`	the first letter	first letter in text	●	●	●	●	●
`:first-line`, `::first-line`	the first line of text	they are the first line of text	●	●	●	●	●
`:after`, `::after`	After	space immediately before element	●8	●	●	●	●
`:before`, `::before`	Before	space immediately after element	●8	●	●	●	●

Code 4.11 Styles are set for the first letter and first line of the first paragraph in an article **B**.

```
<!DOCTYPE html>
<html lang="en">
<head>
<meta charset="UTF-8">
<title>Alice&#8217;s Adventures in
→ Wonderland</title>
<style type="text/css" media="all">
    article p {
        color: gray;
        font-size: 1em;
        line-height: 1.5;
        margin: .875em 2em;
        }
    article p:first-of-type::first-letter {
        color: red;
        font-size: 3em;
        float: left;
        margin: -.25em .05em 0 0; }
    article p:first-of-type::first-line {
        color: black;
        font-size: 1.25em;
        font-weight: bold; }
</style>
</head>
<body>
<article class="chaptertext">
<h2>Chapter I
<span class="chaptertitle">Down the
→ Rabbit-Hole</span>
</h2>
<p>Alice was beginning to get very tired
→ of sitting by her sister on the bank,
→ and of having nothing to do: once or
→ twice she had peeped into the book
→ her sister was reading, but it had
→ no pictures or conversations in it,
→ <q>and what is the use of a book,</q>
→ thought Alice, <q>without pictures or
→ conversations?</q></p>
</article>
</body>
</html>
```

2. **Style the first letter of the element if it is the first of its type.** Type the selector you want to style the first letter of (**article p**), a colon (**:**), and then **first-letter**.

   ```
   article p:first-of-type::
   → first-letter {...}
   ```

   To affect only the first paragraph in an article, you can add the **:first-of-type** pseudo-class, as in this example.

3. **Style the first line of the element's text if it is the first of its type.** Type the selector (**article p**) for which you want to style the first letter, a colon (**:**), and then **first-line**.

   ```
   article p:first-of-type::
   → first-line {...}
   ```

   In this example, the **first-of-type** pseudo-class is added so that only the first paragraph in an article is styled.

4. **The element's first letter and first line of text is styled if it is the first of its type in the parent element.** Add the class attribute to the relevant HTML tag.

   ```
   <p>...</p>
   ```

   Although you do not have to use a class, you generally will want to selectively style the first letter of elements rather than style them all universally.

TIP Drop-cap styled letters are a time-honored way to start a new section or chapter by making the first letter of a paragraph larger than subsequent letters and moving several lines of text to accommodate the larger letter. Medieval monks used drop caps with illuminated manuscripts. Now you can use them on the Web.

Setting content before and after an element

The `:before` and `:after` pseudo-elements can be used to generate content that appears above or below a selector. Generally, these pseudo-classes are used with the **content** property. (See "Adding Content Using CSS" in Chapter 9.) The pseudo-elements let you add and style repetitive content to the page in a consistent way.

To set content before and after an element:

1. **Style the element.**

   ```
   h2 {...}
   ```

   Although not required, it's generally a good idea to set the default style of the selector for which you will be styling the `:before` and `:after` pseudo-elements. (See **Code 4.12**.)

2. **Add content before the element.** Type the selector (HTML, class, or ID) you want to add content before, a colon (**:**), and then the keyword **before**.

   ```
   h2:before { content:... }
   ```

   Next, declare the **content** property and define what generated content goes before the element and how it should be styled.

Code 4.12 Before and after pseudo-elements are used to add content—images **C** in this case—to the page header **D**.

```
<!DOCTYPE html>
<html lang="en">
<head>
<meta charset="UTF-8">
<title>Alice&#8217;s Adventures in
→ Wonderland</title>
<style type="text/css" media="all">
    h2 {
        font-size: 2em;
        color: red; }
    h2::before {
        content:  url('bullet-01.png'); }
    h2::after {
        content: url('bullet-02.png'); }
</style>
</head>
<body>
<article class="chaptertext">
<h2> Chapter I
<span class="chaptertitle">Down the
→ Rabbit-Hole</span>
</h2>
<p>Alice was beginning to get very tired
→ of sitting by her sister on the bank,
→ and of having nothing to do: once or
→ twice she had peeped into the book
→ her sister was reading, but it had
→ no pictures or conversations in it, <q>
→ and what is the use of a book,</q>
→ thought Alice, <q>without pictures or
→ conversations?</q></p>
</article>
</body>
</html>
```

C bullet-01.png & bullet-02.png will be used as flourishes around titles.

◆ Chapter I Down the Rabbit-Hole ◆

Alice was beginning to get very tired of sitting by her sister on the bank, and of having nothing to do: once or twice she had peeped into the book her sister was reading, but it had no pictures or conversations in it, "and what is the use of a book," thought Alice, "without pictures or conversations?"

So she was considering in her own mind (as well as she could, for the hot day made her feel very sleepy and stupid) whether the pleasure of making a daisy-chain would be worth the trouble of getting up and picking the daisies, when suddenly a White Rabbit with pink eyes ran close by her.

There was nothing so *very* remarkable in that; nor did Alice think it so *very* much out of the way to hear the Rabbit say to itself, "Oh dear! Oh dear! I shall be too late!" (when she thought it over afterwards, it occurred to her that she ought to have wondered at this, but at the time it all seemed quite natural); but when the Rabbit actually *took a watch out of its waistcoat-pocket*, and looked at it, and then hurried on, Alice started to her feet, for it flashed across her mind that she had

---

D The header now has a bit of flourish added before and after by the CSS. These images take up space as if they were in an image tag, but do not show up in the HTML code.

3. Add content after the element. Type the selector (HTML, class, or ID) you want to add content after, a colon (**:**), and then the keyword **after**.

`h2:after { content:... }`

Next, declare the **content** property and define what generated content goes after the element and how it should be styled.

The pseudo-element syntax in CSS3 has undergone a slight change from the CSS2 syntax (which is rare). Pseudo-elements now have a double colon to distinguish them from pseudo-classes. Existing pseudo-elements can use either single or double colons. New and future pseudo-elements should use double colons, but will work with a single colon.

TIP Since IE8 does not support double colon syntax for CSS2 pseudo-elements, it's a good idea to use single colon syntax for older pseudo-elements until all browsers have adopted the syntax. Double colon will not work in IE8 anyway.

TIP Be careful when using **before** and **after** to add content to your page. This content will not appear to search engines or screen readers, so do not rely on it for anything vital.

Defining Styles Based on Tag Attributes

Although style attributes should all be handled by CSS, many HTML tags still have attributes that define how they behave. For example, the image tag, **img**, always includes the **src** attribute to define the source for the image file to be loaded.

Styles can be assigned to an HTML element based on an attribute or an attribute value, allowing you to set styles if the attribute has been set, is or is not a specific value, or contains a specific value (**Table 4.6**).

To set styles based on an element's attributes:

1. **Set styles if the element has a specific property.** To set styles based on the existence of an attribute, type the selector you want to style (HTML, class, or ID), a left bracket (**[**), the name of the attribute you want to check for, and a right bracket (**]**) (**Code 4.13**) 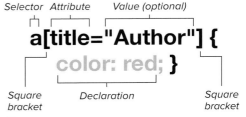.

    a[title] {...}

Selector Attribute Value (optional)

a[title="Author"] {
color: red; }

Square bracket Declaration Square bracket

Ⓐ The general syntax of an attribute selector.

About The Book:

- Alice's Adventures in Wonderland
- Lewis Carroll
- John Tenniel
- Arthur Rackham
- Download Examples
- More Info
- Order The Book

Ⓑ **The results of Code 4.13.** This shows how styles are applied to elements based on their properties.

TABLE 4.6 Attribute Selectors

Format	Name	Elements Are Styled If That Element:	🜁	🜂	🜃	🜄	🜅
[attr]	Attribute	has specified attribute	●	●	●	●	●
[attr="value"]	Exact value	has specified attribute equal to exact value	●	●	●	●	●
[attr~="value"]	Spaced list	has specified attribute equal to exact value within space-separated list	●	●	●	●	●
[attr|="value"]	Hyphenated list	has specified attribute equal to exact value within hyphen-separated list	●	●	●	●	●
[attr^="value"]	Begins with	has specified attribute equal to exact value at beginning	●	●	●	●	●
[attr$="value"]	Ends with	has specified attribute equal to exact value at end	●	●	●	●	●
[attr*="value"]	Contains	has specified attribute equal to exact value anywhere	●	●	●	●	●

Code 4.13 HTML tags can have different attributes, and you can add styles to an element based on its attributes **B**.

```
<!DOCTYPE html>
<html lang="en">
<head>
<meta charset="UTF-8">
<title>Alice&#8217;s Adventures in
→ Wonderland</title>
<style type="text/css" media="all">
   a { display: block; font-size: 2em;}
   a[title] { color: red; }
   a[title="Author"] {color: orange; }
   a[title~="white"] { color: yellow; }
   a[title|="illustrations"] { color:
   → green; }
   a[href^="http://"] {color: blue; }
   a[href*="order"] {color: indigo; }
   a[href$="css3-vqs"] {color: violet; }

</style>
</head>
<body>
<article class="chaptertext">
<h1>About The Book:</h1>
<ul>
   <li><a href="index.html" title="Alice's
   → Adventures in Wonderland">
   → Alice&#8217;s Adventures in
   → Wonderland</a></li>
   <li><a href="index.html"
   → title="Author">Lewis Carroll</a></li>
   <li><a href="index.html" title=
   → "illustrations black white">John
   → Tenniel</a></li>
   <li><a href="index.html" title=
   → "illustrations-full-color">Arthur
   → Rackham</a></li>
   <li><a href="http://www.jasonspeaking
   → .com">Download Examples</a></li>
   <li><a href="http://www.jasonspeaking
   → .com/css3-vqs/order">More Info</a>
   → </li>
   <li><a href="http://www.jasonspeaking
   → .com/css3-vqs">Order The Book</a></li>
</article>
</body>
</html>
```

This will assign the styles you declare only if the tag has this attribute assigned to it regardless of the value.

2. **Set styles if a string exactly matches the property's value.** To set styles based on an attribute's exact value, type the selector you want to style (HTML, class, or ID), a left bracket (**[**), the name of the attribute you want to check for, an equals sign (**=**), the value you are testing for in quotes (**'...'**), and a right bracket (**]**). The value is case sensitive.

   `a[title='home'] {...}`

   This will assign the styles you declare only if the tag has this attribute assigned to it with the exact assigned value.

3. **Set styles if a string is in a space-separated list of values.** To set styles based on an attribute's value that is within a list of space-separated values (for example, a particular word in a sentence), type the selector you want to style (HTML, class, or ID), a left bracket (**[**), the name of the attribute you want to check for, a tilde (**~**), an equals sign (**=**), the value you are testing for in quotes (**'...'**), and a right bracket (**]**).

   `a[title~="email"] {...}`

   This will assign the styles you declare only if the tag has the attribute assigned to it with a value that contains the string as part of a space-separated list. Generally, this means that it is a word in a sentence. Partial words do not count. So in this example, testing for **'mail'** would not work.

continues on next page

4. **Sets the style if the string is in a hyphenated list of values assigned to the property.** To set styles based on an attribute's value being the first in a list separated by hyphens, type the selector you want to style (HTML, class, or ID), a left bracket (**[**), the name of the attribute you want to check for, a bar (**|**), an equals sign (**=**), the value you are testing for in quotes (**'...'**), and a right bracket (**]**).

   `a[title|="resume"]`

   This will assign the styles you declare only if the tag has this attribute assigned to it with a value that contains the string at the beginning of a hyphen-separated list. Generally, this is used for styling languages as an alternative to using the language pseudo-class.

5. ★**Set styles if a string is the value's prefix.** To set styles based on the value at the beginning of an attribute, type the selector you want to style (HTML, class, or ID), a left bracket (**[**), the name of the attribute you want to check for, a carat (**^**), an equals sign (**=**), the value you are testing for in quotes (**'...'**), and a right bracket (**]**).

   `a[href^="http://"]`

   This will assign the styles you declare only if the value string occurs exactly as it is in the quotes at the beginning of the attribute value.

6. ★**Set styles if a string is the property value's suffix.** To set styles based on an attribute's value being the first in a hyphen-separated list, type the selector you want to style (HTML, class, or ID), a left bracket (**[**), the name of the attribute you want to check for, a dollar sign (**$**), an equals sign (**=**), the value you are testing for in quotes (**'...'**), and a right bracket (**]**).

`a[href$=".info"]`

This will assign the styles you declare only if the value occurs at the end of the attribute's value.

7. **Set styles if a string is anywhere in the property value.** To set styles based on an attribute's value being the first in a hyphen-separated list, type the selector you want to style (HTML, class, or ID), a left bracket (**[**), the name of the attribute you want to check for, an asterisk (*****), an equals sign (**=**), the value you are testing for in quotes (**'...'**), and a right bracket (**]**).

`a[href*="speakinginstyles"]`

This will assign the styles you declare if the value occurs anywhere in the attribute's value.

Values are case sensitive. In other words, "Alice" and "alice" are two different values.

★Querying the Media

In Chapter 3 you learned how to specify style sheets for a particular media type, allowing you to set styles depending on whether the HTML is output to a screen, print, TV, or a handheld or other device (**Table 4.7**). CSS3 adds an important new capability that allows you to set styles based on common interface properties such as width, height, aspect ratio, and number of available colors.

Media queries and the `@media` rule can be used to tailor your page, not just to a general device type but to the specific device your site visitor is using. This includes sizing for print, for mobile devices, or to best fit the size of the open browser window.

Media queries

If you want to know the current size of the browser window, why not just ask the browser? JavaScript gives you the ability to do this, but it's a cumbersome way to get some basic facts about the Webbed environment your design is trying to fit into.

Media queries provide you with several common media properties that you can test **A** and then deliver the style sheet that best suits the environment.

Although media queries have many properties (**Table 4.8**), they come in five basic flavors:

- **Aspect-ratio** looks for the relative dimensions of the device expressed as a ratio: 16:9, for example.

- **Width** and **height** looks for the dimensions of the display area. These can also be expressed as maximum and minimum values.

continues on page 106

TABLE 4.7 Media Values

Value	Intended for
screen	Computer displays
tty	Teletypes, computer terminals, and older portable devices
tv	Television displays
projection	Projectors
handheld	Portable phones and PDAs
print	Paper
braille	Braille tactile readers
speech	Speech synthesizers
all	All devices

```
media="
    screen
    and (min-width: 740px)
    and (max-width: 980px)"
```

A The general syntax for media queries.

TABLE 4.8 Media Query Properties

Property	Value					
aspect-ratio	<ratio>	●9	●	●	●	●
max-aspect-ratio	<ratio>	●9	●	●	●	●
min-aspect-ratio	<ratio>	●9	●	●	●	●
device-aspect-ratio	<ratio>	●9	●	●	●	●
max-device-aspect-ratio	<ratio>	●9	●	●	●	●
min-device-aspect-ratio	<ratio>	●9	●	●	●	●
color	<integer>	●9	●	●	●	●
max-color	<integer>	●9	●	●	●	●
min-color	<integer>	●9	●	●	●	●
color-index	<integer>	●9	●	●	●	●
max-color-index	<integer>	●9	●	●	●	●
min-color-index	<integer>	●9	●	●	●	●
device-height	<length>	●9	●	●	●	●
max-device-height	<length>	●9	●	●	●	●
min-device-height	<length>	●9	●	●	●	●
device-width	<length>	●9	●	●	●	●
max-device-width	<length>	●9	●	●	●	●
min-device-width	<length>	●9	●	●	●	●
height	<length>	●9	●	●	●	●
max-height	<length>	●9	●	●	●	●
min-height	<length>	●9	●	●	●	●
monochrome	<integer>	●9	●	●	●	●
max-monochrome	<integer>	●9	●	●	●	●
min-monochrome	<integer>	●9	●	●	●	●
orientation	portrait, landscape	●9	●	●	●	●
resolution	<resolution>	●9	●	●	●	●
max-resolution	<resolution>	●9	●	●	●	●
min-resolution	<resolution>	●9	●	●	●	●
scan	progressive, interlaced	●9	●	●	●	●
width	<length>	●9	●	●	●	●
max-width	<length>	●9	●	●	●	●
min-width	<length>	●9	●	●	●	●

- **Orientation** looks for *landscape* (height greater than width) or *portrait* (width greater than height) layout. This allows you to tailor designs for devices that can flip.

- **Color**, **color-index**, and **monochrome** finds the number of colors or bits per color. These allow you to tailor your design for black-and-white mobile devices.

- **Resolution** looks at the density of pixels in the output. This is especially useful when you want to take advantage of display devices that have a higher resolution than 72 dpi.

By default, media queries are for the viewport (see Chapter 11 for details on the viewport) with the exception of those that specify *device*, in which case they are for the entire screen or output area. For example, width is the width of the visible browser viewport within the screen, whereas device-width is the width of the entire screen.

Code 4.14 *default.css*—These styles are applied regardless of the screen size; but we are tailoring the styles for small devices, most likely mobile devices such as smart phones. We start with the small sizes first, and then tailor for larger sizes in the next two CSS files.

```
/*** Default Screen Styles ***/
body {
    color: charcoal;
    font: normal 1.5em/1 helvetica, arial,
    ↳ sans-serif;
    background: silver url('alice23c.gif')
    ↳ no-repeat center 0;
    padding: 120px 20px; }
h1 { color: purple; font-size: 1.5em; }
h2 { color: black; font-size: 1.25em; }
p {    line-height: 2;  font-size: 1em; }
```

Code 4.15 *medium.css*—A custom view for medium-size screens. Generally, these styles will be used by tablet devices.

```
/*** Medium Device Styles ***/

body {
    color: dimgray;
    background-color: gray;
    font-size: 1.25em;
    padding: 200px 2em; }
h1 { color: gold; }
h2 { color: silver; }
```

Code 4.16 *large.css*—The final style sheet will be used to serve a page tailored to larger computer screens.

```
/*** Large Device Styles ***/

body {
    color: silver;
    font: normal 1.1em/2 georgia,times,serif;
    background: black url('alice23b.gif')
    ↳ no-repeat 0 0;
    padding: 200px 175px; }
h1 {
    color: red;
    font-style: italic; }
h2 { color: gray; }
```

Using media queries to specify styles:

1. **Create your style sheets**. Create a default media style sheet that captures all the general styles for your design and save it. I like to call mine **default.css** (Code 4.14).

   Create style sheets for the various media or specific devices for which you will be designing. Print is generally good to include (**Code 4.17**). You can call the sheet **print.css**, but you might also want to create style sheets specifically for tablets (**Code 4.15**) and for desktop computers (**Code 4.16**).

   continues on next page

Code 4.17 *print.css*—These styles are tailored for the printed page, changing the background to white (assuming white paper), serif fonts, black text, and a different background image.

```
/*** For Print ***/

body {
    color: rgb(0,0,0);
    background: white url('alice23a.gif')
    ↳ no-repeat 0 0;
    padding: 200px 0 0 175px;
}
h1 { color: gray; }
p { font: normal 12pt/2 Constantia, palatino,
↳ times, "times new roman", serif; }
```

2. **Add the viewport meta tag.** In the head of your HTML document (**Code 4.18**), add a meta tag with a name equal to viewport and content, as shown.

```
<meta name="viewport"
→ content="width=device-width,
→ initial-scale=1, maximum-
→ scale=1, minimum-scale=1,
→ user-scalable=no" />
```

This will prevent devices with smaller screens, most notably the iPhone, from resizing the page, overriding your styles to be set in Step 5.

3. **Link to your *default* style sheet.** In the head of your HTML document (**Code 4.18**), type a `<link>` tag that references the default version of the CSS and define `media` as `all`.

```
<link rel="stylesheet" media="all"
→ href="default.css" >
```

continues on page 110

B **Code 4.18** output to a computer screen. This version uses a dark background and an inverted version of the *Alice's Adventures in Wonderland* illustration. On an LCD screen, the lightly colored text will look fine.

C **Code 4.18** on a tablet device, in this case an iPad.

Code 4.18 The HTML code links to all three of the style sheets, which are displayed in default **B**, tablet **C**, smart phone **D**, and print **E**. The iPhone style sheet uses media queries to set a device's width range in keeping with the iPhone. Notice that I used screen for the media type because the iPhone identifies itself as a screen, not a handheld device.

```html
<!DOCTYPE html>
<html lang="en">
<head>
<meta charset="UTF-8">
<meta name="viewport" content="width=device-width, initial-scale=1, maximum-scale=1,
 minimum-scale=1, user-scalable=no" />
<title>Alice&#8217;s Adventures in Wonderland</title>
<link rel="stylesheet" media="screen" href="14.css">
<link rel="stylesheet" media="screen and (min-width: 740px) and (min-device-width: 740px),
 (max-device-width: 800px) and (min-width: 740px) and (orientation:landscape)"
 href="15.css">
<link rel="stylesheet" media="screen and (min-width: 980px) and (min-device-width: 980px)"
 href="16.css">
<link rel="stylesheet" media="print" href="17.css">
</head>
<body>
<hgroup>
<h1>Alice&#8217;s Adventures In Wonderland</h1>
<h2 id="ch01">Chapter 1 <span class="chaptertitle">Down the Rabbit-Hole</span></h2>
</hgroup>
<article>
<p>Alice was beginning to get very tired of sitting by her sister on the bank, and of having
 nothing to do: once or twice she had peeped into the book her sister was reading, but it had no
 pictures or conversations in it, <q>and what is the use of a book,</q> thought Alice, <q>without
 pictures or conversations?</q></p>
</article>
<footer><nav> Next:
<a class="chaptertitle" href="AAIWL-ch02.html">The Pool of Tears</a>
</nav></footer>
</body>
</html>
```

D Code 4.18 on a mobile device, in this case an iPhone. A specially tailored version to fit the width of smaller devices uses a custom header of the Cheshire cat.

E Code 4.18 output to a printer. The background is white, and the background image is no longer inverted. This works better in print.

4. **Use a media query to link to a style sheet.** Immediately after the previous `<link>` tag, add more `<link>` tags that reference the style sheets for a specific media type and then add media queries (**Table 4.8**) in parentheses connecting multiple queries with **and**.

```
<style type="text/css" media=
→ "screen and (min-width: 740px)
→ and (min-device-width: 740px),
→ (max-device-width: 800px)
→ and (min-width: 740px) and
→ (orientation:landscape)">@import
→ url("css/medium.css");</style>


<style type="text/css" media=
→ "screen and (min-width: 980px)
→ and (min-device-width: 980px)">
→ @import url("css/medium.css");
→ @import url("css/large.css");
→ </style>
```

5. Link to your *print* style sheet. Immediately after the `<link>` tag, add another `<link>` tag that references the print version of the CSS and define `media` as `print`.

```
<link rel="stylesheet" media=
→ "print" href="print.css">
```

TIP Before media queries were introduced, Web developers used JavaScript to detect browser dimensions and colors. Media queries render those techniques obsolete, at least for styling purposes.

TIP In this example, media queries are applied to the media property value of the `<link>` tag, but you can just as easily apply them to the media property of the `<style>` tag.

Using the @media rule

Media queries allow you specify styles in the media property of `<link>` and `<style>` tags, but the `@media` rule  allows you to embed media queries directly into a style sheet.

Using @media to specify styles:

1. **Create your style sheets.** Create an external style sheet or embed a style sheet in the body of your document (**Code 4.19**).

2. **Use the `@media` rule to specify styles with media queries.** In the head of your HTML document, type @ and media. Then specify the media type (**Table 4.7**) and any media queries (**Table 4.8**) for the styles.

   ```
   @media screen and
   → (max-device-width: 480px) {...}
   ```

   For example, you might specify that these styles are for screens with a width up to 480px wide. Finish with curly brackets. Add any media-specific styles between the curly brackets.

3. **Add other styles as necessary.**

   ```
   body {...}
   ```

   You can add more **@media** rules or other nonmedia-specific rules. However, all CSS rules that are not in **@rules** (**@media**, **@font-face**, **@import**, and so on) must come after the **@rules**.

   TIP Remember that @media rules can go in external or embedded style sheets.

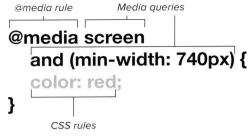

@media rule   Media queries

@media screen
and (min-width: 740px) {
color: red;
}

CSS rules

 The general syntax of the **@media** rule.

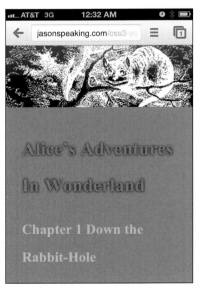

G Code 4.19 on a computer screen.

H Code 4.19 on a mobile device screen. The styles and background have been modified based on the device width.

Code 4.19 The HTML code links to the various style sheets for different media types ⒼG and ⒽH.

```html
<!DOCTYPE html>
<html lang="en">
<head>
<meta charset="UTF-8">
<meta name="viewport" content="width=device-width, initial-scale=1, maximum-scale=1, minimum-scale=1,
→ user-scalable=no" />
<title>Alice&#8217;s Adventures in Wonderland</title>

<style type="text/css">
   body {
      font: normal 12pt/2 times, "times new roman", serif;
      background: white url('alice23a.gif') no-repeat 0 0;
      padding: 200px 175px; }
   h1 { color: gray; }
   h2 { color: silver; }
   p { color: black; }
   @media screen and (max-width: 480px) {
      /*** Small screen Styles ***/
      body {
         -webkit-text-size-adjust:none;
         color: red;
         background: gray url('alice23c.gif') no-repeat center 0;
            padding: 120px 20px 20px 20px; }
      h1 {
         color: red;
         text-shadow: 0 0 5px black; }
      h2 { color: silver; }
      p {
         font-size: 1.5em;
         color: white;    }
   }
</style>
</head>
<body>
<hgroup>
<h1>Alice&#8217;s Adventures In Wonderland</h1>
<h2 id="ch01">Chapter 1 <span class="chaptertitle">Down the Rabbit-Hole</span></h2>
</hgroup>
<article>
<p>Alice was beginning to get very tired of sitting by her sister on the bank, and of having
→ nothing to do: once or twice she had peeped into the book her sister was reading, but it had no
→ pictures or conversations in it, <q>and what is the use of a book,</q> thought Alice, <q>without
→ pictures or conversations?</q></p>
</article>
<footer><nav> Next:
<a class="chaptertitle" href="AAIWL-ch02.html">The Pool of Tears</a>
</nav></footer>
</body>
</html>
```

Styling for Print

With the advent of laser and inkjet printers, we seem to be buried under mounds of perfectly printed paper. Even the Web seems to have *inc*reased the amount of paper we use. If an article on the Web is longer than a couple of scrolls, many people print it.

But the Web was created to display information on the screen, not on paper. Web graphics look blocky when printed, and straight HTML lacks much in the way of layout controls. That said, you can take steps to improve the appearance of printed Web pages. Looking good in print and on the Web may take a little extra effort, but your audience will thank you in the long run.

Here are six simple things you can do to improve the appearance of your Web page when it is printed:

- **Use page breaks before page headers** to keep them with their text.
- **Separate content from navigation.** Try to keep the main content—the part your audience is interested in reading—in a separate area of the design from the site navigation. You can then use CSS to hide navigation in the printed version with a

  ```
  nav { display: none }
  ```

  included in the print style sheet.
- **Avoid using transparent colors in graphics.** This is especially true if the graphic is on a background color or a graphic other than white. The transparent area of a GIF image usually prints as white regardless of the color behind it in the window. This situation is not a problem if the graphic is on a white background to begin with, but the result is messy if the graphic is supposed to be on a dark background.
- **Avoid using text in graphics.** The irony of printing content from the Web is that text in graphics, which may look smooth in the window, can look blocky when printed; but regular HTML text, which may look blocky on some PC screens, can print smoothly on any decent printer. Try to stick with HTML text as much as possible.
- **Avoid dark-colored backgrounds and light-colored text.** Generally you want to keep white as your background color for most of the printed page, and black or dark gray for the text.
- **Do not rely on color to convey your message when printed.** Although color printers are quite common these days, many people are still printing with black-and-white printers or printing in black and white on color printers to save money.

Inheriting Properties from a Parent

No, this book hasn't suddenly become the *Visual QuickStart Guide to Real Estate*. Child and descendent HTML tags generally assume the styles of their parents—*inherit* them—whether the style is set using CSS or is inherited from a browser style. This is called *inheritance of styles*.

For example, if you set an ID called *copy* and give it a font-family value of Times, all of its descendents would inherit the Times font style. If you set a **bold** tag to red with CSS, all of its descendents will inherit both the applied red and the inherent bold style Ⓐ.

In some cases, a style property is not inherited from its parent—obvious properties such as margins, width, and borders. You will probably have no trouble figuring out

{CSS}
strong { color: red; }
.chaptertext { font-family: georgia; }

```
<HTML>
Georgia }  <div class="chaptertext">
                  ↓ inherit
red (bold) }    <strong>
                    ↓ inherit
(italics) }       <em>
                      Curiouser and curiouser!
                  </em>
                </strong>
            </div>
```

Results

Curiouser and curiouser!

Ⓐ The final result of the styles applied and inherited is bold, red, and italicized text in Times font. Styles in parentheses are inherent styles applied by the browser for the particular HTML tag.

which properties are inherited and which are not. For example, if you set a padding of four pixels for the paragraph tag, you would not expect bold tags within the paragraph to also add a padding of four pixels. If you have any doubts, see Appendix A, which lists all the CSS properties and how they are inherited.

If you did want to force an element to inherit a property of its parent, many CSS properties include the `inherit` value. So, in the previous example, to force all the bold tags in a paragraph to take on the 4px padding, you could set their `padding` value to `inherit`.

Managing existing or inherited property values

When defining the styles for a selector, you do not cause it to lose any of its inherited or inherent attributes unless you specifically override those styles. All those properties are displayed unless you change the specific existing properties that make up its appearance.

In addition to overriding the relevant property with another value, many CSS properties have values that allow you to override inheritance:

- `inherit`—Forces a property to be inherited that would normally not be inherited, or overrides other applied style values and inherits the parent's value.

- `none`—Hides a border, image, or other visual element.

- `normal`—Forces the default style to be applied.

- `auto`—Allows the browser to determine how the element should be displayed based on context.

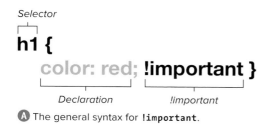

Selector

```
h1 {
    color: red; !important }
```

Declaration *!important*

A The general syntax for **!important**.

Code 4.20 The **!important** value has been added to the color property in the first **h2**, but not in the second **B**. Typically, the second **h2** would override the first, but not in this case.

```
<!DOCTYPE html>
<html lang="en">
<head>
<meta charset="UTF-8">
<title>Alice&#8217;s Adventures in
 → Wonderland</title>
<style type="text/css" media="all">
    h2 {
        color: green !important;
        font-size: 3em;    }
    h2 {
        color: red;
        font-size: 2em; }
</style>
</head>
<body>
<article class="chaptertext">
<h2> Chapter I
<span class="chaptertitle">Down the
 → Rabbit-Hole</span>
</h2>
<p>Alice was beginning to get very tired of
 → sitting by her sister on the bank, and of
 → having nothing to do: once or twice
 → she had peeped into the book her sister
 → was reading, but it had no pictures or
 → conversations in it, <q>and what is the
 → use of a book,</q> thought Alice, <q>
 → without pictures or conversations?</q></p>
</article>
</body>
</html>
```

Making a Declaration !important

You can add the **!important** declaration to a property-value declaration to give it the maximum weight when determining the cascade order **A**. Doing so ensures that a declaration is applied regardless of the other rules in play. (See "Determining the Cascade Order" in this chapter.)

To force use of a declaration:

1. Add your CSS rule (Code 4.20).

   `h2 {...}`

   You can use an HTML, class, or ID selector. CSS rules can be defined within the **<style>** tags in the head of your document (see "Embedded: Adding Styles to a Web Page" in Chapter 3) or in an external CSS file that is then imported or linked to the HTML document (see "External: Adding Styles to a Web Site" in Chapter 3).

2. **Make it important.** Type a style declaration, a space, **!important**, and a semicolon (;) to close the declaration.

   `color: green !important;`

   continues on next page

Chapter I Down the Rabbit-Hole

Alice was beginning to get very tired of sitting by her sister on the bank, and of having nothing to do: once or twice she had peeped into the book her sister was reading, but it had no pictures or conversations in it, "and what is the use of a book," thought Alice, "without pictures or conversations?"

B The result of Code 4.20. The style that is most important wins the day, so the text is green rather than red, despite the fact that the red declaration comes later in the cascade.

3. Add other styles.

```
font-size: 3em;
```

Add any other declarations you wish for this rule, making them **!important** or not, as you desire.

!important is a powerful tool, second only to inline styles for determining style cascade. **!important** is great for debugging your CSS; but, because it can interfere with making changes later, it should never be used in the final Web site code.

Setting a shorthand property to **!important** (**background**, for example) is the same as setting each sub-property (such as **background-color**) to be **!important**.

TIP A common mistake is to locate !important after the semicolon in the declaration. This causes the browser to ignore the declaration and, possibly, the entire rule.

TIP If you are debugging your style sheet and can't get a particular style to work, try adding !important to it. If it still doesn't work, the problem is most likely a typo rather than another overriding style.

TIP Many browsers allow users to define their own style sheets for use by the browser. Most browsers follow the CSS 2.1 specification in which a user-defined style sheet overrides an author-defined style sheet.

Determining the Cascade Order

Within a single Web page, style sheets may be linked, imported, or embedded. Styles may also be declared inline in the HTML.

In addition, many browsers allow visitors to have their own style sheets that can override yours. It's guaranteed, of course, that simultaneous style sheets from two or more sources will have conflicting declarations. Who comes out on top?

The cascade order refers to the way styles begin at the top of the page and, as they cascade down, collect and replace each other as they are inherited. The general rule of thumb is that the last style defined is the one that is used.

However, at times, two or more styles will conflict. Use the following procedure to determine which style will come out on top and be applied to a given element.

To determine the cascade-order value for an element:

Collect all styles that will be applied to the element. Find all the inherent, applied, and inherited styles that will be applied to the element, and then use the following criteria to determine which styles are applied in the cascade order, with the criteria at the top being most important 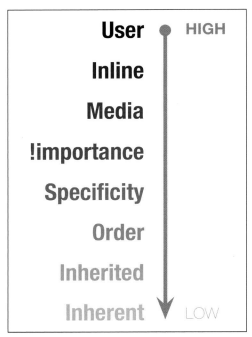.

1. **User styles**

   Most Web browsers allow users to specify their own default style sheets. In principle, these always have precedence over other styles.

2. **Inline styles**

   If the style is inline (see Chapter 3), it is always applied regardless of all other factors. That's why you should *never* use them in your final HTML code.

3. **Media type**

   Obviously, if the media type is set for a style and element that is not being displayed in that media type, the style will not be used.

4. **Importance**

   Including **!important** with a declaration gives it top billing when displayed. (See "Making a Declaration !important" in this chapter.)

   Many browsers let users define their own style sheets for use by the browser. If both the page author and the visitor have included **!important** in their declarations, the user's declaration wins.

   In theory, an author's style sheets override a visitor's style sheets unless the visitor uses the **!important** value. In practice, however, most browsers favor a user's style sheet when determining which declarations are used for a tag.

A The cascade order from most important to least important.

5. Specificity

The more contextually specific a rule is, the higher its cascade priority. So the more HTML, class, and ID selectors a particular rule has, the more important it is. In determining this priority, ID selectors count as 100, classes count as 10, and HTML selectors are worth only 1. Thus,

`#copy p b { color: red; }`

is worth 102, whereas

`b { color : lime; }`

is worth only 1. So, the first rule would have higher specificity and the color would be red.

This priority setting may seem a bit silly at first, but it allows context-sensitive and ID rules to carry more weight, ensuring that they will be used.

6. Order

If the conflicting declarations applied to an element are equal at this point, CSS gives priority to the last rule listed, in order. Remember that inline styles always win.

7. Inherited

These styles are inherited from the parent.

8. Inherent

These styles are applied by the browser to HTML tags and are the least important.

Font Properties

Typography is one of your most powerful tools for presenting organized, clean-looking documents. It's also the best tool for presenting chaotic, grungy-looking documents.

The fonts you use go a long way toward getting your message across in just the way you want—whether that message is classical, grunge, or anything in between. I often say that fonts are to type what voice is to speech. Typeface, font weight, italic, and other typographic effects not only help designers to guide a visitor's eye around the page, but they also add a layer of meaning.

CSS gives you the ability to control the appearance of fonts, also known as *letterforms*, in your Web pages. You can set the font family, boldface, and italic attributes, and the limited font sizes available with HTML tags. CSS3 refines the ability to download font files (called *Web fonts*) from your server and apply them to the text in your Web page, giving you the power to use virtually any font you want in your designs.

Getting Started

In this chapter, we'll be styling the first chapter of Lewis Carroll's *Alice's Adventures In Wonderland*. **Code 5.1** shows an expurgated version of the HTML, with all but the first paragraph stripped out. We'll start adding to the CSS file *font-properties.css* starting with **Code 5.2**, add to it in each section, and present it in full in **Code 5.11**.

Code 5.1 The HTML code for this chapter is taken from Chapter 1 of *Alice's Adventures in Wonderland* Ⓐ. You'll be adding CSS code to this external style sheet throughout the chapter to build the final CSS file *font-properties.css* shown at the end of the chapter in "Putting it All Together."

```
<!DOCTYPE html>
<html lang="en">
<head>
   <meta charset="utf-8">
   <title>
      Alice&#8217;s Adventures In Wonderland | Chapter I
   </title>
   <link href="../css/font-properties.css" type="text/css" rel="stylesheet" media="all">
</head>
<body id="chapter1" class="book aaiw chapter">
   <hgroup>
      <h1>Alice&#8217;s Adventures in Wonderland</h1>
      <h2>By <cite>Lewis Carroll</cite></h2>
   </hgroup>
   <article>
   <h2>Chapter I
      <span class="chaptertitle">Down the Rabbit-Hole</span>
   </h2>
   <p>Alice was beginning to get very tired of sitting by her sister on the bank, and of having
   → nothing to do: once or twice she had peeped into the book her sister was reading, but it had
   → no pictures or conversations in it, "and what is the use of a book," thought Alice, "without
   → pictures or conversations?"</p>
   <article>
<footer>
<nav>
   <a href="toc.html">Table of Contents</a>
   <a href="AAIWL-ch02.html" class="next">The Pool of Tears</a>
</nav>
</footer>
</body>
</html>
```

A This is what your Web page (**Code 5.1**) looks like before any CSS is applied to it. In this chapter you will be adding font styling.

Understanding Typography on the Web

A *type family* (commonly referred to in Web design as a *font family*) is a category of typefaces that have similar characteristics. Each character within a font is referred to as a *glyph*. The advantages of HTML text compared to text in Flash or in graphics are that it is easy to edit if changes are required, and it can adjust to the width of the screen on which it is viewed. In addition, content is often stored within databases and then output as HTML text.

However, HTML text has some severe design limitations. By and large, most of the textual control is left up to the visitor's browser, and you cannot currently do some things, such as run text vertically rather than horizontally, without using CSS transformations (Chapter 12), which are not cross-browser yet.

What seems more stifling is that until recently you were limited to the fonts available on the visitor's machine. But this is no longer true. You now have tens of thousands of fonts to choose from using Web fonts.

Specifying the character set

In the previous chapter, you found that when you create an HTML5 document, you need to specify the character set in use by your page. A character set is simply a list or *repertoire* of characters with a unique code or name that the browser will recognize to display the text. These codes are agreed upon as international standards. You do not need to concern yourself with them, except when you choose the character set you use for your own Web pages.

You specify the character set in the head of your HTML page using a meta tag. The most popular international character set is the UTF-8 (8-bit Unicode Transformation Format) character set:

```
<meta charset="utf-8">
```

Alternatively, if you are writing only in English, another common character set is the ISO 8859-1 character set:

```
<meta http-equiv="Content-Type"
→ content="text/html; charset=
→ ISO-8859-1" />
```

Both UTF-8 and ISO 8859-1 work about the same for English, but UTF-8 supports other alphabets. I highly recommend sticking with UTF-8. Web sites (even your local newspaper) are often translated on the fly into different languages.

One other important point: if you specify a character in your HTML that doesn't exist in the specified character set, the browser generally will display an error marker in place of the character Ⓐ. If that happens, you can often *encode* the character yourself, as explained in the upcoming section *Encoding HTML character entities*.

Ⓐ This glyph, or one like it, will appear in place of any characters that the browser does not recognize as a part of the character set.

TABLE 5.1 Generic Font Families

Name	Example
Serif	Times New Roman
Sans-serif	Helvetica and Arial
Monospace	Courier New
Cursive	*Brush Script MT*
Fantasy	Papyrus

Generic font families

CSS defines five generic font families into which most fonts can be categorized (**Table 5.1**).

- **Serif**—A *serif* is the small ornamentation at the end of a letter that gives it a distinguishing quality. Serifs are holdovers from the days of stonecutting and pen strokes. Serifs often improve legibility by making individual letters stand out from their neighbors.

  Serif fonts are generally best suited for the display of larger text onscreen (14px or larger) or for smaller printed text. They are not so good for smaller text on a screen, because the serifs often obscure the letter. Serif fonts often portray a more conservative feel.

- **Sans-serif**—As you might guess, *sans-serif* fonts are those fonts without serifs.

  Although the characters are less distinctive, sans-serif fonts work better for smaller text on a screen. Sans-serif fonts often portray a more modern and often casual feel.

- **Monospace**—Although *monospace* fonts can have serifs or not, their distinguishing feature is that each letter occupies the same amount of space. The lowercase letter *l*, for example, is much thinner than the uppercase letter *M*. In non-monospace fonts, the letter *l* occupies less space than the *M*, but a monospace font adds extra space around the *l* so that it occupies the same amount of space as the *M*.

continues on next page

Monospace fonts work best for text that has to be exactly (but not necessarily quickly) read—such as programming code—in which typos can spell disaster. Although easier to scan, monospace fonts can become monotonous for reading large amounts of text. Monospace fonts often give a technical or typewritten feel to text.

- **Cursive**—*Cursive* fonts attempt to mimic cursive or calligraphic handwriting, usually in a highly stylized manner with the letters generally appearing partially or completely connected.

  Cursive fonts are best reserved for decoration and large headlines; they are not as readable in large chunks of text. Cursive fonts give an energetic and expressive feel to text.

- **Fantasy**—Decorative fonts that don't fit into any of the preceding categories are referred to as *fantasy* fonts. These fonts usually are extremely ornamental but are still letters, so exclude dingbats or picture fonts, illustrations, or icons.

  Like cursive fonts, fantasy fonts are best reserved for decoration. You should use fantasy fonts sparingly and choose them carefully to reinforce the look and feel of your Web site, since each fantasy font invariably has a strong personality.

B Examples of dingbats. These are drawn from the dingbat font, Webdings.

& © ® TM
½ ¼ ¾
« » ± ¤ ÷
∞ ≈ ≤ ⊇
⊕ ⇐ ↔ ⇔

C Examples of a few common character entities. These can be coded into HTML to ensure that they are represented accurately in the final output.

Dingbats

Although it does not have an official CSS designation, there is another important category of fonts to consider. *Dingbats*, also called *symbol* or *picture* fonts, do not represent numbers or letters, but are instead a collection of icons or pictograms each corresponding to a letter on the keyboard. The most common example of this font type is Webdings, which is installed on most computers. Webdings is a collection of common international symbols **B**. Although other dingbat fonts are not commonly installed on most computers, if you use dingbats as Web fonts, as described later in this chapter, you can be relatively sure that you will get what you want, replacing some graphic icons with dingbat icons.

Encoding HTML character entities

An alternative to dingbat fonts are HTML *character* entities **C**. These are a collection of specialized glyphs that, instead of being represented by a single letter, are represented by code that begins with an ampersand (**&**) and ends with a semicolon (**;**). For example, the ampersand is represented in the code as:

`&amp;`

For many characters (such as the ampersand), this is the only way to display them consistently across browsers and operating systems. For a full list of HTML and Unicode character values, see Appendix B.

Setting a Font-Stack

The **font-family** property lets you determine the visual effect of your message by choosing the font for displaying your text (**Table 5.2**). The typeface you use to display your text can make a powerful difference in how readers perceive your message **A**. Whether you use a serif, sans-serif, monospace, cursive, or fantasy typeface can speak volumes before your visitor even reads the first line of text.

To define the font family for an element:

1. Add the **font-family** property to your CSS rule. Type the property name **font-family**, followed by a colon. In this example, **font-family** is applied to the body tag, which will set the font for the entire page (**Code 5.2**).

   `font-family:`

2. Define the name of the *primary font* you want to use, followed by a comma. This name is not case sensitive. Fonts that contain a space in their names must be enclosed in quotation marks, either single or double (**"Times New Roman"** or **'times new roman'** will both work).

   `Constantia,`

TABLE 5.2 Font-Family Values

Value					
<family-name>	●	●	●	●	●
serif	●	●	●	●	●
sans-serif	●	●	●	●	●
cursive	●	●	●	●	●
fantasy	●	●	●	●	●
monospace	●	●	●	●	●

Times
Arial
Courier
Brush Script
Papyrus

A Examples of different typefaces. What voice do you hear?

Font or Font Family?

Keep in mind the difference between a font and a font family. A font family is a series of fonts with similar appearance, such as Times. A font refers to a specific version—Times normal, Times bold, Times italic, Times bold italic, and so on.

Code 5.2 Styles added to *font-properties.css*—Two separate typefaces are applied to the page **B**.

```
/*** font-properties.css ***/
body {    font-family: Constantia, Georgia, "Times New Roman", serif; }
h1, h2, h3, h4, h5, h6, .byline {
    font-family: Corbel, Helvetica, Arial, sans-serif; }
h2 .chaptertitle {
    font-family: Corbel, Helvetica, Arial, sans-serif; }
```

Alice's Adventures in Wonderland

By *Lewis Carroll*

Chapter I Down the Rabbit-Hole

Alice was beginning to get very tired of sitting by her sister on the bank, and of having nothing to do: once or twice she had peeped into the book her sister was reading, but it had no pictures or conversations in it, "and what is the use of a book," thought Alice, "without pictures or conversations?"

So she was considering in her own mind (as well as she could, for the hot day made her feel very sleepy and stupid) whether the pleasure of making a daisy-chain would be worth the trouble of getting up and picking the daisies, when suddenly a White Rabbit with pink eyes ran close by her.

Ⓑ The body copy is displayed in Constantia, Georgia, or Times New Roman, depending on which is available on the visitor's computer. However, headers are displayed in Corbel, Helvetica, or Arial, also depending on availability.

3. **Define a list of alternative fonts, called** *understudy fonts,* **separated by commas.** You can include as many as you want. These fonts will be used (in the order specified) if the previous font in the list is not available on the visitor's computer. See "Why Include Understudy Fonts and Generic Font Families" in this chapter for more details.

   ```
   Georgia, "Times New Roman",
   ```

4. **Define the generic font family.** After the last understudy font, type the name of the generic font family for the particular style of font you're using. **Table 5.1** lists generic values for font families. Although including this value is optional, doing so is a good idea.

   ```
   serif;
   ```

continues on next page

Why Include Understudy Fonts and Generic Font Families?

When you provide a list of fonts, the browser tries to use the first font on that list. If it isn't available, the browser continues through the list until it finds a font that is installed on the visitor's computer. If no match is found, the browser displays the text in the visitor's default font. The advantage of specifying a generic font is that the browser tries to display the text in the same style of font, even if the specific fonts on the list are not available.

As a last resort, you can include the generic font family so that a browser can make an intelligent decision on the closest matching font.

The advantage of using understudy and generic font families is that, even if a desired font is not available, you can still control which font is used in its place or, at least, get a close match.

5. Add typeface overrides. After a font is set for the body of the page, it will be used in all text throughout the entire Web page, with the exception of text in forms. You need to add another font-family declaration to your CSS only if you want to change the font for a particular element. This is because properties cascade to their child elements, as described in Chapter 4.

The exception to the cascade rule are form elements such as input, text, area, button, and so on, which require their fonts to be set in the form element to cascade down.

```
font-family: Corbel, Helvetica,
→ Arial, serif;
```

If you will be using bold, italic/oblique, and/or bold italic/oblique versions of the font, be sure that the font family supports all of these typefaces. If not, the text will not display properly, or worse, the browser will try to synthesize these versions. Either way, the results will not look professional.

TIP Try to choose fonts with a similar size. Different fonts will have different relative sizes even if set to the same font size.

TIP Some typefaces are easiest to read on a screen; others look better when printed. Always consider the destination when choosing your fonts.

★Using Web Fonts

Look around the Web, and what do you see? You usually see five fonts: Arial, Georgia, Verdana, Trebuchet MS, and Times New Roman. This situation came about for one simple reason: Arial, Georgia, Verdana, Trebuchet MS, and Times New Roman are preinstalled on virtually every Mac and PC.

I am sick of them.

Don't get me wrong—these are great fonts, easy to read at many sizes. But as I said earlier, typography adds a language to text that goes far beyond the written word.

Web-based typography is mired in using Times for serif fonts and Helvetica/Arial for sans-serif fonts. This arrangement mutes the power of typography, and all Web pages begin to look the same.

Web-Safe Fonts

What are the alternatives to the "fatal five?" That depends on the computer the person visiting your site is using. Apple OS X and Windows computers have certain standard fonts that should always be installed. In addition, Internet Explorer (which is installed on most Windows computers these days) installs several additional fonts.

Of course, there's no guarantee that these fonts will be installed, but because they came with the operating system, they are just as likely to be available as Times, Helvetica, or Arial.

You can find a list of Web-safe fonts on my Web site, www.webtypographynow.com/websafe-fonts. It lists these fonts, and includes examples of what they should look like and which similar-looking fonts can be used as replacements 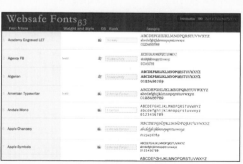.

Web-safe fonts are still good to know about to use as understudy fonts, but increasingly becoming a moot point as Web fonts take over. Web fonts give a much larger selection and are more reliably available.

A The list of Web-safe fonts on www.webtypographynow.com/websafefonts includes a visual example of each typeface. You can sort the list by name, available weights and styles, operating system availability, and rank.

But there is new hope. Two factors are changing the way designers think about their typefaces. The first is that dozens of fonts are commonly preinstalled on Macs and PCs. The second, and most profound change, is that all the major browsers now support the use of downloadable Web fonts.

Web fonts is a recent development in Web design that allows you to include fonts in your Web designs by linking to a font file on your server. Although this seems simple (and it is), this ability has been a long time in coming and will revolutionize Web typography.

Web font formats

For years it has been technically feasible to download a font just as you would an image and use it in your design. However, browser developers have only recently added this feature. The good news is that you can now download Web fonts to the vast majority of Web users. The bad news is that different browsers use different file formats (**Table 5.3**).

Here is a list of the file formats:

- **TTF/OTF.** TrueType and OpenType fonts are the type you are most likely to have on your computer. They are commonly used today and represent the majority of fonts sold. That said, they have no built-in security to prevent their unlicensed use.

- **EOT.** Embedded OpenType is a format developed by Microsoft in the late 1990s to allow secure downloadable fonts for the Web. However, because the technology was proprietary for many years and EOT fonts were hard

TABLE 5.3 Browser Font File Compatibility

Format					
EOT	●				
TTF/OTF			●	●	●
SVG				●	●	●
WOFF		●	●	●	●	●

to create, the format didn't catch on. Because it is the only format supported by IE and has been supported since IE4, it has gained new life for implanting Web fonts for IE.

- **SVG.** A separate W3C standard from CSS, Scalable Vector Graphics can include font information. Some browsers, such as Safari mobile, support only this format.

- **WOFF.** Web Open Font Format may be the new kid on the block, developed in mid-2009, but it is already becoming the frontrunner as the default Web font file format with support in all major Web browsers. This format includes some protection for the font—such as licensing—but is not nearly as cumbersome as EOT.

Setting a better font stack with Web fonts

When deploying Web fonts in your design, the key is to include links to multiple font files; the browser will then use the format that works for it. The good news is that, with a bit of clever coding, this can easily be accomplished. To learn how to download or convert fonts to these multiple font file formats, see "Using Font Squirrel to Convert Font Files" in this chapter.

Let's look again at the font stack and how to leverage Web-safe fonts and Web fonts to create a design that rises above the visual monotony that you commonly see on the Web.

Code 5.3 Added to *font-properties.css*—I've added Web fonts for the body copy (Déjà vu Serif) and the title copy (Little Trouble Girl), **B**.

```css
/*** font-properties.css ***/
@font-face {
   font-family: 'BodyCopy';
   src: url('../fonts/DVS/DejaVuSerif.eot');
   src: url('../fonts/DVS/DejaVuSerif.eot?#iefix') format('embedded-opentype'),
      url('../fonts/DVS/DejaVuSerif.woff') format('woff'),
      url('../fonts/DVS/DejaVuSerif.ttf') format('truetype');
   font-weight: normal;
   font-style: normal;
   font-stretch: normal; }
@font-face {
   font-family: 'BodyCopy';
   src: url('../fonts/DVS/DejaVuSerif-Bold.eot');
   src: url('../fonts/DVS/DejaVuSerif-Bold.eot?#iefix') format('embedded-opentype'),
      url('../fonts/DVS/DejaVuSerif-Bold.woff') format('woff'),
      url('../fonts/DVS/DejaVuSerif-Bold.ttf') format('truetype');
   font-weight: bold;
   font-style: normal;
   font-stretch: normal; }
@font-face {
   font-family: 'BodyCopy';
   src: url('../fonts/DVS/DejaVuSerif-Italic.eot');
   src: url('../fonts/DVS/DejaVuSerif-Italic.eot?#iefix') format('embedded-opentype'),
      url('../fonts/DVS/DejaVuSerif-Italic.woff') format('woff'),
      url('../fonts/DVS/DejaVuSerif-Italic.ttf') format('truetype');
   font-weight: normal;
   font-style: italic;
   font-stretch: normal; }
@font-face {
   font-family: 'BodyCopy';
   src: url('../fonts/DVS/DejaVuSerif-BoldItalic.eot');
   src: url('../fonts/DVS/DejaVuSerif-BoldItalic.eot?#iefix') format('embedded-opentype'),
      url('../fonts/DVS/DejaVuSerif-BoldItalic.woff') format('woff'),
      url('../fonts/DVS/DejaVuSerif-BoldItalic.ttf') format('truetype');
   font-weight: bold;
   font-style: italic;
   font-stretch: normal; }
@font-face {
   font-family: 'TitleCopy';
   src: url('../fonts/LTG/littletroublegirl.eot');
   src: url('../fonts/LTG/littletroublegirl.eot?#iefix') format('embedded-opentype'),
      url('../fonts/LTG/littletroublegirl.woff') format('woff'),
      url('../fonts/LTG/littletroublegirl.ttf') format('truetype'); }
body {   font-family: 'BodyCopy', Constantia, Georgia, 'Times New Roman' serif; }
h1 {   font-family: 'TitleCopy', Corbel, Helvetica, Arial, sans-serif; }
h2 .chaptertitle {   font-family: 'TitleCopy', Corbel, Helvetica, Arial, sans-serif; }
```

Alice's Adventures In Wonderland

By *Lewis Carroll*

Chapter I Down the Rabbit-Hole

Alice was beginning to get very tired of sitting by her sister on the bank, and of having nothing to do: once or twice she had peeped into the book her sister was reading, but it had no pictures or conversations in it, "and what is the use of a book," thought Alice, "without pictures or conversations?"

So she was considering in her own mind (as well as she could, for the hot day made her feel very sleepy and stupid) whether the pleasure of making a daisy-chain would be worth the trouble of getting up and picking the daisies, when suddenly a White Rabbit with pink eyes ran close by her.

There was nothing so *very* remarkable in that; nor did Alice think it so *very* much out of the way to hear the Rabbit say to itself, "Oh dear! Oh dear! I shall be too late!" (when she thought it over afterwards, it occurred to her that she ought to have wondered at this, but at the time it all seemed quite natural); but when the Rabbit actually *took a watch out of its waistcoat-pocket*, and looked at it, and then hurried on, Alice started to her feet, for it flashed across her mind that she had never before seen a rabbit with either a waistcoat-pocket, or a watch to take out of it, and burning with curiosity, she ran across the field after it, and was just in time to see it pop down a large rabbit-hole under the hedge.

In another moment down went Alice after it, never once considering how in the world she was to get out again.

The rabbit-hole went straight on like a tunnel for some way, and then dipped suddenly down, so suddenly that Alice had not a moment to think about stopping herself before she found herself

B The page is now looking a bit more distinctive typographically by including fonts that are not often seen on the Web.

To define a Web font to your font stack:

1. **Add the font face rule to your CSS.** Begin by typing the **@font-face** rule, where you will define the name and location of the font file you want to use in your designs (**Code 5.3**).

   `@font-face {`

2. **Define the name of your font family.** Type the name of the font family you want to import. This can actually be anything you choose, as long as you reference it consistently in your font stack.

   `font-family: 'BodyCopy';`

   Many developers choose to use just the name of the font, but I recommend creating a name that indicates how the font is used in the design. Then, if the typeface is changed, you don't have to change the font name everywhere it is referenced.

   Remember: if you want to use a font name with two or more words separated by a space, put the whole name in quotes.

3. **Define the source of the EOT format of the font file for older versions of Internet Explorer.** Add your font file sources. Always begin with the EOT file for use in Internet Explorer, but *do not* add a format attribute.

   `src: url('../fonts/DVS/`
   `⇢DejaVuSerif.eot');`

   continues on next page

4. **Define the source for newer versions of Internet Explorer.** Because of a bug in Internet Explorer versions earlier than IE9, you need to define the source of the EOT file *again* and include a little code trick after the path: **?#iefix**. This prevents older versions of IE from causing problems with loading the correct format.

```
src: url('../fonts/DVS/
→ DejaVuSerif.eot?#iefix')
→ format('embedded-opentype'),
```

5. **Define the source of the WOFF, TrueType or OpenType, and SVG format of the font file.** Now add the location of your WOFF and TTF/OTF font files. Each browser will use the one best suited for it.

```
url('../fonts/DVS/DejaVuSerif.woff')
→ format('woff'),
```

```
url('../fonts/DVS/DejaVuSerif.ttf')
→ format('truetype');
```

6. *Optional* **Add weight, style, and stretch associated with this font.** This will mean the font is used only if these properties are also applied with the specific value. For the exact values, see the relevant sections for each in this chapter.

```
font-weight: normal;
```

```
font-style: normal;
```

```
font-stretch: normal }
```

7. **Add the Web font name to your font stack.** To leverage a downloaded Web font and trigger its download, place the name you gave it at as the first value of the font stack.

```
font-family:'BodyCopy', Constantia,
→ Georgia, "Times New Roman",
→ serif;
```

8. **Add @font-face for different weights, styles, and stretch.** Particularly if you will be using italic or bold text, you must define the font files for each of these, as well as the normal/regular style.

9. **Add @font-face for different typefaces.** You can use multiple typefaces; in this case I'm including one for the titles.

TIP Although the SVG format can be used as a Web font, I tend not to include it as it is known to cause problems in some older Web browsers.

TIP For this example, I've loaded a lot of different font files. Although they are not huge—the ones I used are 20–35 KB and could be reduced in size by sub-setting the font. However, the file sizes can add up quickly, so be careful not to bloat your page size.

TIP Once loaded, though, the font files are cached, so they will not be downloaded again for subsequent pages that use them.

TIP For more information on Mac fonts, see developer.apple.com/textfonts/.

TIP For more information on Windows fonts, see www.microsoft.com/typography/fonts/. For a more detailed examination of Web fonts and Web typography in general, check out my book *Fluid Web Typography* (www.webtypographynow.info).

TIP The font *Little Trouble Girl* was created by Jess Latham (bvfonts.com).

Using Font Squirrel to Convert Font Files

Although you are now free to start downloading Web fonts for use in your designs, you still face two major hurdles:

1. **Legal.** While you might assume that you can use a purchased font as a Web font, that is rarely the case. Most fonts have usage restrictions outlined in their End User License Agreements (EULA). If the EULA does not specifically state that you can use a font for **@font-face** linking, you can't do so legally. To be sure, check with the font vendor before proceeding.

2. **Technical.** How do you get all of those different font formats? Currently, even if licensed to do so, most font foundries or resellers do not provide these formats.

What to do?

One great resource I use regularly is the Font Squirrel Web site (www.fontsquirrel.com), which provides an index to over 500 freely licensed, downloadable Web fonts. Each is complete with all the font formats as well as sample CSS code **C**.

The site also provides an insanely useful tool—the @font-face Kit Generator **D**—that can convert any OTF or TTF file into EOT, SVG, and WOFF formats (www.fontsquirrel.com/fontface/generator). It's easy to use and fast. Just make sure that your EULA is in order before using it.

C Font Squirrel (www.fontsquirrel.com) offers over 500 free fonts that are ready for use in your Web site.

D Use the @font-face Kit Generator (www.fontsquirrel.com/fontface/generator) to convert any licensed fonts for use on the Web.

Web font service bureaus

Another up-and-coming option for adding specific fonts to a Web design is Web font service bureaus (WFSB). They provide licensed fonts for your use (generally at a cost) but retain the actual files on their own servers while allowing you to reference them in your code. Some enable this with a straightforward CSS link; others use their own proprietary methods, generally incorporating JavaScript.

The advantages to using WFSBs include:

- Fonts are licensed, so you don't have to worry about violating a EULA and getting sued.

- Fonts are hosted on the bureaus' servers, which means you are taking up less bandwidth on your own servers.

- Browser support is handled by the bureau, as are potential updates and upgrades.

However, there are disadvantages as well:

- Since the fonts are on a third-party server, you are depending on someone else's system to always be fast and reliable.

- If you do not have a copy of the font on your own computer, you will not be able to create graphical comps to show clients.

- Price scales vary from service to service. Some charge a one-time fee; others require a yearly subscription. If you forget to pay, your font goes bye-bye.

Web font service bureaus are growing and changing, while new bureaus are still coming online. Without doubt the most popular and fastest growing is Google Web Fonts, which provides hundreds of free fonts. However, don't overlook the paid services, which often offer higher quality fonts at reasonable prices.

Tables 5.4 and **5.5** list some of the best Web font service bureaus along with some factors to consider when choosing one:

- **Technology used**: Although I've described how to use @font-face (@ff) to use Web fonts, most WFSBs will provide either a link to an external CSS file (<link>) on their server or JavaScript code (.js) that serves a similar function. The problem is that, unless you are using @font-face, you have no control

TABLE 5.4 Web Font Stores

	FontSquirrel	FontSpring	FontShop	MyFonts
Tech	@ff	@ff	@ff	@ff
Local	●	●	●	●
Subset	●	●	●	
Price	Free	$80–160/WS	Free–$100/WS	$10–60/WS
URL	*fontsquirrel.com*	*fontspring.com*	*fontshop.com*	*myfonts.com*

TABLE 5.5 Web Font Service Bureaus

	Typekit	FontDeck	Fonts.com	Google	Webink
Tech	.js	<link>	.js or @ff	<link>	@ff
Local			●	●	●
Subset	●		●	●	●
Billing	$25/Year*	$2.50–20/Year/Font*	$10–100/Year*	Free	$20–120/Year*
URL	*typekit.com*	*fontdeck.com*	*fonts.com*	*google.com/ webfonts*	*webink.com*

* Free trial version or free testing available

over the font name, and are forced to use the WFSBs naming. Additionally, JavaScript may cause load issues. My preference is for WFSBs that use @font-face.

- **Local version**: Many WFSBs do not provide a local version to design and develop offline. This is especially problematic if you are creating comps in Photoshop or Fireworks.

- **Sub-setting**: Some WFSBs will allow you to reduce the font file size (thus speeding load times) by removing

characters from the font that you will not be using.

- **Price and billing**: Billing systems are not consistent between WFSBs. Most will charge a flat fee or base the fee on the number of fonts used, number of downloads, or the amount of bandwidth used. Consider how these factors may affect your final cost before choosing a bureau.

TIP For more details on Web fonts and Web font service bureaus, visit www.webtypographynow.com **E**.

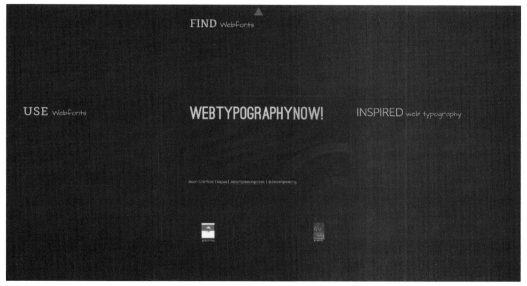

E Web Typography NOW! (www.webtypographynow.com) presents the latest techniques, resources, and inspiration for Web designers.

Setting the Font Size

With CSS, you can specify the size of the text on the screen using several notations or methods **Ⓐ**, including the traditional print-based point-size notation, percentage, absolute size, and even a size relative to the surrounding text (**Table 5.6**).

Fonts can be set as either absolute sizes, which define the size based against a standard length measurement, or relative sizes, which are in relation to defaults set for the browser.

To define the font size for an element:

1. **Add the font size property to your CSS.** Type the property name **font-size**, followed by a colon (**Code 5.4**).

   ```
   font-size:
   ```

2. **Define the font size.**

   ```
   100%;
   ```

   Type a value for the font size, which could be any of the following options:

   ▸ A relative or absolute length unit (often, the font size in pixels or ems). See "Values and Units Used in This Book" in the Introduction for more detail.

   ▸ An absolute size keyword relative to the default page size: xx-small, x-small, small, medium, large, x-large, and xx-large.

   ▸ A relative size keyword of smaller or larger to describe the font size in relation to its parent element.

   ▸ A percentage representing how much larger (values over 100%) or smaller (values less than 100%) the text is relative to the size of its parent element.

Ⓐ The height (size) of a font is measured from the descender to the ascender (usually the cap height). The x-height is the height of lowercase letters.

TABLE 5.6 Font-Size Values

Value					
<length>	○	○	○	○	○
<percentage>	○	○	○	○	○
smaller	○	○	○	○	○
larger	○	○	○	○	○
xx-small	○	○	○	○	○
x-small	○	○	○	○	○
small	○	○	○	○	○
medium	○	○	○	○	○
large	○	○	○	○	○
x-large	○	○	○	○	○
xx-large	○	○	○	○	○
inherit	○	○	○	○	○

Code 5.4 *font-properties.css*—I've defined the default size of text on the page as 100% (the default size the user has set) and then set other font sizes on the page relative to that font size **Ⓑ**.

```
/*** font-properties.css ***/

body { font-size: 100%; }
h1 { font-size: 3em; }
h2 { font-size: 1em; }
h2 cite { font-size: 1.5em; }
h2 .chaptertitle { font-size: 3em; }
em { font-size: 1.1em; }
figcaption { font-size: .875em; }
article p:first-of-type:first-letter
→ { font-size: 5em; }
footer a { font-size: 1em; }
```

Alice's Adventures in Wonderland

By *Lewis Carroll*

Chapter I **Down the Rabbit-Hole**

Alice was beginning to get very tired of sitting by her sister on the bank, and of having nothing to do: once or twice she had peeped into the book her sister was reading, but it had no pictures or conversations in it, "and what is the use of a book," thought Alice, "without pictures or conversations?"

So she was considering in her own mind (as well as she could, for the hot day made her feel very sleepy and stupid) whether the pleasure of making a daisy-chain would be worth the trouble of getting up and picking the daisies, when suddenly a White Rabbit with pink eyes ran close by her.

There was nothing so *very* remarkable in that; nor did Alice think it so *very* much out of the way to hear the Rabbit say to itself, "Oh dear! Oh dear! I shall be too late!" (when she thought it over afterwards, it occurred to her that she ought to have wondered at this, but at the time it all seemed quite natural); but when the Rabbit actually *took a watch out of its waistcoat-pocket*, and looked at it, and then hurried on, Alice started to her feet, for it flashed across her mind that she had never before seen a rabbit with either a waistcoat-pocket, or a watch to take

B The font size helps determine its legibility on the page. Titles are usually larger than body copy; but some text, such as the `<strong>` and `<em>` tags, may need a little more attention.

Choosing Font Size Value Type for Screen or Print

Although they give you more precise control, absolute value types (such as *points*) are unreliable for the screen and can limit how the visitor's browser displays your work.

The point (abbreviated *pt*) is one way to refer to a font's absolute size. A 12-point font is an average size for print use and is comfortable for most readers. The size of a point onscreen, however, varies slightly between operating systems, so a 12-point font displayed on a Windows computer appears larger than the same font as displayed on a Mac. Although using point sizes is an acceptable choice in CSS for print media (see "Querying the Media" in Chapter 4), it is a poor choice for screen display.

I recommend sticking with relative value types (especially em) for screen and absolute value types for print.

The value you use will depend on your need; however, it is generally recommended to set relative font sizes to allow visitors final control of how large they are displayed.

3. **Add font size overrides as needed.**

   `h1 { font-size: 3em; }`

The only reason you would need to reset the font-size is if you need to increase or decrease it compared to the size set in the body. If you are using ems to set size, which I recommend, then remember that this is relative to the size of the parent. So a size of 2em would be twice as large as the parent, whereas a size of .5em would be half the size.

Avoid defining screen media font sizes using points or other absolute font sizes because these tend to render inconsistently across platforms. However, they're fine to use for print style sheets.

TIP When setting font sizes, your best strategy is to set a relative-length size for the `<body>` tag (such as 100%), and then use absolute font sizes (such as *small*) or relative font sizes (such as *larger*) to adjust the size. Doing so ensures the most consistent and versatile page viewing regardless of the actual media used (computer screen, printed page, handheld, and so on.)

★Adjusting Font Size for Understudy Fonts

Font sizes are measured based on the height of capital letters, but it is the lowercase letters that often vary the most from font to font. If you are relying on understudy fonts, your font sizes might look very different, even though the same physical size is set Ⓐ. To help alleviate this, CSS3 introduces the **font-size-adjust** property, which allows you to set the font size relative to lowercase letters rather than uppercase.

To do this, you specify a numeric value that lowercase fonts should be sized to as a multiple of the font size (**Table 5.7**). For example, if the font size is 18 pixels and you set a font-size-adjust of .5, lowercase letters will be sized at 9 pixels. As a result, all the fonts will have the same apparent size relative to each other, even if their x-heights vary greatly.

To adjust the font size for an element:

1. **Add the font size adjust property to your CSS.** Type the property name **font-size-adjust**, followed by a colon (**Code 5.5**).

    ```
    font-size-adjust:
    ```

2. **Define a size value.**

    ```
    .5;
    ```

    Type a value to adjust the font size by:

    ▸ A numeric value of 0 or greater as a multiplier for the current font-size to adjust the text size based on the x-height.

    ▸ **None**, to leave the font-size unadjusted

Ⓐ Verdana has a much taller x-height than Arial (top), but using font-size-adjust, you can set the lowercase letters to use the same height, ensuring greater consistency regardless of which font the browser uses.

TABLE 5.7 Font-Size-Adjust Values

Value					
<number>			●		
inherit			●		

Code 5.5 Styles added to *font-properties.css*— The font size has been adjusted so that lowercase letters are half the size of uppercase letters.

```
body {  font-size-adjust: .5;  }
```

TIP You can calculate these values by dividing the set font-size by the font's x-height, or you can just "eyeball" it until the value for the font-size-adjust appears to have no effect on the font size of the primary font.

TIP Font-size-adjust will adjust the size of all your glyphs (capitals as well as lowercase), but does so relative to the lowercase letters rather than uppercase.

normal *italic oblique*

A Italic or oblique? To really tell the difference, take a careful look at the letter "i" in both words.

TABLE 5.8 Font-Style Values

Value					
normal	●	●	●	●	●
italic	●	●	●	●	●
oblique	●	●	●	●	●

Code 5.6 Styles added to *font-properties.css*—The **h1** and **h2** tags both have italic set for them with this being overridden in the strong tag within an **h2** **B**. We also need to change the font-style in the @font-face rule. This does not actually italicize the downloaded font, it just tells the browser to use this in place of an italicized version.

```
/*** font-properties.css ***/

h1 { font-style: italic; }
h2 { font-style: normal; }
h2 cite { font-style: italic; }
figcaption { font-style: italic; }
```

Alice's Adventures in Wonderland

By *Lewis Carroll*

Chapter I **Down the Rabbit-Hole**

Alice was beginning to get very tired of sitting by her sister on the bank, and of having nothing to do: once or twice she had peeped into the book her sister was reading, but it had no pictures or conversations in it, "and what is the use of a book," thought Alice, "without pictures or conversations?"

So she was considering in her own mind (as well as she could, for the hot day made her feel very sleepy and stupid) whether the pleasure of making a daisy-chain would be worth the trouble of getting up and picking the daisies, when suddenly a White Rabbit with pink eyes ran close by her.

There was nothing so *very* remarkable in that; nor did Alice think it so *very* much out of the way to hear the Rabbit say to itself, "Oh dear! Oh dear! I shall be too late!" (when she thought it over afterwards, it occurred to her that she ought to have wondered at this, but at the time it all seemed quite natural); but when the Rabbit actually *took a watch out of its waistcoat-pocket*, and looked at it, and then hurried on, Alice started to her feet, for it flashed across her mind that she had never before seen a rabbit with either a waistcoat-pocket, or a watch to take

B Italics are often used to help set off text or to add emphasis, as with the chapter title.

Making Text Italic

Two kinds of styled text that are often confused are *italic* and *oblique*. An italic font is a special version of a particular font, redesigned with more pronounced serifs and usually a slight slant to the right. An oblique font, on the other hand, is simply a font that is slanted to the right but otherwise identical to the normal version.

Using the **font-style** property (**Table 5.8**), you can define a font as italic, oblique, or normal. When a font is set to italic but does not have an explicit italic version, the font defaults to oblique **A**.

To set font-style for an element:

1. **Add the font-style property to your CSS.** Type the property name **font-style** (**Code 5.6**), followed by a colon (:).

    font-style: italic;

2. **Define a style value.** Type a value for the **font-style**. Your options are:

    ▸ **italic**, which displays the type in an italic version of the font

    ▸ **oblique**, which slants the text to the right

    ▸ **normal**, which overrides any other styles set

    h2 strong { font-style: normal; }

    continues on next page

3. **Add style overrides as needed.** You can override italics or oblique by setting the font style for a child element to `normal`.

   Many browsers do not differentiate between italic and oblique but will simply use the fonts' italic version (if available), even when they are set to oblique.

TIP If an italicized or oblique version of the typeface does not exist, many browsers will attempt to synthesize one by slanting the normal version of the font to the right. This rarely looks good and should be avoided.

TIP Many Web designers underline words to draw visual attention to them. I recommend using italic or oblique text instead. Underlining often causes the page to look cluttered. More important, underlined text might be confused with hypertext links.

TIP Italicized text generally fits into a more compact space than non-italic text (called roman in traditional typesetting terms) and could be used to save screen space. But be careful—at small point sizes, italic can be difficult to read on the screen.

normal **bold**

Ⓐ The difference between normal and bold text is evident here.

TABLE 5.9 Font-Weight Values

Value	🖙	🖙	🖙	🖙	O
normal	●	●	●	●	●
bold	●	●	●	●	●
lighter	●	●	●	●	●
bolder	●	●	●	●	●
100–900*	●	●	●	●	●

* Depending on available font weights

Code 5.7 *font-properties.css*—The author's name is bold to make it stand out Ⓑ.

```
/*** font-properties.css ***/

.byline .author {
   font-weight: bold; }
```

Alice's Adventures in Wonderland

By **Lewis Carroll**

Chapter I Down the Rabbit-Hole

Alice was beginning to get very tired of sitting by her sister on the bank, and of having nothing to do: once or twice she had peeped into the book her sister was reading, but it had no pictures or conversations in it, "and what is the use of a book," thought Alice, "without pictures or conversations?"

Ⓑ The author's name is bold to stand out.

Font-Weight Numbers

Most fonts do not have nine weights, so if the specified weight is not available, another weight is used:

- **100** to **300** lighter or darker.
- **400** and **500** normal.
- **600** to **900** use the next darker weight, if available, or the next lighter weight.

Setting Bold, Bolder, Boldest

CSS provides several options that allow you to set different levels of boldness for text. Many fonts have various weights associated with them; these weights have the effect of making the text look more or less bold (**Table 5.9**). CSS can take advantage of this feature Ⓐ.

To define bold text in a CSS rule:

1. **Add the font weight property to your CSS.** Type the property name **font-weight** (**Code 5.7**), followed by a colon (:).

   ```
   font-weight:
   ```

2. **Define the weight.**

   ```
   bold;
   ```

   Type the value for the **font-weight** property, using one of the following options:

   - **bold**, which sets the font to boldface
   - **bolder** or **lighter**, which sets the font's weight to be bolder or lighter relative to its parent element's weight
   - A value from **100** to **900**, in increments of 100, which increases the weight, based on alternative versions of the font that are available
   - **normal**, which overrides other weight specifications

TIP Use font-weight to add emphasis to text, but use it sparingly. If everything is bold, nothing stands out.

TIP In reality, most fonts support only normal and bold, so relative values have an absolute effect

★Using Condensed and Expanded Fonts

Although the bold and italic versions of fonts are most common, many fonts have versions that are condensed (narrower) or extended (wider) **A**. The **font-stretch** property allows you to reference particular font widths (**Table 5.10**). Some fonts include font widths that stretch or compress the font and are different from bold, which simply makes the letterform consistently thicker. Most fonts will not have these properties, but for those that do, using **font-stretch** will be the best way to access them.

To define condensed or extended fonts in a CSS rule:

1. Add the **font-stretch** property to your CSS. Type the property name **font-stretch** (**Code 5.8**), followed by a colon (**:**).

   font-stretch:

2. Define the weight.

   condensed;

   Type the value for the **font-stretch** property, using one of the following options:

   ▸ A value from Table 5.10.

   ▸ **normal**, which overrides other weight specifications

normal condensed expanded

A Condensed and expanded fonts.

TABLE 5.10 Font-Stretch Values

Value					
ultra-condensed	●9	●9			
extra-condensed	●9	●9			
condensed	●9	●9			
semi-condensed	●9	●9			
semi-expanded(?)	●9	●9			
expanded	●9	●9			
extra-expanded	●9	●9			
ultra-expanded	●9	●9			
normal	●9	●9			
inherit	●9	●9			

Code 5.8 Added to *font-properties.css*—The author's name is set in condensed text **B**.

```
h2 cite { font-stretch: condensed; }
```

Alice's Adventures in Wonderland

By *Lewis Carroll*

Chapter I Down the Rabbit-Hole

Alice was beginning to get very tired of sitting by her sister on the bank, and of having nothing to do: once or twice she had peeped

B The author's name is condensed.

Normal SMALLCAPS

A With small caps, all the letters are uppercase, but the first letter is larger than the others.

TABLE 5.11 Font-Variant Values

Value					
normal	●	●	●	●	●
small-caps	●	●	●	●	●

Code 5.9. Styles added to *font-properties.css*—Small caps are applied to both header 1 and header 2, but disabled in the strong element within the **h2**. Note that the font-variant declaration was changed in the @font-face to small-caps rule so that the downloaded font will display in the **h1** **B**.

```
h1 { font-variant: small-caps; }
h2 { font-variant: small-caps; }
```

ALICE'S ADVENTURES IN WONDERLAND

BY LEWIS CARROLL

CHAPTER I DOWN THE RABBIT-HOLE

Alice was beginning to get very tired of sitting by her sister on the bank, and of having nothing to do: once or twice she had peeped into the book her sister was reading, but it had no pictures or conversations in it, "and what is the use of a book," thought Alice, "without pictures or conversations?"

So she was considering in her own mind (as well as she could, for the hot day made her feel very sleepy and stupid) whether the pleasure of making a daisy-chain would be worth the trouble of getting up and picking the daisies, when suddenly a White Rabbit with pink eyes ran close by her.

There was nothing so *very* remarkable in that; nor did Alice think it so *very* much out of the way to hear the Rabbit say to itself, "Oh dear! Oh dear! I shall be too late!" (when she thought it over afterwards, it occurred to her that she ought to have wondered at this, but at the time it all seemed quite natural); but when the Rabbit actually *took a watch out of its waistcoat-pocket*, and looked at it, and then hurried on, Alice started to her feet, for it flashed across her mind that she had never before seen a rabbit with either a waistcoat-pocket, or a watch to take

B Using small caps for the title is an elegant way to set it off from the rest of the text.

Creating Small Caps

Small caps (sometimes referred to as *mini-caps*) are useful for emphasizing titles (**Table 5.11**). With small caps, lowercase letters are converted to uppercase but in a slightly smaller size than regular uppercase letters **A**.

To set small caps for an element:

1. **Add the font variant property to your CSS.** Type the property name **font-variant** (Code 5.9), followed by a colon (**:**).

   `font-variant:`

2. **Define a value for the variant.**

   `small-caps;`

   Type the value of the **font-variant** property, using one of the following options:

   - **small-caps**, which sets lowercase letters as smaller versions of true uppercase letters
   - **normal**, which overrides other font-variant values that might be inherited

TIP Small caps are best reserved for titles or other special text; they can be hard to read at smaller sizes.

Setting Multiple Font Values at the Same Time

Although you can set font properties independently, it is often useful, not to mention more concise, to put all font elements in a single declaration (**Table 5.12**). To do this, use the shorthand **font** property.

To define several font attributes simultaneously in a rule:

1. **Add the font property to your CSS.** Type the property name **font** (**Code 5.10**), followed by a colon (**:**). Then type the values in the same order that they are typed in the remaining steps of this exercise.

   ```
   font:
   ```

2. *Optional* **Define a style value.** Type a **font-style** value, followed by a space. (See "Making Text Italic" in this chapter.)

   ```
   italic
   ```

TABLE 5.12 Font Values

Value					
<font-style>	●	●	●	●	●
<font-variant>	●	●	●	●	●
<font-weight>	●	●	●	●	●
<font-size>	●	●	●	●	●
<line-height>	●	●	●	●	●
<font-family>	●	●	●	●	●
visitor styles	●	○	○	○	●

Code 5.10 Changes to *font-properties.css*— Wherever possible, the font properties have been combined into the shorthand **font** property. This requires that the size, font family, and at least one of the other font properties are defined **Ⓐ**.

```
/*** font-properties.css ***/
body {   font: normal 100%/1.5 'BodyCopy',
Constantia, Georgia, "Times New Roman",
serif; }
h1 { font: italic bold small-caps 5em/.9
'TitleCopy', Corbel, Helvetica, Arial,
sans-serif;     }
```

Mimicking the Visitor's Styles

Wouldn't it be nice if you could match your visitor's system font styles? You can do this by simply declaring the font style to be one of the following keywords (for example, **font: icon;**):

- **caption**: the font style used by controls, such as buttons
- **icon**: the font style used to label icons
- **menu**: the font style used in drop-down menus and menu lists
- **message-box**: the font style used in dialog boxes
- **small-caption**: the font style used for labeling small controls
- **status-bar**: the font style used in the window's status bar at the top of the window

ALICE'S ADVENTURES IN WONDERLAND

By Lewis Carroll

CHAPTER I DOWN THE RABBIT-HOLE

Alice was beginning to get very tired of sitting by her sister on the bank, and of having nothing to do: once or twice she had peeped into the book her sister was reading, but it had no pictures or conversations in it, "and what is the use of a book," thought Alice, "without pictures or conversations?"

So she was considering in her own mind (as well as she could, for the hot day made her feel very sleepy and stupid) whether the pleasure of making a daisy-chain would be worth the trouble of getting up and picking the daisies, when suddenly a White Rabbit with pink eyes ran close by her.

There was nothing so very remarkable in that; nor did Alice think it so very much out of the way to hear the Rabbit say to itself, "Oh dear! Oh dear! I shall be too late!" (when she thought it over afterwards, it occurred to her that she ought to have wondered at this, but at the time it all seemed quite natural); but when the Rabbit actually took a watch out of its waistcoat-pocket, and looked at it, and then hurried on, Alice started to her feet, for it flashed across her mind that she had never before seen a rabbit with either a waistcoat-pocket, or a watch to take out of it, and burning with curiosity, she ran across the field after it, and was just in time to see it pop down a large rabbit-hole under the hedge.

In another moment down went Alice after it, never once considering how in the world she was to get out again.

The rabbit-hole went straight on like a tunnel for some way, and then dipped suddenly down, so suddenly that Alice had not a moment to think about stopping herself before she found herself falling down what seemed to be a very deep well.

Either the well was very deep, or she fell very slowly, for she had plenty of time as she went down to look about her, and to wonder what was going to happen next. First, she tried to look down and make out what she was coming to, but it was too dark to see anything; then she looked at the sides of the well, and noticed that they were filled with cupboards and book-shelves: here and there she saw maps and pictures hung upon pegs. She took down a jar from one of the shelves as she passed; it was labelled "ORANGE MARMALADE," but to her disappointment it was empty: she did not like to drop the jar for fear of killing somebody underneath, so managed to put it into one of the cupboards as she fell past it.

"Well!" thought Alice to herself. "After such a fall as this, I shall think nothing of tumbling down stairs! How brave they'll all think me at home! Why, I wouldn't say anything about it, even if I fell off the top of the house!" (Which was very likely true.)

Down, down, down. Would the fall never come to an end? "I wonder how many miles I've fallen by this time?" she said aloud. "I must be getting somewhere near the centre of the earth. Let me see: that would be four thousand miles down. I think—" (for, you see, Alice had learnt several things of this sort in her lessons in the schoolroom, and though this was not a very good opportunity for showing off her knowledge, as there was no one to listen to her, still it was good practice to say it over) "—yes, that's about the right distance—but then I wonder what Latitude or Longitude I've got to?" (Alice had no idea what Latitude was, or Longitude either, but thought they were nice grand words to say.)

Presently she began again. "I wonder if I shall fall right through the earth! How funny it'll seem to come out among the people that walk with their heads downwards! The Antipathies, I think—" (she was rather glad there was no one listening, this time, as it didn't sound at all the right word) "—but I shall have to ask them what the name of the country is, you know. Please, Ma'am, is this New Zealand or Australia?" (and she tried to curtsey as she spoke—fancy curtseying as you're falling through the air! Do you think you could manage it?) "And what an ignorant little girl she'll think me! No, it'll never do to ask: perhaps I shall see it written up somewhere."

Down, down, down. There was nothing else to do, so Alice soon began talking again. "Dinah'll miss me very much to-night, I should think!" (Dinah was the cat.) "I hope they'll remember her saucer of milk at tea-time. Dinah, my dear, I wish you were down here with me! There are no mice in the air, I'm afraid, but you might catch a bat, and that's very like a mouse, you know. But do cats eat bats, I wonder?" And here Alice began to get rather sleepy, and went on saying to herself, in a dreamy sort of way, "Do cats eat bats? Do cats eat bats?" and sometimes, "Do bats eat cats?" for, you see, as she couldn't answer either question, it didn't much matter which way she put it. She felt that she was dozing off, and had just begun to dream that she was walking hand in hand with Dinah, and saying to her very earnestly, "Now, Dinah, tell me the truth: did you ever eat a bat?" when suddenly, thump! thump! down she came upon a heap of sticks and dry leaves, and the fall was over.

Alice was not a bit hurt, and she jumped up on to her feet in a moment: she looked up, but it was all dark overhead; before her was another long passage, and the White Rabbit was still in sight, hurrying down it. There was not a moment to be lost: away went Alice like the wind, and was just in time to hear it say, as it turned a corner, "Oh my ears and whiskers, how late it's getting!" She was close behind it when she turned the corner, but the Rabbit was no longer to be seen: she found herself in a long, low hall, which was lit up by a row of lamps hanging from the roof.

There were doors all round the hall, but they were all locked; and when Alice had been all the way down one side and up the other, trying every door, she walked sadly down the middle, wondering how she was ever to get out again.

Suddenly she came upon a little three-legged table, all made of solid glass; there was nothing on it but a tiny golden key, and Alice's first idea was that this might belong to one of the doors of the hall; but, alas! either the locks were too large, or the key was too small, but at any rate it would not open any of them. However, on the second time round, she came upon a low curtain she had not noticed before, and behind it was a little door about fifteen inches high: she tried the little golden key in the lock, and to her great delight it fitted!

Alice opened the door and found that it led into a small passage, not much larger than a rat-hole: she knelt down and looked along the passage into the loveliest garden you ever saw. How she longed to get out of that dark hall, and wander about among those beds of bright flowers and those cool fountains, but she could not even get her head through the doorway; "and even if my head would go through," thought poor Alice, "it would be of very little use without my shoulders. Oh, how I

Ⓐ This version should look similar to the previous section except for the space between lines of text.

---

3. *Optional* **Define a weight value.** Type a `font-weight` value, followed by a space. (See "Setting Bold, Bolder, Boldest" in this chapter.)

   `bold`

4. *Optional* **Define a variant value.** Type a `font-variant` value, followed by a space. (See "Creating Small Caps" in this chapter.)

   `small-caps`

5. **Define a size value.** Type a `font-size` value. (See "Setting the Font Size" in this chapter.)

   `100%`

6. *Optional* **Define a line height value.** Type a forward slash (`/`), a `line-height` value, and a space. (See "Adjusting Text Spacing" in Chapter 6.)

   `/.9`

continues on next page

7. **Define a font family value.** Type a **font-family** value and closing semi-colon. (See "Setting a Font Stack" in this chapter.)

```
'TitleCopy', Corbel, Helvetica,
Arial, sans-serif;
```

TIP The **font** shorthand property is a real time-saver, and I try to use it as often as possible. It not only takes less time to type and edit, but can reduce the size of your code and speed up your load time.

TIP Code editing software, such as **Coda** and **Dreamweaver**, tend to default to the individual properties rather than the shorthand.

TIP If you don't want to set a particular style, variant, or weight value in the list, just leave it out. The browser will use its default value instead. However, you do have to include at least one value, even if it's just **normal**.

TIP If you need to override a value set by the **font** shorthand property, it's generally best to use the full property (such as **font-style**, **font-variant**, **font-weight**, and **font-family**).

Putting It All Together

Code **5.11** shows the final results for *font-properties.css*, It brings together the Web fonts at the top (they must always be placed at the top of the CSS file or `<style>` tag), and then the styles and weights are listed. Wherever possible, font values have been combined into the **font** shorthand property.

Code 5.11 Final *font-properties.css*

```
/*** fontproperties.css ***/

@font-face {
    font-family: 'BodyCopy';
    src: url('../fonts/DVS/DejaVuSerif.eot');
    src: url('../fonts/DVS/DejaVuSerif.eot?#iefix') format('embedded-opentype'),
        url('../fonts/DVS/DejaVuSerif.woff') format('woff'),
        url('../fonts/DVS/DejaVuSerif.ttf') format('truetype');
    font-weight: normal;
    font-style: normal; }
@font-face {
    font-family: 'BodyCopy';
    src: url('../fonts/DVS/DejaVuSerif-Bold.eot');
    src: url('../fonts/DVS/DejaVuSerif-Bold.eot?#iefix') format('embedded-opentype'),
        url('../fonts/DVS/DejaVuSerif-Bold.woff') format('woff'),
        url('../fonts/DVS/DejaVuSerif-Bold.ttf') format('truetype');
    font-weight: bold;
    font-style: normal; }
@font-face {
    font-family: 'BodyCopy';
    src: url('../fonts/DVS/DejaVuSerif-Italic.eot');
    src: url('../fonts/DVS/DejaVuSerif-Italic.eot?#iefix') format('embedded-opentype'),
        url('../fonts/DVS/DejaVuSerif-Italic.woff') format('woff'),
        url('../fonts/DVS/DejaVuSerif-Italic.ttf') format('truetype');
    font-weight: normal;
    font-style: italic; }
@font-face {
    font-family: 'BodyCopy';
    src: url('../fonts/DVS/DejaVuSerif-BoldItalic.eot');
    src: url('../fonts/DVS/DejaVuSerif-BoldItalic.eot?#iefix') format('embedded-opentype'),
        url('../fonts/DVS/DejaVuSerif-BoldItalic.woff') format('woff'),
        url('../fonts/DVS/DejaVuSerif-BoldItalic.ttf') format('truetype');
    font-weight: bold;
    font-style: italic; }
```

code continues on next page

Code 5.11 *continued*

```css
@font-face {
   font-family: 'BodyCopy';
   src: url('../fonts/DVS/DejaVuSerifCondensed-BoldItalic.eot');
   src: url('../fonts/DVS/DejaVuSerifCondensed-BoldItalic.eot?#iefix') format('embedded-opentype'),
      url('../fonts/DVS/DejaVuSerifCondensed-BoldItalic.woff') format('woff'),
      url('../fonts/DVS/DejaVuSerifCondensed-BoldItalic.ttf') format('truetype');
   font-weight: bold;
   font-style: italic;
   font-stretch: condensed; }
@font-face {
   font-family: 'TitleCopy';
   src: url('../fonts/LTG/littletroublegirl.eot');
   src: url('../fonts/LTG/littletroublegirl.eot?#iefix') format('embedded-opentype'),
      url('../fonts/LTG/littletroublegirl.woff') format('woff'),
      url('../fonts/LTG/littletroublegirl.ttf') format('truetype'); }
body {
   font: normal 100%/1.5 'BodyCopy', Constantia, Georgia, "Times New Roman", serif;
   font-size-adjust: .5; }
h1 {
   font: italic bold small-caps 5em/.9 'TitleCopy', Corbel, Helvetica, Arial, sans-serif; }
h2 {
   font-size: 1em;
   font-style: normal;
   font-variant: small-caps; }
h2 cite{
   font-size: 1.5em;
   font-variant: normal;
   font-weight: bold;
   font-style: italic;
   font-stretch: condensed;
}
h2 .chaptertitle {
   font: normal 3em 'TitleCopy', Corbel, Helvetica, Arial, sans-serif; }
em {
   font-size: 1.1em; }
figcaption {
   font-size: .875em;
   font-style: italic;
   font-stretch: condensed;
   font-weight: bold;
}
```

6

Text Properties

Text is everywhere and is used for everything from the ingredients in breakfast cereal to an ode to a Grecian urn. It is the best system that humans have ever devised for recording complex thoughts. Many people think of text as simply a way to record words, but typography adds a voice to the meaning of the words. Typography affects how text appears by controlling not only the shapes and sizes of the letters used (the font), but also the spaces between letters, words, lines, and paragraphs.

Unfortunately, many of the challenges of typography on the Web have come about as a result of a need to circumvent the limitations of the medium. The challenge of Web typography is to improve screen text legibility, as well as to guide the viewer's attention to important content. It's a difficult balancing act, but this chapter prepares you with the right tools.

In This Chapter

Getting Started

I'll be pulling the sample code for this chapter from Chapter II of Alice's Adventures in Wonderland. An expurgated version is shown in **Code 6.1**. I've included the address label that is a part of the chapter so we can play around with text spacing.

This code links to the final CSS code from Chapter 5 and also links a new file—*text-properties.css*—that we will be building in this chapter and is presented in full at the chapter's end.

Code 6.1 The HTML5 code used for the examples in this chapter.

```
<!DOCTYPE html>
<html lang="en">
<head>
    <meta charset="utf-8">
    <title>Alice&#8217;s Adventures In Wonderland | Chapter II</title>
    <link href="../css/font-properties.css" type="text/css" rel="stylesheet" media="all">
    <link href="../css/text-properties.css" type="text/css" rel="stylesheet" media="all">
</head>
<body id="chapter2" class="book aaiw chapter">
<section>
<header class="pageheader">
<hgroup>
      <h1>Alice&#8217;s Adventures in Wonderland</h1>
      <h2>By <cite>Lewis Carroll</cite></h2>
</hgroup>
</header>

<article>
    <h2>Chapter II
    <span class="chaptertitle">Pool of Tears</span>
    </h2>

    <p>Curiouser and curiouser!" cried Alice (she was so much surprised, that for a moment she
    → quite forgot how to speak good English)...</p>
    <p>And she went on planning to herself how she would manage it…</p>
    <address>
        Alice&#8217;s Right Foot, Esq.<br />
    Hearthrug,<br />
        near the Fender,<br />
            (with Alice&#8217;s love).<br />
</address>
</article>
<footer>
<a href="AAIWL-ch03.html">Chapter I: Down the Rabbit Hold</a>
<a href="TOC.html">Table of Contents</a>
<a href="AAIWL-ch03.html">Chapter III - A Caucus-race and a Long Tale</a>
/footer>
</body>
</html>
```

TABLE 6.1 Letter-Spacing Values

Value					
normal	●	●	●	●	●
\<length\>	●	●	●	●	●

Code 6.2 Added to *text-properties.css*—Space has been compressed in the level 1 heading (the book title) to create a cramped effect **A**. The chapter name has been spaced out; however, the spacing was overridden in the chapter number ("Chapter II"), so it appears normal. I've also closed up the spacing after the first letter in the first paragraph, which is being set as a drop cap.

```
/*** text-properties.css ***/
h1 {
    letter-spacing: -.05em; }
h2 {
    letter-spacing: 2px; }
h2 .chaptertitle {
    letter-spacing: 0; }
h2 + p:first-letter {
    letter-spacing: -.05em; }
```

A Code 6.2 applied to Code 6.1: By changing its spacing, the book title takes on a slightly more distinctive, logo-like appearance, and spacing out the chapter title makes it stand out slightly.

Adjusting Text Spacing

CSS gives you the ability to easily adjust text spacing, including the space between individual letters (*tracking*), words, and lines of text in a paragraph (*leading*). Of course, you could apply non-breaking spaces and the line break tag to get a similar effect in straight HTML, but these "kludges" are difficult to implement, control, and change. With CSS, you have exact control over these elements.

Adjusting the space between letters (tracking)

Tracking is the amount of space between letters in a word, which, in CSS, is controlled with the **letter-spacing** property (**Table 6.1**). More space between letters often improves text readability. On the other hand, too much space can hamper reading by making individual words appear less distinct.

To define tracking:

1. Add the letter-spacing property to your CSS rule. Type **letter-spacing** in the CSS declaration list, followed by a colon (**:**) (**Code 6.2**).

   `letter-spacing:`

2. Specify the amount of space between your letters.

   `-.05em;`

   Type a value for the **letter-spacing** property, using either of the following:

   ▸ A positive or negative length value, such as **-.05em**, which sets the distance between letters. For more information, see "Values and Units Used in This Book" in the Introduction.

   ▸ **normal**, which overrides inherited spacing attributes.

TIP Tracking should not be confused with kerning. Although both can add space between letters to improve legibility, they work in different ways. See the sidebar "Tracking or Kerning?"

TIP Generally, setting letter spacing in ems is preferred because it spaces the letters based on font size. When the text size is changed, the letter spacing automatically adjusts with it.

TIP A positive value for `letter-spacing` adds space between letters; a negative value closes the space. A value of 0 does not add or subtract space but prevents justification of the text. (See "Aligning Text Horizontally" in this chapter.)

Tracking or Kerning?

Whereas *tracking* refers to the spacing between letters in a word, *kerning* refers to the spacing between individual letter pairs in a proportional font. Is this splitting hairs? There actually is a distinction.

Tracking is applied to a word to equally space all the letters; kerning is applied between each letter to give each space the same visual appearance. However, using tracking may mean that some letters are spaced farther apart than others if it improves the readability. Although you could use CSS letter spacing to manually set the space between each letter, I do not recommend it. True text kerning is generally done using specialized layout software because it's very hard to do just by "eyeballing" the letters.

Although not yet ready for use, the W3C has started work on kerning properties for CSS3.

TABLE 6.2 Word-Spacing Values

Value					
normal	●	●	●	●	●
\<length\>	●	●	●	●	●

Code 6.3 Added to *text-properties.css*—When applied to **Code 6.1**, The words in the level 1 heading are spaced almost on top of each other, but this works because the words are visually separated by the capital letters **Ⓑ**. The words in the chapter title class are spaced out. The copy (body text) is slightly spaced out, which has the overall effect of lightening the page by creating more white space.

```
/*** text-properties.css ***/
h1 {    word-spacing: -.1em; }
h2 {    word-spacing: 3px; }
p {     word-spacing: .075em; }
.pageheader h2 {
    word-spacing: -.3em; }
.pageheader h2 .cite {
    word-spacing: 0; }
```

Ⓑ Code 6.3 applied to Code 6.1: The space between the words has been changed for effect in the titles and slightly increased to lighten the copy.

Adjusting space between words

Just as tracking and word spacing adjustments can both help and hinder legibility, adding a little space between words on the screen using the **word-spacing** property (**Table 6.2**) can make your text easier to read. But too much space interrupts the path of the reader's eye across the screen and interferes with reading.

To define word spacing:

1. Add the word-spacing property to your declaration list. Type **word-spacing** in the CSS declaration list, followed by a colon (**:**) (**Code 6.3**).

   ```
   word-spacing:
   ```

2. Specify the amount of space between words.

   ```
   -.1em;
   ```

   Set the value for **word-spacing**, using one of the following:

   ▸ A positive or negative length value, representing the amount of space between words (**-.1em**, for example). For more information, see "Values and Units Used in This Book" in the Introduction.

   ▸ **normal**, which overrides inherited values.

TIP Like letter spacing, use word spacing very sparingly. Generally, the natural word spacing has been optimized for readability. Changing that spacing often does more harm than good.

Adjusting space between lines of text (leading)

Anyone who has typed a term paper knows that they are usually double-spaced to make reading easier and allow space for comments. The leading between lines also can be increased for a dramatic effect by creating negative space between the text. The **line-height** property (**Table 6.3**) adds space between the text *baselines* (the bottoms of most letters).

To define leading:

1. Add the line-height property to your rule. Type **line-height** in the CSS declaration list, followed by a colon (**:**) (**Code 6.4**).

   ```
   line-height:
   ```

2. Specify the space between lines of text.

   ```
   1.5;
   ```

   Type a value for **line-height**, using one of the following options:

   ▸ A number to be multiplied by the font size to get the spacing value (**2.0** for double-spacing, for example). Although a value of **2** works, it will not validate properly, so always include the decimal.

   ▸ A length value, such as **24px**. The space for each line of text is set to this size regardless of the designated font size. So if the font size is set to **12px** and the line height is set to **24px**, the text will be double-spaced. See "Values and Units Used in This Book" in the Introduction.

   ▸ A percentage, which sets the line height proportionate to the font size used for the text.

   ▸ **normal**, which overrides inherited spacing values.

TABLE 6.3 Line-Height Values

Value					
normal	●	●	●	●	●
<number>	●	●	●	●	●
<length>	●	●	●	●	●
<percentage>	●	●	●	●	●

Code 6.4 Added to *text-properties.css*—The default **line-height** has been set in the body to be 1.5, but paragraph copy has been set to 2em. That will double-space the text **C**.

```
/*** text-properties.css ***/
body {   line-height: 1.5; }
p {   line-height: 2em; }
h2 + p:first-letter {
    line-height: 24px; }
```

TIP Adding space between lines of text enhances legibility—especially with large amounts of text. Generally, a line height of 1.5 to 2 times the font size is appropriate.

TIP To double-space text, set the `line-height` value to 2 or 200%. Likewise, a value of 3 or 300% results in triple-spaced text.

TIP You can use a percentage value lower than 100% or length values smaller than the font size to smash lines together. Although this effect may look neat in moderation, it won't ingratiate you with your readers if they can't actually read the text.

TIP Line height can also be defined at the same time as the font size using the `font` shorthand property. (See "Setting Multiple Font Values at the Same Time" in Chapter 5.)

ALICE'S ADVENTURES IN WONDERLAND

By *Lewis Carroll*

CHAPTER II Pool of Tears

"Curiouser and curiouser!" cried Alice (she was so much surprised, that for a moment she quite forgot how to speak good English); "now I'm opening out like the largest telescope that ever was! Good-bye, feet!" (for when she looked down at her feet, they seemed to be almost out of sight, they were getting so far off). "Oh, my poor little feet I wonder who will put on your shoes and stockings for you now, dears? I'm sure *I* sha'n't be able! I shall be a great deal too far off to trouble myself about you: you must manage the best way you can—but I must be kind to them," thought Alice, "or perhaps they won't walk the way I want to go! Let me see: I'll give them a new pair of boots every Christmas."

And she went on planning to herself how she would manage it. "They must go by the carrier," she thought; "and how funny it'll seem, sending presents to one's own feet! And how odd the directions will look!

Alice's Right Foot, Esq. Hearthrug, near the Fender, (with Alice's love).

After a time she heard a little pattering of feet in the distance, and she hastily dried her eyes to see what was coming. It was the White Rabbit returning, splendidly dressed, with a pair of white kid gloves in one hand and a large fan in the other: he came trotting along in a great hurry, muttering to himself as he came, "Oh! the Duchess, the Duchess! Oh! won't she be savage if I've kept her waiting!" Alice felt so desperate that she was ready to ask help of any one; so, when the Rabbit came near her, she began, in a low, timid voice, "If you please, sir——" The Rabbit started violently, dropped

---

C Code 6.4 applied to Code 6.1: The line height in the paragraphs has been loosened to make it easier to read and scan.

Setting Text Case

When you're dealing with dynamically generated output, such as from a database, you can never be sure whether the text will appear in uppercase, lowercase, or a combination of the two. With the **text-transform** property (**Table 6.4**), you can control the ultimate case of the text no matter how it begins.

To define the text case:

1. Add the text-transform property to your CSS. Type **text-transform** in the CSS declaration list, followed by a colon (**:**) (**Code 6.5**).

   `text-transform:`

2. Specify the text case.

   `uppercase;`

   Type one of the following **text-transform** values to specify how you want the text to be treated:

   ▸ **capitalize** sets the first letter of each word to uppercase.

   ▸ **uppercase** forces all letters to uppercase.

   ▸ **lowercase** forces all letters to lowercase.

   ▸ **none** overrides inherited text-case values and leaves the text unaltered.

TABLE 6.4 Text-Transform Values

Value					
capitalize	●	●	●	●	●
uppercase	●	●	●	●	●
lowercase	●	●	●	●	●1

Code 6.5 Added to *text-properties.css*—The **text-transform** property lets you take control of the text case Ⓐ.

```
/*** text-properties.css ***/
address {
    text-transform: uppercase; }
.pageheader h2 cite  {
    text-transform: uppercase; }
```

TIP The `text-transform` property is best reserved for formatting dynamically generated text. If the names in a database are all uppercase, for example, you can use `text-transform` to make them more legible.

TIP Keep in mind that `capitalize` will capitalize all letters in the text, even words such as "of" and "the" that should remain lowercase. In reality, `capitalize` is primarily useful for names.

TIP DON'T TYPE YOUR TEXT IN ALL CAPS. When HTML text is in caps, it makes it a lot harder to control in CSS. Plus, anyone using an assistive device for reading will hear this as shouting. It's better to use normal text plus text transform to style text as uppercase.

ALICE'S ADVENTURES IN WONDERLAND

By *LEWIS CARROLL*

Chapter II **Pool of Tears**

"Curiouser and curiouser!" cried Alice (she was so much surprised, that for a moment she quite forgot how to speak good English); "now I'm opening out like the largest telescope that ever was! Good-bye, feet!" (for when she looked down at her feet, they seemed to be almost out of sight, they were getting so far off). "Oh, my poor little feet I wonder who will put on your shoes and stockings for you now, dears? I'm sure I sha'n't be able! I shall be a great deal too far off to trouble myself about you: you must manage the best way you can—but I must be kind to them," thought Alice, "or perhaps they won't walk the way I want to go! Let me see: I'll give them a new pair of boots every Christmas."

And she went on planning to herself how she would manage it. "They must go by the carrier," she thought; "and how funny it'll seem, sending presents to one's own feet! And how odd the directions will look!

ALICE'S RIGHT FOOT, ESQ. HEARTHRUG, NEAR THE FENDER, (WITH ALICE'S LOVE).

After a time she heard a little pattering of feet in the distance, and she hastily dried her eyes to see what was coming. It was the White Rabbit returning, splendidly dressed, with a pair of white kid gloves in one hand and a large fan in the other: he came trotting along in a great hurry, muttering to himself as he came, "Oh! the Duchess, the Duchess! Oh! won't she be savage if I've kept her waiting!" Alice felt so desperate that she was ready to ask help of any one; so, when the Rabbit came near her, she began, in a low, timid voice, "If you please, sir———" The Rabbit started violently, dropped

Ⓐ **Code 6.5 applied to Code 6.1:** Lewis Carroll's name under the book title is all in caps (as opposed to small caps, explained in Chapter 5).

★Adding a Text Drop Shadow

The drop shadow is a time-honored method for adding depth and texture to two-dimensional designs. Most browsers support the **text-shadow** property, part of CSS3 (**Table 6.5**), which allows you to define the color, offset (x and y), spread, and blur for any text drop shadow. Although this property will not currently work in other browsers, neither will it interfere with them.

To define the text shadow:

1. **Add the text-shadow property to your CSS rule.** Type **text-shadow** in the CSS declaration list, followed by a colon (:) (**Code 6.6**).

   text-shadow:

2. **Specify the x, y offset.** Type a space followed by two positive or negative length values separated by a space.

   2px 3px

   The first value is the vertical distance to offset the shadow (positive is down; negative is up). The second value is the horizontal offset (positive is right; negative is left).

3. **Specify the amount of blur.** Type a space and then a positive length value for the amount of blur to apply to the shadow. All negative values will be treated as 0.

   5px

TABLE 6.5 Text-Shadow Values

Value					
<color>		●	●	●	●
<x-offset>		●	●	●	●
<y-offset>		●	●	●	●
<blur>		●	●	●	●
none		●	●	●	●

Code 6.6 Added to *text-properties.css*—The **text-shadow** property allows you to set the x,y offset and the blur radius.

```
/*** text-properties.css ***/
h1 {
    text-shadow: 2px 3px 5px
    → rgba(0,0,0,.75); }
article h2 {
    text-shadow: 0px 1px 1px
    → rgba(255,255,255,.6), 0px -1px 1px
    → rgba(0,0,0,.6); }
h2 + p:first-letter {
    text-shadow: -3px -3px 6px
    → rgba(153,0,0,.9), 2px 3px 5px
    → rgba(0,0,0,.5); }
```

TIP Using RGBA works best for shadows. Anything under that shadow will realistically show through.

TIP Although this is a "shadow," you can use any color for it. Therefore, if your text is on a dark background, you could use a light color to create a drop "glow."

TIP In Chapter 11, you'll learn how to set a `box-shadow` that works a lot like the `text-shadow` property but is applied to the element's box.

TIP Shadows do not affect the position of the text they are placed behind.

TIP Text shadows make links pop off the page when used with the `:hover` pseudo class.

4. **Specify the color.** Type a space and then a color value for the shadow.

   ```
   rgba(0,0,0,.75);
   ```

   For more information on color values, see "Choosing Color Values" in Chapter 7.

5. **Add more shadows.** You can add multiple shadows (as many as you want) to any block of text. To do so, you can add another text-shadow declaration to the rule, or add a comma followed by another definition.

   ```
   text-shadow: -3px -3px 6px
    → rgba(153,0,0,.9),

   2px 3px 5px rgba(0,0,0,.5);
   ```

   You can set the value to **none** to override a shadow that was previously set in the CSS.

ALICE'S ADVENTURES IN WONDERLAND

By *LEWIS CARROLL*

CHAPTER II **Pool of Tears**

"**C**uriouser and curiouser!" cried Alice (she was so much surprised, that for a moment she quite forgot how to speak good English); "now I'm opening out like the largest telescope that ever was! Good-bye, feet!" (for when she looked down at her feet, they seemed to be almost out of sight, they were getting so far off). "Oh, my poor little feet I wonder who will put on your shoes and stockings for you now, dears? I'm sure *I* sha'n't be able! I shall be a great deal too far off to trouble myself about you: you must manage the best way you can—but I must be kind to them," thought Alice, "or perhaps they won't walk the way I want to go! Let me see: I'll give them a new pair of boots every Christmas."

And she went on planning to herself how she would manage it. "They must go by the carrier," she thought; "and how funny it'll seem, sending presents to one's own feet! And how odd the directions will look!

ALICE'S RIGHT FOOT, ESQ. HEARTHRUG, NEAR THE FENDER, (WITH ALICE'S LOVE).

After a time she heard a little pattering of feet in the distance, and she hastily dried her eyes to see what was coming. It was the White Rabbit returning, splendidly dressed, with a pair of white kid gloves in one hand and a large fan in the other: he came trotting along in a great hurry, muttering to himself as he came, "Oh! the Duchess, the Duchess! Oh! won't she be savage if I've kept her waiting!" Alice felt so desperate that she was ready to ask help of any one; so, when the Rabbit came near her, she began, in a low, timid voice, "If you please, sir——" The Rabbit started violently, dropped

A Code 6.6 applied to Code 6.1: Shadows give the illusion of depth to the page.

Text shadow effects

Although it may seem like a simple effect, the text shadow offers a lot of power to designers beyond producing simple three-dimensional shadows. Because the shadow can be any color and you can stack numerous shadows on top of each other, you can create a wide variety of great special effects with them.

Here are just a few examples that I created classes for:

Blur

Blur creates the illusion that the text is out of focus. Stack shadows with the same color as the text, but with increasing amounts of blur to make the text look blurry.

```
.blur {
    background-color: #ccc;
    color: rgba(0,0,0,1),;
    text-shadow: 0px 0px 2px
     rgba(0,0,0,1),
    0px 0px 4px rgba(0,0,0,1),
    0px 0px 8px rgba(0,0,0,1);}
```

Letterpress

Letterpress text looks as if old-style print press letters were used. To create the effect, use low contrast or no-contrast between the text and background colors, and then add a drop shadow with 1px offset down and white with 30% opacity. If you are using dark colors, use up and black with 30% opacity.

```
.letterpress {
    background-color: #333;
    color: #222;
    text-shadow: 0px 1px 1px
     rgba(255,255,255,.3),
    0px -1px 1px rgba(0,0,0,.3);}
```

Emboss

Emboss reverses the letterpress effect, giving the illusion that the text is rising off of the page.

```
.emboss {
    background-color: #ccc;

    color: #ccc;

    text-shadow: -1px -1px 1px
      rgba(255, 255, 255, 0.75),

    1px 1px 1px rgba(0, 0, 0, 0.75); }
```

Neon Glow

The neon glow effect gives a soft, colorful glow to text, as if it is made from neon tubes. To create this effect, use white text and then stack drop shadows with increasing blur, starting with white and shifting to the desired neon color.

```
.neon {
    background-color: #000;

    color: #fff;

    text-shadow: 0 0 5px #fff,

    0 0 10px #fff,

    0 0 15px #fff,

    0 0 20px #ff2d95,

    0 0 30px #ff2d95,

    0 0 40px #ff2d95,

    0 0 50px #ff2d95,

    0 0 75px #ff2d95;

    letter-spacing: 5px; }
```

Fire

The fire effect creates the illusion of heat coming off the letters. To create the effect, start with white text, and then stack shadows, going from white to yellow to orange to red, while increasing the y-offset and blur with each.

```
.fire {

    background-color: #333;

    color: #fff;

    text-shadow: 0px -1px 4px white,

    0px -2px 10px yellow,

    0px -10px 20px orange,

    0px -18px 40px red; }
```

3D Text Blocks

The 3D text block effect creates the illusion that the letters have depth and mass, like lettering in retro science-fiction movies. To create the effect, start with white text and then stack successively darker shadows, increasing the increment by 1px for as many levels as you want to achieve the desired depth. The offset will depend on the direction you want the text to be angled.

```
.d3 {

    background-color: #ccc;

    color: #fff;

    text-shadow: 0px 1px 0px #999,

    0px 2px 0px #888,

    0px 3px 0px #777,

    0px 4px 0px #666,

    0px 5px 0px #555,

    0px 6px 0px #444,

    0px 7px 0px #333,

    0px 8px 7px #001135; }
```

TABLE 6.6 Text-Align Values

Value					
left	●	●	●	●	●
right	●	●	●	●	●
center	●	●	●	●	●
justify	●	●	●	●	●
inherit	●	●	●	●	●
auto	●	●	●	●	●

Code 6.7 Added to *text-properties.css*—The **h2** in the header is right justified Ⓐ, whereas paragraphs are fully justified.

```
/*** text-properties.css ***/
body {   text-align: left; }
h2 {   text-align: center; }
header h2 {
    text-align: right; }
p {   text-align: justify;
text-align-last: left;
text-justify: distribute; }
```

Ⓐ **Code 6.7 applied to Code 6.1:** Although it's a bit zig-zaggy with left-, right-, center-, and fully-justified text, we'll be changing the title and byline formatting later in this book when I talk about positioning.

★Aligning Text Horizontally

Traditionally, text is aligned at its left margin (left justified) or fully justified, which aligns the text at both the left and right margins (often called *newspaper style*). In addition, for emphasis or special effect, text can be centered on the screen or even right justified. The **text-align** property (**Table 6.6**) gives you control of the text's alignment and justification.

Although the text-align property was not updated for CSS3, two new properties were added that can directly affect it. The **text-align-last** property allows you to treat the justification in the last line of a block of text separately from the rest of the block (**Table 6.7**). This is especially useful for realizing interesting design effects, such as square blocks of text, created by allowing full justification of the last text line.

Additionally, when you are justifying text, you can now specify the justification method used, which is especially useful for text in non-Western languages (**Table 6.8**).

To define text alignment and spacing, and justify the last line of text:

1. Add the text-align property to your CSS. Type **text-align** in the CSS declaration list, followed by a colon (**:**) (**Code 6.7**) and then specify the horizontal alignment.

   ```
   text-align: center
   ```

   Use one of the following alignment styles:

   ▸ **left** to align the text on the left margin.

continues on next page

- **right** to align the text on the right margin.
- **center** to center the text within its area.
- **justify** to align the text on both the left and right margins.
- **inherit** makes the text take its parents' alignment.
- **auto** uses the default alignment, generally left.

2. **If you want the last line of a paragraph to be treated differently from the rest of the text, add the text-align-last property.** Type **text-align-last** in the CSS declaration list, followed by a colon (:) (**Code 6.7**) and specify how text in the last line of a block of text is treated:

```
text-align-last: center;
```

Use one of the following alignment styles:

- **left** to align the text in the last line to the left margin.
- **right** to align the text in the last line to the right margin.
- **center** to center the text within the width of the text area.
- **justify** to align the text on both the left and right margins, adding extra space between words and letters.
- **inherit** to make the text take its parents' alignment.
- **auto** to use the default alignment (generally left alignment).

You should also include the **-moz** extension version for full compatibility.

```
-moz-text-align-last: center;
```

TABLE 6.7 Text-Align-Last Values

Value					
left		●	◇		
right		●	◇		
center		●	◇		
justify		●	◇		
inherit		●	◇		
auto		●	◇		

TABLE 6.8 Text-Justify Values

Value					
kashida	○	○	○	○	○
distribute	○	○	○	○	○
inter-cluster	○	○	○	○	○
inter-ideograph	○	○	○	○	○
inter-word	○	○	○	○	○
none	○	○	○	○	○
auto	○	○	○	○	○

3. If you are using justified text (text-align: justify), add the text-justify property. Type **text-justify** in the CSS declaration list, followed by a colon (**:**) (**Code 6.7**) and specify how justified text is treated:

```
text-justify: distribute;
```

Use one of the following justification styles:

▸ **kashida** to justify text in cursive scripts by elongating their connections.

▸ **distribute** to add space between words and letters.

▸ **inter-cluster** to add space in content that has no inter-word spacing, such as many Asian languages.

▸ **inter-ideograph** to add space between words or block scripts as with certain Asian scripts.

▸ **inter-word** to add space between words only.

▸ **none** to disable justification.

▸ **auto** to use the default alignment (generally left alignment).

TIP Text is left justified by default.

TIP Fully justifying text may produce some strange results on the screen because spaces between words must be added to make each line the same length. In addition, opinions differ as to whether full justification helps or hinders readability.

Aligning Text Vertically

Using the **vertical-align** property, you can specify the vertical position of one inline element relative to the elements above or below it **A**. This means that the **vertical-align** property (**Table 6.9**) can be used only with inline tags and table tags—that is, tags without a break before or after them, such as the anchor (**<a>**), image (**<img>**), emphasized text (**<em>**), strong text (**<strong>**), and table data (**<td>**) tags.

To define vertical alignment:

1. Add the vertical align property to your rule. Type **vertical-align** in the declaration list, followed by a colon (**:**) (**Code 6.8**).

    vertical-align:

Mad Hatter — baseline

Mad ^Hatter — superscript

Mad _Hatter — subscript

Mad ^Hatter — top

Mad Hatter — middle

Mad Hatter — bottom

Mad ^Hatter — text-top

Mad Hatter — text-bottom

A The different alignment types. The lines are shown only as guides.

TABLE 6.9 Vertical-Align Values

Value					
super	●	●	●	●	●
sub	●	●	●	●	●
baseline	●	●	●	●	●
<relative>	●	●	●	●	●
<length>	●	●	●	●	●
<percentage>	●	●	●	●	●

Code 6.8 Added to *text-properties.css*—Use **vertical-align** with relative or absolute values, depending on the results you desire **B**.

```
/*** text-properties.css ***/
h2 .chaptertitle {
   vertical-align: super; }
.pageheader h2 cite {
   vertical-align: -.6em; }
```

ⓑ Code 6.8 applied to Code 6.1: The chapter number and "by" in the byline have been moved up relative to the text to which they refer.

TABLE 6.10 Setting an Element's Position Relative to the Parent Element

Type	To align the element
top	Top to highest element in line
middle	Middle to middle of parent
bottom	Bottom to lowest element in line
text-top	Top to top of parent element's text
text-bottom	Bottom to bottom of parent element's text

Math and Science

Superscript and subscript are used for scientific notation. To express the Pythagorean theorem, for example, you would use superscripts:

$a^2 + b^2 = c^2$

A water molecule might be expressed with subscripts as follows:

H_2O

However, keep in mind that neither subscript nor superscript will reduce the text size, so you may also want to include **font-size** in your definition to achieve a true scientific notation style. (See "Setting the Font Size" in Chapter 5.)

2. **Specify the vertical alignment.**

`super;`

Type a value for the vertical text alignment using one of these options:

▸ **super** superscripts the text above the baseline.

▸ **sub** subscripts the text below the baseline.

▸ **baseline** places the text on the baseline (its default state).

▸ A relative value from **Table 6.10** that sets the element's alignment relative to its parent's alignment. To align the top of your text with the top of the parent element's text, for example, you would use **text-top**.

▸ A percentage value that raises or lowers the element's baseline proportionate to the parent element's font size (**25%**, for example).

TIP Superscript is great for footnotes that can be hyperlinked to notes at the bottom of the current page or to another Web page.

TIP The sup and sub tags can also be used for superscript and subscript, but should not be used for design (as in this case) but for footnotes or mathematical notation.

TIP If you are creating a multicolumn layout, you might encounter problems with vertical alignment when it doesn't appear where it should be. In those cases, a good fallback is to use relative positioning, as explained in Chapter 10.

Indenting Paragraphs

Indenting the first word of a paragraph several spaces (five spaces, traditionally) is the time-honored method of introducing a new paragraph.

On the Web, however, indented paragraphs haven't worked because most browsers compress multiple spaces into a single space. Instead, paragraphs have been separated by an extra line break.

Using the **text-indent** property (**Table 6.11**), you can specify extra horizontal space at the beginning of the first line of text in a paragraph and restore the traditional paragraph style.

To define text indentation:

1. **Add the text indent property to your CSS.** Type **text-indent** in the CSS declaration list, followed by a colon (**:**) (**Code 6.9**).

   text-indent:

2. **Specify the amount of indentation.**

   3em;

   Type a value for the indent, using one of the following options:

   ▸ A length value such as **3em** creates a nice, clear indent. (See "Values and Units Used in This Book" in the Introduction.)

   ▸ A percentage value indents the text proportionate to the parent's (paragraph) width (**10%**, for example).

> **TIP** If you are using indentation to indicate paragraphs, you should set the margin and padding of paragraphs to 0 to override the <p> tag's natural tendency to add space between paragraphs. You'll learn more about margins and padding in Chapter 8.

TABLE 6.11 Text-Indent Values

Value					
<length>	◉	◉	◉	◉	◉
<percentage>	◉	◉	◉	◉	◉
inherit	◉	◉	◉	◉	◉

Code 6.9 Added to *text-properties.css*—Although you can indent any block of text, indentation is generally associated with paragraphs, and I've set all of the paragraphs to indent 3em Ⓐ. However, the first paragraph in a section is generally not indented; therefore, I've set the first paragraph after a header to always have an indention of 0.

```
/*** text-properties.css ***/
p {   text-indent: 3em; }
header + p {
    text-indent: 0; }
```

Ⓐ **Code 6.9 applied to Code 6.1:** All paragraphs except the first paragraph are indented a space that is equivalent to two letters. The indent space will adjust with the font size.

> **TIP** Because indenting is more common in the print world than the online world, you may want to consider using indents for only the printer-friendly versions of your page.

TABLE 6.12 White-Space Values

Value					
normal	●	●	●	●	●
pre	●	●	●	●	●
nowrap	●	●	●	●	●

Controlling White Space

As you've learned, browsers traditionally collapsed multiple spaces into a single space unless a `<pre>` tag was used. CSS lets you allow or disallow that space collapsing, as well as designate whether text can break at a space (similar to the `<nobr>` tag) using the `white-space` property (**Table 6.12**).

An excellent example of this is the mouse tail poem from Chapter 3 of *Alice's Adventures in Wonderland*. This poem is shaped like a curvy mouse tail **A**. If the `white-space` property value is assigned `pre` for the `poem` class, all those spaces collapse **B**. However, if it's assigned a value of `nowrap`, the spaces and line breaks are ignored, and the text stretches as far to the right on the page as necessary **C**.

A The **pre** value keeps all spaces so the poem retains its distinctive mouse tail shape rather than collapsing.

B Without the **pre** value, the spaces collapse along with the mouse tail.

C With the **no-wrap** value, the poem stretches vertically across the window, forcing a horizontal scroll to accommodate its width.

To define white space:

1. **Add the white space property to your CSS rule.** Type **white-space** in the CSS declaration list, followed by a colon (**:**) (Code 6.10).

   ```
   white-space:
   ```

2. **Specify how you want white space treated.**

   ```
   pre;
   ```

   Type one of the following options:

   ▸ **pre** preserves multiple spaces.

   ▸ **nowrap** prevents line wrapping without a **
** tag.

   ▸ **normal** allows the browser to determine how spaces are treated. This setting usually forces multiple spaces to collapse into a single space.

   TIP Do not confuse the **<nobr>** and **<pre>** tags with the **white-space** property values of **nowrap** and **pre**. Although they basically do the same thing, the no break tag is being phased out (deprecated) and should not be used.

   TIP The text content of any tag that receives the **nowrap** value runs horizontally as far as necessary regardless of the browser window's width. The user may be forced to scroll horizontally to read all the text, so this setting is usually avoided.

   TIP **nowrap** is great for preventing content from wrapping in table data cells.

Code 6.10 Added to *text-properties.css*—The address tag is set up to preserve the HTML text as it appears in the code by setting the **white-space** to **pre**. This is useful for formatting the note that Alice is sending to her foot in the formatting that the author intended **D**.

```
/*** text-properties.css ***/
.asis {    white-space: pre; }
```

D Code 6.10 applied to Code 6.1: The note has been set along a diagonal by adding spaces. These would collapse if not for the **pre** value applied to it.

TABLE 6.13 Text-Decoration Values

Value					
none	●	●	●	●	●
underline	●	●	●	●	●
overline	●	●	●	●	●
line-through	●	●	●	●	●

Code 6.11 Added to *text-properties.css*—I use text decoration to set up a class called **.strike** that can be used to strike out unwanted text **A** and to turn off the unwanted underline on hypertext links **B**. Don't worry, though. We'll add underlining back with more control using the border-bottom property in Chapter 10.

```
/*** text-properties.css ***/
a {    text-decoration: none; }
.strike {
    text-decoration: line-through; }
```

ALICE'S ADVENTURES IN WONDERLAND

^{By} *LEWIS CARROLL*

CHAPTER II Pool of Tears

"**C**uriouser and curiouser!" cried Alice (she was so much surprised, that for a moment she quite forgot how to speak good English); "now I'm opening out like the largest telescope that ever was! Good-bye, feet!" (for when she looked down at her feet, they seemed to be almost out of sight, they were getting so far off). "Oh, my poor little feet, I wonder who will put on your shoes and stockings for you now, dears? I'm sure I shan't be able! I shall be a great deal too far off to trouble myself about you: you must manage the best way you can—but I must be kind to them," thought Alice, "or perhaps they won't walk the way I want to go! Let me see: I'll give them a new pair of boots every Christmas."

And she went on planning to herself how she would manage it. "They must go by the carrier," she thought; "and how funny it'll seem, sending presents to one's own feet! And how odd the directions will look!

ALICE'S RIGHT FOOT, ESQ.
~~HEARTHRUG,~~
~~NEAR THE FENDER,~~
~~(WITH ALICE'S LOVE).~~

After a time she heard a little pattering of feet in the distance, and she hastily dried her eyes to see what was coming. It was the White Rabbit

A Code 6.11 applied to Code 6.1: The address has been struck out.

The Pool of Tears

"I won't indeed!" said Alice, in a great hurry to change the subject of conversation. "Are you—are you fond—of—of dogs?" The Mouse did not answer, so Alice went on eagerly: "There is such a nice little dog near our house I should like to show you! A little bright-eyed terrier, you know, with oh, such long curly brown hair! And it'll fetch things when you throw them, and it'll sit up and beg for its dinner, and all sorts of things—I can't remember half of them—and it belongs to a farmer, you know, and he says it's so useful, it's worth a hundred pounds! He says it kills all the rats and—oh dear!" cried Alice in a sorrowful tone, "I'm afraid I've offended it again!" For the Mouse was swimming away from her as hard as it could go, and making quite a commotion in the pool as it went.

So she called softly after it, "Mouse dear! Do come back again, and we won't talk about cats or dogs either, if you don't like them!"

When the Mouse heard this, it turned round and swam slowly back to her: its face was quite pale (with passion, Alice thought), and it said in a low trembling voice, "Let us get to the shore, and then I'll tell you my history, and you'll understand why it is I hate cats and dogs."

It was high time to go, for the pool was getting quite crowded with the birds and animals that had fallen into it: there were a Duck and a Dodo, a Lory and an Eaglet, and several other curious creatures. Alice led the way, and the whole party swam to the shore.

Next: Chapter III - A Caucus-race and a Long Tale ›

B Code 6.11 applied to Code 6.1: The links in the footer of the page are no longer underlined.

Decorating Text

Using the **text-decoration** property (Table 6.13), you can adorn text in one of three ways: underline, overline, or line-through. Used to add emphasis, these decorations attract the reader's eye to important areas or passages on your Web page.

To decorate (or undecorate) text:

1. Add the text decoration property. Type **text-decoration** in the CSS declaration list, followed by a colon (**:**) (**Code 6.11**).

   ```
   text-decoration:
   ```

2. Specify the text decoration you want (or not).

   ```
   none;
   ```

   Type a value for the **text-decoration** property. Choose one of the following:

   ▸ **underline** places a line below the text.

   ▸ **overline** places a line above the text.

   ▸ **line-through** places a line through the middle of the text (also called strikethrough).

   ▸ **none** overrides decorations set elsewhere.

TIP You can also type a space and add another `text-decoration` value (Table 6.13). As long as the first value is not `none`, you can use multiple text decorations by adding more values in a list separated by spaces, as follows:

```
overline underline line-through
```

TIP Ding dong, the blink is dead. With CSS3, the `blink` value has been officially removed as a text decoration option, and the `<blink>` HTML tag is long gone. Now if you want to annoy your visitors with blinking text, you'll have to use Adobe Flash.

TIP Text decorations are applied across an entire text block element rather than on a letter-by-letter basis. This means that a child element cannot override the text decoration set by its parent.

TIP Although a child element cannot override its parent's text decoration, child elements can have additional text decoration added to them. In the example, notice that the emphasis tag uses strikethrough, which is added to the underlining already supplied by the paragraph tag.

TIP Striking through text is useful for text that you want to show as deleted. For example, I've used strikethrough in online catalogs that include sale prices. I show the original price in strikethrough with the sale price next to it. That said, using the `<del>` tag is a better option because it communicates deletion.

TIP Honestly, the only time I use text decoration is to turn off hypertext link underlining. Underlining is just too indiscriminate, placing a hard line under the text in the same color as the text. Some work is being done to provide more underline control to set the space, color, and style of the underline.

Underlining Links?

Setting **text-decoration: none**; in the `<a>` tag overrides the underline in hypertext links, even if the visitor's browser is set to underline links. In my experience, many visitors look for underlining to identify links. Although I don't like underlining for links—it clutters the page, and CSS offers many superior alternatives—I receive angry emails from visitors when I turn off underlining.

One alternative to the **text-decoration** property is to use the **border-bottom** property with the link tag to provide faux underlining. This gives you much better control over the underline appearance, and it even allows you to use different colors.

★Coming Soon!

Several text properties are still under development by the W3C and have yet to be substantially implemented in browsers. You may see them soon, but at the time of this writing I can't give a specific way to implement them across browsers:

Outlining text—Adding an outline around the text (also called a *text stroke*) is another way to make text distinctive, most often for titles. Webkit already includes a rudimentary property for this, but the syntax is likely to change in the final W3C version.

Kerning—Remember that letter spacing is not kerning. The new `font-kerning` property will provide some rudimentary kerning capabilities.

Hanging punctuation—One common problem in typography is what to do when alphanumeric characters are not present at the beginning of a block of text, as with quotation marks. The `hanging-punctuation` property will allow you to define how these characters are treated, either placing them in the edge of the text block or outside.

Text line decoration—As mentioned in my explanation of the `text-decoration` property, several new associated properties are being developed to style the text decoration, including `text-line-color`, `text-line-style`, `text-line-skip`, and `text-underline-position`.

To follow the development of these styles, visit the CSS3 Text Module at www.w3.org/TR/css3-text.

Putting It All Together

Code 6.12 Shows the final results for the file *text-properties.css*, which we have been building this chapter.

Code 6.12 *text-properties.css* in its entirety.

```
/*** text-properties.css ***/
body {
   line-height: 1.5; }
h1 {
   letter-spacing: -.05em;
   word-spacing: -.1em;
   line-height: .9em;
   text-shadow: 2px 3px 5px rgba(0,0,0,.75); }
h2 {
   letter-spacing: 2px;
   word-spacing: 3px;
   line-height: 1em;
   text-align: center; }
header h2 {
   text-align: right; }
article h2 {
   text-shadow: 0px 1px 1px rgba(255,255,255,.6), 0px -1px 1px rgba(0,0,0,.6); }
h2 .chaptertitle {
   letter-spacing: 0;
   vertical-align: middle; }
p {
   line-height: 2em;
   text-align: justify;
   text-indent: 3em; }
h2 + p {
   text-indent: 0; }
h2 + p:first-letter {
   letter-spacing: -.05em;
   line-height: 24px;
   text-shadow: -3px -3px 6px rgba(153,0,0,.9), 2px 3px 5px rgba(0,0,0,.5); }
address, blockquote {
   text-transform: uppercase;
   white-space: pre; }
a {
   text-decoration: none; }
.delete {
   text-decoration: line-through; }
.pageheader h2 {
   word-spacing: -.3em;
   text-align: right; }
.pageheader h2 cite {
   word-spacing: 0;
   text-transform: uppercase;
   vertical-align: -.6em; }
```

Color and Background Properties

Colors form the cornerstone of all design, even if they're only black and white. They create the first impression of your site. Bright, vibrant, jewel-like colors make a radically different statement than earth tones. Even if you choose to use only black and white, your design will make a statement. Beyond their decorative impact, colors can also guide the viewer's eye around the page, helping to highlight some important areas while downplaying others.

In this chapter, you will learn the primary methods used to add and control color with CSS. Keep in mind, however, you can specify color using several CSS properties. (See the sidebar "Other Ways to Add Color.") But before you learn how to code colors, let's quickly explore how to choose them.

In This Chapter

Getting Started

I'll be pulling the sample code for this chapter from Chapter 3 of *Alice's Adventures in Wonderland*. An expurgated version is shown in **Code 7.1**, including a navigational footer at the bottom. It imports the final CSS code from Chapters 5 and 6, and imports a new file called *color-background-properties.css*, that will contain the CSS code from this chapter.

Code 7.1 The HTML5 code used for the examples in this chapter.

```
<!DOCTYPE html>
<html lang="en">
<head>
<meta charset="utf-8">
<title>Alice&#8217;s Adventures In Wonderland | Chapter III</title>
<link href="../css/font-properties.css" type="text/css" rel="stylesheet" media="all">
<link href="../css/text-properties.css" type="text/css" rel="stylesheet" media="all">
<link href="../css/color-background-properties.css" type="text/css" rel="stylesheet" media="all">
</head>
<body id="chapter3" class="book aaiw chapter">
<header class="page">
<hgroup>
    <h1>Alice&#8217;s Adventures in Wonderland</h1>
    <h2>By <cite>Lewis Carroll</cite></h2>
</hgroup>
</header>
<article>
<h2>Chapter III
<span class="chaptertitle">A Caucus-race and a Long Tale</span>
</h2>
<p>They were indeed a queer-looking party that assembled on the bank&mdash;the birds with draggled
 → feathers,the animals with their fur clinging close to them, and all dripping wet, cross, and
 → uncomfortable.</p>
<footer>
&laquo; <a href="AAIWL-ch03">Chapter II - The Pool of Tears</a>
<a href="../index.html">Table of Contents</a>
<a href="AAIWL-ch03">Chapter IV - The Rabbit sends in a Little Bill</a> &raquo;
</footer>
</body>
</html>
```

Choosing Color Values

You can define colors in a variety of ways in CSS. Several methods simply represent how the primary colors—red, green, and blue—should be mixed, but that is by no means the only way colors are defined in CSS (**Table 7.1**).

Color keywords

You have access to many predefined color values derived from lists defined in the HTML4 and SVG specifications. **Table 7.2** shows the list of keywords along with the equivalent hex and decimal values.

continues on page 188

TABLE 7.1 Color Values

Name	Form	Example	@				O
Keyword	<keyword>	coral	●	●	●	●	●
Transparent	transparent	transparent	●	●	●	●	●
Current color	currentcolor	currentcolor	●9	●	●	●	●
RGB hex	#rrggbb, #rgb	#ff7f50, #f90	●	●	●	●	●
RGB decimal	rgb(rrr,ggg,bbb)	rgb(255,127,80)	●	●	●	●	●
RGB percentage	rgb(rrr%,ggg%,bbb%)	rgb(100%, 50%,31%)	●	●	●	●	●
RGBA	rgba(rrr,ggg,bbb,d.d)	rgba(255,127,80,.86)	●9	●	●	●	●
HSL	hsl(hhh,sss%,lll%)	hsl(16,65%,100%)	●9	●	●	●	●
HSLA	hsla(hhh,sss%,lll%,d.d)	hsla(16,65%,100%,.23)	●9	●	●	●	●

TABLE 7.2 Color Keywords

Keyword	Hex	Decimal
aliceblue	#F0F8FF	240,248,255
antiquewhite	#FAEBD7	250,235,215
aqua	#00FFFF	0,255,255
aquamarine	#7FFFD4	127,255,212
azure	#F0FFFF	240,255,255
beige	#F5F5DC	245,245,220
bisque	#FFE4C4	255,228,196
black	#000000	0,0,0
blanchedalmond	#FFEBCD	255,235,205
blue	#0000FF	0,0,255
blueviolet	#8A2BE2	138,43,226
brown	#A52A2A	165,42,42
burlywood	#DEB887	222,184,135
cadetblue	#5F9EA0	95,158,160
chartreuse	#7FFF00	127,255,0
chocolate	#D2691E	210,105,30
coral	#FF7F50	255,127,80
cornflowerblue	#6495ED	100,149,237
cornsilk	#FFF8DC	255,248,220
crimson	#DC143C	220,20,60
cyan	#00FFFF	0,255,255
darkblue	#00008B	0,0,139
darkcyan	#008B8B	0,139,139
darkgoldenrod	#B8860B	184,134,11
darkgray	#A9A9A9	169,169,169
darkgreen	#006400	0,100,0
darkgrey	#A9A9A9	169,169,169
darkkhaki	#BDB76B	189,183,107
darkmagenta	#8B008B	139,0,139
darkolivegreen	#556B2F	85,107,47
darkorange	#FF8C00	255,140,0
darkorchid	#9932CC	153,50,204
darkred	#8B0000	139,0,0
darksalmon	#E9967A	233,150,122

TABLE 7.2 Color Keywords *(continued)*

Keyword	Hex	Decimal
darkseagreen	#8FBC8F	143,188,143
darkslateblue	#483D8B	72,61,139
darkslategray	#2F4F4F	47,79,79
darkturquoise	#00CED1	0,206,209
darkviolet	#9400D3	148,0,211
deeppink	#FF1493	255,20,147
deepskyblue	#00BFFF	0,191,255
dimgray	#696969	105,105,105
dodgerblue	#1E90FF	30,144,255
firebrick	#B22222	178,34,34
floralwhite	#FFFAF0	255,250,240
forestgreen	#228B22	34,139,34
fuchsia	#FF00FF	255,0,255
gainsboro	#DCDCDC	220,220,220
ghostwhite	#F8F8FF	248,248,255
gold	#FFD700	255,215,0
goldenrod	#DAA520	218,165,32
gray	#808080	128,128,128
green	#008000	0,128,0
greenyellow	#ADFF2F	173,255,47
gray	#808080	128,128,128
honeydew	#F0FFF0	240,255,240
hotpink	#FF69B4	255,105,180
indianred	#CD5C5C	205,92,92
indigo	#4B0082	75,0,130
ivory	#FFFFF0	255,255,240
khaki	#F0E68C	240,230,140
lavender	#E6E6FA	230,230,250
lavenderblush	#FFF0F5	255,240,245
lawngreen	#7CFC00	124,252,0
lemonchiffon	#FFFACD	255,250,205
lightblue	#ADD8E6	173,216,230
lightcoral	#F08080	240,128,128
lightcyan	#E0FFFF	224,255,255

table continues on next page

TABLE 7.2 **Color Keywords** (continued)

Keyword	Hex	Decimal	
lightgoldenrodyellow	#FAFAD2	250,250,210	
lightgray	#D3D3D3	211,211,211	
lightgreen	#90EE90	144,238,144	
lightpink	#FFB6C1	255,182,193	
lightsalmon	#FFA07A	255,160,122	
lightseagreen	#20B2AA	32,178,170	
lightskyblue	#87CEFA	135,206,250	
lightslategray	#778899	119,136,153	
lightsteelblue	#B0C4DE	176,196,222	
lightyellow	#FFFFE0	255,255,224	
lime	#00FF00	0,255,0	
limegreen	#32CD32	50,205,50	
linen	#FAF0E6	250,240,230	
magenta	#FF00FF	255,0,255	
maroon	#800000	128,0,0	
mediumaquamarine	#66CDAA	102,205,170	
mediumblue	#0000CD	0,0,205	
mediumorchid	#BA55D3	186,85,211	
mediumpurple	#9370DB	147,112,219	
mediumseagreen	#3CB371	60,179,113	
mediumslateblue	#7B68EE	123,104,238	
mediumspringgreen	#00FA9A	0,250,154	
mediumturquoise	#48D1CC	72,209,204	
mediumvioletred	#C71585	199,21,133	
midnightblue	#191970	25,25,112	
mintcream	#F5FFFA	245,255,250	
mistyrose	#FFE4E1	255,228,225	
moccasin	#FFE4B5	255,228,181	
navajowhite	#FFDEAD	255,222,173	
navy	#000080	0,0,128	
oldlace	#FDF5E6	253,245,230	
olive	#808000	128,128,0	
olivedrab	#6B8E23	107,142,35	
orange	#FFA500	255,165,0	

TABLE 7.2 **Color Keywords** (continued)

Keyword	Hex	Decimal	
orangered	#FF4500	255,69,0	
orchid	#DA70D6	218,112,214	
palegoldenrod	#EEE8AA	238,232,170	
palegreen	#98FB98	152,251,152	
paleturquoise	#AFEEEE	175,238,238	
palevioletred	#DB7093	219,112,147	
papayawhip	#FFEFD5	255,239,213	
peachpuff	#FFDAB9	255,218,185	
peru	#CD853F	205,133,63	
pink	#FFC0CB	255,192,203	
plum	#DDA0DD	221,160,221	
powderblue	#B0E0E6	176,224,230	
purple	#800080	128,0,128	
red	#FF0000	255,0,0	
rosybrown	#BC8F8F	188,143,143	
royalblue	#4169E1	65,105,225	
saddlebrown	#8B4513	139,69,19	
salmon	#FA8072	250,128,114	
sandybrown	#F4A460	244,164,96	
seagreen	#2E8B57	46,139,87	
seashell	#FFF5EE	255,245,238	
sienna	#A0522D	160,82,45	
silver	#C0C0C0	192,192,192	
skyblue	#87CEEB	135,206,235	
slateblue	#6A5ACD	106,90,205	
slategray	#708090	112,128,144	
snow	#FFFAFA	255,250,250	
springgreen	#00FF7F	0,255,127	
steelblue	#4682B4	70,130,180	
tan	#D2B48C	210,180,140	
teal	#008080	0,128,128	
thistle	#D8BFD8	216,191,216	
tomato	#FF6347	255,99,71	
turquoise	#40E0D0	64,224,208	

table continues on next page

Currentcolor keyword

In addition to the color keyword list, you can use the **currentcolor** keyword. Using **currentcolor** to set any color value will use the element's current **color** value. For example, to create an aqua border color, use:

```
color: aqua;
```

```
border-color: currentcolor;
```

If you assign **currentcolor** specifically to the **color** property, it will inherit its parent element's color value just like using **color: inherit**.

Transparent keyword

Another important keyword is **transparent**, which is the equivalent of a 0 alpha. That is, it's completely transparent. This keyword allows anything behind that element to show through.

RGB hex values

Hexadecimal values can range from 0–9 and a–f. Values include three couplets of hexadecimal values representing the levels of red, green, and blue (in that order) in the desired color. The color value couplets range from 00 (no color) to FF (full color) 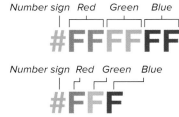. However, if the couplets contain the same hex value, only three values are needed to define the color. For example, these two sets of values represent the same pure blue:

#0000ff

#00f

TABLE 7.2 Color Keywords *(continued)*

Keyword	Hex	Decimal	
violet	#EE82EE	238,130,238	
wheat	#F5DEB3	245,222,179	
white	#FFFFFF	255,255,255	
whitesmoke	#F5F5F5	245,245,245	
yellow	#FFFF00	255,255,0	
yellowgreen	#9ACD32	154,205,50	

Number sign   Red   Green   Blue

#FFFFFF

Number sign   Red   Green   Blue

#FFF

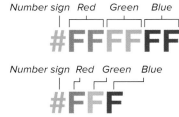

Ⓐ RGB hex color values are represented by three couplet values, or by three single values ranging from 0–9 or A–F that indicate the levels of red, green, and blue that combine to create the color.

Red   Green   Blue

rgb(**255**, **255**, **255**)

Ⓑ RGB decimal color values range from 0–255 to indicate the levels of red, green, and blue that combine to create the color.

Red Green Blue

rgb(**100%**, **100%**, **100%**)

C RGB percentage color values range from 0–100 to indicate the amount of red, green, and blue that is combined to create the color.

Hue Saturation Lightness

hsl(**360**, **100%**, **100%**)

D HSL color values represent hue as the angle on a standard color wheel (0–360), saturation as a percentage, and lightness as a percentage.

Hex or Decimal?

Until recently, it was assumed that colors should always be declared in RGB hexadecimal notation. In fact, I still meet designers and developers who are completely unaware that they have alternatives. RGB decimal has been around for quite awhile and will work in any browser you want to throw it at.

But which is "better"?

I personally find that it's much easier to envision a color in decimal numbers (which I've used all my life) than in hex values. I can look at the value **135, 127, 107** and know it's a reddish beige much faster than if I see **877f6b**. Additionally, since there is no alpha version for hex, if you want transparent colors, you have to use decimal values (**Table 7.2**).

The only argument in favor of hex color values is that they are more compact (a smaller file size) than decimal values. But even over a large-scale Web site, you might save only a few bytes (millionths of a second in load time).

RGB decimal values

Often, simply referred to as the *RGB values*, RGB uses decimal values from 0 (no color) to 255 (full color) to represent the levels of red, green, and blue (in that order) present in the desired color **B**.

Percentage values

RGB values can also be expressed as whole percentages from 0% (no color) to 100% (full color) to represent the levels of red, green, and blue (in that order) present in the desired color **C**.

★HSL values

Although their notations are different, hex, decimal, and percentage values are just different ways to define the levels of red, green, and blue in a color. CSS3 adds a completely different method for defining color by its hue, saturation, and lightness (HSL) **D**:

- **Hue**—A degree value from 0 to 360, although the degree symbol is not included. The hue is based on a color's position in the standard color wheel where red is at 0°, yellow at 60°, green at 120°, cyan at 180°, blue at 240°, and magenta at 300°.

- **Saturation**—A percentage from 0% (no color) to 100% (full color).

- **Lightness**—A percentage from 0% (black) to 100% (white).

TIP Hex values are currently the most popular way to define color values, but they are by no means the best way to add colors. I find it much easier to imagine colors using Base 10 decimal values rather than Base 16 hexadecimal values.

TIP Although HSL is a bit difficult to master at first, it can be easier to use when setting complementary colors. Just add 180° to the hue.

★Setting Alpha Values for Color Transparency

Although the opacity property allows you to make elements transparent, this is applied to the entire element. CSS3 now allows you to make specific colors transparent. An alpha value is generally a fourth value in a color, but rather than representing a color, it sets the opacity of the color—a value from 0 (transparent) to 1 (opaque). So, an alpha of .5 is the equivalent of 50% opacity **E**.

TIP You can set an alpha channel for either RGB decimal or HSL color values, but currently there is no way to add alpha values to RGB hex values.

TIP In addition to setting the color opacity, CSS includes the ability to set the opacity of an entire object and any of its content. See "Setting an Element's Opacity" in Chapter 11 for more information.

Alpha (opacity: 0–1)

rgba(255, 255, **255**, **1.0**)

hsla(**360**, **100%**, **100%**, **1.0**)

Alpha (opacity: 0–1)

E RGBA and HSLA add an alpha value as a decimal (0–1) to represent the opacity of a color with 0 completely transparent and 1 completely opaque.

Other Ways to Add Color

Although this chapter presents the primary methods for setting colors in your design, several other CSS properties include color values:

- **text-shadow** & **box-shadow**—Although generally thought of as black or gray, you can set a text-shadow to any color. I often use this with brighter colors to create a glow (see Chapter 6).

- **border**—An element's border colors can be set as part of any of the border properties or directly in the **border-color** property (see Chapter 10).

- **outline**—Like the **border** property, **outline** allows you to define a color around the edge of an element (see Chapter 10).

Linear

Radial

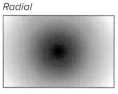

A Linear and radial gradients are available in all modern browsers, including IE9+.

linear-gradient(

45deg, ———————— *Angle*

purple 25%, ———————— *Color stop 1*

rgb(23, 136, 12), ——— *Color stop 2*

#c00) ———————————— *Color stop 3*

B Linear gradients have an optional angle value, followed by two or more color stops separated by commas. The angle can be in degrees, or one or two keywords to indicate the starting side or corner. The color stop is a color value and an optional length or percentage value for the position of the stop—where it is at full color—along the gradient line.

★Creating Color Gradients

Although not yet a finished part of the CSS3 standard, the ability to fill an element's background with a gradient has been introduced as extensions in Opera, Internet Explorer, Webkit, and Mozilla—which means you can add linear and radial gradients compatible with Opera, Internet Explorer, Safari, Chrome, and Firefox **A**.

To ensure maximum compatibility, you need to include the CSS3 standard version of the gradient property along with the browser extension versions: **-o**, **-ms**, **-webkit**, and **-moz**. Don't worry, they all take the same values. If you need to support really old browsers (Safari 3 and earlier or Internet Explorer 8 or earlier), you may also need to include values for them. For more details, see the sidebar "Older Gradient Syntax?"

Linear Gradients

Linear gradients have two different value types, the angle of the gradient and the colors that make up the gradient **B**.

- **Angle (degrees)**—The angle for the gradient expressed as a numeric value, using degrees (**deg**): such as **45deg**.

- **Angle (keyword)**—Instead of an angle numeric value, you can use one or two keywords—separated by a spaces—defining the side or corner where the gradient should start and stop—and preceded by the word **to**. Values can include **top**, **right**, **bottom**, and/or **left**. If two values are used (separated by a space), they specify a corner, such as **to top left**. such as **to bottom right**.

continues on next page

- **Color stop**—The values of two or more colors at a particular point along the gradient with values separated by spaces. You should include at least two values (otherwise you'll get a solid color), but you can follow them with as many values as you want. These may include any color value type as shown in **Table 7.1**, including transparent colors using RGBA or HSLA, and an optional percentage or length value to set where the color should be positioned along the gradient axis, such as **green 67%: rgba(221,160,221)**.

C There's more than one way to create the same gradient.

At its simplest, a linear gradient can be two color values with the default angle at 270°, the start stop at 0%, and the end stop at 100%:

```
linear-gradient(navy, gold);
```

This is the same as:

```
linear-gradient(270deg, rgb(0,0,128),
→rgb(255,215,0));
```

```
linear-gradient(to bottom, navy,
→gold);
```

```
linear-gradient(to top, gold, navy);
```

```
linear-gradient(#008 0%, #ffd700
→100%);
```

```
linear-gradient(180deg, gold 0%,
→navy 100%);
```

All of these values produce the same gradient C.

radial-gradient(

center center, ———— *Origin position*

circle farthest-corner, – *Shape/size*

purple 25%, ———— *Color stop 1*

rgb(23, 136, 12), ———— *Color stop 2*

#c00) ———————— *Color stop 3*

D Radial gradients have optional values for the origin of the gradient, the shape and size, and two or more color stops. The position can be two values for the horizontal and vertical location. The shape is either **circle** or **elliptical** and the size can be keyword or two values. The color stop has a color value and an optional length or percentage value for the position of the stop—where it is at full color—along the gradient.

TABLE 7.3 Radial Gradient Size Values

Value	Description
closest-side	Gradient shaped to meet closest side from its center
closest-corner	Gradient shaped to meet closest corner from its center
farthest-side	Gradient shaped to meet farthest side from its center
farthest-corner	Gradient shaped to meet farthest corner from its center

Radial Gradients

Radial gradients get a little more complicated than linear gradients because they have four possible value types **D**:

- **Position**—The location of the center of the gradient within its box (see Chapter 10). The value(s) are a numeric distance value (such as **5em**), a percentage (such as **23%**) or a keyword (such as **center**) that sets the center of the radial gradient (which is the same as setting background image positions shown later in **Table 7.10**). You can use two values to define the horizontal and vertical positions independently (such as at **2em 5em**, at **23% 46%**, or at **left center**). You can mix value types (such as at **2em center**). The position is optional, and if omitted defaults to **center**.

- **Size (keyword)**—The size sets the radial gradient's endpoint, using a keyword (**Table 7.3**). Currently, the webkit version of the property uses a different and more limited set of keywords, but they have equivalents in the new standard.

- **Size (length)**—If the shape is not explicitly stated, the size can be set as one or two length (such as **20px**) or percentage (such as **89% 42%**) values. If two values are used, the first is the horizontal length and the second is the vertical length. Negative values are not allowed.

- **Shape**—The shape of a radial gradient, either **circle** or **ellipse**. The shape value is optional; but if omitted, the value defaults to **circle**. Otherwise, the size is a single length, and **ellipse**.

continues on next page

- **Color stop**—The values of two or more colors at particular points along the gradient with values separated by spaces. You should include at least two values (otherwise you'll get a solid color), but you can follow them with as many values as you want. These may include any color value type shown in **Table 7.1**—including transparent colors using RGBA or HSLA—and an optional percentage or length value to set where the color should be positioned along the gradient axis, such as **green 67%, rgba(221,160,221,0.5)**.

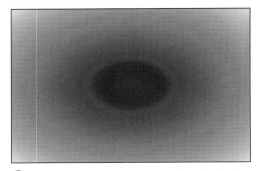

E There are many ways to create this elliptical gradient.

At its simplest, a radial gradient can be two color values with the default position in the center, the shape an **ellipse**, the size set by the farthest-corner, and the start stop at 0% and end stop at 100%:

```
radial-gradient(navy,gold);
```

This is the same as:

```
radial-gradient(ellipse rgb(0,0,128),
→ rgb(255,215,0);
radial-gradient(center, navy, gold);
radial-gradient(farthest-corner, #008
→ 0%, #ffd700 100%);
radial-gradient(center center,
→ ellipse farthest-corner, navy 0%,
→ gold 100%);
```

All of these values produce the same gradient **E**.

Repeating Gradients

Both linear and radial gradients can repeat, rather than fill the area with the end color. To repeat gradients, simply use:

`-repeating-linear-gradient()`

`-repeating-radial-gradient()`

TIP If you specify a gradient as a background, also specify a background color to ensure that text will be legible in browsers that do not support gradients.

TIP Currently, gradients work only in the background of elements.

TIP Use the `background-image` property to set gradients in the background of an element. You could also use the `background` property, but `background-image` works more consistently across multiple browsers.

Older Gradient Syntax?

Although work is well underway for the official W3C CSS gradient standard as a part of the new Image Module (http://dev.w3.org/csswg/css3-images), the bad news is that Safari, Chrome, Firefox, and Internet Explorer have dabbled in creating their own versions of the standard. The good news is that, for the most part, these older syntaxes are no longer relevant. A possible exception is the older webkit syntax, which some developers still include. Given that a decreasing number of browsers are likely to use this style, I recommend leaving it out.

If you really need to support an older syntax, though, the best way to get the code is to use the CSS3 Gradient Generator Tool (http://gradients.glrzad.com) 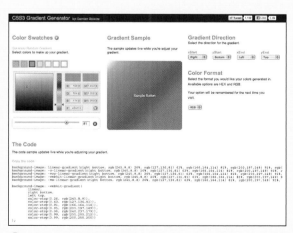.

E A great tool for plotting gradients can be found at http://gradients.glrzad.com.

Choosing Your Color Palette

Graphic designers have a saying, "No color is better than bad color." If you are not careful, color can work against you by obscuring your message and confusing your visitors. The effective use of color in design takes a lot of practice to get right, and designers have been practicing for centuries to get it right 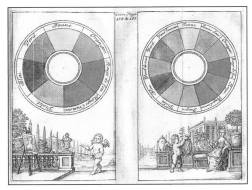.

Colors have powerful emotional meanings that cannot always be predicted, especially when used in different combinations. **Table 7.4** presents some of the most common color associations in Western culture. When you put two colors together, the meanings begin to interrelate, much like words in a sentence.

You want to make sure you don't just slap colors down on your page. If you do, they'll probably clash. The most important thing you can do to avoid this is to take time to plan your color choices. Begin by choosing the specific colors you will use and their exact RGB or HSL values. Then apply these colors consistently throughout your project.

You will need to consider the colors that you will be applying to the basic parts of your Web page (including the colors in the background images) **B**. You do not have to choose a different color hue for each part, but you should define what color will be applied to each component:

- **Body background**—Covering the entire visible area of the browser window, the background generally should provide the most contrast with the foreground text colors.

- **Content background**—Often, you will use a different color for the background directly around the content of the page,

A Eighteenth-century color wheels. Although modern color wheels have a lot more colors **C**, the basic concept remains unchanged.

TABLE 7.4 Western Color Associations

Color	Emotional Associations	Color
Red	assertive, powerful, intense	■
Blue	consoling, fidelity, defense	■
Yellow	concern, rebirth, clarity	■
Green	wealth, fitness, food, nature	■
Brown	nature, maturity, wisdom	■
Orange	hospitality, exhilaration, vigor	■
Pink	vital, innocent, feminine	■
Purple	royalty, refinement, calm	■
Black	stark, stylish, somber	■
Gray	business-like, cool, detached	■
White	clean, pure, straightforward	□

allowing the body background color to absorb extra horizontal space in the browser window.

- **Border/rule**—You may want to use contrasting colors around the borders of content areas, headers, navigation blocks, lists, and tables, or use rules to separate different chunks of content. Choose a color that contrasts with the area that the lines are meant to separate.

- **Header**—You may choose not to change the background color for section headers, but always make sure that the text color clearly contrasts with the background colors you choose.

- **Copy**—Your copy (generally sentences or paragraphs of text) should have the highest contrast with the background to maximize legibility.

- **Link/navigation**—You may choose different colors for your site navigation and for links in the copy, but these link colors should be easily discernible from other text while still contrasting with the background.

- **List/table**—You may choose different background colors behind lists and tables or even alternating row colors, called *zebra striping*, to improve readability.

- **Form**—You can specify the border, foreground, and background colors of many form elements to give them a more distinctive look for your site, apart from their default appearance. However, be careful not to customize them so much that the visitor does not know what they are.

B Consider which colors you will use for each component of your Web page. (Site: SEIA.org)

Color wheel basics

A color wheel is a disc or circle that shows the spectrum of color values, providing you with a quick overview of all the possibilities from red, orange, and yellow, to green, blue, indigo, and violet, and back to red again. Some color wheels also allow you to view brightness (dark to light) and saturation (full color tone to gray) levels 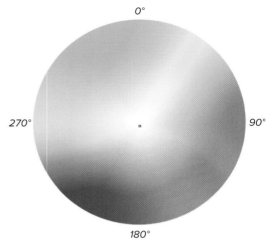.

When you get down to it, though, color is a matter of preference. Colors that I think look great together may make my wife gag (and usually result in changing my outfit). To be safe, you can count on a single color (monochrome) or one of the following color-combination schemes as (more or less) fail-safe:

C The color wheel. This is especially important to know if you want to use HSL color values. The wheel goes from 0° to 90° to 180° to 270° back to 0°.

Analogous—Three or more colors and their tones with one primary color and two secondary colors that are the same angle from the primary color, from 0 degrees to 60 degrees.

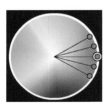

Monochromatic—A single color with different brightness or saturation values for contrast.

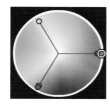

Triad—Three colors and their tones with one primary and two secondary colors that are at equal angles in the color wheel, 120 degrees to 180 degrees from the primary.

Complementary—Two colors from opposite sides of the color wheel (180 degrees), providing the highest contrast.

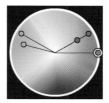

Compound—Four colors that include one primary color, one secondary color (in direct contrast to the primary color), and two colors that are the same angle from the primary or secondary color, from 0 degrees to 90 degrees.

All of these color schemes allow you to choose the basic hue and then use various brightness and/or saturation values for the colors to add additional shades to your palette.

Online color scheme tools

Not sure where to start planning your color scheme? Here are some excellent online tools that you can use:

- **Build a palette**—Adobe's Kuler (http://kuler.adobe.com) provides an excellent tool for comparing colors side by side in an interactive environment 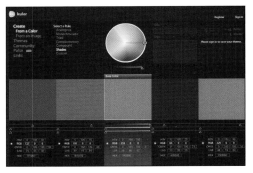.

- **ColRD: Palette Creator**—Explore color palettes and gradients on ColRD (http://colrd.com/create/palette) 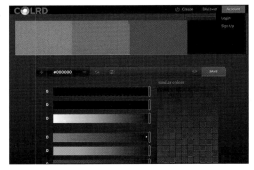.

- **DeGraeve's Color Palette Generator**—When you are using graphics or photography with a particular color scheme in them, the Degrave.com Color Palette Generator (degraeve.com/color-palette) will analyze the image and then produce a color palette based on those colors in the image 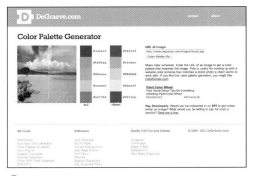.

- **Color Scheme Designer**—If you need an advanced color wheel tool, I recommend the Color Scheme Designer (colorschemedesigner.com) 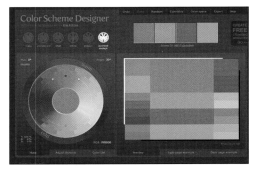.

D Adobe's Kuler (http://kuler.adobe.com)

E ColRD: Palette Creator
(http://colrd.com/create/palette)

F DeGraeve's Color Palette Generator
(degraeve.com/color-palette)

G Color Scheme Designer
(colorschemedesigner.com)

Color and Accessibility

Beyond attractive and compelling design, another critical consideration with color is accessibility for people who are visually impaired. The most important considerations are to provide enough contrast between foreground and background colors so that the information is readable and to make sure that color is not critical for understanding information. For example, if you are using color for links, also set off those links using some other formatting such as underlining or bold.

For more details on color and accessibility, see section 9 of the W3C's white paper "CSS Techniques for Web Content Accessibility Guidelines" at w3.org/TR/WCAG10-CSS-TECHS/#style-colors.

I also recommend that you check your foreground and background colors for accessibility at http://snook.ca/technical/colour_contrast/colour.html 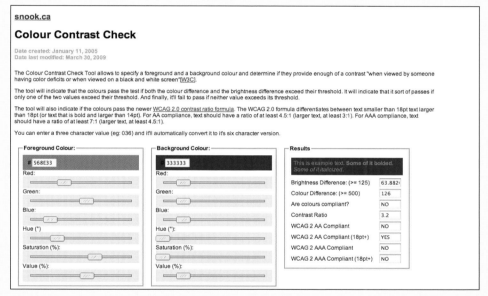.

 Check your color contrast to make sure it's accessible (http://snook.ca/technical/colour_contrast/colour.html).

Setting Text Color

The **color** property is used to set the *text color* (sometimes called the *foreground color*) of an element (**Table 7.5**). This color will be inherited by all of the element's children (see Chapter 4), so you need only set it once in the body element and then provide overrides as needed. For example, if you set the color to gray in the **<body>**, then all text on the page will be gray. If you then set the **<p>** element to red, all paragraph text and any elements in it will be red, overriding the gray.

To define the text color:

1. **Add the text color property to your CSS declarations.** Type **color** in the CSS rule, followed by a colon (**:**) (**Code 7.2**).

   ```
   color:
   ```

2. **Specify a color value.** Type a value for the color based on color values from Table 7.1. This includes RGB, HSL, transparent, or current color.

   ```
   rgb(51, 51, 51);
   ```

   It's a good idea to set a default page color for the body, table, and input tags independently—even if it's just to black—to ensure that colors are consistent across the page.

TABLE 7.5 Color Value

Value					
<color>	●	●	●	●	●
inherit	●	●	●	●	●

Code 7.2 Added to *color-background-properties.css*—The header text is rendered in a variety of shades of red, the text is a dark gray, and the form button and the text that gets typed into the form field are red Ⓐ. The brighter red text is much more prominent than the lighter red and the gray text.

```
/*** color-background-properties.css ***/

body {   color: rgb(51,51,51); }
header h1 {
    color: hsla(7,62%,40%,.8); }
header h2 {
    color: rgba(242,237,217,.25); }
header h2 cite {
    color: rgba(242,237,217,.5); }
article h2 .chaptertitle {
    color: rgba(135,127,107,.5); }
article p:first-of-type:first-letter {
    color: rgb(153,0,0); }
footer {
    color: white; }
a:link {
    color: rgb(204,0,0); }
a:visited {
    color: rgb(153,0,0); }
a:hover {
    color: rgb(255,0,0); }
a:active {
    color: rgb(153,153,153); }
```

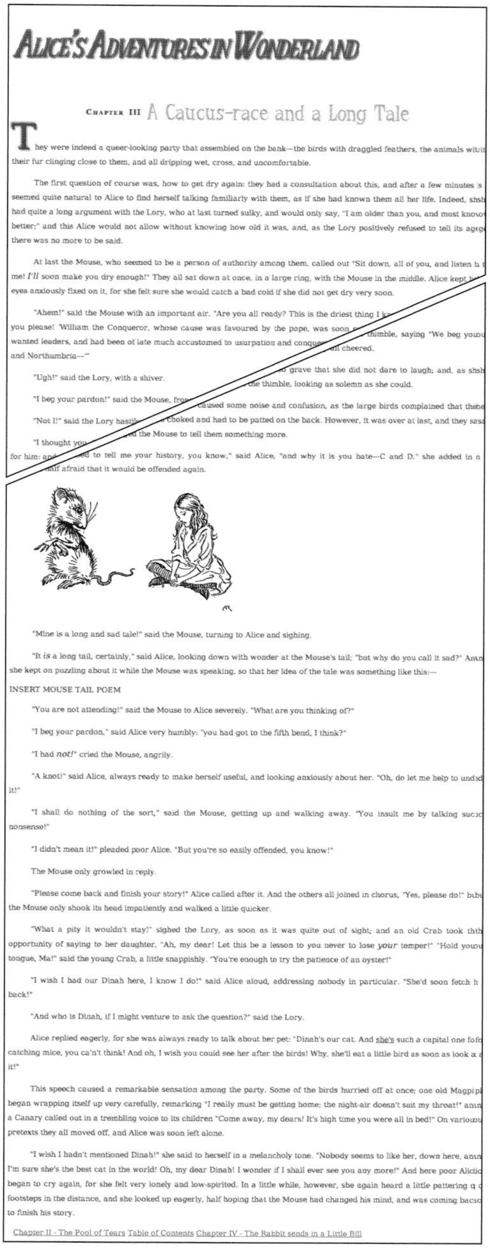

ALICE'S ADVENTURES IN WONDERLAND

CHAPTER III A Caucus-race and a Long Tale

They were indeed a queer-looking party that assembled on the bank—the birds with draggled feathers, the animals with their fur clinging close to them, and all dripping wet, cross, and uncomfortable.

The first question of course was, how to get dry again: they had a consultation about this, and after a few minutes it seemed quite natural to Alice to find herself talking familiarly with them, as if she had known them all her life. Indeed, she had quite a long argument with the Lory, who at last turned sulky, and would only say, "I am older than you, and must know better;" and this Alice would not allow without knowing how old it was, and, as the Lory positively refused to tell its age, there was no more to be said.

At last the Mouse, who seemed to be a person of authority among them, called out "Sit down, all of you, and listen to me! I'll soon make you dry enough!" They all sat down at once, in a large ring, with the Mouse in the middle. Alice kept her eyes anxiously fixed on it, for she felt sure she would catch a bad cold if she did not get dry very soon.

"Ahem!" said the Mouse with an important air. "Are you all ready? This is the driest thing I know. Silence all round, if you please! William the Conqueror, whose cause was favoured by the pope, was soon submitted to by the English, who wanted leaders, and had been of late much accustomed to usurpation and conquest. Edwin and Morcar, the earls of Mercia and Northumbria—"

"Ugh!" said the Lory, with a shiver.

"I beg your pardon!" said the Mouse, frowning, but very politely: "Did you speak?"

"Not I!" said the Lory hastily.

"I thought you did," said the Mouse. "—I proceed. Edwin and Morcar, the earls of Mercia and Northumbria, declared for him: and even Stigand, the patriotic archbishop of Canterbury, found it advisable—"

[...]

"Mine is a long and sad tale!" said the Mouse, turning to Alice and sighing.

"It is a long tail, certainly," said Alice, looking down with wonder at the Mouse's tail; "but why do you call it sad?" And she kept on puzzling about it while the Mouse was speaking, so that her idea of the tale was something like this:—

INSERT MOUSE TAIL POEM

"You are not attending!" said the Mouse to Alice severely. "What are you thinking of?"

"I beg your pardon," said Alice very humbly: "you had got to the fifth bend, I think?"

"I had not!" cried the Mouse, angrily.

"A knot!" said Alice, always ready to make herself useful, and looking anxiously about her. "Oh, do let me help to undo it!"

"I shall do nothing of the sort," said the Mouse, getting up and walking away. "You insult me by talking such nonsense!"

"I didn't mean it!" pleaded poor Alice. "But you're so easily offended, you know!"

The Mouse only growled in reply.

"Please come back and finish your story!" Alice called after it. And the others all joined in chorus, "Yes, please do!" but the Mouse only shook its head impatiently and walked a little quicker.

"What a pity it wouldn't stay!" sighed the Lory, as soon as it was quite out of sight; and an old Crab took the opportunity of saying to her daughter "Ah, my dear! Let this be a lesson to you never to lose your temper!" "Hold your tongue, Ma!" said the young Crab, a little snappishly. "You're enough to try the patience of an oyster!"

"I wish I had our Dinah here, I know I do!" said Alice aloud, addressing nobody in particular. "She'd soon fetch it back!"

"And who is Dinah, if I might venture to ask the question?" said the Lory.

Alice replied eagerly, for she was always ready to talk about her pet: "Dinah's our cat. And she's such a capital one for catching mice you ca'n't think! And oh, I wish you could see her after the birds! Why, she'll eat a little bird as soon as look at it!"

This speech caused a remarkable sensation among the party. Some of the birds hurried off at once: one old Magpie began wrapping itself up very carefully, remarking "I really must be getting home; the night-air doesn't suit my throat!" and a Canary called out in a trembling voice to its children "Come away, my dears! It's high time you were all in bed!" On various pretexts they all moved off, and Alice was soon left alone.

"I wish I hadn't mentioned Dinah!" she said to herself in a melancholy tone. "Nobody seems to like her, down here, and I'm sure she's the best cat in the world! Oh, my dear Dinah! I wonder if I shall ever see you any more!" And here poor Alice began to cry again, for she felt very lonely and low-spirited. In a little while, however, she again heard a little pattering of footsteps in the distance, and she looked up eagerly, half hoping that the Mouse had changed his mind, and was coming back to finish his story.

A **Code 7.2 when applied to code 7.1:** The contrast of the page text has been reduced by making it dark gray with titles and the drop cap rendered in shades of red. Link colors in the footer are red.

3. **Add colors with alpha channels, as needed.** If you want the color to be partially transparent, then under the color value you can add the same again using the RGBA or HSVA value. For browsers that do not support alpha values, the first color value will be used and the second will be ignored:

```
color: hsla(7, 62%, 40%, 0.8);
```

TIP When choosing foreground text colors, be careful to use colors that contrast with the background color or image. The lower the contrast (that is, the less difference in the brightness of the foreground and background colors), the more your readers will have to strain their eyes when reading. If you are unsure, you can use the Colour Contrast Check tool (http://snook.ca/technical/colour_contrast/colour.html).

TIP Notice that I broke the color contrast rule in the title for this page. I've used a dark red title on a dark red background. To be legit, I should lighten the red color.

TIP Color change is one important way of showing the different states of a hypertext link, but it is by no means the only style you can change. Chapter 14 will show you best practices for styling links, navigation, and controls using the anchor tag.

Setting a Background Color

The ability to set the background color on an HTML page has been around almost since the first Web browsers. However, with CSS you can define the background color, not only for the entire page, but also for individual elements using the **background-color** property (**Table 7.6**). Unlike the color property, though, background colors are applied only to the element, and are not directly inherited by its children. That said, by the very fact they are within the parent, they will be set against that background.

To define the background color of an element:

1. **Add the background color property to your declaration list.** Start your declaration by typing **background-color** (**Code 7.3**), followed by a colon (:).

   `background-color:`

2. **Specify the color value.** Type a value for the background color. This value can be the name of the color or an RGB value.

   `rgb(102,0,0);`

   Alternatively, you could type **transparent**, which would allow the parent element's background color to show through, or **currentcolor** to use the value of the **color** property.

   TIP The default state for an element's background color is **transparent**, so the parent element's background will show through unless the background color or image for that particular child element is set.

TABLE 7.6 Background-Color Values

Value					
<color>	●	●	●	●	●
inherit	●	●	●	●	●

Code 7.3 Added to *color-background-properties. css*—Background colors can be set as solid or transparent Ⓐ.

```
/*** color-background-properties.css ***/
body {
    background: rgb(76,76,76); }
header.page {
    background: rgb(102,0,0); }
article {
    background-color: rgb(242, 237, 217);}
figure {
    background-color: rgb(242, 237, 217); }
footer {
    background-color: rgb(0,0,0); }
```

TIP You can also set the background color using the **background** property, as described later in this chapter in "Using Background Shorthand to Add Multiple Background Images and Gradients."

TIP Some older browsers had incomplete HTML5 support, so you may see variation in the displayed appearance of your code. For example, Safari 4 did not support backgrounds in HTML5-specific tags such as <header> unless they have **display: block** set (see Chapter 10).

A Code 7.3 when applied to code 7.1: The colors begin to define distinct areas of the page, including the page header, the article, and the footer.

★Setting Background Images

Beyond the ability to set an image as the background of an element, CSS includes several properties that offer you great flexibility in the exact placement of the image:

- **Repeat**—Sets whether the image tiles appear only once or repeat only horizontally or vertically.

- **Attachment**—Sets whether the image scrolls with the rest of the page or stays in one place.

- **Position**—Moves the image to the left and down (positive values) or to the right and up (negative values) from the top-left corner of the parent element.

- ★**Size**—Sets the width and height of the image within the element's background as an absolute length, percentage, or the keywords `cover`, `contain`, or `auto` (which maintains the aspect ratio).

- ★**Clip**—Sets whether the background fits to the border or just within the content area.

- ★**Origin**—Sets the position of the background relative to the border, padding, or content. This is especially useful for setting the background of inline elements that might break across multiple lines.

- ★**Multiple background images**—Although not a specific property, CSS now allows you to layer multiple background images using a comma-separated list.

You can also use the **background-image** property to set gradients in the background of an element. You could use the **background** property, but **background-image** works more consistently across browsers.

To define a background image:

1. Add the background image property to your CSS code with the image file source. Type **background-image**, followed by a colon (**:**), **url()**, and a URL in the parentheses for the location of the image file (GIF, JPEG, or PNG) that you want to use as the background. It can be either a complete Web address or a relative path (**Code 7.4**).

   ```
   background: url(../images/chrome/
   dark-victorian.jpg);
   ```

   Alternatively, you could type **none** instead of **url()** along with a path to instruct the browser not to use a background image (**Table 7.7**).

Code 7.4 Added to *color-background-properties. css*—Background images are added over the background colors Ⓐ.

```
/*** color-background-properties.css ***/

body {
background: url(../images/chrome/dark-
victorian.jpg);
background-repeat: repeat;
background-attatchment: fixed;
background-position: 0 0; }
header.page {
    background: url(../images/chrome/
    → bg-book-spine.jpg);
background-repeat: repeat-x;
background-position: 0 0; }
article {
    background-image: url(../images/chrome/
    → paper-01.jpg);
background-repeat: repeat;
background-position: 0 0; }
article p:first-of-type:first-letter {
    background-image: url(../images/chrome/
    → alice02b.png);
background-repeat: no-repeat;
background-position: center center;

    -webkit-background-size: contain;
    -moz-background-size: contain;
    -ie-background-size: contain;
    -o-background-size: contain;
    background-size: contain;

    -webkit-background-clip: padding-box;
    -moz-background-clip: padding;
    -ie-background-clip: padding-box;
    -o-background-clip: padding-box;
background-size: padding-box;

    -webkit-background-origin: padding-box;
    -moz-background-origin: padding;
    -ie-background-origin: padding-box;
    -o-background-origin: padding-box;
background-origin: padding-box; }
figure {
    background-image: url(../images/chrome/
    → paper-01.jpg);
backgound-repeat: repeat;
background-position: 0 0; }
```

TABLE 7.7 Background-Image Values

Value					
<url>	●	●	●	●	●
none	●	●	●	●	●

TABLE 7.8 Background-Repeat Values

Value					
repeat	●	●	●	●	●
repeat-x	●	●	●	●	●
repeat-y	●	●	●	●	●
no-repeat	●	●	●	●	●
space	●				
round	●				

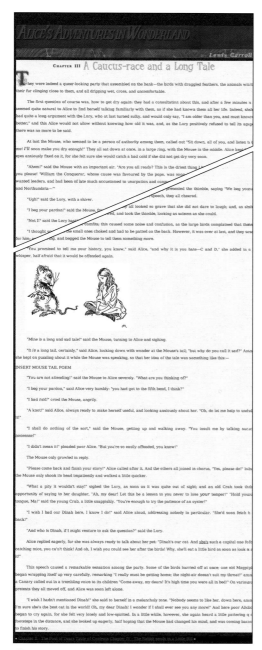

A Code 7.4 when applied to code 7.1: Adding background images begins to add texture to the page.

2. **Add the background repeat property and specify** how the background should be tiled (or not). Type **background-repeat**, followed by a colon (**:**)

```
background-repeat: repeat;
```

Then define how you want your background to repeat by typing one of the following options (**Table 7.8**):

▸ **repeat** instructs the browser to tile the graphic throughout the background of the element horizontally and vertically. This is the default value if the property is omitted.

▸ **repeat-x** instructs the browser to tile the background graphic horizontally only, so that the graphic repeats in one straight horizontal line along the top of the element.

▸ **repeat-y** instructs the browser to tile the background graphic vertically only, so the graphic repeats in one straight vertical line along the left side of the element.

▸ **no-repeat** causes the background graphic to appear only once (and not tile).

▸ **round** resizes the image so that it repeats without clipping.

▸ **space** spaces the image to fill the area so that it is not clipped.

continues on next page

3. **Add the background attachment property and specify how the background should scroll with the element.** Type **background-attachment**, followed by a colon (**:**).

   `background-attachment: fixed;`

   Then define how you want the background to be treated when the page scrolls by typing one of the following options (**Table 7.9**):

   ▸ **scroll** instructs the background graphic to scroll with the element. This is the default value if the property is omitted.

   ▸ **fixed** instructs the browser not to scroll the background content with the rest of the element. However, it will scroll with parent elements.

   ▸ **local** is similar to fixed, but the background is fixed to the content of the element, rather than the element itself.

4. **Add the background position property and specify the positioning of the background.** Type **background-position**, followed by a colon (**:**).

   `background-position: 0 0;`

   Then type one value or two values separated by a space to indicate where you want the background to appear in relation to the top-left corner of the element. If one value is entered, it is used for x, and y is centered. Use one of the following values (**Table 7.10**):

   ▸ **Length values**, such as **–10px**. The values can be positive or negative. The first number tells the browser the distance the element should appear from the left edge of its parent; the second value specifies the position from the top edge of the parent.

TABLE 7.9 Background-Attachment Values

Value					
scroll	●	●	●	●	●
fixed	●	●	●	●	●
local			●	●	●

TABLE 7.10 Background-Position Values

Value					
<length>	●	●	●	●	●
<percentage>	●	●	●	●	●
top	●	●	●	●	●
bottom	●	●	●	●	●
left	●	●	●	●	●
right	●	●	●	●	●
center	●	●	●	●	●

TABLE 7.11 Background-Size Values

Value					
<length>	●9	●	●	●	●
<percentage>	●9	●	●	●	●
cover	●9	●	●	●	
contain	●9	●	●	●	
auto	●9	●	●	●	

See "Values and Units Used in This Book" in the Introduction for more information.

▸ **Percentage values**, such as **25%**. The first percentage indicates the horizontal position proportional to the parent element's size; the second value indicates the vertical position proportional to the parent element's size.

▸ **Keywords** in plain English: `top`, `bottom`, `left`, `right`, or `center`.

5. **Add the background size property and specify the exact size, percentage, or sizing method.** Type `background-size`, followed by a colon (`:`).

   ```
   -webkit-background-size: contain;
   -moz-background-size: contain;
   -ie-background-size: contain;
   -o-background-size: contain;
   background-size: contain;
   ```

   Then type a value from **Table 7.11**. Two values can be included to define separate x and y sizes:

   ▸ **Length values**, such as **10px**.

   ▸ **Percentage values**, such as **25%**. The first percentage indicates the width proportionate to the parent element's width; the second value indicates the height proportionate to the parent element's height.

   ▸ **cover** fits the image to the width or height of the containing element while preserving the aspect ratio.

   ▸ **contain** scales the image to the smallest size to fit the entire image in the desired area while preserving the aspect ratio.

   continues on next page

6. **Add the background clip property and specify a clipping method.** Type **background-clip**, followed by a colon (:).

```
-webkit-background-clip:
→ padding-box;

-moz-background-clip: padding;

-ie-background-clip: padding-box;

-o-background-clip: padding-box;

background-clip: padding-box;
```

Then type a value from **Table 7.12**. Two values can be included to define separate x and y sizes.

Mozilla and Webkit both use a slightly different syntax than what was finally implemented in the CSS3 standards.

▸ **border/border-box** clips the image to the outer edge of the border.

▸ **padding/padding-box** clips the image to the outer edge of the padding.

▸ **content/content-box** clips the image to the outer edge of the content.

TABLE 7.12 Background-Clip Values

Value	ⓔ	ⓤ	ⓢ	ⓒ	ⓞ
content-box	●9	●	●	●	●
border-box	●9	●	●	●	●
padding-box	●9	●	●	●	●

TABLE 7.13 Background-Origin Values

Value					
padding-box	●9	●	●	●	●
border-box	●9	●	●	●	●
content-box	●9	●	●	●	●

TIP You can mix percentage and length values in the same background position and size declarations, but you cannot mix length or percentages with plain English keywords.

TIP Several of the background images used in this example are transparent **PNGs**, which allow the background to show through them.

TIP Any space in the background that does not have a background graphic will be filled with the background color, so I always recommend specifying a background color with a background image.

TIP Background images are used to create **CSS Sprites**, discussed in Chapter 14, one of the most useful tools in your dynamic Web design arsenal.

7. **Add the background origin property and specify an origin method.** Type **background-origin** followed by a colon (**:**).

```
-webkit-background-origin:
→ padding-box;

-moz-background-origin: padding;

-ie-background-origin:
→ padding-box;

-o-background-origin: padding-box;

background-origin: padding-box;
```

Then type a value from **Table 7.13**. Two values can be included to define separate x and y sizes.

▸ **border/border-box** positions the image relative to the outer edge border, placing it behind the border.

▸ **padding/padding-box** positions the image relative to the inner edge of the padding.

▸ **content/content-box** positions the image relative to the outer edge of the content.

8. **Finally, specify the background image to which the above properties are applied.** To layer background images, add each value in a comma-separated list. Images will be placed *beneath* previous images in the list with background color behind all of them. Be sure to add values for all the properties, as necessary.

```
background: url(../images/chrome/
→ alice02b.png);

background: no-repeat;

background-position: center
→ center;
```

Using Background Shorthand to Add Multiple Background Images and Gradients

The **background** shorthand property (Table 7.14) allows you to define the background image and color for an entire page or individual element, rolling many of the background properties into a single quick and compressed declaration. From a coding standpoint, this method is preferable because it uses less space, but it requires that you remember the purpose of each of the values in the list.

TABLE 7.14 Background Values

Value					
<background-color>	●	●	●	●	●
<background-image>	●	●	●	●	●
<background-position>	●	●	●	●	●
<background-size>	●	●	●	●	●
<background-repeat>	●	●	●	●	●
<background-attachment>	●	●	●	●	●
Multiple backgrounds	●9	●	●	●	●
SVG backgrounds	●9	●	●	●	●

Code 7.5 Added to *color-background-properties.css*—Although the results will be similar to Code 7.4, this version is much more compact, easier to scan, and cuts down on file size Ⓐ.

```css
/*** color-background-properties.css ***/
body {
   background: rgb(76,76,76) url(../images/chrome/dark-victorian.jpg) repeat 0 0; }
header.page {
   background: url(../images/chrome/bg-book-spine-title.png)  no-repeat right top,
   rgb(102,0,0) url(../images/chrome/bg-book-spine.jpg) repeat-x 0 0; }
article {
   background: url(../images/chrome/embelish-01.png) no-repeat right top,
   rgb(242, 237, 217) url(../images/chrome/paper-01.jpg) repeat 0 0; }
footer {
   display: block;
   padding: 1.5em;
   background: rgb(153,153,153);
   background: -webkit-linear-gradient(top,  rgba(0,0,0,0),  rgba(0,0,0,1));
   background: -moz-linear-gradient(top, rgba(0,0,0,0),  rgba(0,0,0,1));
   background: -ms-linear-gradient(top,  rgba(0,0,0,0),  rgba(0,0,0,1));
   background: -o-linear-gradient(top,  rgba(0,0,0,0),  rgba(0,0,0,1));
   background: linear-gradient(to top, rgba(0,0,0,0),  rgba(0,0,0,1)); }
figure {
   background: rgb(242, 237, 217) url(../images/chrome/paper-01.jpg) repeat 0 0; }
```

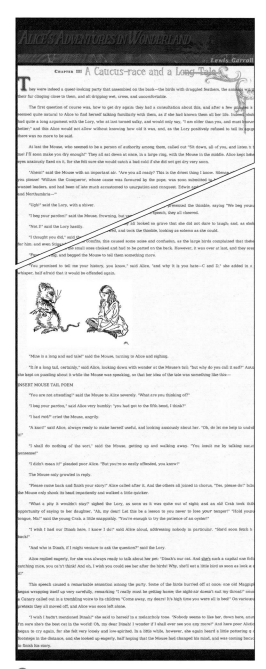

A Code 7.5 when applied to code 7.1: Adding background images makes the design come alive, giving it texture and structure.

To define the background:

1. **Add the background property to your CSS rule declarations list.** Start your declaration by typing **background**, followed by a colon (**:**). Then define a background value (**Code 7.5**).

   <code>background:</code>

2. **Specify the color value.** Type a value for the background color, followed by a space. This value can be the name of the color or an RGB, HSL, or keyword value (**Table 7.1**) Use <code>transparent</code> if you do not want a background color to appear.

   <code>rgb(76, 76, 76)</code>

   continues on next page

3. **Specify the URL for the background image.** Type **url()** and in the parentheses, add an absolute or relative path to the background image (**Table 7.7**), followed by a space. This location is the image file (GIF, JPEG, or PNG file) that you want to use as the background and is either a complete Web address or a local filename **B**.

```
url(../images/chrome/
→ dark-victorian.jpg)
```

Alternatively, you could type **none** instead of a URL, which would instruct the browser not to use a background image.

4. **If you included a background image, specify how it should tile.** Type a value for the way you want your background to repeat, followed by a space.

```
repeat
```

Use one of the following options (**Table 7.8**):

▶ **repeat** instructs the browser to tile the graphic throughout the background of the element, both horizontally and vertically.

▶ **repeat-x** instructs the browser to tile the background graphic horizontally only. In other words, the graphic repeats in one straight horizontal line along the top of the element.

▶ **repeat-y** instructs the browser to tile the background graphic vertically only. In other words, the graphic repeats in one straight vertical line along the left side of the element.

▶ **no-repeat** causes the background graphic to appear only once.

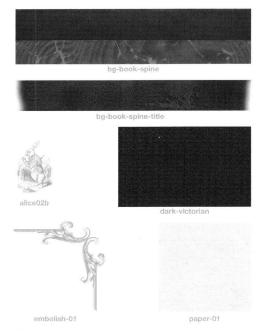

bg-book-spine

bg-book-spine-title

alice02b

dark-victorian

embelish-01　　　　paper-01

B All of the images that go into making this design.

5. **If you are using a background image, specify how it should scroll.**

   `fixed`

   Type a keyword for the way you want the background attached—how it should be treated when the page scrolls—followed by a space. Use one of the following options (**Table 7.9**):

   ▸ `scroll` instructs the background graphic to scroll with the element.

   ▸ `fixed` instructs the browser not to scroll the background content with the rest of the element.

   ▸ `local` is similar to fixed, but the background is fixed to the content of the element, rather than the element itself.

6. **If you are using a background image, specify how it should be positioned.**

   `0 0;`

   Type two values, separated by a space, to specify where you want the background positioned relative to the top-left corner of the element. Use any of the following units; you can use a mixture across the two values if you like (**Table 7.10**):

   ▸ A **length value**, such as **–10px**. The values can be positive or negative. The first number tells the browser the distance the element should appear from the left edge of its parent; the second value specifies the position from the top edge of the parent.

   ▸ A **percentage value**, such as **25%**. The first percentage indicates the horizontal position proportional to the parent element's size; the second value indicates the vertical position proportional to the parent element's size.

   ▸ A position keyword, such as **top**, **bottom**, **left**, **right**, or **center**.

7. **Add multiple backgrounds to an image in a comma-separated list.**

   ```
   background: url(../images/
   → chrome/bg-book-spine-title.png)
   → no-repeat right top,
       rgb(102,0,0) url(../images/
       → chrome/bg-book-spine.jpg)
       → repeat-x 0 0;
   ```

   As with the stand-alone background properties, you can place multiple backgrounds in a single object. Just add the values in a comma-separated list. Place the background color value in the last value set; otherwise, it will cover everything beneath it.

   continues on next page

While it is possible to include the background image size and clip in the shorthand, the browser support for this is spotty at best. I recommend keeping these as separate declarations.

8. **Add gradients to backgrounds.**

```
background: rgb(153,153,153);

background: -webkit-linear-
→ gradient(top, rgba(0,0,0,0),
→ rgba(0,0,0,1));

background: -moz-linear-
→ gradient(top, rgba(0,0,0,0),
→ rgba(0,0,0,1));

background: -ms-linear-
→ gradient(top, rgba(0,0,0,0),
→ rgba(0,0,0,1));

background: -o-linear-
→ gradient(top, rgba(0,0,0,0),
→ rgba(0,0,0,1));

background: linear-
→ gradient(to top,
→ rgba(0,0,0,0),   rgba(0,0,0,1));
```

Add the default background color, which will be used by browsers that do not understand gradients, and then add the gradient property for all of the browsers. Finally add the official CSS3 version at the bottom. Browsers will use whichever version applies to them.

TIP The ability to place graphics behind any element on the screen is a very powerful design tool for Web pages, especially when using the **CSS Sprite technique**, where a single background image can be used for different dynamic states. **See Chapter 14 for more information.**

TIP The default state for an element's background is *none*, so the parent element's background image and/or color will show through unless the background color or background image is set for that child element.

TIP A fixed background can be particularly effective if you're using a graphic background in your layout to help define the layout grid.

Putting It All Together

Code 7.6 shows the final results for the file *color-background-properties.css,* which we have been building in this chapter.

Code 7.6 Final *color-background-properties.css*—The finished code for this chapter, using the background shorthand wherever possible.

```css
/*** color-background-properties.css ***/

body {
   color: rgb(51,51,51);
   background: rgb(76,76,76) url(../images/chrome/dark-victorian.jpg) repeat 0 0; }
header.page {
   background: url(../images/chrome/bg-book-spine-title.png)  no-repeat right top,
   rgb(102,0,0) url(../images/chrome/bg-book-spine.jpg) repeat-x 0 0; }
h1 {
   color: hsla(7,62%,40%,.8); }
header h2 {
   color: rgba(242,237,217,.25); }
header h2 cite {
   color: rgba(242,237,217,.5);}
article {
   background: url(../images/chrome/embelish-01.png) no-repeat right top,
   rgb(242, 237, 217) url(../images/chrome/paper-01.jpg) repeat 0 0; }
article h2 .chaptertitle {
   color: rgba(135,127,107,.5); }

article p:first-of-type:first-letter {
   color: rgb(153,0,0);
   background: transparent url(../images/chrome/alice02b.png) no-repeat center center;

-webkit-background-size: contain;
   -moz-background-size: contain;
   -ie-background-size: contain;
   -o-background-size: contain;
   background-size: contain;

   -webkit-background-clip: padding-box;
   -moz-background-clip: padding;
   -ie-background-clip: padding-box;
   -o-background-clip: padding-box;
background-size: padding-box;

   -webkit-background-origin: padding-box;
   -moz-background-origin: padding;
   -ie-background-origin: padding-box;
   -o-background-origin: padding-box;
background-origin: padding-box; }
```

code continues on next page

```
footer {
   color: white;
   display: block;
   padding: 1.5em;
   background: rgb(153,153,153);
   background: -webkit-linear-gradient(top,  rgba(0,0,0,0),  rgba(0,0,0,1));
   background: -moz-linear-gradient(top, rgba(0,0,0,0),  rgba(0,0,0,1));
   background: -ms-linear-gradient(top,  rgba(0,0,0,0),  rgba(0,0,0,1));
   background: -o-linear-gradient(top,  rgba(0,0,0,0),  rgba(0,0,0,1));
   background: linear-gradient(to top, rgba(0,0,0,0),  rgba(0,0,0,1)); }
a:link {
   color: rgb(204,0,0); }
a:visited {
   color: rgb(153,0,0); }
a:hover {
   color: rgb(255,0,0); }
a:active {
   color: rgb(153,153,153); }
figure {
background: rgb(242, 237, 217) url(../images/chrome/paper-01.jpg) repeat 0 0; }

/* putting it all together */
nav.global a:link, nav.global a:visited {
   color: rgb(248, 240, 227); }
aside {
   background: rgb(242, 237, 217) url(../images/chrome/paper-01.jpg) repeat 0 0; }
td {
   background-color: rgba(200, 200, 180,.25);
   border: 1px solid rgb(200, 200, 180); }
```

List and Table Properties

Most of the CSS properties discussed in this book can be applied to tables and lists. However, CSS also includes a few unique properties specifically for tables and lists. The specifications of table and list properties have not changed from CSS2 to CSS3, although Internet Explorer has improved its implementation in the most recent versions.

Although tables should never be used for page layout, as they once were, they are still used to lay out tabular data. Lists, on the other hand, are not only used to create lists (obviously), but have also become the standard way to structure Web site navigation.

Getting Started

I'll be styling **Code 8.1** in this chapter. It imports the final CSS from Chapters 5, 6, and 7 as well as a new file, *list-table-properties.css*, that you will build in this chapter. It includes the table of contents from *Alice's Adventures in Wonderland* and a list for the colophon and credits. Initially, the page will have standard bullets and an unformatted table Ⓐ. We are going to add a few styles to control the table width, padding, margins, borders, vertical alignment, and font and text styles (**Code 8.1B**). Otherwise, the table would not look nearly as nice.

Code 8.1 The HTML5 code used for examples in this chapter.

```
<!DOCTYPE html>
<html lang="en">
<head>
<meta charset="utf-8">
<title>Alice&#8217;s Adventures In Wonderland | Chapter IV</title>
<link href="../css/font-properties.css" type="text/css" rel="stylesheet" media="all">
<link href="../css/text-properties.css" type="text/css" rel="stylesheet" media="all">
<link href="../css/color-background-properties.css" type="text/css" rel="stylesheet" media="all">
<link href="../css/ch08/10.css" type="text/css" rel="stylesheet" media="all">
</head>
<body id="chapter4" class="book aaiw chapter">

<header class="page">
<hgroup>
    <h1>Alice&#8217;s Adventures in Wonderland</h1>
    <h2>By <cite>Lewis Carroll</cite></h2>
</hgroup>
</header>

<article id="toc">
<table>
<caption>Table of Contents</caption>
<thead>
<tr><th>Chapter</td><th>Title</td><th>Rating</th></tr>
</thead>
<tfoot></tfoot>
```

code continues on next page

```
<tbody>
<tr><td>I. </td><td><a href="AAIWL-ch01.html">Down the Rabbit-hole</a></td><td>&hearts;</td></tr>
<tr><td>II. </td><td><a href="AAIWL-ch02.html">The Pool of Tears</a></td><td>&hearts;&hearts;
 ↪ </td></tr>
<tr><td>III. </td><td><a href="AAIWL-ch03.html">A Caucus-race and a Long Tale</a></td><td></td>
 ↪ </tr>
<tr><td>IV. </td><td><a href="AAIWL-ch04.html">The Rabbit sends in a Little Bill</a></td><td>
 ↪ &hearts;&hearts;</td></tr>
<tr><td>V. </td><td><a href="AAIWL-ch05.html">Advice from a Caterpillar</a></td><td>&hearts;
 ↪ &hearts;&hearts;</td></tr>
<tr><td>VI. </td><td><a href="AAIWL-ch06.html">Pig and Pepper</a></td><td>&hearts;</tr>
<tr><td>VII. </td><td><a href="AAIWL-ch07.html">A Mad Tea-party</a></td><td>&hearts;&hearts;
 ↪ &hearts;&hearts;</td></tr>
<tr><td>VIII. </td><td><a href="AAIWL-ch08.html">The Queen's Croquet-ground</a></
td><td>&hearts;&hearts;</td></tr>
<tr><td>IX. </td><td><a href="AAIWL-ch09.html">The Mock Turtle's Story</a></td><td></td></tr>
<tr><td>X. </td><td><a href="AAIWL-ch010.html">The Lobster Quadrille</a></td><td>&hearts;</td></
tr>
<tr><td>XI. </td><td><a href="AAIWL-ch011.html">Who Stole the Tarts?</a></td><td>&hearts;&hearts;&
hearts;</td></tr>
<tr><td>XII. </td><td><a href="AAIWL-ch012.html">Alice&#8217;s Evidence</a></
td><td>&hearts;&hearts;</td></tr>
</tbody>
</table>
</article>

<article id="colophon">
    <h2>Colophon</h2>
    <h3>Typography</h3>
    <ol class="list">
        <li>DejaVu Serif</li>
        <li>Little Trouble Girl BV</li>
        <li>Helvetica Neu</li>
        <li>Socialico</li>
        <li>Architects Daughter</li>
    </ol>
    <h3>Credits</h3>
    <ul>
        <li>Text by Lewis Carroll</li>
        <li>Art &amp; Illustrations by Arthur Rackham</li>
        <li>Additional Illustrations by John Tenniel</li>
        <li>Design by Jason Cranford Teague</li>
        <li>Thanks to Tara, Dashiel, &amp; Jocelyn</li>
    </ul>
</article>
</body>
</html>
```

Code 8.1B The initial code added to *list-table-properties.css* to create a more attractive table for us to play with.

```css
table {
    width: 75%;
    margin: 40px auto; }
tr {
    font-size: 1.25em; }
td {
    verticalalign: top;
    padding: .5em;
    background-color: rgba(200, 200, 180,.25);
    border: 1px solid rgb(200, 200, 180); }
table thead {
    font-size: 1em;
    font-style: normal;
    font-variant: small-caps;
    text-shadow: 0px 1px 1px
    → rgba(255,255,255,.6), 0px -1px 1px
    → rgba(0,0,0,.6); }
table {
    width: 75%;
    margin: 40px auto; }
table caption {
    font: normal 3em 'TitleCopy', Corbel,
    → Helvetica, Arial, sans-serif; }
article {
    padding: 100px 20px; }
```

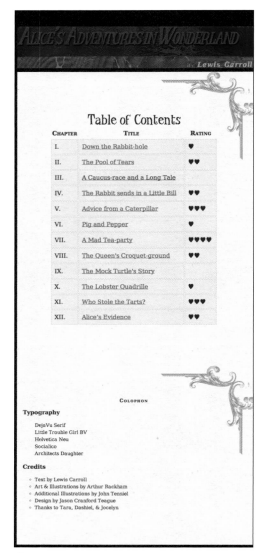

A Our Web page for this chapter before adding any list or table styles. So, the browser default styles are applied, plus a few styles are added to style the table.

TABLE 8.1 List-Style-Type Values

TABLE 8.1 List-Style-Type Values

Value					
<bullet name>*	○	○	○	○	○
none	○	○	○	○	○
inherit	○	○	○	○	○

* See Table 8.2

Code 8.2 Added to *list-table-properties.css*— The `list-style-type` property is used to choose between the different bullet and number styles for your list 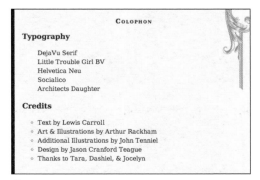.

```
/*** list-table-properties.css ***/
ul {
    list-style-type: circle; }

nl.list {
    list-style-type: none; }
```

TABLE 8.2 List-Style Bullet Names

Name	Appearance (varies depending on system)
disc	•
circle	○
square	■
decimal	1, 2, 3
decimal-leading-zero	01, 02, 03
upper-roman	I, II, III
lower-roman	i, ii, iii
upper-alpha	A, B, C
lower-alpha	a, b, c
lower-greek	α, β, γ

Setting the Bullet Style

The `list-style-type` property (**Table 8.1**) controls the type of bullet to be used for list items—not just circles, discs, and squares, but also letters and numerals and dots and our own custom image bullets.

To define the bullet style:

1. **Add the list style type property to your declaration list.** Type `list-style-type`, followed by a colon (`:`) (**Code 8.2**).

   `list-style-type:`

2. **Specify the bullet type.** Type one of the bullet names listed in **Table 8.2**, or type **none** if you do not want a marker to appear.

   `circle;`

   Although the list item tag `<li>` is used in this example, you can turn any element into a list item by adding the CSS list properties along with the definition `display: list-item`. See Chapter 10 for more information.

> **TIP** You can change the bullet type or image using pseudo-classes such as `:hover`, `:visited`, and `:active`.

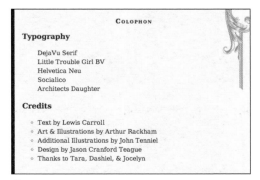

A Code 8.2 applied to Code 8.1: Bullets are changed from discs (default) to circles and the numbers are removed.

Creating Your Own Bullets

You're not limited to the preset bullet styles built into a browser. You can also use your own graphics as bullets from GIF, JPEG, and PNG files by applying the **list-style-image** property (**Table 8.3**).

To define your own graphic bullet:

1. **Add the list-style-image property to your CSS rule.** Type **list-style-image**, followed by a colon (**:**) (**Code 8.3**).

   `list-style-image:`

2. **Specify the location of your image bullet.** To include your own bullet, you have to tell the browser where your bullet graphic file is located.

   `url(bullet-01.png);`

   Type the complete Web address or relative path of the image. In this example, **bullet-01.png** is a local file.

   Alternatively, type **none** to instruct the browser to override any inherited bullet images.

   Bullets are placed out of the layout frame by default, so they often will fall outside of the layout box if they are particularly long.

   TIP Keep in mind that the text being bulleted has to make space for the graphic you use. A taller graphic will force more space between bulleted items, and a wider graphic will force bulleted items farther to the right.

   TIP To be honest, very few developers use the list-style-image property to add image bullets to their designs. Instead, most developers will use the background property with padding to get more precise styling. Want to know how to do this? Check out Chapter 17, "Navigation, Buttons, and Controls."

TABLE 8.3 List-Style-Image Values

Value	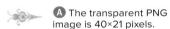				
\<url\>	●	●	●	●	●
none	●	●	●	●	●
inherit	●	●	●	●	●

Code 8.3 Added to *list-table-properties.css*— I created a small arrow graphic **A** (saved as a transparent PNG) to be inserted as the bullet using **list-style-image** **B**.

```
/*** list-table-properties.css ***/
ol.list {
    list-style-image:
    → url(../images/chrome/bullet-01.png); }
```

A The transparent PNG image is 40×21 pixels.

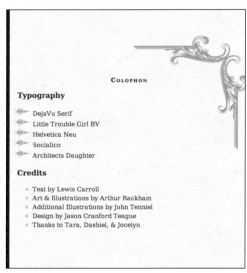

B Code 8.3 applied to Code 8.1: The fancy bullet image is used instead of numbers.

> • **Outside**...Magnus es, domine, et laudabilis valde: magna virtus tua, et sapientiae tuae non est numerus. et laudare te vult homo.
>
> • **Inside**...Magnus es, domine, et laudabilis valde: magna virtus tua, et sapientiae tuae non est numerus. et laudare te vult homo.

 `outside` is generally how bulleted lists are presented. You may want to override that by using `inside`.

Code 8.4 Added to *list-table-properties*: The **list-style-position** property allows you to specify how lines of text flow under the bullet .

```
/*** list-table-properties.css ***/
ul {   list-style-position: outside; }

nl.list {
   list-style-position: inside; }
```

B Code 8.4 applied to Code 8.1: `outside` pushes the image bullet over, while `inside` pulls the disc bullet back.

Setting Bullet Positions

Often, the text of a bulleted list item is longer than one line. Using the **list-style-position** property (**Table 8.4**), you can specify the position of wrapping text in relation to the bullet. Wrapped text that is indented to start below the first letter of the first line of text is called a *hanging indent* **A**.

To define the line position for wrapped text in a list item:

1. Add the list-style-position property to your declarations. Type **list-style-position**, followed by a colon (:) (**Code 8.4**).

   `list-style-position:`

2. Specify the position type.

   `inside;`

   Type one of the following values to set text indentation:

   ▸ **inside** aligns the left edge of the bullet with the left edge of subsequent text.

   ▸ **outside** left aligns the first line of text with subsequent text, placing the bullet as a hanging indent.

TIP Generally, bulleted lists that have a hanging indent (`outside` position) stand out much better than those without a hanging indent (`inside` position).

Setting Multiple List Styles

You can use one line of code to set all list properties described in the previous three sections using the **list-style** short-hand property (**Table 8.5**), which sets the **list-style-type**, **list-style-position**, and **list-style-image** properties.

To define multiple list-style attributes:

1. Add the list-style property to your CSS rules. Type **list-style**, followed by a colon (**:**) (**Code 8.5**).

   ```
   list-style:
   ```

2. **Specify the location of your bullet image (optional).** Next, type a **list-style-image** value.

   ```
   url(arrow_02.png)
   ```

   To include your own bullet, you must create the bullet graphic and then tell the browser where the graphic is located using either the complete Web address or the relative path of the image. (See "Creating Your Own Bullets" in this chapter for more information.)

TABLE 8.5 List-Style Values

Value					
<list-style-type>	●	●	●	●	●
<list-style-position>	●	●	●	●	●
<list-style-image>	●	●	●	●	●

Code 8.5 Added to *list-table-properties*: The **list-style** property lets you set the type, image, and position all in one definition Ⓐ.

```
/*** list-table-properties.css ***/
ul {
   list-style: circle outside; }

ol.list {
   list-style: none url(../../images/chrome/
   → bullet-01.png) inside; }
```

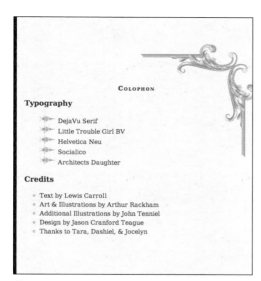

A Code 8.5 applied to Code 8.1: This version is identical to the previous version; only the code is different.

3. **Specify the bullet type.** Type a **list-style-type** value from Table 8.3, followed by a space, or type **none** if you don't want a marker to appear.

```
circle
```

4. **Specify the position type.** Type a **list-style-position** value from Table 8.4.

```
outside;
```

You do not need to include all of the values to ensure that this shorthand selector will work. Omitted values are set to the default. The following example works just fine:

```
list-style: inside;
```

TIP If visitors have turned off graphics in their browsers or if a graphical bullet does not load for some reason, the browser uses the **list-style-type** that you defined in Step 3.

Setting the Table Layout

Different browsers use different methods to calculate how a particular table sis displayed. Two primary **table-layout** (Table 8.6) methods are favored:

- **Fixed** method bases its layout on the width of the table and the width of columns in the first row. This method is generally faster than automatic.

- **Automatic** uses the table column width along with the amount of content in the table data cell to calculate the table data cell width. This will generally render more slowly than the fixed method, but it also produces more accurate results for widths throughout the table.

To set the table layout method:

1. Add the table layout property to a CSS rule for a table element. Type **table-layout**, followed by a colon (**:**) on table elements (**Code 8.6**).

   table-layout:

2. Specify the layout method.

   auto;

   Type one of the following values to specify which method you want to use when displaying your table:

   - **fixed** will use the first row to calculate the overall width of table data cells in that column of the table.

   - **auto** will allow the browser to calculate the widths of table data cells based on their content and the overall width of the table.

TIP Although **fixed** renders faster for longer tables, **auto** generally provides better results unless the rows of data are consistent in size.

TABLE 8.6 Table-Layout Values

Value	⬤	⬤	⬤	⬤	O
fixed	⬤	⬤	⬤	⬤	⬤
auto	⬤	⬤	⬤	⬤	⬤
inherit	⬤	⬤	⬤	⬤	⬤

Code 8.6 Added to *list-table-properties*: The **table-layout** property lets you force the browser to use either the **fixed** or **auto** methods for rendering tables .

```
/*** list-table-properties.css ***/

table {
    table-layout: fixed; }
```

A Code 8.6 applied to Code 8.1 with fixed layout: When content is much longer than subsequent rows, the table looks cramped when using **fixed**.

TIP I recommend **auto** since short tables will not take long to render, and long tables will need more accuracy. Either way, **auto** is preferred.

TABLE 8.7 Border-Spacing Values

Value					
`<length>`	●	●	●	●	●
inherit	●	●	●	●	●

Code 8.7 Added to *list-table-properties*: The **border-spacing** property works like a margin around the table data cell .

```
table {
    border-spacing: 8px; }
```

A Code 8.7 applied to Code 8.1: Spacing out data cells can make them easier for users to scan.

Setting the Space Between Table Cells

Although table data cells and table header cells can use many of the box properties we'll explore in Chapter 10, they cannot use the **margin** property. Instead, CSS has the **border-spacing** (Table 8.7) property, which sets an equal amount of space between data cells' top, bottom, left, and right sides.

To collapse the borders in a table:

1. Add the border spacing property to the CSS rule for a table element. Type **border-spacing**, followed by a colon (**:**) (Code 8.7).

   `border-spacing:`

2. Specify the spacing between table data cells.

   `8px;`

   Type a length value (such as **8px**) to specify the distance between cells. (See "Values and Units Used in This Book" in the Introduction.) Alternatively, use **inherit** to use the same border spacing as a cell's parent element.

Collapsing Borders Between Table Cells

Every table data cell defined by the `<td>` tag has four borders: top, right, bottom, and left. The **border-collapse** property (**Table 8.8**) allows you to set a table so that each table data cell will share its borders with an adjacent table data cell rather than creating a separate border for each.

To collapse the borders in a table:

1. Add the border collapse property to a table element. Type **border-collapse**, followed by a colon (**:**) (**Code 8.8**).

   `border-collapse:`

2. Specify how borders should collapse.

   `separate;`

   Type one of the following to determine how you want to display the borders in the table:

   - **collapse** will make adjacent table data cells share a common border; however, you won't be able to set **border-spacing** if borders are collapsed.

   - **separate** will maintain individual borders for each table data cell.

TABLE 8.8 Border-Collapse Values

Value					
collapse	●	●	●	●	●
separate	●	●	●	●	●
inherit	●	●	●	●	●

Code 8.8 Added to *list-table-properties.css—* The **border-collapse** property lets you remove *all* space between the table data cells, giving each side a single border Ⓐ, but border spacing will be ignored. Use **separate** to allow **border-spacing** to work Ⓑ.

```
table {
    border-collapse: separate; }
```

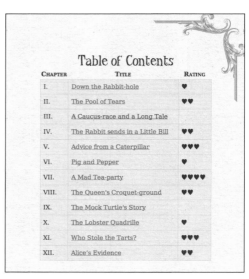

Ⓐ By using **collapse**, the border between data cells has been reduced to a single, thin line.

Table of Contents

CHAPTER	TITLE	RATING
I.	Down the Rabbit-hole	♥
II.	The Pool of Tears	♥♥
III.	A Caucus-race and a Long Tale	
IV.	The Rabbit sends in a Little Bill	♥♥
V.	Advice from a Caterpillar	♥♥♥
VI.	Pig and Pepper	♥
VII.	A Mad Tea-party	♥♥♥♥
VIII.	The Queen's Croquet-ground	♥♥
IX.	The Mock Turtle's Story	
X.	The Lobster Quadrille	♥
XI.	Who Stole the Tarts?	♥♥♥
XII.	Alice's Evidence	♥♥

B Code 8.8 applied to Code 8.1: With `separate` set, you can set **border-spacing**.

TIP The displayed results can vary between different browsers unless you set the border style using CSS.

TIP If the borders being collapsed do not share the same border thickness, the thicker border will be shown and its style used.

TIP If borders have the same thickness but different styles, the border style for the data cell to the left is used.

Dealing with Empty Table Cells

If a table data cell has no data (not even spaces or nonbreaking spaces), it simply appears as a blank box at the default width and height of the column and row. The `empty-cells` property (**Table 8.9**) allows you to specify how that empty data cell (and, most importantly, its border) is presented.

To hide empty table data cells:

1. **Add the `empty-cells` property to a table elements CSS rule.** Type `empty-cells`, followed by a colon (`:`) (**Code 8.9**).

   `empty-cells:`

2. **Specify how empty table cells should be treated.**

   `hide;`

   Type one of the following to specify how the cells will be treated:

   ▸ `show` will force the empty data cell to display its background and border.

   ▸ `hide` will leave a visual gap in place of the data cell.

TABLE 8.9 Empty-Cells Values

Value	@				O
show	●	●	●	●	●
hide	●	●	●	●	●
inherit	●	●	●	●	●

Code 8.9 Added to *list-table-properties.css*— The `empty-cells` property lets you show (default) or hide empty table data cells .

```
/*** list-table-properties.css ***/
table {
    empty-cells: hide; }
```

A Code 8.9 applied to Code 8.1: Empty table data cells have been hidden so that their border and background colors are not displayed, leaving an empty gap in the table.

TABLE 8.10 Caption-Side Values

Value					
top	●	●	●	●	●
bottom	●	●	●	●	●
inherit	●	●	●	●	●

Code 8.10 Added to *list-table-properties.css*— The **caption-side** property lets you specify whether the caption should appear above (**top**) or below (**bottom**) the table 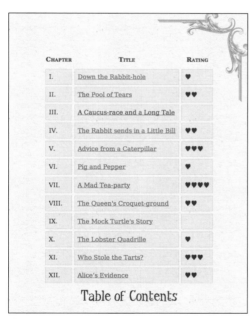.

```
/*** list-table-properties.css ***/
table {
    caption-side: bottom; }
```

A The caption is forced to the bottom of the table rather than its natural position at the top.

Setting the Position of a Table Caption

The **<caption>** tag lets you embed identifying text in a table. You can set the **align** attribute in the tag to define where the caption should appear in relation to the table, but this is being deprecated in favor of the CSS **caption-side** property (**Table 8.10**), which does the same thing.

To set the position of a caption in relation to its table:

1. **Add the caption side property to your CSS.** Type **caption-side**, followed by a colon (**:**) (**Code 8.10**).

   ```
   caption-side:
   ```

2. **Type a keyword** indicating which side of the table you want the caption to appear: **top** or **bottom**.

   ```
   bottom;
   ```

Putting It All Together

Code 8.11 shows the final version of *list-table-properties.css* using the list short-hand property wherever possible. The **caption-side** property lets you specify whether the caption should appear above (**top**) or below (**bottom**) the table .

Code 8.11 Final *list-table-properties.css*

```
/*** list-table-properties.css ***/

ul {
    list-style: circle inside; }
ol.list {
    list-style: none url(../images/chrome/
    ↪ bullet-01.png) inside; }
table {
    table-layout: auto;
    border-spacing: 8px;
    border-collapse: separate;
    empty-cells: hide;
    caption-side: top;
    width: 75%;
    margin: 40px auto; }
tr {
    font-size: 1.25em; }
td {
    vertical-align: top;
    padding: .5em;
    background-color: rgba(200, 200, 180,.25);
    border: 1px solid rgb(200, 200, 180); }

table caption {
    font: normal 3em 'TitleCopy', Corbel,
    ↪ Helvetica, Arial, sans-serif; }
table thead {
    font-size: 1em;
    font-style: normal;
    font-variant: small-caps;
    text-shadow: 0px 1px 1px
    ↪ rgba(255,255,255,.6), 0px -1px 1px
    ↪ rgba(0,0,0,.6); }
article {
    padding: 100px 20px; }
```

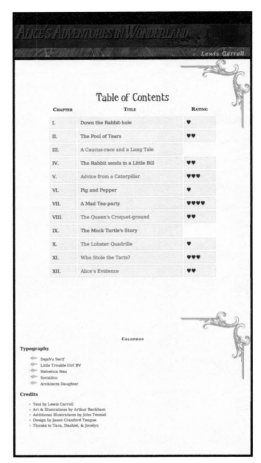

 The final appearance of the Table of Contents.

User Interface and Generated Content Properties

The user interface cannot, for the most part, be controlled by CSS. It is dependent on the specific operating system and browser in use. Objects such as the scroll bars are out of your control. However, CSS does provide some control over the appearance of the mouse pointer and style of quotes.

Additionally, CSS includes several properties that let you specify content to be placed on the page (generated) for specific instances. For example, you might want all chapter titles to include the word "Chapter" before them. Although you'll usually want to place all of your Web page content directly into the HTML code, on occasion you'll find it useful to have some redundant content generated for you or have it tailored to a specific language.

In This Chapter

Getting Started

For this chapter, we'll be using our Chapter 5 content from *Alice's Adventures in Wonderland* (**Code 9.1**). The HTML imports the final CSS from Chapters 5, 6, 7, and 8, as well as a new file you will be building in this chapter, *ui-generatedcontent-properties.css*. I've also converted all quote marks within paragraphs to use the `<q>` tag, allowing us to specify the quote style for different languages. Technically, this is how all quotations other than block quotes should be tagged, but it's rare to see them used **A**.

A The Web page for this chapter as it looks before adding any of the generated content.

Code 9.1 The HTML5 code used in the examples in this chapter.

```
<!DOCTYPE html>
<html lang="en">
<head>
<meta charset="utf-8">
<title>Alice&#8217;s Adventures In Wonderland | Chapter V</title>
<link href="../css/font-properties.css" type="text/css" rel="stylesheet" media="all">
<link href="../css/text-properties.css" type="text/css" rel="stylesheet" media="all">
<link href="../css/color-background-properties.css" type="text/css" rel="stylesheet" media="all">
<link href="../css/list-table-properties.css" type="text/css" rel="stylesheet" media="all">
<link href="../css/ch09/01a.css" type="text/css" rel="stylesheet" media="all">
</head>
<body id="chapter5" class="book aaiw chapter">

<header class="page">
<hgroup>
    <h1>Alice&#8217;s Adventures in Wonderland</h1>
    <h2>By <cite>Lewis Carroll</cite></h2>
</hgroup>
</header>
<article>
<h2>CHAPTER V
<span class="chaptertitle">Advice from a Caterpillar</span>
</h2>
<p>The Caterpillar and Alice looked at each other for some time in silence: at last the Caterpillar
→ took the hookah out of its mouth, and addressed her in a languid, sleepy voice.</p>
<p><q>Who are <em>you?</em></q> said the Caterpillar.</p> <p>This was not an encouraging opening for
→ a conversation. Alice replied, rather shyly, <q>I hardly know, sir, just at present&mdash;at least
→ I know who I <em>was</em> when I got up this morning, but I think I must have been changed
→ several times since then.</q></p>
<p><q>What do you mean by that?</q> said the
Caterpillar sternly. <q>Explain yourself!</q></p>
</article>
<footer>
<a href="AAIWL-ch04.html" class="prev">The Rabbit sends in a Little Bill</a>
<a href="toc.html">Table of Contents</a>
<a href="AAIWL-ch06.html" class="next">Pig and Pepper</a>
</footer>
</body>
</html>
```

Changing the Mouse Pointer Appearance

Normally, the browser determines the appearance of the mouse pointer according to the content currently under it. If the pointer is over text, for example, the pointer becomes a text selector. Or, if the browser is working and the visitor can't do anything, the pointer becomes a timer, indicating that the visitor needs to wait.

Sometimes, it's useful to override the browser's behavior and set the appearance of the pointer yourself using the **cursor** property (**Table 9.1**). This can be applied to any element on the screen, not just links. Also, you do not *have* to associate it with the dynamic hover state for it to work; just apply it directly to the element's CSS rule.

To set the mouse pointer's appearance:

1. **Add the cursor property to your CSS declarations.** Type **cursor** in the CSS declaration block, followed by a colon (**:**) (**Code 9.2**).

   cursor:

2. **Specify the mouse pointer.** Type one of the mouse pointer names listed in **Table 9.2** to specify the pointer's appearance.

   crosshair;

   Alternatively, type one of these values for **cursor:**

   ▸ **auto** to have the browser choose which mouse pointer to use.

   ▸ **none** to hide the pointer altogether.

TABLE 9.1 Cursor Values

Value					
<cursor type name>	●	●	●	●	●
<URL>	●	●	●	●	●
auto	●	●	●	●	●
none	●	●	●	●	●

Code 9.2 Added to *ui-generatedcontent-properties.css*—I set up different pointer types that depend on the type of object or link over which the pointer is hovering Ⓐ.

```
/*** ui-generatedcontent-properties.css ***/
h1 {
    cursor: crosshair; }
footer a {
    cursor: url('../images/chrome/
    ↪ cursor-02.png') 20 20, help; }
```

Ⓐ **Code 9.2 applied to Code 9.1:** the pointer turns into the Cheshire Cat's head when over the book title.

TABLE 9.2 Cursor Types

Name	Appearance (varies depending on OS)
crosshair	+
e-resize	→
help	?
move	⊕
ne-resize	↗
n-resize	↑
nw-resize	↖
pointer	👆
progress	🅐
se-resize	↘
s-resize	↓
sw-resize	↙
text	I
wait	⌛
w-resize	←

3. **Add a graphic mouse pointer.** You can also create your own pointer by adding the URL reference to an image file (generally in PNG format) to use as a custom cursor. You can specify the complete Web address or the local filename of the image.

```
cursor: url(../images/chrome/
  cursor-02.png) 20 20, crosshair;
```

★**Hotspot:** CSS3 adds the ability to define the pointer's hotspot (the point at which the active click will happen) as determined from the upper-left corner of the image. Always include a backup pointer type.

Firefox, Safari, Opera, and Chrome allow you to use CUR, ANI, GIF, PNG, or JPEG images as a custom pointer by specifying the URL for the image file. Unfortunately, Internet Explorer supports only CUR and ANI file formats for custom pointers.

TIP **CUR and ANI are not standard image formats and can only be created using specialized software.**

TIP **Remember that the exact appearance of the pointer depends on the operating system and the Web browser in use.**

TIP **Although it's fun to play around with switching the mouse pointers, I've tested this feature on my own Web site and have received several emails asking me to cut it out. Most Web users have learned to recognize the common functions of specific pointers and when they should appear. Breaking these conventions tends to confuse users.**

Adding Content Using CSS

For the purposes of search engine optimization and accessibility, it is usually best to keep all content within the **<body>** element of your Web page. If it is dynamically generated, then it will not be seen by Web crawlers and many screen readers. However, at times you might have repetitive content that will not help (or may even hinder) your placement in a search index.

To add content, you can use the **content** property (**Table 9.3**), which allows you to specify a text string, image or sound file URL, counter, quote, or even an attribute value that should be displayed on the page.

To define generated content:

1. **Specify whether the content should go before or after the element.** Type a selector with the **:before** or **:after** pseudo-class (see "Setting content before and after an element" in Chapter 4) to define where the content will be positioned in relation to the selector (**Code 9.3**).

   ```
   footer a.prev:before {...}
   ```

2. **Add the content property to your CSS.** In your declaration block, type the **content** property name, followed by a colon (:) and one of the values listed in Step 3.

   ```
   content:
   ```

TABLE 9.3 Content Values

Value					
normal	●8	●	●	●	●
none	●8	●	●	●	●
<string>	●8	●	●	●	●
<url>	●8	●	●	●	●
<counter>	●8	●	●	●	●
attr(<selector>)	●8	●	●	●	●
open-quote	●8	●	●	●	●
close-quote	●8	●	●	●	●
no-open-quote	●8	●	●	●	●
no-close-quote	●8	●	●	●	●
inherit	●8	●	●	●	●

Code 9.3 Added to *ui-generatedcontent-properties.css*—The left arrow image (**bullet-02**) is inserted along with the word "Chapter," before the title of the previous chapter. Next, the word "Chapter" is inserted before the next chapter title with a right-pointing arrow (**bullet-01**) after Ⓐ.

```
/*** ui-generatedcontent-properties.css ***/

footer a.prev:before {
   content:  url('../images/chrome/
   → bullet-02.png')' ' Chapter '
   → counter(chapterNum) ': '; }

footer a.next:before {
content: 'Chapter ' counter(chapterNum) ': '; }

footer a.next:after {
   content:  ' ' url('../images/chrome/
   → bullet-01.png');
}
```

A Code 9.3 applied to Code 9.1: The previous and next chapters now have back and forth arrows.

TIP Because the `content` property was not supported until Internet Explorer 8, it is best not to rely on this property for critical information.

TIP Information rendered using the `content` property will not be searchable by search engine spiders, so never use it to insert information that defines your page.

TIP Content added this way is also invisible to screen readers, so don't include anything that they will miss.

TIP One idea is to use content to add figure captions pulled from the image's alt tag. Because this is visible to screen readers and search engines, it's a good way to cut down on repetitive content.

3. **Specify the content to be added.**

```
url('../images/chrome/
 bullet-01.png') 'Chapter
 'counter(chapterNum) ': ';
```

To define the content that is being added, type one or more of the following values, separating each value with a space:

▸ Type a string value, such as **Chapter**, within single or double quotes. Anything within the quotes will be displayed just as you typed it, including HTML code, although spaces are collapsed (that is, more than two spaces are collapsed into a single space when displayed).

▸ **url()**, with an absolute or relative URL within the parentheses pointing to an external file, such as an image or sound file. For example, **url(bg_flourish.png)** will load an image.

▸ **counter()**, with a counter name in parentheses. For example, **counter(chapterNum)** adds the counter number for the **chapterNum** counter. (Counters are explained in the next section.)

▸ **open-quote** or **close-quote** to add a quotation mark using the current quotation style. (See "Specifying the Quote Style" later in this chapter.)

▸ **no-open-quote** or **no-close-quote** to increase the level of quoting by one level.

▸ **attr()** to display the value of the indicated attribute. For example, **attr(alt)** will display the value for the alt attribute of the element being styled.

▸ **inherit**, which will use the content defined for the parent element.

▸ **normal** or **none**, which will not add any content or apply any other values.

Teaching the Browser to Count

Browsers can automatically create sequentially numbered lists, starting at 1 and counting by ones. You will explore this later in the chapter. However, what if you need to start numbering from 6 instead of 1? Or, what if you need to create two sequential lists that are nested inside each other?

CSS allows you to set up multiple counter lists to be used with the **counter** value of the **content** property (see the previous section). The **counter-reset** property (**Table 9.4**) is used to set the initial value for the count, and the **counter-increment** property (**Table 9.5**) is used to increase the counter by a specific value (**Code 9.4**).

To use a counter:

1. Add the **counter-reset** property to your declaration block.

    ```
    counter-reset: chapterNum 4;
    ```

    Type **counter-reset**, a colon (**:**), and then the name of the counter identifier you are defining (which can be any name you want). Then insert a space and the number you want to start the list.

TABLE 9.4 Counter-Reset Values

Value					
<counterName>	●8	●	●	●	●
<num>	●8	●	●	●	●
none	●8	●	●	●	●
inherit	●8	●	●	●	●

TABLE 9.5 Counter-Increment Values

Value					
<counterName>	●8	●	●	●	●
<num>	●8	●	●	●	●
none	●8	●	●	●	●
inherit	●8	●	●	●	●

Code 9.4 Added to *ui-generatedcontent-properties.css*—The numbering in the footer is reset to 4 (the previous chapter) in Chapter 5 and then incremented by two to show the next chapter Ⓐ.

```
/*** ui-generatedcontent-properties.css ***/

footer a.next:before {
    content: 'Chapter '
  → counter(chapterNum) ': ';
    counter-increment: chapterNum 2; }

#chapter5 footer{
    counter-reset: chapterNum 4; }
```

Ⓐ **Code 9.4 applied to Code 9.1:** The chapters number themselves correctly.

2. **Add the `counter-increment` property to the declaration block and include the name of the counter identifier.**

   `counter-increment: chapterNum 2;`

   Insert a space and then enter a value to indicate how much you want to increase the count for each instance. The default is 1, but you can increase the count by any desired value.

   Again, be very careful when using **counter-reset** because it can hamper accessibility. In fact, the example I use here is not really very good from the standpoint of universal accessibility. Shame on me!

Specifying the Quote Style

Although most writers will use the keyboard to add quotation marks to text, HTML includes the quotation tag: **<q>...</q>**. This tag places browser-default quotation marks around the indicated text. With CSS, you can define the exact characters to be used as quotation marks using the **quotes** property (**Table 9.6**). Although English uses single ('...') or double ("...") quotation marks, this is by no means the norm for all languages.

To define the bullet style:

1. **Add the quotes property to your declaration block.** Type **quotes**, followed by a colon (**:**).

   quotes:

   You can add this to any specific element, or you can key it off of a specific language as explained in "Styling for a particular language" (Chapter 4).

TABLE 9.6 Quotes Values

Value					
'<string>'	○8	○	○	○	○
none	○8	○	○	○	○
inherit	○8	○	○	○	○

Code 9.5 Added to *ui-generatedcontent-properties.css*—In this example , the quotation marks are set to use « ... », which is standard for many European languages, including French.

```
/*** ui-generatedcontent-properties.css ***/
* { quotes: '«' '»' '‹' '›'; }
```

A Code 9.5 applied to Code 9.1: The quotes are now set using angle quotation marks, which is standard for many European languages. I've magnified the image so that you can get a better look.

2. Set one of the values or value pairs listed in Table 9.6 within standard single or double English quotation marks (**Code 9.5**).

```
'«  '  '  »'
```

3. After a space, you can add another grouping of quotation styles for the second level quotes (quotes that occur within quotes).

```
'‹  '  '  ›';
```

4. For the quote style to work, you will actually need to use the quote tag (**<q>**) to indicate quotes in your HTML document.

```
<q>...</q>
```

This property can come in handy even for English. UK and US English use the same quotes, but reversed in order. The US uses double quotes for a main quote and single for second level quotes, whereas in the UK, this is reversed.

Putting It All Together

Code 9.6 shows the final code for *ui-generatedcontent-properties.css* created in this chapter. Notice that I've had to add individual cases for each chapter in the book so that they are all numbered correctly in the footer.

Code 9.6 Final *ui-generatedcontent-properties.css*

```
/*** ui-generatedcontent-properties.css ***/
* {
   quotes: '«' '»' '‹' '›'; }
h1 {
   cursor: crosshair; }
footer a {
   cursor: url('../images/chrome/cursor-02.png') 20 20, help; }
footer a.prev:before {
   content: url('../images/chrome/bullet-02.png')  ' Chapter ' counter(chapterNum) ': '; }
footer a.next:before {
   content: 'Chapter ' counter(chapterNum) ': ';
   counter-increment: chapterNum 2; }
footer a.next:after {
   content:  ' ' url('../images/chrome/bullet-01.png'); }
#chapter1 footer{
   counter-reset: chapterNum 0; }
#chapter2 footer{
   counter-reset: chapterNum 1; }
#chapter3 footer{
   counter-reset: chapterNum 2; }
#chapter4 footer{
   counter-reset: chapterNum 3; }
#chapter5 footer{
   counter-reset: chapterNum 4; }
#chapter6 footer{
   counter-reset: chapterNum 5; }
#chapter7 footer{
   counter-reset: chapterNum 6; }
#chapter8 footer{
   counter-reset: chapterNum 7; }
#chapter9 footer{
   counter-reset: chapterNum 8; }
#chapter10 footer{
   counter-reset: chapterNum 9; }
#chapter11 footer{
   counter-reset: chapterNum 10; }
#chapter12 footer{
   counter-reset: chapterNum 11; }
```

10

Box Properties

In the physical world, atoms are the building blocks of all larger objects. Every type of atom, or element, has unique properties, but when bonded with other atoms, they create molecules—larger structures with properties different from the parts.

Likewise, HTML tags are the building blocks of your Web page. Each tag, or element, has its own capabilities. Tags can be combined to create a Web page that is greater than the sum of its parts. Whether a tag is by itself or nested deep within other tags, it can be treated as a discrete element on the screen and controlled by CSS.

Web designers use the concept of the *box* as a metaphor to describe the various things that you can do to an HTML element, whether it is a single tag or several nested tags. A box can have several properties—including margins, borders, padding, width, and height—that can be influenced by CSS.

This chapter shows you how to control the box and its properties (**Code 10.1**).

In This Chapter

Code 10.1 The HTML5 code used for the examples in this chapter. It imports the final CSS from Chapters 5, 6, 7, 8, and 9 as well as a new file we will be building in this chapter called *box-properties.css*. For this section, I've added two figures (color with a caption and black and white) and an aside to the article Ⓐ.

```
<!DOCTYPE html>
<html lang="en">
<head>
<meta charset="utf-8">
<title>Alice&#8217;s Adventures In Wonderland | Chapter VI</title>
<link href="../css/font-properties.css" type="text/css" rel="stylesheet" media="all">
<link href="../css/text-properties.css" type="text/css" rel="stylesheet" media="all">
<link href="../css/color-background-properties.css" type="text/css" rel="stylesheet" media="all">
<link href="../css/list-table-properties.css" type="text/css" rel="stylesheet" media="all">
<link href="../css/ui-generatedcontent-properties.css" type="text/css" rel="stylesheet" media="all">
<link href="../css/box-properties.css" type="text/css" rel="stylesheet" media="all">
</head>
<body id="chapter6" class="book aaiw chapter">

<header class="page">
<hgroup>
    <h1>Alice&#8217;s Adventures in Wonderland</h1>
    <h2>By <cite>Lewis Carrol</cite></h2>
</hgroup>
</header>

<article>
<h2>Chapter VI
<span class="chaptertitle">Pig and Pepper</span>
</h2>

<p>For a minute or two she stood looking at the house, and wondering what to do next, when suddenly
→ a footman in livery came running out of the wood&mdash;(she considered him to be a footman
→ because he was in livery: otherwise, judging by his face only, she would have called him a
→ fish)&mdash;and rapped loudly at the door with his knuckles. It was opened by another footman in
→ livery, with a round face and large eyes like a frog; and both footmen, Alice noticed, had
→ powdered hair that curled all over their heads. She felt very curious to know what it was all
→ about, and crept a little way out of the wood to listen.</p>

<figure class="illo cl-illo floatright" style="width: 384px;">
<img src="../images/illos/p0070-insert2.jpg" width="384" height="500" alt="An unusually large saucepan
→ flew close by it, and very nearly carried it off" title="">
<figcaption>An unusually large saucepan flew close by it, and very nearly carried it off
→ </figcaption>
</figure>

<figure class="illo bw-illo floatcenter"  style="width: 400px;">
<img src="../images/illos/p0075-image.png" width="400" height="258" alt="Cheshire cat in a tree"
title="">
</figure>
```

Code continues on next page

```
<p>She had not gone much farther before she
→ came in sight of the house of the March
→ Hare: she thought it must be the right
→ house, because the chimneys were shaped
→ like ears and the roof was thatched with
→ fur. It was so large a house, that she did
→ not like to go nearer till she had nibbled
→ some more of the left-hand bit of
→ mushroom, and raised herself, to about two
→ feet high: even then she walked up towards
→ it rather timidly, saying to herself,
→ "Suppose it should be raving mad after
→ all! I almost wish I'd gone to see the
→ Hatter instead!"</p>
</article>

<aside>
<h2>About the Author</h2>
    <p>Charles Lutwidge Dodgson 7 January
    → 1832 - 14 January 1898), better known
    → by the pseudonym Lewis Carroll was an
    → English author, mathematician, logician,
    → Anglican deacon and photographer. His
    → most famous writings are Alice's
    → Adventures in Wonderland and its sequel
    → Through the Looking-Glass, as well as
    → the poems "The Hunting of the Snark"
    → and "Jabberwocky", all examples of the
    → genre of literary nonsense. He is noted
    → for his facility at word play, logic,
    → and fantasy, and there are societies
    → in many parts of the world (including
    → the United Kingdom, Japan, the United
    → States, and New Zealand) dedicated to
    → the enjoyment and promotion of his
    → works and the investigation of his
    → life.</p>
</aside>

<footer>
<nav>
<a href="AAIWL-ch05.html" class="prev">Advice
from a Caterpillar</a>
<a href="toc.html">Table of Contents</a>
<a href="AAIWL-ch07.html"  class="next">A Mad
Tea-party</a>
</nav>
</footer>

</body>
</html>
```

A The Web page for this chapter before adding any of the box properties. It's a scrambled mess right now, but you'll be laying down the design grid, adding margins, and adding padding to give the design some breathing room.

Understanding an Element's Box

As you learned in Chapter 2, an element is a part of an HTML document that is set off by HTML container tags. The following is an HTML element:

```
<p>Alice</p>
```

This is another HTML element:

```
<article><p><em>Alice
   <img src="alice11.gif">
   </em></p></article>
```

The first example is an element made of a single tag. The second example is a collection of nested tags, and each of those nested tags is an individual element. Remember that nested tags are called the *children* of the tags within which they are nested, which are called the *parents* (see "Inheriting Properties from a Parent" in Chapter 4).

Parts of the box

All HTML elements have four sides: top, right, bottom, and left **Ⓐ**. These four sides make up the element's box, to which CSS box properties can be applied. Each side of the box has the following properties:

- **Content**—At the center of the box, this is the substance of the page. The content includes all text (called copy), lists, forms, and images you use.

- **Child Elements**—Elements contained within the parent element that are set off by their own HTML tags. Child elements typically have their own box that can be controlled independently of the parent.

- **Width** and **Height**—The dimensions of the content area. If you leave width and height undefined, these dimensions are determined by the browser (see "Setting the Width and Height of an Element" in this chapter).

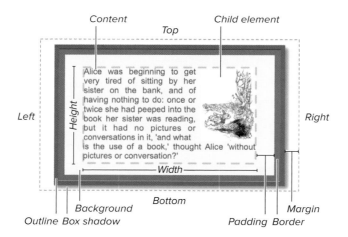

Ⓐ The box model in all its glory. Notice that the outline is part of the margin. If a margin is not present, the outline will appear underneath adjacent elements. Also, if two elements are stacked on each other, the margins between are not added, but collapse to the larger of the two.

- **Padding**—The space between the border and the content of the element (see "Setting an Element's Padding" in this chapter). Background colors and images also fill this space. If left unset, the size of the padding is generally 0.

- **Background**—Space behind the content and padding of the element. This can be a solid color, one or more background images, or a background gradient. (See Chapter 7 for more information about backgrounds.)

- **Border**—A rule (line) that surrounds the element and can be set separately on any of the sides. The border is invisible unless you set its color, width, and style—solid, dotted, dashed, and so on. You can also set a background image. If left unset, the border size is generally 0.

- **Outline**—Similar to border, but does not occupy any space. It appears underneath the margin and any surrounding sibling elements in the background.

- **Margin**—The space between the border of the element and other elements in the window (see "Setting an Element's Margins" in this chapter). If left unset, the browser defines the margin.

By default, setting the content width and content height does not set the width and height of the space that the element occupies on the page. The overall width includes any padding and border on a side:

element width = content width + left padding + left border width + right padding + right border width

Height is a little different. If a content height is set, but overflow is not, then the height will stretch to accommodate the content plus any padding and borders:

element height = height needed to display content + top padding + top border width + bottom padding + bottom border width

If overflow is set to hidden, scroll, or auto, then height is computed:

element height = content height + top padding + top border width + bottom padding + bottom border width

Any content that does not fit within the element will be either hidden or scrollable.

However, CSS3 introduces the new **box-resize** property, which simply sizes the width and height of the box *including* the padding and border.

TIP Every element is rectangular in nature, even if its content is not rectangular shaped. For example, even if the image in an element is a circle, it's bound by a rectangular box.

TIP Every element has content area and a top, right, bottom, and left. Every element can also have background, padding, border, outline, and box-shadow values.

Displaying an Element

In Chapter 1 you learned that all elements can be classified according to the way they're displayed—inline or block (see "Types of HTML Elements" in Chapter 2). By default, every tag has a display style that defines how it will fit with the surrounding tags.

You can use the **display** property to define whether an element includes line breaks above and below (block), is included with other elements without hard line breaks (inline), is treated as part of a list (list), or is displayed at all (none). **Table 10.1** shows the values available for the **display** property.

To set an element's display type:

1. Start your declaration by typing the **display** property name in the CSS declaration block, followed by a colon (:) (Code 10.2).

   `display:`

2. Type one of the display types from Table 10.1.

   `block;`

   Choose a type depending on the desired result:

   ▸ **inline** flows the element horizontally and its siblings from left to right until the edge of the parent element is encountered, at which point a soft break is added wrapping the content to the next line. Hard line breaks immediately before and after the box are always suppressed Ⓐ.

   ▸ **block** places a hard line break above and below the box, flowing the elements vertically. Setting this automatically forces the width of the box to the width of the parent element's box Ⓑ.

TABLE 10.1 Display Values

Value					
list-item	●	●	●	●	●
block	●	●	●	●	●
inline	●	●	●	●	●
inline-block	●	●	●	●	●
table	●8	●	●	●	●
table-cell	●8	●	●	●	●
table-footer-group	●8	●	●	●	●
table-header-group	●8	●	●	●	●
table-row	●8	●	●	●	●
table-row-group	●8	●	●	●	●
inline-table	●8	●	●	●	●
none	●	●	●	●	●
inherit	●	●	●	●	●

ELEMENT	ELEMENT	ELEMENT

Ⓐ Inline level elements flow horizontally.

ELEMENT
ELEMENT
ELEMENT

Ⓑ Block level elements flow vertically.

	ELEMENT	
	ELEMENT	
ELEMENT	ELEMENT	ELEMENT

C Inline-block elements can stack vertically in the box, but the box is flowed inline.

Code 10.2 Added to *box-properties.css*—When applied to **Code 10.1**, adding the **display** property allows you to redefine how different elements flow within the document **D**. Defining the **figure**, **figcaption**, and the first letter of the first paragraph in an article as block elements will ensure that you can control their width, height, and float.

```
/*** box-properties.css ***/
header, section, nav, article, aside, figure,
→ figcaption, footer, hgroup {
   display: block; }
article h2 + p:first-letter {
   display: block; }
```

D **Code 10.2 applied to Code 10.1:** The figure caption is now a block level element so it will appear below the image, rather than beside it.

- ▸ **inline-block** defines this element as inline, but the content within it is treated as a block **C**.

- ▸ **run-in** is contextual, acting as a block element *unless* its next sibling is also a block element, in which case it will act as an inline element to its sibling. The sibling cannot be a run-in or have floating applied to it for this to work.

- ▸ **table**, or any one of the other **table** values shown in Table 10.1, allows you to turn any tag into part of a data table.

- ▸ **list-item** places a list item marker on the first line of text, as well as a break above and below the text. This code allows the item to be used as part of a list even if you're not specifically using a list element. Using **list-item** to create lists out of non-list elements is discussed in Chapter 8.

- ▸ **inherit** uses the display value set or implicit for the element's parent.

- ▸ **none** causes this element not to display in CSS browsers. It will appear as though the content doesn't exist on the page.

TIP HTML5 structure tags (header, section, article, footer, and so on) will need to have `display: block` set for them.

TIP Although you can turn any element into a list item or table, *don't*. This is bad coding from a semantic and accessibility standpoint. Stick to HTML tags for creating lists and tables.

TIP The `compact` property was dropped in CSS2.1 but may make a comeback in CSS3. At present, only a placeholder exists in the CSS Work Groups Box Model documentation for CSS3.

TIP Any elements that are assigned `display:none` will be ignored by the browser. Be careful when using `none`, however. Although it is not an inherited attribute, `none` turns off the element display as well as the display of any child elements.

TIP `display:none` is useful for creating dynamic elements—such as drop-down menus—that show and hide as the user interacts with the page. However, keep in mind that this also hides the element from screen readers, which can hinder usability.

TIP Another great use for `none` is to use it to create a print-specific style sheet that hides elements not needed when the page is printed, such as navigation and form fields. Who needs navigation links, search forms, and low-resolution graphics in a printout?

TIP The `display` property should not be confused with the `visibility` property (see "Setting the Visibility of an Element" in Chapter 11). Unlike the `visibility` property, which leaves a space for the element, `display:none` completely removes the element from the page, although the browser still loads its content.

Code 10.3 *box-properties.css*—When applied to Code 10.1, `width` and `height` are used to control element dimensions. Max  and min  values can be used to allow the design to fluidly grow or shrink to meet the user's needs.

```
/*** box-properties.css ***/
header, footer {
    width: 100%; }
header {
    height: 135px; }
footer {
    height: 60px;
box-sizing: border-box; }
h1 {
width: 95%;
    max-width: 980px;
min-width: 660px; }
article h2 {
    width: 95%; }
article {
    max-width: 980px;
    min-width: 660px; }
aside {
    width: 300px;
    height: 400px; }
```

A **Code 10.3 applied to Code 10.1:** Shows the example with the window open to 1280px wide.

B **Code 10.3 applied to Code 10.1:** Shows the example with the window open to 640px wide.

Setting the Width and Height of an Element

By default, the browser automatically sets the width and height of an element to 100 percent of the available width and whatever height is needed to display all the content. You can use CSS to override both the width and height of block elements. Generally, you will be setting the width of an element more often than the height unless you know the exact size of the content of a block or are willing to allow scrolling.

In addition to setting a specific width and height, you can specify a width and height range by setting a minimum and maximum width and height for an element. This can be indispensible for creating flexible designs (*responsive designs* as described in Chapter 14) that will never stretch to unreasonable proportions of the screen in which they are displayed.

To define the width of an element:

1. Type the `width` property name in the CSS declaration block, followed by a colon (:) (Code 10.3).

   `width:`

continues on next page

2. Type a value for the element's width.

   `80%;`

   Use one of the following values
   (Table 10.2):

   ▸ A length value, generally in pixels

   ▸ A percentage, which sets the width
     proportional to the parent element's
     width

   ▸ **auto**, which uses the width calculated
     by the browser for the element—
     usually the maximum distance that
     the element can stretch to the right
     before hitting the edge of the window
     or the edge of a parent element

To define the height of an element:

1. Type the `height` property name in the
   CSS declaration block, followed by a
   colon (`:`).

   `height:`

2. Type a value for the element's height.

   `135px;`

   Use one of the following values
   (Table 10.2):

   ▸ A length value

   ▸ A percentage, which sets the height
     proportional to the parent element's
     height

   ▸ **auto**, which uses a calculated height
     determined by the browser—what-
     ever space the element needs to
     display all the content

TABLE 10.2 Width and Height Values

Value					
\<length\>	●	●	●	●	●
\<percentage\>	●	●	●	●	●
auto	●	●	●	●	●
inherit	●	●	●	●	●

TABLE 10.3 Max/Min-Width and Max/Min-Height Values

Value					
<length>	●	●	●	●	●
<percentage>	●	●	●	●	●
inherit	●	●	●	●	●
none*	●	●	●	●	●

*height only

To set the maximum and minimum width:

1. Type the `min-width` and/or `max-width` property name, a colon (:), and an appropriate value from Table 10.3.

   ```
   max-width: 980px;
   → min-width: 660px;
   ```

   The element will never grow wider or narrower than these values regardless of the browser window width.

2. Type the `min-height` and/or `min-height` property name, a colon (:), and an appropriate value from Table 10.3.

   ```
   max-height: 300px;
   → min-height: 100px;
   ```

   The max/min-height properties work very much the same as max/min-width, but depend on the content displayed rather than the dimensions of the browser window.

TIP When you have too much content to display in the defined area, use the `over-flow` property (see "Controlling Overflowing Content" in this chapter) to allow the viewer to scroll the additional material.

TIP You can resize an image (GIF, PNG, or JPEG) using the `width` and `height` properties, and override the intrinsic width and height.

TIP Use `width` and `height` to keep form fields and buttons at a consistent size.

TIP If you are setting the height of an element and forcing a scrollbar, be careful not to let that element get too close to the browser window's scrollbar because it can lead to confusion and an unpleasant experience for viewers.

TIP You don't have to include both the minimum and maximum values.

TIP If you set the width of the body tag to less than the `max-width` of an element, the `max-width` property is ignored because the body never stretches wide enough.

TIP Generally, the `max-height` will act like the `height` attribute and the `min-height` is ignored because, unlike the max/min width, the element will not resize with the browser window.

★Setting How a Box Sizes

As mentioned at the beginning of this chapter, the actual space a box takes up is based on the width/height, plus the padding, plus the border. However, calculating space this way can be problematic because it assumes you always know the border and padding values. The **box-sizing** property lets you change how the box size is calculated, so that the size is calculated from border to border.

TABLE 10.4 Box-Size Values

Value					
content-box	●8	●	●	●	●
border-box	●8	●	●	●	●

To specify the model used to calculate the width and height of an element, use one of the following values with the **box-sizing** property (**Table 10.4**):

- **content-box** will size *only* the content area. The padding and border widths are added separately to the space needed to display the element. This is the default value.

- **border-box** will set the size of the element from the outer edges of the border to the facing border.

Internet Explorer used to calculate width and height using the border box method. This made sense to many people, but because IE was the only browser to use this method, it caused a lot of problems for Web designers.

Firefox is experimenting with the padding-box, which will size the element from the outer edge of the padding, and ignore the border width. No other browsers are currently supporting this value.

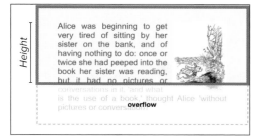

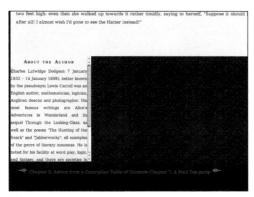

A The overflow is any area (horizontally or vertically) that cannot be displayed within the given area for an element.

Code 10.4 Added to *box-properties.css*—When applied to **Code 10.1**, the content in the aside now has a scrollbar **B**.

```
/*** box-properties.css ***/
aside {
    overflow: auto }
```

B **Code 10.4 applied to Code 10.1:** The aside area's height is restricted to 400px, but more content exists than can fit in that area, so a vertical scrollbar is added automatically.

★Controlling Overflowing Content

When an element is clipped or when the parent element's width and height are less than the area needed to display everything, some content is not displayed **A**. The **overflow** property allows you to specify how this cropped content is treated.

★Overflow for the width or height can be controlled independently using **overflow-x** and/or **overflow-y**.

To define the overflow control:

1. Type the **overflow**, **overflow-x**, or **overflow-y** property name, followed by a colon (:) (Code 10.4).

   overflow:

   continues on next page

2. Add a keyword to tell the browser how to treat overflow from the clip.

```
auto;
```

Use one of the following keywords (**Table 10.5** and **Table 10.6**):

- ▸ **visible** forces the cropped part of the element to be displayed, essentially instructing the browser to ignore the cropping, pushing the content to flow outside of the box **C**.

- ▸ **hidden** hides the overflow and prevents the scrollbars from appearing **D**.

- ▸ **scroll** sets scrollbars around the visible area to allow the visitor to scroll through the element's content. When you set this value, space will be reserved for the scrollbars, even if they are not needed **E**.

- ▸ **auto** allows the browser to decide whether scrollbars need to be displayed **F**.

TABLE 10.5 Overflow Values

Value					
visible	●	●	●	●	●
hidden	●	●	●	●	●
scroll	●	●	●	●	●
auto	●	●	●	●	●

TABLE 10.6 Overflow-x and Overflow-y Values

Value					
visible	●	●	●	●	●
hidden	●	●	●	●	●
scroll	●	●	●	●	●
auto	●	●	●	●	●

C **Visible** will override the height of the element, forcing it to display all content.

E **Scroll** places both horizontal and vertical scrollbars to access additional content in the element. However, placeholder scrollbars are added even if they're not needed.

D **Hidden** will crop the element but provide no way to access the rest of the element's content.

F **Auto** is generally the best option because it displays scrollbars only as needed.

★Setting How Text Overflows

Although being able to set box overflow is useful, often the text that is overflowing is rudely clipped in the middle of a word or even a letter.

In typography, though, incomplete text is indicated using an ellipsis (…).

The **text-overflow** property controls how text is displayed where the available space cannot display all of the content, generally because the width and height have been set with overflow hidden Ⓖ.

In this case, use one of the following values (**Table 10.7**):

- **clip** will truncate the text wherever the space for the display area is exceeded. This can mean that text is clipped in a word or even in part of a letter.

- **ellipsis** will add the ellipsis as the last character, shortening the text so that it can be completely displayed. This may come at the end of a word or within a word, but will not clip a letter.

Opera and Internet Explorer currently use browser extensions. Safari used a browser extension until version 5.1.

Clip

Ellipses

Ⓖ **Clip** or **ellipsis** are used to control how text is treated in overflow mode.

TABLE 10.7 Text-Overflow Values

Value	🌐	🌐	🌐	🌐	🌐
clip	◇	●	●	●	◇
ellipsis	◇	●	●	●	◇
inherit	◇	●	●	●	◇

TIP Generally, `auto` is preferred for overflow because it will show the scrollbars only as needed and hide the scrollbar chrome when there is nothing to scroll.

TIP The `overflow` property is also used to define how clipping overflow is treated.

TIP Although not commonly used, I recommend implementing the ellipsis property for all text. This insures that if for some reason it is cut off, at least it will not look unattractive.

Floating Elements in the Window

In addition to precisely positioning elements within the document, CSS also allows you to set how an element interacts with other elements by *floating* it.

Using the CSS **float** property, you flow text around content or float block elements next to each other to create columns.

To float an element:

1. Start your definition by typing the **float** property name, followed by a colon (:) (Code 10.5).

   ```
   float:
   ```

Code 10.5 Added to *box-properties.css*—When applied to **Code 10.1**, the **float** properties will cause the text to wrap around the figure **Ⓐ**. Additionally, this code will cause the first letter in the first paragraph of an article to become a true drop cap **Ⓑ**.

```
/*** box-properties.css ***/

article {
float: left; }
article h2 + p:first-letter {
    float: left; }
.floatleft {
    float: left; }
.floatright {
    float: right; }
```

Ⓐ Code 10.5 applied to Code 10.1: The figure now floats with the text around it.

Ⓑ Code 10.5 applied to Code 10.1: The drop cap.

TABLE 10.8 Float Values

Value					
left	●	●	●	●	●
right	●	●	●	●	●
none	●	●	●	●	●

2. Type a keyword to tell the browser on which side of the screen the element should float.

`right;`

Choose one of the following keywords (**Table 10.8**):

▸ **right** aligns this element to the right of other elements, causing subsequent elements to wrap horizontally to the left of this element.

▸ **left** aligns this element to the left of other elements, causing subsequent elements to wrap horizontally to the right of this element.

▸ **none** overrides floating for this element.

TIP In order to work, elements being floated have to have a specific width, so an element with no width or `width: auto` set will not appear to float.

TIP Floating elements within other elements can often have odd consequences if both the child and parent are block elements. The child tends to ignore the height of the parent, which can have undesirable consequences. The child element will appear to begin in the parent element but will then extend beyond the bottom of the parent element. The fix for this is discussed in the Chapter 13 section, "Fixing the Float."

TIP In Chapter 13, you'll learn how to use the `float` property to set up separate columns to replace a traditional table-based layout.

Clearing a floated element

Sometimes, you may find it necessary to override the **float** property to prevent elements that appear after a floating element from wrapping. Similar to the **clear** attribute of the HTML break tag, the CSS **clear** property allows you to specify whether you want to deny floating around the left, right, or both sides of an element (**Table 10.9**).

To prevent an element from floating:

1. Type the **clear** property name in the CSS rule, followed by a colon (:) to start your declaration (Code 10.6).

   ```
   clear:
   ```

2. Type the keyword for the side that you want to prevent floating.

   ```
   right;
   ```

   Choose one of the following keywords:

   - **left** to prevent wrapping on the left side of the element

   - **right** to prevent wrapping on the right side of the element

   - **both** to prevent wrapping on both sides of the element

   - **none** to override a previously set **clear** property

   TIP I like to set up float classes: `.floatleft` and `.floatright`. These can come in handy for creating versatile Web designs.

   TIP It's usually a good idea to set headers and titles to `clear:both`, so that they don't wrap around other objects.

TABLE 10.9 Clear Values

Value					
left	●	●	●	●	●
right	●	●	●	●	●
both	●	●	●	●	●
none	●	●	●	●	●

Code 10.6 Added to *box-properties.css*—When applied to **Code 10.1**, figures are prevented from floating next to each other, which might create an unattractive design

```
/*** box-properties.css ***/

figure {
   clear: both; }
```

TABLE 10.10 Margin Values

Value					
<length>	●	●	●	●	●
<percentage>	●	●	●	●	●
auto	●	●	●	●	●

Code 10.7 Added to *box-properties.css*—When applied to **Code 10.1**, `margin` is set to 0 in the body, and margins are added to help space out other elements in the screen .

```
/*** box-properties.css ***/
body {
   margin: 0; }
h1 {
   margin: 0 20px 10px 5%; }
hgroup h2 {
   margin: 30px; }
article h2 {
   margin-bottom: 60px; }
article p {
   margin: 0; }
article h2 + p {
   margin-bottom: 1em; }
article h2 + p :first-letter {
   margin-bottom: .35em .2em .2em 0; }
article a {
   margin: 0 1em; }
figure img {
   margin: 0; }
.floatleft {
   margin: 1em 2em 1em 0; }
.floatright {
   margin: 1em 0 1em 2em; }
.floatcenter {
   margin: 1em auto; }
```

Setting an Element's Margins

The `margin` (Table 10.10) of an element allows you to set the space between that element and other elements in the window by specifying one to four values that correspond to all four sides together, the top/bottom and left/right sides as pairs, or all four sides independently.

To define the margins of an element:

1. Start your declaration by typing the `margin` shortcut property name in the declaration block, followed by a colon (:) (Code 10.7).

   ```
   margin:
   ```

   continues on next page

 **Code 10.7 applied to Code 10.1:** Among other elements that are spaced out, all of the paragraphs now have no space between them, and instead, the text-indent from Chapter 6 now visually defines new paragraphs.

2. **Type a value for the margin.**

   `.35em .2em .2em 0;`

   Use one of the following values:

   - A length value
   - A percentage, which creates a margin proportional to the parent element's width
   - `auto`, which returns control of the margins to the browser's discretion

   You can enter one to four values, separated by spaces, to define the margins as follows:

   - One value sets the margin for all four sides equally.
   - Two values set the top/bottom margins and left/right margins.
   - Three values set the top margin, the left/right margins (the same), and the bottom margin.
   - Four values set each margin clockwise, starting from top: top, right, bottom, and left.

3. **You can also set the margin for just one side of the box independently without setting the other three margins.**

   `margin-bottom: 60px;`

   This is useful when used with an inline style to override margins set elsewhere. To do this, specify the margin side you want to define (**margin-top**, **margin-bottom**, **margin-left**, or **margin-right**) and enter a legitimate margin value from Table 10.10.

   You can also set margins for the **<body>** tag; in which case the margins define the distance that elements nested in the body should appear from the top and left sides of the browser window.

Setting Negative Margins

Although you can use negative margins (for example, `margin:-5em;`) to create interesting effects for overlapping pieces of text, this method is frowned upon because various browsers present different results.

Overlapping text is better achieved using CSS positioning (see Chapter 11).

Be careful when setting negative margins around a hypertext link. If one element has margins that cause it to cover the link, the link will not work as expected.

Margin Collapse

When two elements stacked vertically on top of each other determine the vertical margin between them, rather than adding the bottom and top margin together, the larger margin will be used, with the smaller margin collapsing to 0. This allows you to keep consistent margins at the top and bottom of a collection of stacked elements.

TIP In addition to the `.floatleft` and `.floatright` classes, I've added a `.floatcenter`, using an auto margin for left and right. This isn't a true float, where text wraps around the object, since that's not possible in CSS. What it does is simply center an element.

TIP I've also added margins to `.floatleft` and `.floatright` in order to make sure those floating elements have some breathing room.

TIP The best way to center an element within its parent element is to set the margins on the left and right to `auto`. This is how most Web pages with the content centered in the browser window are created.

TIP When setting proportional margins, be aware that you might get very different results depending on the size of the user's window. What looks good at a resolution of 800 x 600 might be a mess at larger screen sizes.

TIP The browser has a default margin that it adds to the body of your page so the content doesn't immediately begin at the edge of the screen. However, the default is not the same on all browsers, which can be a problem when you position elements on the page (see Chapter 11). It's a good idea to set the margins in the body tag so that they remain consistent using a CSS reset, as explained in Chapter 13.

Setting an Element's Outline

The outline (**Table 10.11**) surrounds the border and even uses the same values as the border; unlike the border, it does not increase the apparent dimensions (width or height) of the box and does not actually occupy any space on the screen. Instead, it appears under any margin and out into the page under surrounding content.

An outline can be very useful for link-rollovers, allowing you to highlight them without displacing the surrounding content.

To set a box's outline:

1. The `outline` property looks identical to the `border` property, although it behaves differently. Enter a width, style, and color separated by spaces (**Code 10.8**).

   ```
   outline: rgba(135,127,107,.65)
   → 10px double;
   ```

2. Alternatively, you can define each outline value, which is useful when you need to override one element value without changing the others.

   ```
   outline-color: rgba(135,127,107,.65);
   ```

   ```
   outline-width: 10px;
   ```

   ```
   outline-style: double;
   ```

   Unlike **border**, **outline** cannot be set independently for the sides.

TIP I tend to use `outline` only when I am debugging element positioning on my page, and I want to see exactly how much space each block is taking up and where they extend.

TIP Another good use of `outline` is using attribute selectors (Chapter 4) to highlight particular elements without disturbing their positioning.

TABLE 10.11 Outline Values

Value					
<border-width>	●8	●	●	●	●
<border-style>	●8	●	●	●	●
<border-color>	●8	●	●	●	●

Code 10.8 Added to *box-properties.css*—When applied to **Code 10.1**, the **outline** style can be used to highlight links being hovered over without disturbing the surrounding elements **A**.

```
/*** box-properties.css ***/
footer a:hover {
   outline: rgba(135,127,107,.65) 10px
   → double; }
```

A Code 10.8 applied to Code 10.1: The link "Table of Contents" in the footer navigation is highlighted using the outline.

★Outline Offset

Add the **outline-offset** property to add some distance between the outline and the border or content edge (**Table 10.12**). Think of this as padding for the outline:

outline-offset: 2px;

TABLE 10.12 Outline-Offset Values

Value					
<length>	●	●	●	●	●
inherit	●	●	●	●	●

Code 10.9 Added to *box-properties.css*—When applied to **Code 10.1**, the border property sets a line—sometimes called a *rule* by designers—on any side of an element's box with a specific style, color, and thickness .

```
/*** box-properties.css ***/
figure {
    border: 6px double rgb(142, 137, 129); }
figcaption {
    border-top: 2px solid
    → rgb(142, 137, 129); }
article {
    border-top: 10px transparent solid;
    border-right: 10px transparent solid;
}
```

The Cat only grinned when it saw Alice. It looked good-natured, she thought: still it had *very* long claws and a great many teeth, so she felt that it ought to be treated with respect.

"Cheshire Puss," she began, rather timidly, as she did not at all know whether it would like the name: however, it only grinned a little wider. "Come, it's pleased so far," thought Alice, and she went on. "Would you tell me, please, which way I ought to go from here?"

"That depends a good deal on where you want to get to," said the Cat.

"I don't much care where——" said Alice.

"Then it doesn't matter which way you go," said the Cat.

It grunted again so violently that she looked down into its face in some alarm

A **Code 10.9 applied to Code 10.1:** The figure is now surrounded by a double-lined border with the caption adding a border at the top to set it off from the image above. The chapter title also receives a border, as does the aside header.

TABLE 10.13 Border Values

Value					
<border-width>	●	●	●	●	●
<border-style>	●	●	●	●	●
<border-color>	●	●	●	●	●

Setting an Element's Border

The **border** property allows you to set a rule (line) around all four sides of your box in any color and thickness using a variety of line styles (**Table 10.13**). Also, using additional **border** properties, you can independently set the borders on any of the four sides, giving you amazing design versatility.

To set the border:

1. To set the border on all four sides, type the **border** property name in the CSS declaration block, followed by a colon (**:**) (**Code 10.9**).

   `border:`

   continues on next page

2. Type a `border-width` value, followed by a space.

`6px`

This value can be one of the following (**Table 10.14**):

- ▸ A length value; a value of **0** prevents the border from appearing, even if the style and color are set.
- ▸ A relative-size keyword, such as **thin**, **medium**, or **thick** (Table 10.14).
- ▸ **inherit** will cause the element to use the same border styles as its parent element.

3. Type the name of the style you want to assign to your border.

`double`

Table 10.15 shows a complete list of available border styles.

Alternatively, you can type **none**, which prevents the border from appearing.

4. Type a color value, which is the color you want the border to be as defined in Table 10.16.

`rgb(142, 137, 129);`

This can be the name of the color or an RGB value.

TABLE 10.14 Border-Width Values

Value					
\<length\>	●	●	●	●	●
thin	●	●	●	●	●
medium	●	●	●	●	●
thick	●	●	●	●	●
inherit	●	●	●	●	●

TABLE 10.15 Border-Style Values

Value	Appearance					
dotted	··········	●	●	●	●	●
dashed	▬ ▬ ▬ ▬ ▬	●	●	●	●	●
solid	▬▬▬▬	●	●	●	●	●
double	══════	●	●	●	●	●
groove	▬▬▬▬	●	●	●	●	●
ridge	▬▬▬▬	●	●	●	●	●
inset	▬▬▬▬	●	●	●	●	●
outset	▬▬▬▬	●	●	●	●	●
none		●	●	●	●	●
inherit		●	●	●	●	●

TABLE 10.16 Border-Color Values

Value					
\<color\>	●	●	●	●	●
transparent	●	●	●	●	●
inherit	●	●	●	●	●

5. You aren't stuck using the same border on all four sides. You can set each side (**border-top**, **border-bottom**, **border-left**, and/or **border-right**).

```
border-top: 2px solid
→ rgb(142, 137, 129);
```

If those options aren't enough, see the sidebar "Additional Ways to Set a Border."

You do not have to include all the individual border attributes in your definition list, but if you don't, the default value will be used.

TIP I've also added a little invisible border around the article, which has the affect of pushing the background image embellishment away from the edge.

Additional Ways to Set a Border

CSS gives you the freedom to define aspects of the border's appearance one side at a time, as follows:

```
border-style: solid dashed double ridge;
```

```
border-width: 1px 2px 4px 8px;
```

```
border-color: red green blue purple;
```

The values for these are shown in **Tables 10.4** through **10.6**.

As with margins, you can include one to four values for each of these properties to set each border side independently, as follows:

- One value sets the property for all four sides.
- Two values set the property for the top/bottom and left/right sides.
- Three values set the top property, the left/right properties (the same), and the bottom property.
- Four values set the property for each side in this order: top, right, bottom, and left.

This method is useful for overriding the values set by the single **border** property.

Your final option for setting a border on a single side (as if you really needed another option!) is to set the individual properties for a specific side (top, bottom, left, right):

```
border-top-width: 3px;
```

```
border-top-style: solid;
```

```
border-top-color: #f00;
```

★Rounding Border Corners

Rounded corners can help soften an otherwise sharp design, but they have been difficult to achieve using images. CSS3 includes a simple method for rounding off one or all of the corners of an element's box: **border-radius**.

Both Mozilla and Webkit have implemented their own versions of **border-radius** in advance of the final W3C pronouncement, and you need to take these browser extensions into account for the widest interoperability (**Table 10.17**).

To set rounded corners:

1. Add the Webkit, Mozilla, and standard CSS3 **border-radius** properties (Code 10.10).

   `border-radius:`

   Although the order doesn't matter, it's generally preferred to have the CSS3 version last because it's the version that *should* be used.

2. Type a **border-radius** value, followed by a semicolon, using the same value for all three instances.

   `5px;`

   This value can be one of the following depending on browser compatibility (Table 10.17):

   ▸ A length value, which sets the radius of an imaginary circle at the corner, which is used to round it off. The larger the value, the rounder the edge.

   ▸ A percentage (**0%** to **50%**), which uses the size of the element to set the corner radius. Higher values produce rounder corners, with **50%** joining

TABLE 10.17 Border-Radius Values

Value					
<length>	●9	●	●	●	●
<percentage>	●9	●	●5.1	●	●

Code 10.10 Added to *box-properties.css*—When applied to **Code 10.1**, the **border-radius** property is used to round the corners of different elements Ⓐ Ⓑ.

```
/*** box-properties.css ***/
article {
   border-top-right-radius: 20px; }
figure {
   border-radius: 5px; }
aside {
   border-radius: 20px/40px; }
```

Ⓐ **Code 10.10 applied to Code 10.1:** The figure area border also has slightly rounded corners but only on the outer line of the double line border.

Setting Elliptical Corners

One final option is to create elliptical rather than circular corners by defining two radius points. Include two values, separated by a slash:

`border-radius: 20px/40px;`

Safari and Chrome support only a single value for the four corners in border radius, so setting elliptical corners is problematic. If you need to set separate elliptical corners, use the long form for each corner instead.

Also, I find, however, that the anti-aliasing distortion becomes even more exaggerated in some browsers when an elliptical corner is used, so I avoid these.

B **Code 10.10 applied to Code 10.1:** The main article has been rounded off, giving it the look of a notebook.

corners into a semicircle. Percentage is *not* supported in Webkit.

3. **Each corner's border radius can be set independently without specifying the other corner radii.**

   `border-top-right-radius: 20px;`

4. **You can include up to four values.**

   border-radius: 20px 0 0 20px;

   Separate each value by a space as a shortcut for setting the border radius:

   ▸ One value sets all four corner radii the same.

   ▸ Two values set the radius for the top-left/bottom-right and bottom-left/top-right corners.

   ▸ Three values set the corner radius for the top left, bottom left/top right (the same), and the bottom right corners.

   ▸ Four values set the radius for each corner in this order: top left, top right, bottom right, and bottom left.

With Webkit you must set corners separately because it treats a second value as the second point in the radius to create elliptical (rather than circular) corners.

TIP Although `border-radius` does anti-alias the curves to make them appear smooth, the results can be hit or miss. I recommend keeping the contrast between your lines and background low to improve the curve appearance.

TIP Curved borders will *not* clip the content in the box. So, an image that might normally be in the corner of the box will still be there, sticking out into the curve.

★Setting a Border Image

A new feature in CSS3 is the ability to use a rectangular image that can be applied to the box's border, overriding the line style. Mozilla and Webkit have implemented almost identical systems, and CSS3 has (thankfully) followed their lead. Although some differences exist, setting a basic image border background is identical among the three systems.

The **border-image** (Table 10.18) takes a rectangular image and slices it into nine parts. The eight parts around the edges are used as the side and corner images, and the center is hidden to allow the content within the element to show through. The corners are applied to the corners of the element box with a size based on the offset you set. Then the middle of the sides of the image are *stretched* or *tiled* to fill the width and height.

To set the border background image:

1. **Create your background image and save it, preferably as a transparent PNG, although any format will work.** For this example, I've divided the image into a grid of 27px squares, fitting the corners and edges of my background into each of these. This will make the math easier.

2. **Add the Webkit, Mozilla, and standard CSS3 border-image properties.**

   ```
   -webkit-border-image:

   -moz-border-image:

   -o-border-image:

   border-image:
   ```

TABLE 10.18 Border-Image Values

Value					
<url>		◇	◇	◇	◇
<offsetnumber>		◇	◇	◇	◇
round		◇	◇	◇	◇
repeat		◇	◇	◇	◇
stretch		◇	◇	◇	◇

Code 10.11 Added to *box-properties.css*—When applied to **Code 10.1**, the header in the aside column uses the file border-02.png as its source for adding a border **A**.

```
/*** box-properties.css ***/
figure.bw-illo {
    border: 1em double rgb(142, 137, 129);
    -webkit-border-image: url(../images/
    ↪ chrome/border-02.png) 27 round;
    -moz-border-image: url(../images/
    ↪ chrome/border-02.png) 27 round;
    -o-border-image: url(../images/chrome/
    ↪ border-02.png) 27 round;
    border-image: url(../images/chrome/
    ↪ border-02.png) 27 round; }
```

A Code 10.11 applied to Code 10.1: The border tiles on the sides as needed to surround the element.

TIP More properties and values for setting the border image are in the CSS3 specification, but they are not yet supported in most browsers.

TIP Opera 10.5 supports the CSS3 version of the `border-image` property.

Although the order doesn't matter, it's generally preferred to have the CSS3 version last because it's the version that *should* be used (**Code 10.11**).

3. Add the URL that indicates the path to the image file you created in step 1.

`url(../_images/border-02.png)`

4. You can include up to four values that specify the border image offset—basically how far into the image the background should extend (how wide the border slices should be)—separated by a space.

27

If you set up your image as a grid, this will be the size of a square in your grid:

▸ One value sets all four sides.

▸ Two values set the offset for the top/bottom and left/right, respectively.

▸ Three values set the offset for the top, left/right, and bottom, respectively.

▸ Four values set the offset for each side in this order: top, right, bottom, and left.

5. Set one or two values to dictate how the images in the middle of a side should be tiled or stretched.

`round;`

Choose from the following values:

▸ `stretch` (default value) scales images to fit the width or height of the box.

▸ `repeat` tiles the images to the width and height of the element.

▸ `round` is similar to `repeat`. It tiles the images but scales them so they fit exactly within the width or height.

Setting an Element's Padding

At first glance, **padding** (Table 10.19) seems to have an effect identical to **margins**: It adds space around the element's content. The difference is that **padding** sets the space between the border of the element and its content rather than between the element and the other elements in the window. Padding is useful when you're using borders and background colors and don't want the content butting right up to the edges.

To set padding:

1. **Start your declaration by typing the padding property name, followed by a colon (:) (Code 10.12).**

   padding:

2. **Type a value for the element's padding.**

   10px;

   Use one of the following values:

   ▸ Length values, which create padding of the exact size you specify

   ▸ A percentage, which creates padding proportional to the parent element's width

   ▸ **inherit** to use the parent's **padding** value

TABLE 10.19 Padding Values

Value					
<length>	●	●	●	●	●
<percentage>	●	●	●	●	●
inherit	●	●	●	●	●

Code 10.12 Added to *box-properties.css*—When applied to **Code 10.1**, the padding property allows you to add space between the border of an element and its content Ⓐ.

```
/***  box-properties.css ***/
body {
    padding: 0; }
h1 {
    padding-top: 10px; }
footer {
    padding: 30px 0 10px 0; }
article {
    padding: 20px; }
article h2 + p {
    padding-bottom: 1em; }
article h2 + p:first-letter {
    padding: 0; }
figcaption {
    padding: 10px; }
```

A Code 10.12 applied to Code 10.1: With padding added, the aside no longer looks so cramped.

To set each side's padding value separately, you can type from one to four values.

- ▶ One value sets the padding for all four sides.
- ▶ Two values set the padding for the top/bottom and left/right sides.
- ▶ Three values set the top padding, the padding for the left/right sides (the same), and the bottom padding.
- ▶ Four values set the padding for each side in this order: top, right, bottom, and left.

3. **As with margins, padding can also be set independently on all four sides of the box** (top, right, bottom, and left).

```
padding-right: 10px;
```

TIP If there is no border around or background-color behind the element, setting the margin will have the same visual effect as padding, and you won't run into the issues surrounding box model measurements. (See the Chapter 13 sidebar, "Fixing the Box Model for Older Versions of Internet Explorer.")

★Creating a Multi-Column Text Layout

Although you'll learn how to create a column grid layout in Chapter 13, you can use the new column properties to create balanced columns of text, similar to a newspaper style. Although not useful for extremely long columns of text, text columns can be a great way to give intro blurbs some style.

To set up multi-column text:

1. Start your declaration by typing the **column-count** property name, followed by a colon (**:**) along with the number of columns (**Tables 10.20** and **10.23**) you want as an integer (**Code 10.13**).

   ```
   -webkit-column-count: 2;

   -moz-column-count: 2;

   column-count: 2;
   ```

2. Add the **column-gap** property name, followed by a colon (**:**) along with the width of the separation (called a gutter) you want between the columns (**Table 10.22**). This can be any standard length value.

   ```
   -webkit-column-gap: 4em;

   -moz-column-gap: 4em;

   column-gap: 4em;
   ```

Code 10.13 Added to *box-properties.css*—When applied to **Code 10.1**, the first paragraph splits into two columns with a line between them Ⓐ.

```
/*** box-properties.css ***/
article h2 + p {
    -webkit-column-count: 2;
    -moz-column-count: 2;
    column-count: 2;
    -webkit-column-gap: 50px;
    -moz-column-gap: 5%;
    column-gap: 5%;
    -webkit-column-rule: 2px groove
    ⇢ rgba(0,0,0,.5);
    -moz-column-rule: 2px groove
    ⇢ rgba(0,0,0,.5);
    column-rule: 2px groove rgba(0,0,0,.5);
}
```

TABLE 10.20 Column-Count Values

Value					
<integer>	●10	◇	◇	◇	●
auto	●10	◇	◇	◇	●

TABLE 10.21 Column-Rule Values

Value					
<border-width>	●10	◇	◇	◇	●
<border-style>	●10	◇	◇	◇	●
<color>	●10	◇	◇	◇	●

A Code 10.13 applied to Code 10.1: The first paragraph will split across two equally balanced columns.

3. Start your declaration by typing the **column-rule** property name, followed by a colon (**:**) along with a width, style (**Table 10.21**), and color you want for line-separating the columns. Your can also set each of these values separately using **column-rule-width**, **column rule-style**, and **column-rule-color**.

```
-webkit-column-rule: 2px groove
→ rgba(0,0,0,.5);
```

```
-moz-column-rule: 2px groove
→ rgba(0,0,0,.5);
```

```
column-rule: 2px groove
→ rgba(0,0,0,.5);
```

TABLE 10.22 Column-Width/Gap Values

Value	ⓔ	ⓦ	◉	◉	�O
<length>	●10	◇	◇	◇	●
auto	●10	◇	◇	◇	●

TABLE 10.23 Column Values

Value	ⓔ	ⓦ	◉	◉	ⓞ
<column-count>	●10	◇	◇	◇	●
<column-width>	●10	◇	◇	◇	●

Coming Soon!

Watch for a number of new properties and features that are planned for CSS in the future. These include:

Resize. Allows you to set a box as being resizable by the user. This is especially useful in text for fields where someone may have a lot to say.

New width and height values. One problem with width is that you often want the content to take up enough space to display, but no more. Several experimental values will allow you to size the box to its content.

Putting It All Together

Code 10.14 shows the final external CSS file created in this chapter. The box properties include the majority of your layout grid.

Code 10.14 Final *ui-box-properties.css*.

```
/*** box-properties.css ***/
body {
   margin: 0;
   padding: 0; }
header, section, nav, article, aside, figure, figcaption, footer, hgroup {
   display: block; }
header, footer {
   clear: both;
   width: 100%; }
header {
   height: 135px; }
footer {
   height: 40px;
   padding: 30px 0 10px 0;
   text-align: center; }
h1 {
   width: 95%;
   max-width: 980px;
   min-width: 660px;
   margin: 0 20px 10px 5%;
   padding-top: 10px; }
hgroup h2 {
   margin: 30px; }
article h2 {
   width: 95%;
   margin-bottom: 60px; }article {
   width: 80%;
   max-width: 980px;
   min-width: 660px;
   margin: 150px 0 10px 0;
   border-top-right-radius: 20px;
   border-top: 10px transparent solid;
   border-right: 10px transparent solid;
   padding: 80px; }
article p {
   margin: 0; }
article h2 + p {
   margin-bottom: 1em;
   padding-bottom: 1em;
   -webkit-column-count: 2;
   -moz-column-count: 2;
   column-count: 2;
```

Code continues on next page

```
     -webkit-column-gap: 4em;
     -moz-column-gap: 4em;
     column-gap: 4em;
     -webkit-column-rule: 2px groove rgba(0,0,0,.5);
     -moz-column-rule: 2px groove rgba(0,0,0,.5);
     column-rule: 2px groove rgba(0,0,0,.5); }
article h2 + p:first-letter {
     float: left;
     display: block;
     margin: .35em .2em .2em 0;
     padding: 0; }
aside {
     width: 200px;
     height: 400px;
     overflow: auto;
     border-radius: 20px/40px;
padding: 20px; }
footer nav a {
     margin: 0 1em; }
footer nav a:hover {
     outline: rgba(135,127,107,.65) 10px double; }
figure {
     border: 6px double rgba(142, 137, 129,.5);
     clear: both; }
figure img {
     margin: 0; }
figure.cl-illo {
     border-radius: 10px; }
figure.bw-illo {
     border: 1em double rgba(142, 137, 129,.5);
     -webkit-border-image: url('../images/chrome/border-02.png') 27 round;
     -moz-border-image: url('../images/chrome/border-02.png') 27 round;
     -o-border-image: url('../images/chrome/border-02.png') 27 round;
     border-image: url('../images/chrome/border-02.png') 27 round; }
figcaption {
     border-top: 2px solid rgba(142, 137, 129, .5);
     padding: 10px; }
.floatleft {
     float:left;
     margin: 1em 2em 1em 0; }
.floatright {
     float:right;
     margin: 1em 0 1em 2em; }
.floatcenter {
     margin: 1em auto ; }
```

Visual Formatting Properties

Whether your designs are meant to be pixel perfect or fluid, element positioning is the key to any good design. You've already learned how to use CSS to control margins and padding in your composition (Chapter 10). With CSS, you can also position elements in the window, either exactly (absolutely or fixed) or in relation to other elements in the document (relatively). You can also set the visibility of any element in the window, making it visible, hidden, transparent, or even clipped on its sides.

This chapter introduces you to the methods you can use to position HTML elements using CSS, including how to stack elements on top of one another and float elements next to each other.

In This Chapter

Getting Started

For this chapter's example, I'll be using the text and images from Chapter 7 of *Alice's Adventures in Wonderland* (**Code 11.1A**). This also includes the aside "About The Author" that we'll be styling in this chapter. We'll be building the CSS file *visualformatting-properties.css* (**Code 11.1B**). See the final version of this file at the end of the chapter in "Putting It All Together."

Code 11.1A The HTML5 code for Chapter 11 is similar to the previous chapter but includes a new "gallery" element at the bottom of the article. It imports the final CSS from Chapters 5, 6, 7, 8, 9, and 10, as well as a new file you will build in this chapter, *visualformatting-properties.css*.

```
<!DOCTYPE html>
<html lang="en">
<head>
<meta charset="utf-8">
<title>Alice&#8217;s Adventures In Wonderland | Chapter VII</title>
<link href="../css/font-properties.css" type="text/css" rel="stylesheet" media="all">
<link href="../css/text-properties.css" type="text/css" rel="stylesheet" media="all">
<link href="../css/color-background-properties.css" type="text/css" rel="stylesheet" media="all">
<link href="../css/list-table-properties.css" type="text/css" rel="stylesheet" media="all">
<link href="../css/ui-generatedcontent-properties.css" type="text/css" rel="stylesheet" media="all">
<link href="../css/box-properties.css" type="text/css" rel="stylesheet" media="all">
<link href="../css/visualformatting-properties.css" type="text/css" rel="stylesheet" media="all">

</head>
<body id="chapter7" class="book aaiw chapter">

<header class="page">
<hgroup>
    <h1>Alice&#8217;s Adventures in Wonderland</h1>
    <h2>By <cite>Lewis Carroll</cite></h2>
</hgroup>
</header>

<article>
<h2>Chapter VII
<span class="chaptertitle">A Mad Tea-party</span>
</h2>

<p>There was a table set out under a tree in front of the house, and the March Hare and the Hatter
→ were having tea at it: a Dormouse was sitting between them, fast asleep, and the other two were
→ using it as a cushion resting their elbows on it, and talking over its head. "Very uncomfortable
→ for the Dormouse," thought Alice; "only as it's asleep, suppose it doesn't mind."</p>
```

code continues on next page

Code 11.1A *continued*

```
...
</article>

<aside>
<h2>About the Author</h2>
    <p><b>Charles Lutwidge Dodgson</b> (7
    ➝ January 1832 – 14 January 1898), better
    ➝ known by the pseudonym Lewis Carroll
    ➝ was an English author, mathematician,
    ➝ logician, Anglican deacon and
    ➝ photographer. His most famous writings
    ➝ are Alice's Adventures in Wonderland
    ➝ and its sequel Through the Looking-
    ➝ Glass, as well as the poems "The
    ➝ Hunting of the Snark" and "Jabberwocky",
    ➝ all examples of the genre of literary
    ➝ nonsense. He is noted for his facility
    ➝ at word play, logic, and fantasy, and
    ➝ there are societies in many parts of
    ➝ the world (including the United Kingdom,
    ➝ Japan, the United States, and New
    ➝ Zealand) dedicated to the enjoyment
    ➝ and promotion of his works and the
    ➝ investigation of his life.</p>
</aside>

<footer>
<nav>
<a href="AAIWL-ch06.html" class="prev">Advice
➝ from a Caterpillar</a>
<a href="toc.html">Table of Contents</a>
<a href="AAIWL-ch08.html"  class="next">A Mad
➝ Tea-party</a>
</nav>
</footer>

</body>
</html>
```

Code 11.1B Starting *visualformatting-properties. css*—This file starts out empty, although I like to have a note at the top with the file name Ⓐ.

```
/*** visualformatting-properties.css ***/
```

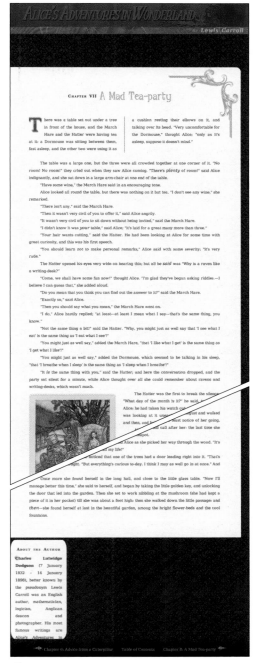

Ⓐ How the page looks before the CSS file *visualformatting-properties.css* is applied.

Understanding the Window and Document

A Web page (also referred to as the *document*) is displayed within a browser window's *viewport*. Everything that you can present to the viewer is displayed in that area, although the document will require scrolling if it is larger than the viewport.

You can open multiple windows (each displaying its own documents in its own viewport), resize and position windows on the screen, or insert smaller viewports called *iframes*. Everything that you present, however, is displayed within a browser window as part of a document.

Like the elements contained within it (see "Understanding an Element's Box" in Chapter 10), the window has a width and height, as well as a top, bottom, left, and right. In fact, you can think of the browser window as the ultimate element in your Web design—the parent of all other elements 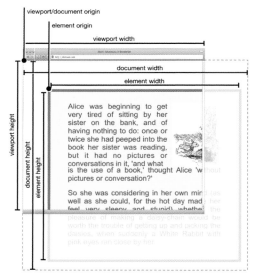. Browser windows and the documents they contain have several distinct parts:

- **Browser width and height** refers to the dimensions of the entire window, including any browser controls and other interface items.

- **Viewport** is the area of the display area. All fixed-position elements are placed in relation to the viewport edges.

Ⓐ The browser window displaying a document that will require some vertical scrolling to reveal the rest of its content.

- **Viewport width and height** refers to the live *display area* of the browser window's viewport. The live dimensions, obviously, are always less than the full window dimensions. Generally, when I refer to "the window," I'm referring to the viewport.

- **Document width and height**, sometimes called the *rendered* width and height, refers to the overall dimensions of the Web page contained within the body tag. If the document's width and/or height are larger than the viewport width and/or height, you'll see scroll bars that let you view the rest of the document.

- **The element edge** is the edge of an element *within* the border. Elements are positioned relative to their parent element's edges *if* the parent element has also been positioned. Otherwise, the element is positioned relative to the document edge.

- **Element width and height** should not be confused with *content* width and height (defined in Chapter 10). This is the total space occupied when border and padding are added to the content width and height.

TIP The document width is most often the same as the viewport width since horizontal scrolling is generally not preferred.

TIP Normal flow refers to where an element will appear in the Web page if no positioning is applied to it.

Setting the Positioning Type

CSS positioning allows you to set several properties associated with the HTML element's position not only in 2D but also in 3D, clipping, and visibility. But first, you have to declare *how* the element's positing should be treated.

An element can have one of four position values—**static**, **relative**, **absolute**, or **fixed** (Table 11.1). The position value tells the browser how to treat the element when placing it into the document.

In addition to setting the position of an element, other position-dependent properties include:

- **Stacking order**, which is available for absolutely and fixed-position elements, allowing you to move elements in 3D.

- **Visibility**, which hides an element's content but not the element itself, effectively setting its opacity to 0.

- **Clipping**, which hides parts of the content, "clipping" its sides.

Static positioning

By default, elements are positioned as static in the document unless you define them as positioned absolutely, relatively, or fixed. Static elements, like the relatively positioned elements explained in the following section, flow into a document one after the next. Static positioning differs, however, in that a static element cannot be explicitly positioned or repositioned, cannot be clipped, and cannot have its visibility changed Ⓐ.

TABLE 11.1 Position Values

Value					
static	●	●	●	●	●
relative	●	●	●	●	●
absolute	●	●	●	●	●
fixed	●	●	●	●	●
inherit	●	●	●	●	●

ELEMENT	ELEMENT	ELEMENT

Ⓐ A statically positioned element stays right where it is.

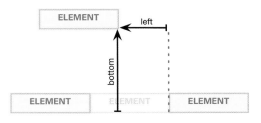

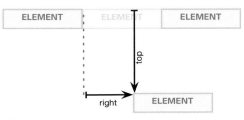

B A relatively positioned element is moved relative to the indicated side—top, right, bottom, and/or left—where it would have appeared if untouched. Negative values move the element in the opposite direction but still relative to the same side.

Relative positioning

A relative element is positioned in the context of its natural position in the document. A relatively positioned element is offset based on its position in the normal flow of the document. The space it occupied will remain in place but appear empty **B**.

Absolute positioning

Absolute positioning takes an element out of the normal flow of the document, while leaving no space. An element that is defined in this way is placed at an exact point in the window by means of x and y coordinates relative to its most recently positioned parent element's edges, or the body if none of its parents are positioned **C**.

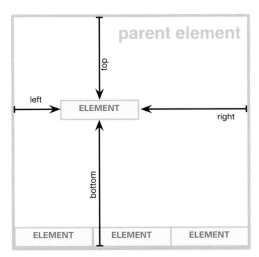

C An absolutely positioned element is removed from the normal flow and positioned from a positioned parent element's sides (or the document sides if it has no positioned parents).

Fixed positioning

Fixing an element's position in the window is similar to absolute positioning except that it is always in a locked position relative to the viewport edge (rather than its parent). When a document scrolls in the viewport, fixed elements stay in their initial positions and do not scroll with the rest of the document. This allows you to establish constant elements in the screen that do not scroll with the rest of the content 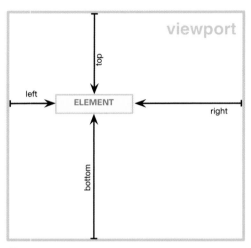.

To set an element's position type:

1. **Add the position property to your declaration list.** Type **position** in a rule's declaration block or in the **style** attribute of an HTML tag, followed by a colon (**:**) (**Code 11.2**).

   ```
   position:
   ```

2. **Specify the positioning.**

   ```
   relative;
   ```

   Type a position-type value, which can be one of the following:

   ▸ **static** flows the content normally; however, none of the position properties can be set for this element.

   ▸ **relative** also flows the element normally, but allows the position to be set relative to its normal position using the values set on the **top**, **left**, **right**, and **bottom** properties.

   ▸ **absolute** places the element relative to the edge of its most recently positioned parent element. This element will be the body of the document, or the element it is nested within if that element's positioning has been set.

   ▸ **fixed** places the element relative to the edges of the viewport, independent of any other content on the page and ignoring its parent

D A fixed-positioned element is always positioned relative to the viewport's edge.

Code 11.2 Added to *visualformatting-properties. css*—Sets the position type for several elements **E**. Keep in mind that you won't see any difference until you start setting the top, right, bottom, or left position.

```
/*** visualformatting-properties.css ***/

header, footer {
    position: fixed; }
footer nav {
    position: relative; }
hgroup h2 {
    position: relative; }
aside {
    position: absolute; }
strong {
    position: relative; }
div.gallery {
    position: relative; }
div.gallery figure {
    position: absolute; }
```

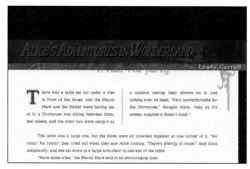

ⓔ Code 11.2 applied to Code 11.1. Position types have been set, but—without actually setting positions—the elements look to be a jumble. The footer, which is fixed, is now at the top of the page! Also, note how low the text marked with the strong tag is. This was caused by increasing its font size relative to the surrounding text. You will fix that in the next section.

Inheriting Position Types

`inherit` is another value for positioning. It tells the element to use the same positioning type as its parent, overriding the default static value. This can be tricky to use, though, because tying the child's position type to its parent can radically alter the layout if you change the parent's position type.

elements. Unlike an absolutely positioned element, when the window is scrolled, the fixed element stays where it is in the viewport as the rest of the content moves.

▸ `inherit` uses the position type of the element's immediate parent. If no position is set, this will default to static (see the sidebar "Inheriting Position Types").

TIP Absolutely positioned and fixed-positioned elements take up no space within the parent element. So if you have an element—such as an image—that is absolutely positioned, its width and height are *not* included as part of the width and height of the parent content.

TIP You can position elements within other positioned elements. For example, you can set the relative position of a child element that is within an absolutely positioned parent or set the absolute position of an element within an absolutely positioned parent.

TIP Remember that the browser adds a default margin to the body of your Web page, but the default value is not consistent across all browsers. To correct this, you should always set your own margin in the body tag, which allows you to position elements consistently. See Chapter 12 for details on using a browser reset.

TIP Positioning can also vary from browser to browser due to rounding errors. It's generally best to use "clean" numbers, rounded to the nearest even number.

TIP When an element's position type has been set to anything other than `static`, you can use JavaScript or other scripting languages to move the element, change the clip, change the stacking order, hide it, or display it.

TIP Browsers that do not understand the `fixed` position type default to `static` for the position type.

Setting an Element's Position

All positioned elements can have a top value, a right value, a bottom value, and a left value to position the element from those four sides (**Tables 11.2** and **11.3**). A relative element will be offset relative to its own edges. An absolute element will be offset relative to its parent's edges. A fixed element will be offset relative to the viewport's edges.

To define an element's position:

1. **Specify a position type.** For details, see "Setting the Positioning Type" earlier in this chapter.

2. **Add a position side property to your CSS declaration list.** Type `left`, `right`, `top`, or `bottom` in the CSS rule, followed by a colon (**:**) (**Code 11.3**).

   `top:`

3. **Specify the position.**

   `0;`

   Type a value for the element's offset. You can enter any of the following:

   ▸ A length value such as **120px**, **2.3em**, or **1.25cm**.

   ▸ A percentage value, such as **1%**, which creates a fluid offset.

   ▸ **auto**, which allows the browser to calculate the value if the position is set to absolute; otherwise, the default value will be **0**.

TABLE 11.2 Top and Left Values

Value					
<length>	●	●	●	●	●
<percentage>	●	●	●	●	●
auto	●	●	●	●	●
inherit	●	●	●	●	●

TABLE 11.3 Bottom and Right Values

Value					
<length>	●	●	●	●	●
<percentage>	●	●	●	●	●
auto	●	●	●	●	●
inherit	●	●	●	●	●

Code 11.3 Added to *visualformatting-properties. css*—When applied to Code 11.1, this CSS positions the footer at the bottom of the viewport (and keeps it there); positions the aside in a convenient location in the top-right corner of the screen; and offsets the gallery images slightly. It also pulls up the strong text, so that its baseline matches the surrounding text. It looks *much* better **A**.

```
/*** visualformatting-properties.css ***/

header {
    top: 0;
    left: 0; }
footer {
    bottom: 0;
    left: 0; }
footer nav {
    top: 10px; }
aside {
    right: 4%;
    top: 150px; }
hgroup h2 {
    top: 15px;
    right: 25px; }
strong {
    top: -.15em; }
#f1 {
    left: -10%; }
#f2 {
    left: 25%; }
#f3 {
    right: -10%; }
```

TIP You don't have to include the `top`, `right`, `bottom`, and `left` declarations, but if they are not included, they are treated as `auto`.

TIP You can use negative values to move the content up and to the left instead of down and to the right.

TIP Child elements that are not absolutely positioned always move with their parent element.

TIP What happens if you set the `top`/`left` and `bottom`/`right` positions for the same element? The answer depends on the browser. Internet Explorer always defaults to the `top` and `left` positions. But most others will stretch elements that do not have a definite width or height to accommodate the values that are set.

A Code 11.3 applied to Code 11.1. The page is starting to come together. Notice that the strong text is now aligned with the rest of the paragraph **B**.

B Even when scrolling, the footer still stays at the bottom of the screen. But notice that the aside is scrolling over the header. We'll fix that in a few pages.

Stacking Objects in 3D

Although the screen is a two-dimensional area, positioned elements can be given a third dimension: a relative stacking order.

Positioned elements are assigned stacking numbers automatically, starting with 0 and continuing incrementally—1, 2, 3, and so on—in the order in which the elements appear in the HTML and relative to their parents and siblings 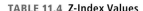. Elements with higher numbers appear above those with lower numbers. This system is called the *z-index* (**Table 11.4**). An element's z-index number establishes its 3D relationship to other elements in its parent element **B**.

When the content of elements overlap, the element with a higher z-index number will appear on top of the element with a lower number **C**. The z-index is always relative to an element's siblings, *not* to its parents.

You can override the natural order of the z-index by setting a value for the **z-index** property.

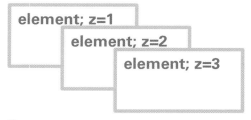

A The natural z order of three elements.

TABLE 11.4 Z-Index Values

Value					
<number>	●	●	●	●	●
auto	●	●	●	●	●
inherit	●	●	●	●	●

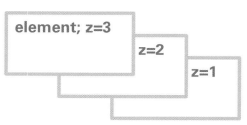

B The natural z order has been overridden using the z-index property.

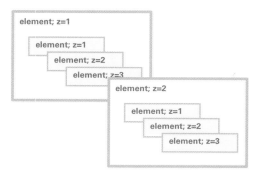

C The z-index order is relative to an element's siblings.

Code 11.4 Added to *visualformatting-properties. css*—When applied to Code 11.1, this CSS will raise the header and footer above everything else 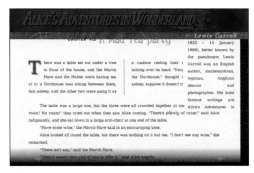. We are also setting up the z-index for the image gallery that we'll play around with in Chapter 12, such that images will rise to the top when hovered over.

```
/*** visualformatting-properties.css ***/

header, footer {
   z-index: 99; }
div.gallery figure {
   z-index: 0; }
div.gallery figure:hover {
   z-index: 999; }
```

D Code 11.4 applied to Code 11.1. Compare the aside to the one shown in the previous section. It's now below the header.

To define an element's z-index:

1. **Specify a position type.** For details, see "Setting the Positioning Type" earlier in this chapter (**Code 11.4**).

2. **Add the z-index property to your CSS rule.** Type **z-index** in the same declaration block, followed by a colon (**:**).

    `z-index:`

3. **Specify the position number.** Type a positive or negative number (no decimals allowed), or **0**.

    `99;`

    This step sets the element's z-index in relation to its siblings, where **0** is on the same level.

    Alternatively, you can use **auto** to allow the browser to determine the element's z-index order.

    Using a negative number for the z-index causes an element to be stacked that many levels below its parent.

Setting the Visibility of an Element

The **visibility** property designates whether an element is visible in the window. If visibility is set to **hidden** (**Table 11.5**), the element is invisible but still occupies space in the document, and an empty rectangle appears where the element is located **A**.

To set an element's visibility:

1. **Specify a position type.** For details, see "Setting the Positioning Type" earlier in this chapter.

2. **Add the visibility property to your CSS.** Type **visibility** in the element's CSS declaration block, followed by a colon (**:**).

   `visibility:`

3. **Specify how the element's visibility should be treated.**

   `hidden;`

   Type one of the following keywords to specify how you want this element to be treated:

   ▸ **hidden** makes the element invisible when the document is initially rendered on the screen.

   ▸ **visible** makes the element visible.

   ▸ **inherit** causes the element to inherit the visibility of its parent element.

TABLE 11.5 Visibility Values

Value					
hidden	●	●	●	●	●
visible	●	●	●	●	●
inherit	●9	●	●	●	●

ELEMENT	ELEMENT

A The hidden element no longer appears, although its location is shown as an empty space indicated by the dotted line in this figure (no, there will not actually be a dotted line).

TIP Although the properties seem similar, `visibility` differs radically from `display` (Chapter 10). When `display` is set to none, the element is scrubbed from the document, and no space is reserved for it. `Visibility` reserves and displays the empty space like the invisible man in his bandages.

TIP Generally, `display:none` is used for JavaScript effects, such as drop-down menus and pop-up text, in which elements are alternately hidden and shown. Because this property will remove the element, it prevents the element from interfering with the layout of the page when not needed.

TIP I recommend using `display:none` to hide elements, such as navigation, when creating a print style sheet.

TIP One downside to hidden elements is that Web search engines will not see them nor will screen readers used by the vision impaired. If you do hide content, make sure it's not something that is vital for SEO.

Clipping an Element's Visible Area

Unlike setting the width and the height of an element, which controls the element's dimensions (see Chapter 10), clipping an absolute- or fixed-position element designates how much of that element's content will be visible (**Table 11.6**). The part that is not designated as visible will still be present, but viewers won't be able to see it, and the browser will treat it as empty space .

TABLE 11.6 Clip Values

Value	🌐	🦊	🧭	⊚	O
rect (<top> <right> <bottom> <left>)	●	●	●	●	●
auto	●	●	●	●	●
inherit	●	●	●	●	●

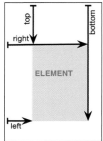

Ⓐ The center area is clipped based on the top, right, bottom, and left values provided to the clip property. The transparent area will not be visible.

Code 11.5 Added to *visualformatting-properties. css*—When applied to Code 11.1, this CSS cuts the aside down to just the headline **B**.

```
/*** visualformatting-properties.css ***/
aside {
   clip: rect(30px, 230px, 60px, 10px); }
aside:hover {
   clip: auto; }
```

B **Code 11.5 applied to Code 11.1.** The "About the Author" aside is now just a title, until the reader places the mouse pointer over it, in which case it expands to full size.

To define the clip area of an element:

1. **Specify a position type.** For details, see "Setting the Positioning Type" earlier in this chapter.

2. **Add the clip property to your declaration list.** Type the **clip** property name, followed by a colon (**:**), as shown in **Code 11.5**.

   ```
   clip:
   ```

3. **Specify the rectangular clipping region.** Type **rect** to define the shape of the clip as a rectangle, an opening parenthesis (**(**), four values separated by spaces, a closing parenthesis (**)**), and a semicolon (**;**).

   ```
   clip: rect(30px, 230px, 60px,
   → 10px);
   ```

   The numbers define the *top*, *right*, *bottom*, and *left* lengths of the clip area, respectively. All these values are distances from the element's origin (top left corner), not from the indicated side.

   Each value can be a length value or **auto**, which allows the browser to determine the clip size (usually, 100 percent).

   The element's borders and padding, but not its margin, are clipped along with the content of the element.

   TIP Currently, clips can only be rectangular.

   TIP **Auto** should restore an element to its unclipped original state. However, Safari and Chrome will only restore the clip to the outer edges of the border while still slipping the outline or box shadow.

★Setting an Element's Opacity

One of the earliest and most widely implemented CSS3 features was the ability to set element opacity, which let you transform an element from opaque to transparent and any translucency in between **A**. However, different browsers implement opacity in different ways.

For example, rather than implementing the W3C CSS syntax, Internet Explorer builds on its existing **filter** functionality, whereas other W3C-compliant browsers simply add the **opacity** property (**Table 11.7**). Because Internet Explorer ignores the other browsers' code, you can place both declarations in the rule list for an element to control its opacity.

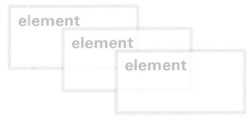

A Changing opacity allows you to see through to the element underneath.

TABLE 11.7 Opacity Values

Value	🅔	🅕	🅢	🅖	🅞
<alphavalue>	●9	●	●	●	●
inherit	●9	●	●	●	●

Code 11.6 Added to *visualformatting-properties. css*—When applied to Code 11.1, this CSS makes the aside transparent until the mouse pointer is over it, when it will turn fully opaque  .

```
/*** visualformatting-properties.css ***/

aside {
   opacity: 0.5; }
aside:hover {
   opacity: 1.0; }
```

B Code 11.6 applied to Code 11.1. The aside now has a neat affect where it is reduced by the clip and transparent until the user mouses over it, at which time it will pop open.

To set the opacity of an element:

1. **Add the opacity property to your CSS.** To control the opacity of an element, type **opacity** followed by a colon (**:**) (**Code 11.6**).

   opacity:

2. **Specify the opacity.** Enter an alpha value for the opacity of the element, which can range between **0.0** (completely transparent) and **1.0** (completely opaque).

   0.5;

   You could also use **inherit**, which will set the element's opacity to the same value as its parent. So, if the parent has an opacity of 0.75, **inherit** will cause the child element to reduce its opacity 75 percent *in addition to* the 75 percent already set for the parent.

   Opacity is applied to the entire element and to all of its children, with no way to override it in child elements. However, you can independently set the opacity of two sibling elements and then position one on top of the other.

TIP Opacities are cumulative, so if an element with 0.5 opacity is within an element with 0.5 opacity, it will have a cumulative opacity of 0.25.

★Setting an Element's Shadows

Just as with text shadows (Chapter 6), you can add one or more drop shadows to the box of any element on the screen—positioned or not 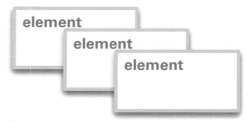. The term "shadow" is a bit misleading, though, since you can make the color anything you like—including light colors—to create a glow effect.

To set an element shadow:

1. **Add the box shadow property to your CSS rule.** Type the **box-shadow** property names, followed by a colon (**:**) (**Code 11.7**).

   ```
   box-shadow:
   ```

2. **Specify the shadow offset, blur, choke, color, and inset.**

   ```
   1px 1px 5px 1px rgba(0,0,0,.25)
   → inset
   ```

   Type the following keywords or values (**Table 11.8**) to specify how you want this element's shadow to be treated (from right to left):

   ▸ **x** and **y** offset length values set the position of the shadow relative to the box. Positive values offset the shadow down and to the right, whereas negative values move the shadow up and to the left. These values are required.

A Shadows provide a sense of depth and texture.

TABLE 11.8 **Box-Shadow Values**

Value					
inset	●9	●	●	●	●
<x-offset>	●9	●	●	●	●
<y-offset>	●9	●	●	●	●
<blur>	●9	●	●	●	●
<spread>	●9	●	●	●	●
<color>	●9	●	●	●	●

Code 11.7 Added to *visualformatting-properties.css*—When applied to Code 11.1, this CSS adds a drop shadow to the article and both a drop and interior shadow to the aside. It also adds shadows to the gallery images, but because they are clipped, they don't show up **B**.

```
/*** visualformatting-properties.css ***/
header {   box-shadow: 0 10px 10px
↪ rgba(0,0,0,.5);}
article {   box-shadow: 5px 5px 10px
↪ rgba(0,0,0,.7); }
aside {    box-shadow: 1px 1px 5px 1px
↪ rgba(0,0,0,.25) inset, 3px 3px 15px
↪ rgba(0,0,0,.5); }
figure {   box-shadow: 5px 5px 10px
↪ rgba(0,0,0,.7); }
```

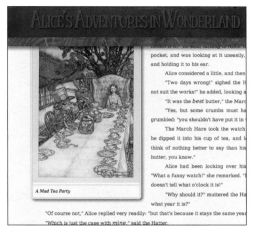

B **Code 11.7 applied to Code 11.1.** The shadows add to the illusion of pages in a book, giving them a sense of weight and thickness.

- ▸ A **blur** length value is a positive value that increases the fuzziness of the shadow and spreads it out. The higher the value, the bigger and lighter the shadow. This value is optional but defaults to **0** when left unset.

- ▸ A **spread** length value—sometimes called the *choke*—is a positive value used to specify the break point for the shadow's fade. It has the effect of increasing the darker area of the shadow before it begins to fade. This value is optional but defaults to **0** when left unset.

- ▸ A **color** value is any of the standard color values outlined in Chapter 7. This value is optional but defaults to **transparent** when left unset, rendering the shadow invisible.

- ▸ **inset** causes the shadow to appear within the element's edges, creating an inner shadow. This is optional.

3. **Add more shadows as desired.**

   `, 3px 3px 15px rgba(0,0,0,.5);`

   You can repeat the shadow code as many times as desired to create multiple shadows under or within the element, separating each value list by a comma (,) and always remembering to end your CSS rule with a semicolon (;).

   If only one length value is included after the x/y offset length values, it will be assumed to be the blur, not the spread.

Box "Shadow" Effects

The box shadow can do some great effects that might all but replace the border and outline properties. Here are just a few examples that I created classes for:

Frame

The frame effect uses drop shadows with the spread set to 0 to create a frame around the box. This has an advantage over border because you can have multiple borders, and has the advantage of the outline property in that it will not take up any space in the design .

```
.frame {
    box-shadow: 0 0 0 5px
    → hsl(0,100%,0%),

    0 0 0 10px hsl(90,100%,20%),

    0 0 0 15px hsl(180,100%,40%),

    0 0 0 20px hsl(270,100%,80%),

    0 0 0 25px hsl(0,100%,80%),

    0 0 0 30px hsl(90,100%,100%); }
```

Inset Frame

Like the frame effect, only the border is inside the element 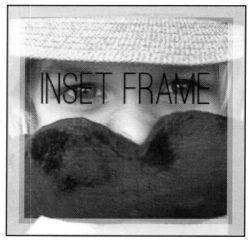. You *cannot* do this with the border property.

```
.insetframe {
    background: rgb(53,53,53);

    box-shadow: 0 0 0 15px
    → hsla(0,0%,100%,.5) inset,

    0 0 0 10px hsla(0,0%,100%,.5)
    → inset;     }
```

C Using multiple Box-shadows to create a multiple border effect.

D Using Box-shadows to create a transparent border inside the image.

Code 11.8 Final *visualformatting-properties.css*

```css
/*** visualformatting-properties.css ***/

header, footer {
    position: fixed;
    z-index: 999; }
header {
    top: 0;
    left: 0;
    box-shadow: 0 10px 10px rgba(0,0,0,.5); }
footer {
    bottom: 0;
    left: 0; }
hgroup h2 {
    position: relative;
    top: 15px;
    right: 25px; }
article {
    box-shadow: 5px 5px 10px rgba(0,0,0,.7); }
aside {
    position: absolute;
    right: 4%;
    top: 150px;
    opacity: .5;
    clip: rect(30px 230px 60px 10px);
    box-shadow: 1px 1px 5px 1px rgba(0,0,0,.25)
      inset, 3px 3px 15px rgba(0,0,0,.5); }
aside:hover {
    clip: auto;
    opacity: 1.0; }
figure {
    box-shadow: 5px 5px 10px rgba(0,0,0,.7); }
footer nav {
    position: relative;
    top: 20px; }
strong {
    position: relative;
    top: -.15em; }
```

Putting It All Together

The completed code for *visualformatting-properties.css* should look something like **Code 11.8**.

Transformation and Transition Properties

Although the use of transform and transition properties is still somewhat controversial, the ability to apply these changes to elements without using JavaScript will be a boon for Web designers and developers. Think of these as temporal styles that not only change the appearance of an element—as do other styles—but also change that element's appearance over time and space.

The styles presented in this chapter are extremely new, at least by Web standards. Although Webkit has had them in one form or another for a while and Firefox and Opera have started adopting them, it is only recently that many of them have been added to Internet Explorer and that work has started toward making them part of the standard CSS3 canon. I'd approach these with some caution while making sure they degrade gracefully in older browsers, but I can't wait to see how you use them.

In This Chapter

Getting Started

For this chapter's example, I'll be using the text and images from Chapter 8 of *Alice's Adventures in Wonderland* (**Code 12.1A**), which includes several black-and-white figures that I've collected into a "gallery" so that we can play around with using transforms and transitions on them. We'll be building the CSS file *transformation-transition-properties.css* (**Code 12.1B**) in this chapter. Start out by adding a few styles that position the images in our figure (IDed as f1, f2, and f3). See the finished version of this CSS file in the section "Putting It All Together" at the end of the chapter.

Code 12.1A The HTML5 code for Chapter 12 is similar to the previous chapter. It links to the final CSS from Chapters 5, 6, 7, 8, 9, 10, and 11, as well as a new file we will be building in this chapter called *transformation-transition-properties.css*.

```
<!DOCTYPE html>
<html lang="en">
<head>
<meta charset="utf-8">
<title>Alice&#8217;s Adventures In Wonderland | Chapter VIII</title>
<link href="../css/font-properties.css" type="text/css" rel="stylesheet" media="all">
<link href="../css/text-properties.css" type="text/css" rel="stylesheet" media="all">
<link href="../css/color-background-properties.css" type="text/css" rel="stylesheet" media="all">
<link href="../css/list-table-properties.css" type="text/css" rel="stylesheet" media="all">
<link href="../css/ui-generatedcontent-properties.css" type="text/css" rel="stylesheet" media="all">
<link href="../css/box-properties.css" type="text/css" rel="stylesheet" media="all">
<link href="../css/visualformatting-properties.css" type="text/css" rel="stylesheet" media="all">
<link href="../css/transformation-transition-properties.css" type="text/css" rel="stylesheet"
 → media="all">
</head>
<body id="chapter8" class="book aaiw chapter">

<header class="page">
<hgroup>
    <h1>Alice&#8217;s Adventures in Wonderland</h1>
    <h2>By <cite>Lewis Carroll</cite></h2>
</hgroup>
</header>
```

code continues on next page

Code 12.1A *continued*

```
<article>
<h2>Chapter VIII
<span class="chaptertitle">The Queen's Croquet-Ground</span>
</h2>

<p>A large rose-tree stood near the entrance of the garden: the roses growing on it were white,
 → but there were three gardeners at it, busily painting them red. Alice thought this a very curious
 → thing, and she went nearer to watch them, and just as she came up to them she heard one of them
 → say <q>Look out now, Five! Don't go splashing paint over me like that!</q></p>
...

<p>The Cat's head began fading away the moment he was gone, and by the time he had come back with
 → the Duchess, it had entirely disappeared; so the King and the executioner ran wildly up and down
 → looking for it, while the rest of the party went back to the game.</p>
<div class="gallery">
<figure id="f1" class="illo bw-illo" style="width: 300px;">
<img src="../images/illos/p0103-image.png" width="300" height="400" alt="Playing croquet" title="" />
</figure>
<figure id="f2" class="illo bw-illo"  style="width: 380px;">
<img src="../images/illos/p0106-image.png" width="380" height="179" alt="The cat" title="" />
</figure>
<figure id="f3" class="illo bw-illo" style="width: 286px;">
<img src="../images/illos/p0109-image.png" width="286" height="300" alt="The Executioner" title="">
</figure>
</div>
</article>
<aside>
<h2>About the Author</h2>
    <p><b>Charles Lutwidge Dodgson</b> (7 January 1832 - 14 January 1898), better known by the
    → pseudonym Lewis Carroll was an English author, mathematician, logician, Anglican deacon and
    → photographer. His most famous writings are Alice's Adventures in Wonderland and its sequel
    → Through the Looking-Glass, as well as the poems "The Hunting of the Snark" and "Jabberwocky",
    → all examples of the genre of literary nonsense. He is noted for his facility at word play,
    → logic, and fantasy, and there are societies in many parts of the world (including the United
    → Kingdom, Japan, the United States, and New Zealand) dedicated to the enjoyment and promotion
    → of his works and the investigation of his life.</p>
</aside>
<footer>
<nav>
<a href="AAIWL-ch07.html" class="prev">The Mock Turtle's Story</a>
<a href="toc.html">Table of Contents</a>
<a href="AAIWL-ch09.html"  class="next">Who Stole the Tarts?</a>
</nav>
</footer>
</body>
</html>
```

Code 12.1B Starting *transition-properties.css*—We're adding some positioning (Chapter 11) and width (Chapter 10) styles for the figures in the figure gallery 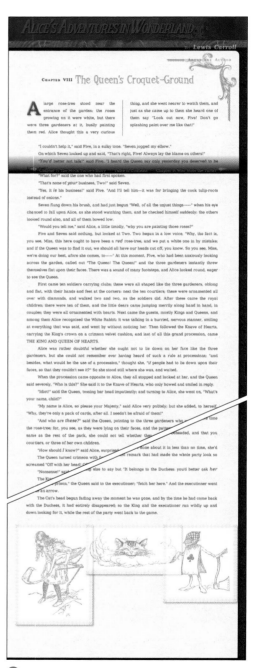.

```
/*** transition-properties.css ***/
div.gallery {
    position: relative;
    width: 100%;
    height: 500px;
    padding: 20px; }
div.gallery figure {
width: auto;
    position: absolute;
    opacity: .5;
    z-index: 0; }
div.gallery figure:hover {
    opacity: 1;
    z-index: 999; }
div.gallery figure#f1 {
    left: -10%; }
div.gallery figure#f2 {
    left: 25%; }
div.gallery figure#f3 {
    right: -10%; }
```

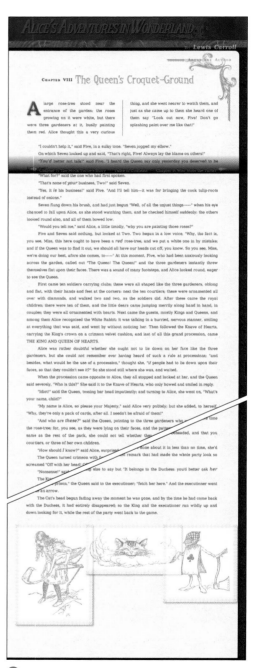

A How the page looks at the start of this chapter. Notice that the gallery of images is still very grid-like in its appearance.

TABLE 12.1 2D Transform Values

Value					
rotate(<angle>)	◇10	◇16	◇	◇	◇
rotateX(<angle>)	◇10	◇16	◇	◇	◇
rotateY(<angle>)	◇10	◇16	◇	◇	◇
scale(<num×2>,)	◇10	◇16	◇	◇	◇
scaleX(<number>)	◇10	◇16	◇	◇	◇12.5
scaleY(<number>)	◇10	◇16	◇	◇	◇12.5
skew(<angle×2>,)	◇10	◇16	◇	◇	◇12.5
skewX(<angle>)	◇10	◇16	◇	◇	◇12.5
skewY(<angle>)	◇10	◇16	◇	◇	◇12.5
translate(<length×2>,)	◇10	◇16	◇	◇	◇12.5
translateX(<length>)	◇10	◇16	◇	◇	◇12.5
translateY(<length>)	◇10	◇16	◇	◇	◇12.5
matrix(<various×6>,)	◇10	◇16	◇	◇	◇12.5

TABLE 12.2 Transform-Origin Values

Value					
<percentage>	◇10	◇16	◇	◇	◇12.5
<length>	◇10	◇16	◇	◇	◇12.5
<keyword>	◇10	◇16	◇	◇	◇12.5

★Transforming an Element

Transforms permits you to manipulate elements beyond the basic position properties, allowing you to finally break out of the rectangular layout grid with values to rotate, scale, skew, and move elements.

Transform values have three basic value types that you might use:

- **Angle** can be defined in degrees (**90deg**), grads (**100grad**), or radians (**1.683rad**). Negative values and values greater that **360deg** are allowed but are translated into positive values.

- **Number** can be any integer or decimal value, positive or negative. Numbers are generally used as multipliers.

- **Length** is a length value, as defined in the introduction of this book. This can include relative values (em, px, %) or absolute values (in, mm, cm).

Many transform values can take multiple parenthetical values, separated by a comma:

```
scale(2,1.65)
```

Generally, two or three values will represent the X, Y, and Z axes. If only one value is included, it is assumed that it should be applied to all three.

As with many advanced CSS3 properties, transformations are currently implemented using extensions to browsers.

Transformations are a bit of a cheat, though. Yes, they enable you to create incredibly cool designs. However, each transform "value" shown in **Table 12.1** (for 2D) and **Table 12.2** (for 3D) could actually be a property in and of itself because each takes its own parenthetical values. But instead, they are all associated with the **transform** property, and we'll have to live with that.

2D transformations

Currently, the most stable and widely available transformations are in two dimensions, but this is a good starting point 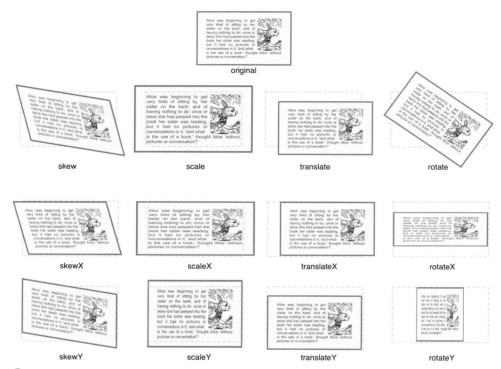.

A The 2D transformations. It sounds like a '70s funk band's name.

Code 12.2 Added to *transition-properties.css*—When applied to Code 12.1, several transformations give the aside a jaunty angle and break up the grid containing the images **B** **C**. Notice that four lines of code are required for maximum cross-browser compatibility.

```
/*** transition-properties.css ***/
aside {
   -webkit-transform: rotate(-2deg);
   -moz-transform: rotate(-2deg);
   -ms-transform:
   -o-transform: rotate(-2deg);
   transform: rotate(-2deg); }
div.gallery figure {
   -webkit-transform-origin: left 25%;
   -moz-transform-origin: left 25%;
   -o-transform-origin: left 25%;
   transform-origin: left 25%; }
div.gallery figure#f1 {
   -webkit-transform: scale(.75)
   ↪ rotate(10deg);
   -moz-transform: scale(.75)
   ↪ rotate(10deg);
   -o-transform: scale(.75) rotate(10deg);
   transform: scale(.75) rotate(10deg); }
div.gallery figure#f3 {
   -webkit-transform: scale(.75)
   ↪ rotate(3deg);
   -moz-transform: scale(.75)rotate(3deg);
   -o-transform: scale(.75) rotate(3deg);
   transform: scale(.75) rotate(3deg); }
```

To add a 2D transformation to an element:

1. Add the `transform` property:

   `-webkit-transform:`

   `-moz-transform:`

   `-ms-transform:`

   `-o-transform:`

   `transform:`

   The exact order is not important, although standard CSS should always come last (**Code 12.2**).

   continues on next page

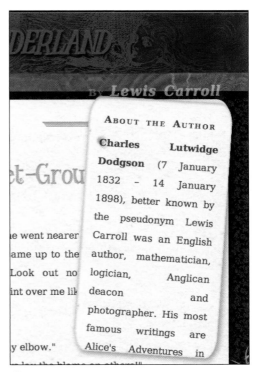

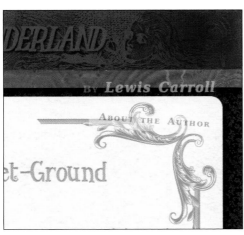

B At the top of the page, the aside title is at a slight angle.

C When expanded, the angle is more noticeable.

2. **Specify the transition type and value.**

`rotate(-2deg);`

For each property, add the same transform value (Table 12.1) with its relevant parenthetical value:

- **rotate()** with an angle value to rotate the element. Positive values turn the element clockwise, whereas negative values turn the element counterclockwise.

- **rotateX()** or **rotateY()** with an angle value to turn the element around the X or Y axis. Positive values turn the element clockwise, whereas negative values turn the element counterclockwise.

- **scale()**, **scaleX()**, or **scaleY()** with numeric values that act as multipliers to the width (X) and/or height (Y) of the element. Positive numbers increase element size. Negative values will still increase size *but also* reflect the element along its axis. Decimal numbers decrease scale.

- **skew()**, **skewX()**, or **skewY()** with angle values that skew the element along the X and/or Y axis of the element. Positive values skew up and to the left, whereas negative values skew down and to the right.

- **translate()**, **translateX()**, or **translateY()** with length values that offset the element along the X axis and/or Y axis of the element. Positive values offset down and to the right, whereas negative values offset up and to the left.

- **matrix()** is a 3×3 matrix of values that can be used as a shorthand to represent any of the preceding transformations alone or in combination.

A Brief Note on Design Enhancements

Let me emphasize one point: Never rely on styles for Web site functionality if the styles are not browser interoperable (that is, available on all common browsers).

One more time for those who missed it: **Never rely on styles for Web site functionality if the styles are not browser interoperable.**

That said, you can and should use styles—such as transitions—as *design enhancements* to improve the user experience without sacrificing usability for those who cannot see them. This is acceptable as long as you can live without the transitions and users can still complete their tasks.

TABLE 12.3 Transform-Origin Keywords

Value
left
right
top
bottom
center

3. **Add more transformations as needed.**

   ```
   transform: scale(.75) rotate(3deg);
   ```

   You can include multiple transformation values separated by a space.

4. **Specify the transformation origin, if it is not the center of the element.**

   ```
   -webkit-transform-origin: 0, 25%;
   ```

   ```
   -moz-transform-origin: 0, 25%;
   ```

   ```
   -o-transform-origin: 0, 25%;
   ```

   ```
   transform-origin: 0, 25%;
   ```

   By default, all transformations use the center of the element as the point of origin. Thus, a rotate transform will rotate around the middle of the element.

   To change this, add the **transform()** property with one or two values for the X and Y location of the origin (Table 12.2) as a percentage, length, or a keyword (**Table 12.3**). If you specify only a single value, it is used for both X and Y values. Positive values move the origin up and to the left of the element, whereas negative values move the origin down and to the right of the center of the element.

3D transformations

As of this writing, 3D transitions are supported only in Safari and Chrome, although that can rapidly change as new versions of Firefox are released. As a result, I don't advocate the use of 3D transitions except when you know the only browser in use supports these properties—for example, in iOS applications or pages created for iPhone, iPod touch, or iPad display. That said, because this is a standard under development by the W3C, you should also include the standard CSS3 syntax for future compatibility.

To transform an element in three dimensions

1. Add the transform style property to your CSS declarations and specify the style.

    `-webkit-transform-style: flat;`

    `-moz-transform-style: flat;`

    `transform-style: flat;`

    Add **transform-style** to the elements being transformed (**Code 12.3**), which allows you to specify whether child elements should be set flat against the parent element or treated separately in their own 3D spaces (**Table 12.4**). Although **transform-style** does work in Internet Explorer, it does so using the CSS3 syntax, not its own browser extension.

TABLE 12.4 Transform-Style Values

Value					
flat	●10	◇16	◇	◇	●
preserve-3d	●10	◇16	◇	◇	●

Code 12.3 Added to *transition-properties.css*— When applied to Code 12.1, this code gives the middle image in the gallery a slight 3D spin that will look like **D**.

```
/*** transition-properties.css ***/
div.gallery figure {
    -webkit-transform-style: flat;
-moz-transform-style: flat;
    transform-style: flat;
    -webkit-perspective: 5000;
    -moz-perspective: 5000;
    perspective: 5000;
    -webkit-perspective-origin: 25% 25%;
-moz-perspective-origin: 25% 25%;
    perspective-origin: 25% 25%;
    -webkit-backface-visibility: visible;
    -moz-backface-visibility: visible;
    backface-visibility: visible; }
div.gallery figure#f2 {
    -webkit-transform: perspective(250px)
    ⇢ scale3d(.5,.75,1.5)
    ⇢ rotate3d(-3,-3,-8,18deg);
    -moz-transform: perspective(250px)
    ⇢ scale3d(.5,.75,1.5)
    ⇢ rotate3d(-3,-3,-8,18deg);
    -o-transform: perspective(250px)
    ⇢ scale3d(.5,.75,1.5)
    ⇢ rotate3d(-3,-3,-8,18deg);
    transform: perspective(250px)
    ⇢ scale3d(.5,.75,1.5)
    ⇢ rotate3d(-3,-3,-8,18deg);}
```

D At the bottom of the page, our photo gallery is now a little more jumbled looking.

E In Webkit browsers, the middle image now appears to be rotated in a 3D space.

2. Add the perspective style property to your CSS declarations and specify the perspective value **D**.

```
-webkit-perspective: 500;

-moz-perspective: 500;

perspective: 500;
```

Perspective works like the transform **perspective()** value described later in this chapter but applies a perspective to an element's positioned children, not the element itself (**Table 12.5**).

3. Add the transform style property to your CSS declarations and one or two values **E**.

```
-webkit-perspective-origin: 25%
25%;

-moz-perspective-origin: 25% 25%;

perspective-origin: 25% 25%;
```

Add **perspective-origin** with one or two values that specify an origin point for the **perspective** property (not the transform value), defining the X and Y position at which the viewer appears to be viewing an element's children (**Table 12.6**). **Perspective-origin** keywords are the same as **transform-origin** keywords (Table 12.3).

continues on next page

TABLE 12.5 Perspective Values

Value	@	⬤	◉	◉	0
<number>	●10	◇16	◇	◇	●
none	●10	◇16	◇	◇	●

TABLE 12.6 Perspective-Origin Values

Value	@	⬤	◉	◉	0
<percentage>	●10	◇16	◇	◇	●
<length>	●10	◇16	◇	◇	●
<keyword>	●10	◇16	◇	◇	

4. **Add the backface visibility property to your CSS declarations and one value.**

   ```
   -webkit-backface-visibility:
   ⤷ visible;

   -moz-backface-visibility: visible;

   backface-visibility: visible;
   ```

   Add **backface-visibility** for the special case in which two elements are placed back to back (like a playing card) and need to be flipped together. This property will hide the back of flipped elements using **rotateZ** or **rotate3D** (**Table 12.7**).

5. **Add the transform property to your CSS declarations for the different browser extensions, including Opera.**

   ```
   -webkit-transform:

   -moz-transform:

   -o-transform:

   transform:
   ```

   3D transformations use the same properties as 2D transformations; only the values are different.

6. **Establish the perspective.**

   ```
   perspective(250px)
   ```

   To create a three-dimensional transformation, a three-dimensional **perspective** property should be established in the element to define a depth. Values start at 0 with lower values giving a more pronounced perspective than higher values, thereby creating a three-dimensional foreshortening.

TABLE 12.7 Backface-Visibility Values

Value					
visible		●10	◇16	◇	◇
hidden		●10	◇16	◇	◇

Do Browser Extensions Ever Go Away?

Yes, browser extensions eventually go away. After a browser implements the standard W3C syntax of a property, the browsers generally support the extension for the next two versions of the browser, although this is by no means a hard and fast rule. This is why—when a standard CSS syntax has been defined—it's best to include it at the bottom of the list of browser extension properties to ensure that it's the version that is used, if supported.

TABLE 12.8 3D Transform-Style Values

Value					
perspective(<number>)		●10	◇16	◇	◇
rotate3d (<number×3>,<angle>)		●10	◇16	◇	◇
rotateZ(<angle>)		●10	◇16	◇	◇
translate3d (<length×3>,)		●10	◇16	◇	◇
translateZ(<length>)		●10	◇16	◇	◇
scale3d(<number×3>,)		●10	◇16	◇	◇
scaleZ(<length>)		●10	◇16	◇	◇
matrix3d(<various×16>)		●10	◇16	◇	◇

7. Add the transform values.

```
scale3d(.5,.75,1.5)
 rotate3d(-3,-3,-8,-18deg);
```

For each browser-specific property, add the same transform value (**Table 12.8**) with its relevant parenthetical value:

▸ **rotate3d()** requires three numbers to define the X, Y, Z axes, and an angle value to turn the element around those axes. Positive values turn the element clockwise, whereas negative values turn the element counterclockwise.

▸ **rotateZ()** uses an angle value to turn the element around the Z axis. Positive values turn the element clockwise, whereas negative values turn the element counterclockwise.

▸ **scale3d()** requires three numeric values that act as multipliers to the width (X) and/or height (Y) and depth (Z) of the element. Positive numbers increase element size. Negative values increase size *and* reflect the element along that axis. Decimal numbers decrease scale.

▸ **scaleZ()** adds a numeric value that acts as a multiplier to the depth (Z) of the element. Positive numbers increase element size. Negative values will increase size *and* reflect the element along that axis. Decimal numbers decrease scale.

▸ **translate3d()** requires three length values that offset the element along the X, Y, and/or Z axes of the element. Positive values offset down, to the right, and forward (larger), whereas negative values offset up, to the left, and backward (smaller).

▸ **translateZ()** adds a length value that offsets the element along the Z axis of the element. Positive values offset forward, whereas negative values offset backward. Unlike the X and Y values, a percentage is not allowed with Z.

▸ **matrix3d()** is a 4×4 matrix of 16 values that can be used as shorthand to represent any of the preceding transformations alone or in combination.

TIP Notice that the 3D transformations work in Internet Explorer with version 10, but do *not* require a browser extension. Instead, they work with the standard CSS3 syntax.

TIP I find 3D transformations a bit mind-blowing when it comes to figuring out what does what. Don't worry if they don't seem intuitive at first. Experimentation is the best remedy for confusion.

★Adding Transitions Between Element States

Despite users' expectations to see change and movement on the screen, CSS and HTML have few controls that allow you to design interactivity, and those that do exist have been binary up to this point:

- A link is one color *or* another.
- A text field is one size *or* another.
- A photo is transparent *or* opaque.

No in-betweens have existed in the past from one state to the next, and no transitions. This has led to most Web pages feeling abrupt, with elements shifting and changing ungracefully.

What we need is a quick and easy way to add simple transitions to a page, and that's where CSS transitions come into the picture.

What can be transitioned?

Almost any CSS property that has a color, length, or position component—including many of the new CSS3 properties—can be given a transition, changing it from one style to another style over time.

Table 12.9 shows a list of the CSS properties available and the values that can be transitioned. (One exception is **box-shadows**.)

For a transition to occur, there has to be a state change in the element using one of the link or dynamic pseudo-classes discussed in Chapter 4. Transitions work by changing a style between different element states over a period of time Ⓐ. For example, the color value of the default state of an element will pass through intermediate colors in the spectrum before appearing as the color value for the hover state Ⓑ.

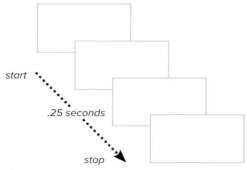

Ⓐ A transition is like several frames in a movie, changing gradually over time rather than instantly. With opacity, the transition is from transparent to opaque.

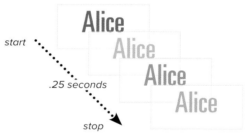

Ⓑ With color, the transition is from one color to another on the color wheel.

TABLE 12.9 CSS Properties with Transitions

CSS Property	What Transitions	CSS Property	What Transitions
background-color	Color	margin-left	Length
background-image	Only gradients	margin-right	Length
background-position	Percentage, length	margin-top	Length
border-bottom-color	Color	max-height	Length, percentage
border-bottom-width	Length	max-width	Length, percentage
border-color	Color	min-height	Length, percentage
border-left-color	Color	min-width	Length, percentage
border-left-width	Length	opacity	Alpha Value
border-right-color	Color	outline-color	Color
border-right-width	Length	outline-offset	Integer
border-spacing	Length	outline-width	Length
border-top-color	Color	padding-bottom	Length
border-top-width	Length	padding-left	Length
border-width	Length	padding-right	Length
bottom	Length, percentage	padding-top	Length
color	Color	right	Length, percentage
clip	Rectangle	text-indent	Length, percentage
font-size	Length, percentage	text-shadow	Shadow
font-weight	Number	top	Length, percentage
grid	Various	vertical-align	Keywords, length, percentage
height	Length, percentage	visibility	Visibility
left	Length, percentage	width	Length, percentage
letter-spacing	Length	word-spacing	Length, percentage
line-height	Number, length, percentage	z-index	Integer
margin-bottom	Length	zoom	Number

To add a transition effect between states:

1. Add the **transition** property.

   `-webkit-transition:`

   `-moz-transition:`

   `-o-transition:`

   `transition:`

   Include versions for the browser extensions including Webkit, Mozilla, Opera, and standard CSS3, including the standard property at the bottom of the list (**Code 12.4**).

Code 12.4 Added to *transition-properties.css*— When applied to Code 12.1, transitions are now applied to the color, opacity, and transformations, resulting in a gradual rather than instant change ⒸC. Notice that I also added a hover state for the figures. You can't have a transition without a style change, and the easiest way to add a change is with the **:hover** pseudo-class.

```
/*** transition-properties.css ***/
aside, figure, a {
   -webkit-transition: color .25s ease-in,
   → opacity .5s ease, -webkit-transform
   → .25s ease-in-out 0;
   -moz-transition: color .25s ease-in,
   → opacity .5s ease, -moz-transform .25s
   → ease-in-out 0;
   -o-transition: color .25s ease-in,
   → opacity .5s ease, -o-transform .25s
   → ease-in-out 0;
   transition: color .25s ease-in,
   → opacity .5s ease, transform .25
   → ease-in-out 0;   }

div.gallery figure#f1:hover, div.gallery
figure#f2:hover, div.gallery figure#f3:hover {
   -webkit-transform: rotate(0);
   -moz-transform: rotate(0);
   -o-transform: rotate(0);
   transform: rotate(0);
   cursor: pointer; }
```

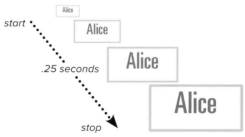

Ⓒ With the scale transform, the transition is through sizes.

TABLE 12.10 Transition Values

Value	e				O
<transition-property>	●10	◇16	◇	◇	◇
<transition-duration>	●10	◇16	◇	◇	◇
<transition-timing-function>	●10	◇16	◇	◇	◇
<transition-delay>	●10	●16	◇	◇	◇

TABLE 12.11 Transition-Property Values

Value	e				O
<CSSPropertyTransition>*	●10	◇16	◇	◇	◇
none	●10	◇16	◇	◇	◇
all	●10	◇16	◇	◇	◇

*See Table 12.9

TABLE 12.12 Transition-Duration Values

Value	e				O
<time>	●10	◇16	◇	◇	◇12.5

TABLE 12.13 Transition-Timing-Function Values

Value	How It Works
cubic-bezier (<number×4>,)	X and Y values are between 0 and 1 to define the shape of a bezier curve used for the timing function.
linear	Constant speed
ease	Gradual slowdown
ease-in	Speed up
ease-out	Slow down
ease-in-out	Speed up and then slow down

2. **Add values for each transition.**

`color .25s ease-in`

Choose from the following values (**Table 12.10**):

▸ A **transition-property** from **Table 12.11** indicates which specific CSS property is affected.

▸ **transition-duration** sets how long the transition should take from beginning to end, generally in seconds (**Table 12.12**). This is optional, and the default will be **0**.

▸ **transition-timing-function** defines the behavior of the transition's speed as it progresses (**Table 12.13**). This value is not required, and defaults to **linear** when not set.

▸ **transition-delay** specifies how long the duration should pause before starting (**Table 12.14**). This is optional and defaults to **0** if not set.

continues on next page

TABLE 12.14 Transition-Delay Values

Value	e				O
<time>	●10	◇16	◇	◇	◇12.5

3. Add more transitions as needed.

```
, opacity .5s ease, transform .25
→ ease-in-out 0;
```

You can add as many transitions as you want, separated by commas. If you are setting a transition for the **transform** value, be sure to use the browser extension version with the right transition browser extension, as shown here.

The example shown in this section uses the transition shorthand, but each of these properties can be set separately, using the **transition-property**, **transition-duration**, **transition-timing-function**, and **transition-delay** properties. Of course, you will need to set all of these properties independently for all three browser extensions as well as the standard CSS version, which can lead to a lot of code. Still, using these properties can be useful to override a particular value.

A Universal Transition

I added default transitions to the universal selector, applying these styles to *every* element on the screen. This ensures a consistent transition across my design and cuts down on the amount of code needed, since I apply it only once. You can then override the transitions, as necessary.

Putting It All Together

The completed code for *transition-properties.css* should look something like **Code 12.5**.

Code 12.5 Final *transition-properties.css*

```
/*** transition-properties.css ***/
aside, figure, a {
   -webkit-transition: color .25s ease-out, opacity .5s ease .1s, -webkit-transform .25s ease-in-out;
   -moz-transition: color .25s ease-out, opacity .5s ease .1s, -moz-transform .25s ease-in-out;
   -o-transition: color .25s ease-out, opacity .5s ease .1s, -o-transform .25s ease-in-out;
   transition: color .25s ease-out, opacity .5s ease .1s, transform .25 ease-in-out; }
aside {
   -webkit-transform: rotate(-2deg);
   -moz-transform: rotate(-2deg);
   -o-transform: rotate(-2deg);
   transform: rotate(-2deg); }
div.gallery {
   position: relative;
   width: 100%;
   display: block;
   overflow: visible;
   height: 300px; }
div.gallery figure:hover {
   opacity: 1;
   z-index: 999; }
div.gallery figure {
   position: absolute;
   opacity: .5;
   z-index: 0;
   width: auto;
   -webkit-transform-origin: left 25%;
   -moz-transform-origin: left 25%;
   transform-origin: left 25%;
   -webkit-transform-style: flat;
   -moz-transform-style: flat;
   transform-style: flat;
   -webkit-perspective: 5000;
   -moz-perspective: 5000;
   perspective: 5000;
   -webkit-perspective-origin: 25% 25%;
   -moz-perspective-origin: 25% 25%;
   perspective-origin: 25% 25%;
   -webkit-backface-visibility: visible;
   -moz-backface-visibility: visible;
   backface-visibility: visible; }
div.gallery figure#f1 {
   top: -60px;
```

code continues on next page

```
    left: -5%;
    -webkit-transform: scale(.5) rotate(10deg);
    -moz-transform: scale(.5) rotate(10deg);
    -o-transform: scale(.5) rotate(10deg);
    transform: scale(.5) rotate(10deg); }
div.gallery figure#f2 {
    top: 60px;
    left: 25%;
    -webkit-transform: perspective(250px) scale3d(.5,.75,1.5) rotate3d(-3,-3,-8,18deg);
    -moz-transform: perspective(250px) scale3d(.5,.75,1.5) rotate3d(-3,-3,-8,18deg);
    -o-transform: perspective(250px) scale3d(.5,.75,1.5) rotate3d(-3,-3,-8,18deg);
    transform: perspective(250px) scale3d(.5,.75,1.5) rotate3d(-3,-3,-8,18deg); }
div.gallery figure#f3 {
    right: -10%;
    -webkit-transform: scale(.75)rotate(3deg);
    -moz-transform: scale(.75)rotate(3deg);
    -o-transform: scale(.75) rotate(3deg);
    transform: scale(.75) rotate(3deg); }
div.gallery figure#f1:hover, div.gallery figure#f2:hover, div.gallery figure#f3:hover {
    -webkit-transform: rotate(0);
    -moz-transform: rotate(0);
    -o-transform: rotate(0);
    transform: rotate(0);
    cursor: pointer; }
aside, figure, a {
    -webkit-transition: color .25s ease-in, opacity .5s ease, -webkit-transform .25s ease-in-out 0;
    -moz-transition: color .25s ease-in, opacity .5s ease, -moz-transform .25s ease-in-out 0;
    -o-transition: color .25s ease-in, opacity .5s ease, -o-transform .25s ease-in-out 0;
    transition: color .25s ease-in, opacity .5s ease, transform .25 ease-in-out 0;  }
div.gallery figure#f1:hover, div.gallery figure#f2:hover, div.gallery figure#f3:hover {
    -webkit-transform: rotate(0);
    -moz-transform: rotate(0);
    -o-transform: rotate(0);
    transform: rotate(0);
    cursor: pointer; }
```

Why Add All of the Browser Extensions?

Notice that Code 12.5 is pretty extensive, mostly because we had to add several browser extensions. A lot of developers out there think, "No one's using Opera or Firefox, so, why bother? I'll just use Webkit." The fact is that both Opera and Firefox have an audience, and cutting them out is just rude. However, browser neglect is becoming a big enough problem that Mozilla, Opera, and even Microsoft are adding support for the Webkit extension. This is understandable from their standpoint, but bad news for developers who now will not know whether their code is being used in the right browser or not.

It takes only a few seconds to add fully compatible code. Don't be lazy. One day, all of this code will be available without browser extensions. Until then, *use them!*

Essential Design and Interface Techniques

There are a few critical recipes that every Web designer needs to know to begin putting their CSS skills to work. These applications of CSS have become so standard that they form the core of the vast majority of Web designs you will see.

Let's look at these core applications of CSS to create columns, style menus, and drop-down menus; and use CSS sprites.

Getting Started

This chapter uses Chapter 9 from *Alice's Adventures in Wonderland* with the styles added in Chapters 5–12. It also includes a table of contents in the **nav** tag and an aside to set up the columns for the layout.

Code 13.1 The HTML5 code you'll be playing with in this chapter Ⓐ.

```
<!DOCTYPE html>
<html lang="en">
<head>
<meta charset="utf-8">
<title>Alice&#8217;s Adventures In Wonderland | Chapter IX</title>
<link href="../css/font-properties.css" type="text/css" rel="stylesheet" media="all">
<link href="../css/text-properties.css" type="text/css" rel="stylesheet" media="all">
<link href="../css/color-background-properties.css" type="text/css" rel="stylesheet" media="all">
<link href="../css/list-table-properties.css" type="text/css" rel="stylesheet" media="all">
<link href="../css/ui-generatedcontent-properties.css" type="text/css" rel="stylesheet" media="all">
<link href="../css/box-properties.css" type="text/css" rel="stylesheet" media="all">
<link href="../css/visualformatting-properties.css" type="text/css" rel="stylesheet" media="all">
<link href="../css/transformation-transition-properties.css" type="text/css" rel="stylesheet"
  media="all">
<link href="../css/design-interface.css" type="text/css" rel="stylesheet" media="all">
</head>
<body id="chapter9" class="book aaiw chapter">
<header class="page">
<hgroup>
    <h1>Alice&#8217;s Adventures in Wonderland</h1>
    <h2>By <cite>Lewis Carroll</cite></h2>
</hgroup>
</header>
<section>
<nav class="toc">
<ul class="menu">
<li><h2>Table of Contents</h2></li>
<ol class="drop">
<li><a href="AAIWL-ch01.html">Down the Rabbit-hole</a></li>
<li><a href="AAIWL-ch02.html">The Pool of Tears</a></li>
<li><a href="AAIWL-ch03.html">A Caucus-race and a Long Tale</a></li>
<li><a href="AAIWL-ch04.html">The Rabbit sends in a Little Bill</a></li>
<li><a href="AAIWL-ch05.html">Advice from a Caterpillar</a></li>
<li><a href="AAIWL-ch06.html">Pig and Pepper</a></li>
<li><a href="AAIWL-ch07.html">A Mad Tea-party</a></li>
<li><a href="AAIWL-ch08.html">The Queen's Croquet-ground</a></li>
<li><a href="AAIWL-ch09.html">The Mock Turtle's Story</a></li>
<li><a href="AAIWL-ch010.html">The Lobster Quadrille</a></li>
<li><a href="AAIWL-ch011.html">Who Stole the Tarts?</a></li>
```

code continues on next page

Code 13.1 *continued*

```html
<li><a href="AAIWL-ch012.html">Alice&#8217;s
 Evidence</a></li>
</ol>
</ul>
</nav>
<article>
<h2>Chapter IX
<span class="chaptertitle">The Mock Turtle's
 Story</span>
</h2>
<p>"You can't think how glad I am to see
 you again, you dear old thing!" said
 the Duchess, as she tucked her arm
 affectionately into Alice&#8217;s, and
 they walked off together.</p>
<p>Alice was <a href="#">very glad to find
 her</a> in such a pleasant temper, and
 thought to herself that perhaps it was only
 the pepper that had made her so savage
 when they met in the kitchen.</p>

...

<p>"That's enough about lessons," the Gryphon
 interrupted in a very decided tone: "tell
 her something about the games now."</p>
</article>
<aside>
<h2>About the Author</h2>
    <p><b><a href="#">Charles Lutwidge
 Dodgson</a></b> (7 January 1832 - 14
 January 1898), better known by the
 pseudonym Lewis Carroll...</p>
</aside>
</section>
<footer>
Illustrator: Arthur Rackham
</footer>
</body>
</html>
```

Ⓐ The Web page (**Code 13.1**) without any styles applied to it. The content is all stacked vertically.

Creating Multicolumn Layouts with Float

The most common way to lay out a page is by establishing a grid, which is generally made up of two or more columns **A**. This allows the designer to present multiple sources of information and functionality in the same horizontal plane, making better use of the screen and reducing the need to scroll.

Although not explicitly intended to perform this duty, the **float** property (discussed in Chapter 10) is now the standard method for creating a grid structure of columns in most modern Web designs. This is done by taking block level elements—elements that would normally flow *vertically*—and "floating" them next to each other so that they flow *horizontally* **B**.

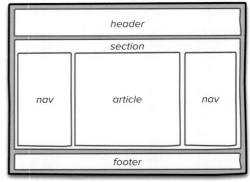

A The basic wireframe for your page showing the three columns within the surrounding section element.

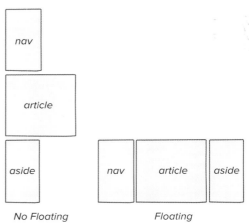

B When floating is applied, the columns flow horizontally next to each other.

Code 13.2 Added to *design-interface.css*—Creates columns when applied to Code 13.1 **C**. In addition to a simple CSS reset, the layout code sets the width of the total page, along with the width and padding of each column (for a fixed-width page this must equal the overall width of the page), and then floats the three columns so that they horizontally flow next to each other rather than stacking.

```
/*** design-interface.css ***/

/* Column Layout
---------------------------------------------------------------- */
header.page, section, footer.page {
   clear: both;
   margin: 0 auto;
   min-width: 980px;
   width: 100%; }
section {
   width: 1280px; }
nav.toc, article, aside {
   position: relative;
   float: left; }
nav.toc:hover, aside:hover {
   z-index: 99; }
nav.toc {
   background: rgb(242, 237, 217) url(../images/chrome/paper-01.jpg) repeat 0 0;
   box-shadow: 1px 1px 5px 1px rgba(0,0,0,.25) inset, 3px 3px 15px rgba(0,0,0,.5);
   padding: 0;
   top: 150px;
   width: 270px;
   z-index: 1;
   -webkit-transform: rotate(2deg);
   -moz-transform: rotate(2deg);
   -o-transform: rotate(2deg);
   transform: rotate(2deg); }
nav.toc ol, nav.toc ul, nav.toc li {
   background: none;
   list-style: none;
   list-style-position: outside;
   margin: 0;
   margin-left: 1em;
   padding: 1em 0;
   width: 100%; }
nav.toc li, nav.toc li li {
   background: none;
   margin: 0;
   padding: 1em 0;
   width: 95%; }
article {
   margin-left: -5%;
   min-width: 480px;
   max-width: 580px;
   z-index: 1; }
aside {
   opacity: 1;
   right: 40px;
   width: 200px;
   z-index: 0; }
```

To set up a multicolumn layout using CSS:

1. **Add rules to define the width of your content area(s).** This is a container around your columns that will help hold them together regardless of the width of the browser window. I like to use the `section` tag to define it (**Code 13.2**). Generally, it involves defining a width for the site's header and footer, as well as the section into which you will add the articles.

   The widths will depend on a number of factors:

   ▸ **Fluid design:** If you are using a fluid grid, you will be setting your width in relative units, most likely a percentage.

   With a fluid design, you need to set the minimum width (using absolute units such as pixels) to which the content can be squeezed before vertical scrolling is needed. You may also want to set the maximum width to which the content can stretch; otherwise text columns will grow so wide that they'll become hard to read.

   ▸ **Fixed design:** When you want a fixed-width design, use absolute units (inches, cms, pixels, and so on). If you have a defined layout grid (highly recommended), then you should consider how wide the grid is and the number of columns it will contain.

   Regardless of whether you are using a fluid or fixed design, you will want to tailor column widths to the target device, as described in Chapter 14.

   ```
   header.site, section,
   → footer.site {...}
   ```

Ⓒ **Code 13.2 applied to Code 13.1.** The columns now line up horizontally and we can see all three columns at once.

2. **Set the `float` property for your columns.** Most columns use a **`float:left`** but **`float:right`** or a combination will work, depending on your needs.

   `nav, article, aside {...}`

   Remember to use one of the float fixes, outlined in this chapter, if you see strange things happening with your box backgrounds and borders.

3. **Set the column widths.** Until these widths are set, the columns will stretch the full width of the parent elements (**`section`**) and not actually float next to each other. Additionally, you will want to set margins and any padding. So you will set a separate width using conditional styles as explained in Chapter 12:

   `nav {...}, article {...}, aside {...}`

TIP My general rule of thumb is to leave one to five pixels or 1 to 2% (for fluid columns) as a "fudge factor" between floated elements. The difference between columns that float and rows stacked on each other can literally come down to a single pixel. However, you will need to test your design on multiple browsers at multiple window sizes to find the exact fudge factor for your design.

TIP When you are using padding, you will run afoul of the box model problem in Internet Explorer explained in the sidebar "Fixing the Box Model for Older Versions of Internet Explorer."

TIP Although I used three columns here, you can add as many columns as you want. Just add more `<aside>` or `<div>` elements with the `float` property and adjust your column.

Fixing the Float

CSS has a nasty little bug that was apparently meant to be a feature: When you float block-level elements within a block-level element (see Chapter 10 for more information), the child elements do not take up any space in their parent  . Make no mistake, the child elements are still on the Web page where you expect them to be; but if you add a background or border to their parent, the parent's box appears to collapse as if no content were present! Believe it or not, this was done on purpose by the browser developers as a response to the CSS specification, but it can be incredibly annoying when you are trying to set up columns.

The problem is that floating elements are taken out of the normal flow of the document so, in effect, nothing anchors the bottom of the element and identifies where the bottom is. Later in this chapter I'll show you how to float two elements next to each other to create a columnar layout. But to make them work effectively, you first need to learn the following techniques.

Several solutions have been developed to combat this little "feature" and force the parent element to acknowledge all of its prodigal children **B** . But I find two solutions to be most reliable. The first is structural in the HTML; the other is pure and simple CSS.

Ⓐ Without a fix, the parent element (article) rolls up like a cheap newspaper, leaving its child elements high and dry.

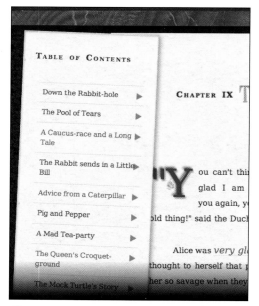

Ⓑ With the fix in place, the parent is there to protect its children.

Code 13.3 The **break** tag clearfix involves adding a new structural element (the **break** tag) to the bottom of the parent element to clear the floating and snap the parent open. The overflow fix requires that you add the overflow property to the parent's selector, in this case the **section** tag, to display everything as it should be.

```
/*** design-interface.css ***/
/* Float Fixes
-------------------------------------------- */
.clearfix { clear: both; }
section { overflow: auto; }
```

Using a break tag "clearall" fix

The float problem is caused when an element is floating and its last child in an element is floating. As a result, the parent can't see its bottom. The most common method for fixing the float problem is to clear floating at the bottom of the element (following all of the elements that are floated within it) so the parent will open to its natural height.

To do this, we create a special "clearfix" class that we can use with any element—most commonly a **break** tag—to force an end to the float.

To add the clearfix:

1. Create a class in your CSS called `clearfix`. This class will include the single declaration to clear all floating (**Code 13.3**):

   `.clearfix { clear: both; }`

2. Add the `clearfix` class to an HTML tag at the bottom of every parent element that contains floating elements. You could also just add a **break** tag with the class at the bottom of every floating element. This class will clear floating, and the element will snap to its natural height:

   `<br class="clearfix">`

   TIP Although I've used `clearfix` here for the specific purpose of fixing the floating box problem, this class can be applied anywhere you want to clear floating.

   TIP Although extremely popular, this trick tends to litter the page with a lot of breaks with `clearfix` class.

Using an overflow fix

The second method for preventing a parent element from collapsing is so simple that if it weren't so important, it would hardly be worth mentioning: To restore the element's height, just set the parent `overflow`. That's it. You can even set the element overflow to `auto`. Apparently setting `overflow` reminds the element to accommodate its children.

To add the overflow fix:

1. **For any element that is collapsing, add the `overflow` property.** You can set the value to anything, including the default value **auto**, to restore the parent to its proper height (Code 13.3):

   ```
   overflow: auto;
   ```

2. **Set up your parent element with floating children.** As long as the parent element includes the **overflow** declaration, you are safe.

   ```
   <section>...</section>
   ```

> **TIP** While you could just set the `overflow` property using the universal selector, I find that this can lead to some problems, as some browsers will throw in scrollbars everywhere, even when there isn't any overflow.

> **TIP** You may notice a little trick I used to center the numbers in the blocks horizontally (easy) and also vertically. Horizontal is achieved by adding `text-align: center`. Vertical is done by setting the line-weight to be the same value as the height of the box. As long as only a single line of text is present, it will stay vertically centered in the element.

Fixing the Box Model for Older Versions of Internet Explorer

All elements are rectangular "boxes" with a margin, border, padding, and content that has a width and height. But remember that this is Web design—it can never be that simple, right?

Right. For a long time, Internet Explorer didn't follow the same rules for calculating the box size that other browsers did.

The W3C definition of a box created using CSS specifies that the width and height define the width and height of only the content area where images and other objects are displayed. However, the *total* area that the element occupies includes the content area *plus* the padding and border sizes. So, the apparent width would be calculated in the following way:

width(content) + left padding + right padding + left border + right border = width (total)

Unfortunately, Internet Explorer through version 5.5 defined width and height values as the apparent width and height including padding and borders. This effectively subtracted the padding and border sizes to determine the content width and height:

width(total) – left padding – right padding – left border – right border = width (content)

So, given the following CSS code:

```
#object1 {
border: 5px solid #000;
padding: 10px;
width: 100px;
}
```

Browsers using the W3C standard (Firefox, Safari, Opera) would set the content area to 100 pixels wide but have a total width of 130 pixels:

100 + 5 + 5 + 10 + 10 = 130

On the other hand, Internet Explorer 5.5 and earlier would set the total width of the element (from border to border) as 100 pixels, shrinking the width of the content to 70 pixels:

100 – 5 – 5 – 10 – 10 = 70

Internet Explorer versions 6 and later fix this problem by following the W3C standards. So you are probably wondering why I'm even mentioning this. A problem can pop up in later versions of IE. When you are using the transitional document type definition (DTD) for your page, which is still very common—or a DTD that the browsers do not recognize, such as HTML5—IE6 and IE7 revert to the "quirky" version of the box model. Unfortunately, more often than not, your site will probably trigger IE's "quirks" mode.

sidebar continues on next page

Fixing the Box Model for Older Versions of Internet Explorer *(continued)*

So what's a good Web designer to do? You have a few options:

- Do not use a border and/or padding with any element that has a set dimension. If you do, don't expect pixel-precise layouts. Generally, this solution isn't practical, but for simple pages it might do the trick.

- Code for the strict DTD so that the browser uses the standards-compliant box model. Generally, this approach is not practical because the slightest error can return the browser to quirks mode and destroy the whole design.

- Use conditional CSS (explained in Chapter 14 to code separate "equalizing" widths and/or heights for older versions of Internet Explorer.

Because IE7 and earlier now make up less than five percent of the browsers currently in use worldwide, this problem increasingly becomes a moot point, but you may still run across it from time to time. Interestingly, a new CSS3 property under discussion, **box-sizing**, explained in Chapter 10, will allow you to choose which of these box models you want to use. This gives *you* control over which method gets used.

Styling Links vs. Navigation

The Web is nothing without links. Many designers are content to rely on default browser styles applied to their links; but this is not only boring, it also makes all the links on your page look exactly the same, whether they are global navigation or content links.

Styling links using pseudo-classes was covered in Chapter 4, but to bring your navigation to life, you need to style your links depending on the context.

To style navigation and links:

1. **Style the default link styles.** In the *design-interface.css* file, add rules for the anchor tag and its **:link**, **:visited**, **:hover**, and **:active** states (**Code 13.4**).

   ```
   a {...}
   a:link {...}
   a:visited {...}
   a:hover {...}
   a:active {...}
   ```

   I recommend setting text decoration to "none" to eliminate the unattractive underlining. You can then add link underlining using the **border-bottom** property as needed.

   continues on next page

2. **Style specific hypertext link styles such as paragraphs, lists, and tables.** Links in paragraphs need a little extra attention because they are surrounded by other text.

    ```
    p a {...}
    p a:link {...}
    p a:visited {...}
    p a:hover {...}
    p a:active {...}
    ```

    In addition to color, some options to differentiate hypertext from text include:

    ▸ **Underline** using `border-bottom` to control the style, thickness, and color of the underline.

    ▸ **Italics or bold** to give the linked text extra style or weight.

    ▸ **A background color or image to create a highlight effect.** See "Using CSS Sprites" in this chapter.

    ▸ Increase size slightly.

3. **Style the navigation links.** Navigation links are most commonly set up as a list to allow the links to appear in a list even if CSS is present (See "Designing with Progressive Enhancements" in Chapter 14.)

    ```
    nav.toc .menu a {...}
    ```

    These are the basic styles applied to the navigation links, but you are not quite done styling the menu itself. You'll get to that in the next two sections.

Ⓐ Shows the Web page (**Code 13.1**) when the *design-interface.css* (**Code 13.4**) styles are added. The difference between hypertext links in paragraphs and navigation links in the menu are now clear.

Code 13.4 Added to *design-interface.css*—Styles the links in Code 13.1, with a default link style applied to all link (**a**) elements, and special styles applied for links in paragraphs and links used for navigation Ⓐ.

```
/*** design-interface.css ***/

/* Default Link Styles
---------------------------------------------------------- */
a {
   text-decoration: none; }
a:link {
   color: rgb(204,0,0); }
a:visited {
   color: rgb(153,0,0); }
a:hover {
   color: rgb(255,0,0); }
a:active {
   color: rgb(0,255,255); }

/* Contextual Link Styles

---------------------------------------------------------- */
p a {
   font-style: italic;
   font-size: 1.2em;}
p a:link, p a:visited {
   border-bottom: 1px dotted rgb(255,153,153); }
p a:hover, p a:active {
   background-color: rgb(255,235,235);
   border-bottom: 1px solid rgb(255,102,102); }

/* Menu Link Styles
---------------------------------------------------------- */
nav.toc .menu a {
   display: block;
   padding: 10px;
   width: 100%;
   height:100%; }
nav.toc .menu a:link, nav.toc .menu a:visted {
   color: rgb(153,0,0); }
nav.toc .menu a:hover {
   color: rgb(255,255,255); }
nav.toc .menu a:active {
   color: rgb(153,0,0); }
nav.toc .menu {
   display: block;
   position: relative;
   height: auto;
   width: 230px;
   cursor: pointer; }
nav.toc .menu .drop {
   display: block;
   position: relative;
   width: auto; }
```

Using CSS Sprites

The *CSS sprite* technique lets you create a single image that contains the different states used for buttons, menus, or interface controls using dynamic pseudo-classes. In that file, you place all of the individual sprites that make up your button, separated by enough space so that they don't run into each other. You then call this image as the background for an element, and set the background position property (using negative values to move the background up and/or left) to position the correct sprite. Because only one image must load, the browser needs to make only one server call, which speeds up your site.

For example, in your menu from the previous section, it might be nice to place a pointer icon to the right of the options to show that you will be loading a new page. The sprite includes all three versions of the icon for all three dynamic states.

To add CSS image rollovers to a Web page:

1. **Create an image with the different dynamic states for your icon.** You will create icons for each of the dynamic states you need (default, hover, and active, in this example) all in the same image file, separated by a small amount of space and name it *sprite-pointer.png* 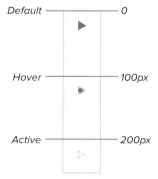. Generally, you will want to regularly space the states' positions, making them easy to remember. For example, I set the top of each graphic at intervals of 100 pixels.

Default ———————— 0

Hover ———————— *100px*

Active ———————— *200px*

A *sprite-pointer.png*—The image used to create the multiple states used for the arrow. They are arranged at regular intervals to help you more quickly and accurately switch them.

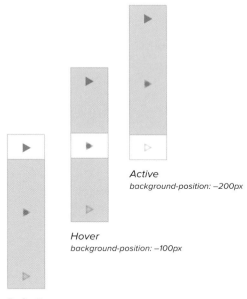

Active
background-position: –200px

Hover
background-position: –100px

Default
background-position: 0

B Shows your Web page (**Code 13.1**) when the *design-interface.css* (**Code 13.5**) styles are included.

2. **Add the sprite to the element you are using as a control (Code 13.5).**

   ```
   nav.toc .menu .drop li {...}
   ```

3. **Set the background image to not repeat.** You will need to set the horizontal position to left or right and then adjust the vertical position up (negative values) or down (positive values) as needed for appearance.

   ```
   background: transparent
    url('../_images/sprite-pointer.
    png') no-repeat right 10px;
   ```

   Although this is a link, you are using the list element to add your sprite because this provides better control over positioning. However, sprites work just as well on links, lists, or any other element.

continues on next page

Code 13.5 added to *design-interface.css*—When applied to your Web page (**Code 13.1**), this code adds a graphic arrow to the menu, providing visual interaction as the visitor uses the menu and further differentiating that link style **B**.

```
/*** design-interface.css ***/

/* CSS Sprites
---------------------------------------------------------- */
nav.toc .menu .drop li {
    font-size: .875em;
    border-top: 1px solid rgb(204,204,204);
    background: transparent url('../images/chrome/sprite-pointer.png') no-repeat right 10px;
    margin: 0;
    padding: 0;
    padding-right: 20px;  }
nav.toc .menu .drop li:hover {
    background-color: rgb(102,0,0);
    background-position: right -90px;   }
nav.toc .menu .drop li:active {
    background-color: rgb(255,255,255);
    background-position: right -190px; } }
```

4. **Move the background image up or down, depending on the state.** Add rules for all the link states (`:link`, `:visited`, `:hover`, `:active`, and `:focus`), setting the **background-position** property with the correct vertical offset values to display the relevant rollover state.

```
nav.toc .menu .drop li:hover {...},
→ nav.toc .menu .drop li:active
→ {...}
```

For example, the visited state would use:

```
background-position: right -100px;
```

So only the visited button state is shown 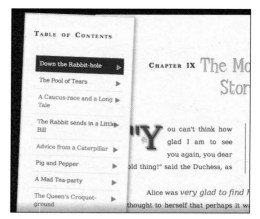.

C With the height of the element set, only a part of the background image is revealed, hiding the rest. By changing the background position within the element, it appears as if the image has changed.

TIP You can, of course, include any other style changes you want. In this example, I'm also changing the background color.

TIP The concept (and the last part of the name) of CSS sprites originated in the early days of video games, when memory and speed were at a premium. To overcome system limitations, video game producers would lay out the thousands of small graphics used to create the game into a grid and then display each sprite as needed, masking out all but the needed part of the larger image.

TIP The example here is a simple one, but it's possible to place dozens, hundreds, or more images on a single sprite to cut down on server requests and speed up your site.

A Code 13.6 applied to Code 13.1. Initially, the menu is hidden.

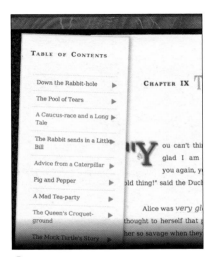

B When the user hovers a pointer over the menu header, the menu drops down and is ready for the user to select a menu option.

Creating a CSS Drop-Down Menu

Drop-down menus are a standard way to reduce navigation noise, allowing you to present a lot of links in a little space. Although generally thought of as the domain of JavaScript, drop-down menus can also be achieved using only a little bit of CSS.

To make a pure CSS drop-down menu:

1. **Hide the drop-down menu.** To show the menu—"dropping" it down—you first need to hide it (**Code 13.6**). Give it a triple whammy by setting its height to 0, overflow to hidden, and opacity to completely transparent.

   ```
   nav.toc .menu .drop {...}
   ```

   continues on next page

Code 13.6 Added to *design-interface.css*—When applied to your Web page (Code 13.1), this collapses the menu, leaving only a menu label **A**, which when the pointer hovers over it, expands the menu to full height **B**.

```
/*** design-interface.css ***/
/* Drop Menu
----------------------------------------------------------- */
nav.toc .menu .drop {
    overflow: hidden;
    height: 0;
    opacity: 0; }
nav.toc .menu:hover>.drop {
    height: auto;
    opacity: 1; }
```

2. **Set the drop menu to appear when the user's pointer hovers over it.** When the pointer hovers over any part of the menu—including the title at the top— set the height to auto and opacity to opaque. You can also couple this with a transition to create a more subtle opening effect.

```
nav.toc .menu:hover>.drop {...}
```

TIP It would be cool if the menu could use a transition to unroll from 0 to the menu's full height. You could do this if you knew the exact height of the menu, but this is rarely the case, especially in a dynamic Web site.

TIP Because this trick relies on the child selector, it will not work in IE6, so you will need to either show the menu (using conditional CSS to set display and opacity) or make other navigational arrangements.

Preventing Navigation Noise

One of my chief gripes about most Web sites is the overabundance of unorganized links. You've probably seen sites with long lists of links that stretch off the window. These links add visual noise to the design and waste precious screen space without assisting navigation.

Web surfers rarely take the time to read an entire Web page. Instead, they scan for relevant information. But human beings can process only so much information at a time. If a Web page is cluttered, visitors must wade through dozens or hundreds of links to find the one path to the information they desire.

Anything designers can do to aid visitors' abilities to scan a page, such as organizing links in lists and hiding sublinks until they're needed, will improve the Web site's usability. Drop-down, sliding, and collapsible menus are a great way to organize your page and prevent navigation noise.

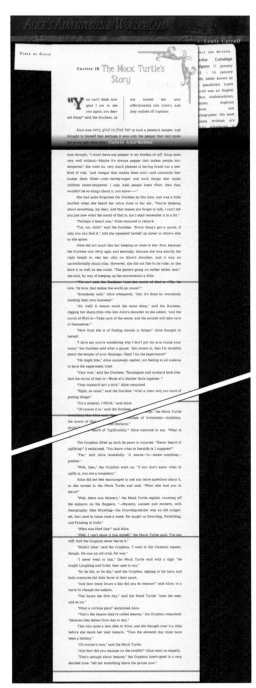

A Code 13.7 applied to **Code 13.1**.

Putting It All Together

Code 13.7 shows the final version of design-interface.css.

Code 13.7 Added to *design-interface.css*—When applied to your Web page (Code 13.1), the final results are three columns **A**.

```
/*** design-interface.css ***/

/* Column Layout
-------------------------------------------------- */
header.page, section, footer.page {
    clear: both;
    margin: 0 auto;
    min-width: 980px;
    width: 100%; }
section {
    width: 1280px; }
nav.toc, article, aside {
    position: relative;
    float: left; }
nav.toc:hover, aside:hover {
    z-index: 99; }
nav.toc {
    background: rgb(242, 237, 217) url(../
      images/chrome/paper-01.jpg) repeat 0 0;
    -shadow: 1px 1px 5px 1px rgba(0,0,0,.25)
      inset, 3px 3px 15px rgba(0,0,0,.5);
    padding: 0;
    top: 150px;
    left: 20px;
    width: 270px;
    z-index: 0;
    -webkit-transform: rotate(2deg);
    -moz-transform: rotate(2deg);
    -o-transform: rotate(2deg);
    transform: rotate(2deg); }
nav.toc ol, nav.toc ul, nav.toc li {
    background: none;
    list-style: none;
    list-style-position: outside;
    margin: 0;
    margin-left: 1em;
    padding: 1em 0;
    width: 100%; }
nav.toc li, nav.toc li li {
    background: none;
    margin: 0;
```

code continues on next page

```
      padding: 1em 0;
      width: 92%; }
   article {
      margin-left: -5%;
      min-width: 480px;
      max-width: 580px;
      z-index: 1; }
   aside {
      opacity: 1;
      right: 40px;
      width: 200px;
      z-index: 0;
   }


   /* Float Fixes
   --------------------------------------------- */
   .clearfix { clear: both; }
   section { overflow: auto; }


   /* Default Link Styles
   --------------------------------------------- */
   a {
      text-decoration: none; }
   a:link {
      color: rgb(204,0,0); }
   a:visited {
      color: rgb(153,0,0); }
   a:hover {
      color: rgb(255,0,0); }
   a:active {
      color: rgb(0,255,255); }

   /* Contextual Link Styles
   --------------------------------------------- */
   p a {
      font-style: italic;
      font-size: 1.2em;}
   p a:link, p a:visited {
      border-bottom: 1px dotted rgb(255,153,153); }

   p a:hover, p a:active {
      background-color: rgb(255,235,235);
      border-bottom: 1px solid rgb(255,102,102); }

   /* Menu Link Styles
   --------------------------------------------- */
   nav.toc .menu a {
      display: block;
```

code continues in next column

```
      padding: 10px;
      width: 100%;
      height:100%; }
   nav.toc .menu a:link, nav.toc .menu a:visted {
      color: rgb(153,0,0); }
   nav.toc .menu a:hover {
      color: rgb(255,255,255); }
   nav.toc .menu a:active {
      color: rgb(153,0,0); }
   nav.toc .menu {
      display: block;
      position: relative;
      height: auto;
      width: 230px;
      cursor: pointer; }
   nav.toc .menu .drop {
      display: block;
      position: relative;
      width: auto; }

   /* CSS Sprites
   --------------------------------------------- */

   nav.toc .menu .drop li {
      font-size: .875em;
      border-top: 1px solid rgb(204,204,204);
      background: transparent url('../images/
   ↪ chrome/sprite-pointer.png') no-repeat
   ↪ right 10px;
      margin: 0;
      padding: 0;
      padding-right: 20px;   }

   nav.toc .menu .drop li:hover {
      background-color: rgb(102,0,0);
      background-position: right -90px;     }

   nav.toc .menu .drop li:active {
      background-color: rgb(255,255,255);
      background-position: right -190px; }

   /* Drop Menu
   --------------------------------------------- */

   nav.toc .menu .drop {
      overflow: hidden;
      height: 0;
      opacity: 0; }
   nav.toc .menu:hover>.drop {
      height: auto;
      opacity: 1; }
```

Responsive Web Design

Web design is at a crossroads. For most of this book, I showed designs and examples presented in a computer-based browser. However, more and more web content is being delivered to smart phone- and tablet-based browsers. It may surprise you to learn that web surfing via these mobile devices may soon overtake and surpass the computer. For Web designers, the problem is that one size does not fit all.

You can use several strategies to deal with the various devices—ignoring them is not a viable strategy—but the best of these solutions is simply to use the same HTML code with layout and content adjusted using CSS and media queries.

In this chapter, you'll learn the basic techniques for responsive design, including resetting styles, adjusting CSS for Internet Explorer, and how to easily adjust your page design to fit the device it is delivered to.

In This Chapter

Getting Started

This chapter uses Chapter 10 from *Alice's Adventures in Wonderland* with the styles added in Chapters 5–13. It includes the Table of Contents and the aside that you placed in columns in Chapter 13. Now we'll need to figure out how they are treated when the screen size is smaller.

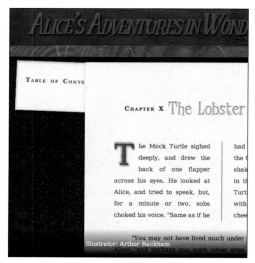

A The Web page (**Code 14.1**) before responsive design is applied.

B When the page width is reduced, the design simply scrolls horizontally off the page.

Code 14.1 The HTML5 code you'll be using in this chapter **A** **B**.

```
<!DOCTYPE html>
<html lang="en">
<head>
<meta charset="utf-8">
<title>Alice&#8217;s Adventures In Wonderland | Chapter X</title>

</head>
<body id="chapter10" class="book aaiw chapter">
<header class="page">
<hgroup>
    <h1>Alice&#8217;s Adventures in Wonderland</h1>
    <h2>By <cite>Lewis Carroll</cite></h2>
</hgroup>
</header>
<section>
<nav class="toc">
<ul class="menu">
<li><h2>Table of Contents</h2></li>
<ol class="drop">
<li><a href="AAIWL-ch01.html">Down the Rabbit-hole</a></li>
<li><a href="AAIWL-ch02.html">The Pool of Tears</a></li>
<li><a href="AAIWL-ch03.html">A Caucus-race and a Long Tale</a></li>
```

code continues on next page

```
<li><a href="AAIWL-ch04.html">The Rabbit sends in a Little Bill</a></li>
<li><a href="AAIWL-ch05.html">Advice from a Caterpillar</a></li>
<li><a href="AAIWL-ch06.html">Pig and Pepper</a></li>
<li><a href="AAIWL-ch07.html">A Mad Tea-party</a></li>
<li><a href="AAIWL-ch08.html">The Queen's Croquet-ground</a></li>
<li><a href="AAIWL-ch09.html">The Mock Turtle's Story</a></li>
<li><a href="AAIWL-ch010.html">The Lobster Quadrille</a></li>
<li><a href="AAIWL-ch011.html">Who Stole the Tarts?</a></li>
<li><a href="AAIWL-ch012.html">Alice&#8217;s Evidence</a></li>
</ol>
</ul>
</nav>

<article>
<h2>Chapter X
<span class="chaptertitle">The Lobster Quadrille</span>
</h2>

<p>The Mock Turtle sighed deeply, and drew the back of one flapper across his eyes. He looked at
→ Alice, and tried to speak, but, for a minute or two, sobs choked his voice. "Same as if he had
→ a bone in his throat," said the Gryphon: and it set to work shaking him and punching him in the
→ back. At last the Mock Turtle recovered his voice, and, with tears running down his cheeks, went
→ on again:</p>
...
</article>

<aside>
<h2>About the Author</h2>
    <p><b><a href="#">Charles Lutwidge Dodgson</a></b> (7 January 1832 – 14 January 1898), better
    → known by the pseudonym Lewis Carroll was an English author, mathematician, logician, Anglican
    → deacon and photographer. His most famous writings are Alice's Adventures in Wonderland and
    → its sequel Through the Looking-Glass, as well as the poems "The Hunting of the Snark" and
    → "Jabberwocky", all examples of the genre of literary nonsense. He is noted for his facility
    → at word play, logic, and fantasy, and there are societies in many parts of the world (including
    → the United Kingdom, Japan, the United States, and New Zealand) dedicated to the enjoyment and
    → promotion of his works and the investigation of his life.</p>
</aside>
</section>
<footer>
Illustrator: Arthur Rackham
</footer>
</body>
</html>
```

What Is Responsive Design?

Clearly, a one-for-all strategy will not work 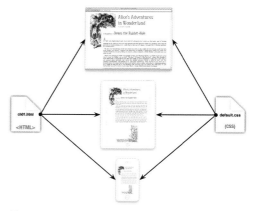. A layout that works in one device may become cramped and unusable in another. Instead, our design must be *responsive,* changing as needed based on the user's context as generally determined by the device she is using and its available screen resolution. Most responsive designs will then use *break points* where the interface needs to radically change for different contexts and adapt to make smaller adjustments for specific devices ⑧.

To do this, we'll use media queries to "ask" the device about itself, and then deliver styles accordingly ⓒ. The server will contain an assortment of style sheets, which are then assembled to match the capabilities of the device.

The approach that is often called "responsive design" is actually a combination of techniques used to create Web pages that optimize themselves to the end user's environment, regardless of her browser, version, or device.

A responsive design includes:

■ **Progressive enhancement**: This is not a specific code to be deployed, but a general design philosophy that you will need to apply to your development decisions. It's built on the idea that designs should scale up or down depending on the environment they are displayed in.

Ⓐ One size does not fit all. The style sheet that looks good on a computer screen does not look as good on a tablet or smart-phone.

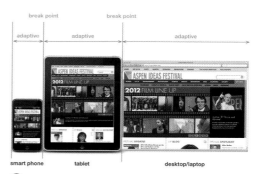

Ⓑ Responsive design uses break points when the interface needs to change radically, and adaptive design to make minor adjustments for different devices.

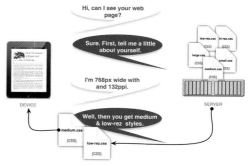

Ⓒ Small, medium, or large? Let the device tell you.

- **Resetting styles**: To ensure that the default browser styles interfere as little as possible with the end design, we will manually reset margins, padding, and other default style values. This has to be done only once per site, but ensures better conformity across all browsers and devices.

- **Conditional styles for Internet Explorer**: Although recent versions of Internet Explorer have come a long way in adopting CSS standards, you may need to adjust your design for older IE versions.

- **Adaptive styles**: Adaptive styles replace pixel perfection with more fluid relative sizes, allowing the layout to stretch and shrink within the confines of the screen dimensions. For example, you would need to make interface changes between an iPhone and an iPad because they have substantially different contexts. However, an iPhone and an Android smart phone share similar contexts, so you could maintain similar designs; but their exact sizes may vary, requiring some design adaptation.

- **Break points**: Adaptive styles get you only so far. Responsive design uses specific break points at which point the design is more radically adjusted, generally between small devices (such as smart phones), medium devices (tablets), large devices (computer monitors), and extra-large devices (high-definition televisions).

Designing with Progressive Enhancements

It's clear that not all browsers are created equal, so why should we expect all Web sites to treat them that way? For years Web designers have tried to design to the lowest common denominator (such as Internet Explorer), and ignore new features in the belief that they had to create the same, pixel-perfect experience in all browsers.

Pixel perfection is a user-experience philosophy that dictates that a Web design must look exactly the same on every version of every browser.

In contrast, *progressive enhancement* is a design philosophy that recommends using newer technologies (such as CSS3) even though the design may not look exactly the same in every browser. What's more important is that on every target device, the design ultimately looks as good as possible with as little extra design and coding work as possible Ⓐ Ⓑ.

How does it work?

Using progressive enhancement is critical when designing across multiple browsers and across multiple devices, because when it comes to designing for smart phones and tablets, the desire to create pixel-perfect designs can actually be counter-productive. Responsive design relies on the fact that the designs will automatically adjust to devices.

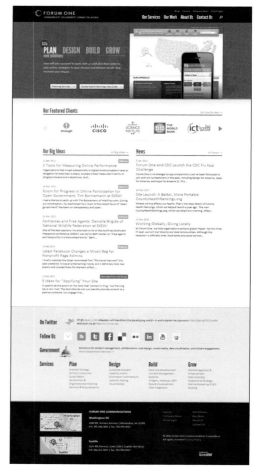

Ⓐ Forum One uses progressive enhancement to style its pages using CSS to add rounded corners to buttons, gradients, and shadows. This is how forumone.com looks in Chrome.

B This is the same page in Internet Explorer 7. Notice that the buttons are no longer rounded and that the gradient is missing from the bottom of the portfolio image. These small touches add texture to the design, but are not essential to the site's content or functionality.

However, designing this way will take some special considerations. I recommend that you follow these simple guidelines:

- **Basic content is accessible to all browsers**: A design may look different from browser to browser and device to device, but all of the same content is available, regardless of its presentation. However, be careful not to add styles that will prevent content from appearing. For example, you might think it looks cool to put white text on a white background with a text-shadow to make it pop. But what happens when the browser does not support text shadows? The text disappears.

- **Basic functionality is accessible to all browsers**: An interaction may not act exactly the same in all contexts, but the user can perform a function with the same outcome. For example, you can enhance menus with CSS transitions, drop-downs, and other flourishes; just make sure that every user can still use the same navigation.

- **Enhanced *layout* is provided by externally linked CSS**: The content should be kept separate from the code used to style it. In other words, always place all styles in external style sheets (see Chapter 3).

- **The end user's *styles* should be honored**: Many Web surfers have customized styles set for their browser—often because of vision impairments—that allow them to use the Web most effectively. You shouldn't get in the way of those styles.

Graceful degradation

This means that you can use styles like border-radius, box-shadow, text-shadow, and others that may not work in older browsers, as long as they do not prevent the user from using the site and all of its functionality when they *do not* appear. The design may not look equally polished in all situations, but the site still performs all necessary tasks.

Graceful degradation might require you to use conditional styles for older versions of Internet Explorer, but generally, it should not take nearly as much extra work as pixel perfection.

Why should I use progressive enhancement?

Pixel perfection has a strong track record in Web design, and it may take a while to convince clients and other teammates that progressive enhancement is a better way. However, I generally find these arguments do the trick:

- *Faster* to develop—Rather than spending time kludging together a bunch of images for rounded corners, drop shadows, and other effects, a few lines of code take care of it all.

- *Cheaper* to maintain—Changing code is much more cost effective than reworking, recutting, and redeploying images.

- *Better* looking—Since the styles are native to the browser, they will display more precisely than images that are shoehorned in.

If these arguments don't sway your client, then compare a budget for designing with progressive enhancements to a pixel perfect budget. Usually the relative costs will convince even the most stubborn client to approve progressive enhancement.

A Multi-Screen Strategy?

The world of Web design is becoming an increasingly complex place to live. Just as computer screens get larger, browsers get more consistent, and connection speeds get faster, the landscape is undergoing a seismic shift to accommodate the smaller screens and slower speeds of mobile devices. The number of different screen sizes and resolutions is constantly growing ⓒ. I won't even bother to list the most common mobile devices in this book, because they will probably change between now and the time the book is published.

So what's a designer to do? You need to develop a multi-screen strategy, ensuring that your audience gets the best experience, regardless of what device is being used. There are several strategies you could deploy, but one is the clear leader:

ⓒ The Solar Energy Industries Association uses a responsive design multi-screen strategy that allows the same Web page to appear optimally across a wide range of screen sizes and user contexts.

- **Mobile app**: You could build separate applications to run in the various devices. Unfortunately, since each device will require separate design and development, this can get expensive, or require you to ignore possible users.

- **Mobile site**: You can build a site—with a separate URL—customized for mobile devices. Generally, these are built separately from the general Web site, take more design and development time, and are generally designed for the lowest-level browser.

- **Responsive design site**: You can build a site that adapts to its environment using media queries. It may require a little extra work to adapt the design to different "break points," but these sites will likely run efficiently on the widest number of devices.

Of these three strategies, responsive design is the most promising. It uses the same HTML files for all browsers, then applies progressive enhancement to tweak the design for each device.

Responsive design works simply by using CSS media queries to ask the device about its specific properties, and then delivering styles to tailor the HTML being displayed to best fit the environment it is being presented in.

Resetting Browser Default Styles

In Chapter 2, you learned about browser default styles. Recall that browser developers set the default styles applied by HTML tags. Before you get too far into the responsive design weeds, start by resetting those default styles to make sure they are the same regardless of the browser you are designing for.

Far too many Web sites are designed by default Ⓐ. The designers and developers allow the browser to have the final word on how the content is displayed. Additionally, all browser default styles are not the same. CSS resets were developed to level the playing field and help prevent "vanilla" designs Ⓑ.

The exact CSS reset you choose will depend on your design needs. I like to keep my reset simple, adding styles to specific tags only as needed. However, several styles are inconsistent or (in my opinion) poorly set in most browsers.

Redefining important CSS properties (generally to none or 0) provides a few benefits:

- **Reduces bad styles.** Undoes some of the questionable and downright annoying styles added by browsers, and eliminates the styles that simply do not work. One example is using an outline to highlight items that are in focus, such as form fields. Although highlighting is useful for keyboard navigation, you should design this yourself.

Ⓐ A page with no CSS applied.

Ⓑ The same page with the simple reset applied.

- **Eliminates design by default.** Sets a level playing field from which to begin a design. Rather than allowing the browser to dictate your page appearance, you take control.

- **Makes browser styles consistent.** Ensures that values across all browser types and versions are the same. Because browsers slightly vary their default style values, a good reset will allow your designs to appear with greater consistency regardless of how your visitor is viewing it.

To use a CSS reset, simply add the desired code at the very top of your CSS code. That's it. The code does the rest.

What Should You Reset?

As a designer, I recommend resetting many of the typographic and box styles and then setting your own defaults. In addition to not allowing the browser to set the direction, another good argument for resetting styles is that different browsers have slightly different values.

- **Padding, borders, and margins**—These are the main styles that designers like to reset, largely because they vary so much from browser to browser.

- **Text underlining**—Never use the `text-decoration` property to underline text. I have never seen a design in which underlining did anything other than add visual noise, even for links. Instead of using `underline`, apply `border-bottom` to achieve a similar effect with more precise control that allows you to specify the thickness, color, and line style of the underline.

- **Line height**—The default value for line height on text is 1em, which means that the text has little or no breathing room. All text can benefit by bumping this up to at least 1.4em.

- **Outline**—Outlines are applied by some browsers to highlight elements, such as form fields, when they come into focus. Although this is a good idea for accessibility reasons, the nature of this highlight should be up to you, not the browser.

- **Vertical alignment**—Vertical alignment is tricky to deal with and rarely works the way you expect. The best procedure is to set the vertical alignment to the baseline and then use relative positioning to move elements up or down manually.

- **Other**—These are the basics, but most CSS resets will go beyond this, cleaning up other perceived problems, generally with specific tag implementation.

A simple CSS reset

The easiest way to reset styles is to use the universal selector and set the default styles you want applied to all tags, as shown in **Code 14.2**. Remember that you want to keep your CSS reset compact. **Code 14.3** does the same thing but removes all spaces and returns.

This is a quick way to reset the most important styles, but it has one drawback: IE6 does not recognize the universal selector. If you are concerned about supporting IE6, you will want to include all the HTML tags in the selector list. The advantage of using the universal selector, other than compactness, is that it will always apply itself to new HTML tags as they become available.

Code 14.2 *cssreset-simple.css*—This version of the CSS uses the universal selector to reset the browser default values of several key properties, including margin, padding, border, outline, line-height, vertical-align, and text-decoration.

```
/*** cssreset-simple.css ***/
* {   margin: 0;
    padding: 0;
    border: 0;
    outline: 0;
    font-size: 100%;
    font-style: normal;
    font-weight: normal;
    line-height: 1;
    vertical-align: baseline;
    text-decoration: none; }
```

Code 14.3 *cssreset-simple.css*—The same code as Code 14.2, but compressed by removing all line breaks and spaces.

```
/*** cssreset-simple.css ***/
*{margin:0;padding:0;border:0;outline:0;
  font-size: 100%;font-style: normal;font-
  weight: normal;line-height: 1;vertical-
  align:baseline;text-decoration:none;}
```

Code 14.4 *cssreset-YUI2.css*—Developed by Yahoo, the YUI2 reset does a more thorough job of overriding specific browser default styles.

```
/*** cssreset-YUI2.css ***/
body,div,dl,dt,dd,ul,ol,li,h1,h2,h3,h4,h5,h6,
 ▸ pre,form,fieldset,input,textarea,p,
 ▸ blockquote,th,td {
    margin:0;
    padding:0; }
table {
    border-collapse:collapse;
    border-spacing:0; }
fieldset,img {
    border:0; }
address,caption,cite,code,dfn,em,strong,th,
 ▸ var {
    font-style:normal;
    font-weight:normal; }
ol,ul {
    list-style:none; }
caption,th {
    text-align:left; }
h1,h2,h3,h4,h5,h6 {
    font-size:100%;
    font-weight:normal; }
q:before,q:after {
    content:''; }
abbr,acronym {
    border:0; }
```

YUI2: Reset CSS

Yahoo developed the YUI2: Reset CSS to remove and neutralize inconsistencies in the default styling of HTML elements, create a level playing field across browsers, and—according to their documentation— provide a sound foundation upon which you can explicitly declare your intentions (*developer.yahoo.com/yui/reset/*).

This CSS reset (**Code 14.4**) addresses the styles of many specific HTML tags by zeroing them out, as well as resolving some problems with font sizes, weights, and the use of quotation marks

Eric Meyer's reset

Partially in response to Yahoo, noted Web pundit Eric Meyer developed his own CSS reset script. According to his blog, he felt that the Yahoo code went too far in some areas and not far enough in others. This script (**Code 14.5**) is useful for resetting typographic styles (*meyerweb.com/eric/tools/css/reset/*).

TIP Applying styles globally to every tag puts a burden on the browser's rendering engine. This is mostly an argument against using the universal selector (*), which applies the styles to every tag. However, I have not seen any data showing exactly that this lag occurs, nor have I detected any noticeable degradation in my own tests, even on complex pages.

Code 14.5 *cssreset-ericmeyer.css*—Developed by Eric Meyer, this reset is simpler than the Yahoo Reset.

```
/*** cssreset-ericmeyer.css ***/
/* v1.0 | 20080212 */
html, body, div, span, applet, object, iframe,
h1, h2, h3, h4, h5, h6, p, blockquote, pre,
a, abbr, acronym, address, big, cite, code,
del, dfn, em, font, img, ins, kbd, q, s, samp,
small, strike, strong, sub, sup, tt, var,
b, u, i, center,
dl, dt, dd, ol, ul, li,
fieldset, form, label, legend,
table, caption, tbody, tfoot, thead, tr,
  th, td {
    margin: 0;
    padding: 0;
    border: 0;
    outline: 0;
    font-size: 100%;
    vertical-align: baseline;
    background: transparent;
}
body {
    line-height: 1;
}
ol, ul {
    list-style: none;
}
blockquote, q {
    quotes: none;
}
blockquote:before, blockquote:after,
q:before, q:after {
    content: '';
    content: none;
}
/* remember to define focus styles! */
:focus {
    outline: 0;
}
/* remember to highlight inserts somehow! */
ins {
    text-decoration: none;
}
del {
    text-decoration: line-through;
}
/* tables still need 'cellspacing="0"' in the
  markup */
table {
    border-collapse: collapse;
    border-spacing: 0;
}
```

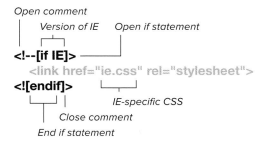

Open comment
Version of IE   *Open if statement*

```
<!--[if IE]>
    <link href="ie.css" rel="stylesheet">
<![endif]>
```

IE-specific CSS
Close comment
End if statement

A General syntax for conditional statements. Anything placed between the comments will be used only by the specified versions of Internet Explorer.

Adjusting CSS for Internet Explorer

Although Internet Explorer no longer has the dominant position it once held over the Web, it is still a major player and not to be ignored. However, you will face problems if you have to support IE6, IE7, and IE8 in quirks mode (see the sidebar "What Is Quirks Mode?"

IE9 and 10 have changed this by adding full CSS3 and HTML5 compatibility and are quickly replacing older versions of the browser. However, the reality is that you will likely need to include code to tailor your design to Internet Explorer for some time to come.

Fortunately, Internet Explorer allows us to add *conditional styles* that will be applied only to Internet Explorer, even only to specific versions of Internet Explorer. Internet Explorer (and *only* Internet Explorer) has the ability to interpret conditional statements (if this … then do that) that are ignored by other browsers **A**. This allows you to insert links to style sheets that can tailor your CSS for any version of Internet Explorer and create designs that respond to those special conditions.

To set up conditional styles for Internet Explorer:

1. **Add a conditional comment, specifying the version of IE you want to target.** Within an HTML comment, use an **if** statement within square brackets and specify which version of Internet Explorer the CSS overrides should be used with (**Code 14.6**):

   ```
   <!--[if IE]>
   ```

   Table 14.1 shows the possible logical operators you can include for targeting specific browsers or a range of browser versions.

   Using just **IE** will cause the CSS to be used in any version of Internet Explorer. Adding a space followed by a number will specify the version number. For example, **IE 6** allows CSS to be used only in Internet Explorer 6 regardless of the doctype.

2. **Add the IE-specific CSS for the browser version(s).** This value will override previous values for that property for standard CSS. This can be embedded in the head of your document using the **<style>** tag or imported using the **<link>** tag or **@import** rule:

   ```
   <style type="text/css" media="all">
       @import url("../css/ie-fix.css");
   </style>
   ```

TABLE 14.1 IE Conditionals

Conditional	Any version of IE
lt IE <version>	Versions less than version
lte IE <version>	Versions less than or equal to version
IE <version>	Specific version
gte IE <version>	Versions greater than or equal to version
gt IE <version>	Versions greater than version
IEMobile	Mobile version of Internet Explorer
!	Not—Can be added to any other conditional

Code 14.6 Add this code to the head of Code 14.1. It loads a specialized style sheet (**Code 14.7**) that corrects a color problem in the header for Internet Explorer, and makes those new HTML5 tags all block level so that they will properly respond to styles. It also loads the JavaScript file you created in Chapter 2 (Code 2.3) that "teaches" the new HTML5 tags to older versions of Internet Explorer **B** **C**.

```
<!--[if IE ]>
   <style type="text/css" media="all">
      @import url("../css/ie-fix.css");
   </style>
<![endif]-->

<!--[if lte IE 8]>
   <script type="text/javascript"
→ src="../script/HTML5forIE.js"></script>
<![endif]-->
```

Code 14.7 *ie-fix.css*—Styles are used to override styles from previous CSS files to display the page as well as possible in Internet Explorer.

```
/*** ie-fix.css ***/
/*** color & background properties ***/
header h1 {
   color: rgb(255,153,153); }
/*** box properties ***/
article,aside,canvas,details,dialog,
→ eventsource,figure,footer,header,hgroup,
→ mark,menu,meter,nav,output,progress,
→ section,time,video { display: block; }
```

3. **Close the conditional comment.** Close your conditional comment with an **endif** in brackets:

```
<![endif]-->
```

TIP Because IE9 is promising HTML5 and CSS3 compatibility, I recommend setting your IE conditional to "let IE 8," which will apply the overrides only to versions of Internet Explorer *less than or equal to* 8.

TIP Although you can add specific code for different versions of Internet Explorer, try to keep the number of links and imports to a minimum. The more external files you bring in, the longer it will take your Web page to load.

TIP Add an exclamation mark before any of the conditionals and it becomes a "not" (for example, !lt IE 9 = *not* less than version 9).

B The header in most modern browsers. The header is a dark red set against a textured background for contrast, but Internet Explorer does not support text shadows.

C The header in Internet Explorer. Although it looks much the same, the header is now a brighter red, since the text shadow property is not available.

Adapting to the Environment

Break points can most easily be thought of as *small*, *medium*, and *large* screen sizes. At first, you may want to create entirely different style sheets for each break point style sheet and apply them separately. However, the fact is that most styles will be the same between the style sheets, so the simplest thing to do is put the common styles in *small*, and then use the *medium* and *large* style sheets to override those styles needed to scale the design up.

However, between those break points, different devices have different dimensions, so your styles should use relative lengths to ensure that they stretch to accommodate . This is referred to as *adaptive design*.

- **small.css** (**Code 14.8**): Applied to all devices. Contains all of the general styles to be applied to the design with layout for small devices .

- **medium.css** (**Code 14.9**): Applied to tablets and computer screens. Contains override styles used to scale the design up for medium screen sizes **C**.

continues on page 368

A 0–739 pixels is the small range. 740–979 pixels is medium range. 980 and above is large.

B Small. **Code 14.8** applied to **Code 14.12**.

C Medium. **Code 14.9** applied to **Code 14.12**.

Code 14.8 *small.css* contains all of the default styles used in the site plus layout styles for smaller screens. To save space, I've added the styles from Chapters 5–10 using @import to bring those other files into this one, but generally this technique is not recommended (see Chapter 3 for details).

```
/*** small.css - Default Styles ***/

@import url("../css/font-properties.css");
@import url("../css/text-properties.css");
@import url("../css/color-background-properties.css");
@import url("../css/list-table-properties.css");
@import url("../css/ui-generatedcontent-properties.css");

h1 {
    font-size: 3em; }
p {
    width: 94%; }
nav.toc{
    color: rgba(255,255,255,.75);
    margin: 0;
    padding: 0;
    width: 93%; }
nav.toc ol, nav.toc ul, nav.toc li {
    background: rgba(0,0,0,.5);
    border-bottom: 1px solid rgb(153,153,153);
    list-style: none;
    margin: 0 0 0 -4%;
    padding: .5em 5%;
    width: 100%; }
aside {
    padding: 5%;
    width: 91%; }
```

Code 14.9 *medium.css* provides adaptive styles for medium-size devices, which in this case means changing the header size.

```
/*** Medium Device Styles ***/
h1 { font-size: 4em; }
```

- *large.css* (**Code 14.10**): Applied to computer screens. Contains override styles used to scale the design up for larger screen sizes 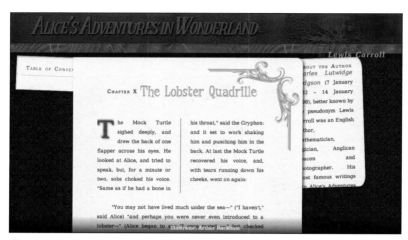.

- *print.css* (**Code 14.11**): Applied to print designs **E**.

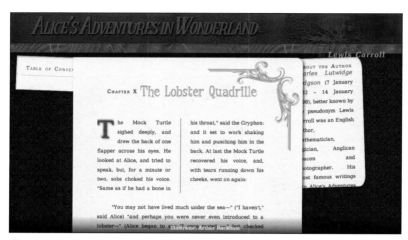

D Large. **Code 14.10** applied to **Code 14.12**.

E Print. **Code. 14.11** applied to **Code 14.12**.

Code 14.10 *large.css* contains adaptive styles for larger devices. Since Chapters 11–13 were built with a large screen in mind, I'm importing those styles into large.

```
/*** Large Device Styles ***/
@import url("../css/box-properties.css");
@import url("../css/visualformatting-properties.css");
@import url("../css/transformation-transition-properties.css");
@import url("../css/design-interface.css");

h1 {
    font-size: 5em; }
nav.toc {
    color: rgba(0,0,0,.75);
```

Code 14.11 *print.css* includes some simple styles to make the page better for printing, as seen in Chapter 3.

```
/*** For Print ***/

body {
    padding: 1em;
    color: rgb(0,0,0);
    background: white url(../chapters/alice23a.gif) no-repeat 0 0;
    padding: 200px 0 0 175px; }

header.page, article {
    margin: 1em 0;
    background: none;
}

h1,h2,h3 { color: black; }
h2.chaptertitle { color: red; }
h2 cite { color: black; }

p { font: normal 12pt/2 Constantia, palatino, times, "times new roman", serif;
    text-indent: 3em; }

nav { display: none; }
```

To set up a simple responsive design with CSS media queries:

1. Add the viewport meta tag (**Code 14.12**):

```
<meta name="viewport"
→ content="width=device-width,
 → initial-scale=1,
 → maximum-scale=1,
 → minimum-scale=1,
 → user-scalable=no">
```

This sets up the file for responsive design, ensuring that the design is appropriately scaled to the user's device and prevents the user from zooming in, which might cause problems and annoyances because the design is already scaled for best fit. If you are worried that some users will want to zoom in, you can instead set **user-scalable** to *yes*.

2. Add a link to *small.css*

```
<link type="text/css"
 → rel="stylesheet" media="all"
 → href="css/small.css" />
```

This file contains the base level and default styles that should be applied to any environment, as well as the styles to make the design best fit within a smaller mobile device such as a smart phone.

3. Add a conditional link that will cover the older versions of IE—not including mobile versions, which get the small version of the CSS—loading *large.css*:

```
<!--[if (lt IE 9)&(!IEMobile)]>
 → ...<![endif]-->
```

Since older versions of Internet Explorer can't use media queries, we want to make sure that they are styled for the computer screen.

continues on page 373

Code 14.12 The final HTML showing all of the structure for the page.

```
<!DOCTYPE html>
<html lang="en">
<head>
<meta charset="utf-8">
<meta name="viewport" content="width=device-width, initial-scale=1, maximum-scale=1, minimum-scale=1,
→ user-scalable=no">

<title>Alice&#8217;s Adventures In Wonderland | Chapter X</title>

<link type="text/css" rel="stylesheet" media="all" href="../css/cssreset.css" />

<!--[if lte IE 8]>
    <script type="text/javascript" src="../script/HTML5forIE.js"></script>
<![endif]-->

<!--[if IE ]>
    <style type="text/css" media="all">
        @import url("../css/ie-fix.css");
    </style>
<![endif]-->

<link type="text/css" rel="stylesheet" media="all" href="../css/small.css" />

    <!--[if (lt IE 9)&(!IEMobile)]>
        <style type="text/css" media="all">
        @import url("../css/medium.css");
        @import url("../css/large.css");
        </style>
    <![endif]-->

<!--[if gte IE 9]><!-->
<style type="text/css" media="screen and (min-width: 740px) and (min-device-width: 740px),
→ (max-device-width: 800px) and (min-width: 740px) and (orientation:landscape)">
    @import url("../css/medium.css");
</style>
<!--<![endif]-->

<!--[if gte IE 9]><!-->
<style type="text/css" media="screen and (min-width: 980px) and (min-device-width: 980px)">
    @import url("../css/medium.css");
    @import url("../css/large.css");
</style>
<!--<![endif]-->

<link type="text/css" rel="stylesheet" media="print" href="../css/print.css" />

</head>
<body id="chapter10" class="book aaiw chapter">
<header class="page">
<hgroup>
    <h1>Alice&#8217;s Adventures in Wonderland</h1>
    <h2>By <cite>Lewis Carroll</cite></h2>
```

code continues on next page

```
</hgroup>
</header>
<section>
<nav class="toc">
<ul class="menu">
<li><h2>Table of Contents</h2></li>
<ol class="drop">
<li><a href="AAIWL-ch01.html">Down the Rabbit-hole</a></li>
<li><a href="AAIWL-ch02.html">The Pool of Tears</a></li>
<li><a href="AAIWL-ch03.html">A Caucus-race and a Long Tale</a></li>
<li><a href="AAIWL-ch04.html">The Rabbit sends in a Little Bill</a></li>
<li><a href="AAIWL-ch05.html">Advice from a Caterpillar</a></li>
<li><a href="AAIWL-ch06.html">Pig and Pepper</a></li>
<li><a href="AAIWL-ch07.html">A Mad Tea-party</a></li>
<li><a href="AAIWL-ch08.html">The Queen's Croquet-ground</a></li>
<li><a href="AAIWL-ch09.html">The Mock Turtle's Story</a></li>
<li><a href="AAIWL-ch010.html">The Lobster Quadrille</a></li>
<li><a href="AAIWL-ch011.html">Who Stole the Tarts?</a></li>
<li><a href="AAIWL-ch012.html">Alice&#8217;s Evidence</a></li>
</ol>
</ul>
</nav>

<article>
<h2>Chapter X
<span class="chaptertitle">The Lobster Quadrille</span>
</h2>

<p>The Mock Turtle sighed deeply, and drew the back of one flapper across his eyes. He looked at
→ Alice, and tried to speak, but, for a minute or two, sobs choked his voice. "Same as if he had
→ a bone in his throat," said the Gryphon: and it set to work shaking him and punching him in the
→ back. At last the Mock Turtle recovered his voice, and, with tears running down his cheeks, went
→ on again:</p>
...
</article>
<aside>
<h2>About the Author</h2>
  <p><b><a href="#">Charles Lutwidge Dodgson</a></b> (7 January 1832 - 14 January 1898), better
→ known by the pseudonym Lewis Carroll was an English author, mathematician, logician, Anglican
→ deacon and photographer. His most famous writings are Alice's Adventures in Wonderland and
→ its sequel Through the Looking-Glass, as well as the poems "The Hunting of the Snark" and
→ "Jabberwocky", all examples of the genre of literary nonsense. He is noted for his facility
→ at word play, logic, and fantasy, and there are societies in many parts of the world (including
→ the United Kingdom, Japan, the United States, and New Zealand) dedicated to the enjoyment and
→ promotion of his works and the investigation of his life.</p>
</aside>
</section>
<footer>
Illustrator: Arthur Rackham
</footer>

</body>
</html>
```

4. Add a style tag with media queries with breaking points at a minimum width of 740 pixels for computer monitors, or a maximum width of 800 pixels and a landscape orientation for tablets.

```
<style type="text/css" media="all
→ and (min-width: 740px) and
→ (min-device-width: 740px),
→ (max-device-width: 800px)
→ and (min-width: 740px) and
→ (orientation:landscape)">...
→ </style>
```

This means that *both* the small and medium style sheets are applied to the design, tailoring it to tablet-size devices in landscape orientation.

5. Add a style tag for devices with screens *over* 980 pixels and import both the medium *and* large style files:

```
<style type="text/css" media="all
→ and (min-width: 980px) and
→ (min-device-width: 980px)">...
→ </style>
```

This means that all three style sheets are loaded, with the large style overriding previous styles.

6. Finally, add a link to *print.css*:

```
<link type="text/css"
→ rel="stylesheet" media="print"
→ href="css/print.css" />
```

This file formats the Web page for printing, as explained in Chapter 4.

CSS Best Practices

It's not enough to write CSS that makes your pages look pretty: to create the best Web pages, you must also write clean code that's easy to read, easy to maintain, and loads quickly.

To manage your style sheets you need to know how to create well-organized code, work with CSS libraries and frameworks, optimize the linking of style sheets, validate your CSS, and compress the code by *minifying* it.

This chapter helps you realize all these goals and finishes with a review of the best practices I've presented throughout the book.

In This Chapter

Create Readable Style Sheets

Although the computer interprets the CSS code to render a Web page, you and other humans have to create and edit it. During development, your code will probably get pretty messy, which makes it hard to track down rule interactions, determine the cascade order, or even locate rules that need changing.

Keeping your code organized *while* you work can actually save you time. Follow these simple suggestions to keep your code as readable as possible during development, and then double-check and clean up your code before you deploy.

Include an introduction and TOC

Place an introduction at the top of your CSS that includes basic information such as the title, site name, version, change date, usage, and other notes (**Code 15.1**). Additionally, some developers like to insert a rough table of contents, outlining the organizational structure of the style sheets.

CSS Libraries and Frameworks

A *CSS library* is simply a collection of common styles that you use throughout one Web site, and potentially, multiple Web sites. The library can include your CSS reset, general typography, general transition styles, or any other style that requires consistency.

CSS frameworks are ready-built CSS libraries that allow you to quickly deploy well-tested and finely crafted CSS code to your own Web site. Generally, CSS frameworks are free, community-based efforts maintained by interested volunteers.

For simple Web sites, frameworks can be overkill, adding a lot of code that will never be used. However, even for medium-sized sites, frameworks can be a real time-saver.

Some of the more popular CSS frameworks include:

- **Blueprint**—Provides a solid layout grid, typographic styles, and a style sheet for printing pages .

  Visit *www.blueprintcss.org.*

- **Emastic**—Uses ems to create elastic layouts.

  Visit *code.google.com/p/emastic.*

- **Intuit CSS**—Uses 12- and 16-column grids at 960px wide and typographic style rules to create a strong vertical rhythm.

  Visit *csswizardry.com/inuitcss.*

- **YUI Grids**—Yahoo!'s CSS Grids framework provides fixed and fluid layouts.

  Visit *yuilibrary.com/yui/docs/cssgrids.*

Ⓐ The home page of Blueprint, one of the more popular CSS frameworks.

Code 15.1 An example of an introduction and TOC for an external CSS file. Notice that the hierarchy of the file shown in the TOC is based on page structure.

```
/*----------------------------------------------------------------
# Default Stylesheet
Filename:     default.css
Site:         speakinginstyles.com
Version:      1.1
Last change: 09/11/12 [added gallery view, jct]
Author:      Jason Cranford Teague (jct)
Desciption:  Default styles to be applied to all pages in the site
## TOC
* HTML Selectors (Defaults)
    ** Headers
    ** Body
    ** Lists
    ** Forms
    ** Tables
* Navigation
    ** Menu
    ** Breadcrumb
    ** Footer
* Content
    ** Aside
        *** Right
        *** Left
    **    Article
        *** Blockquotes
        *** Paragraphs
        *** Lists
        *** Tables
    **    Comments
* Footer
    ----------------------------------------------------------*/
```

Define colors, fonts, and other constants

It's sometimes difficult to keep track of all the values that you are using in your design. It's unlikely that CSS will ever include constants, so it will help to keep notes in an easy-to-reference location in your document. Creating a glossary of colors and types leads to more consistent and attractive designs (**Code 15.2**).

Use section headers

Although section headers and dividers really aren't anything more than CSS comments, they do help organize your CSS and allow you to quickly scan your code to locate particular CSS rule groups. If you have established a TOC, I recommend reflecting that organization here. In this example (**Code 15.3**), I'm using asterisks to indicate a section level.

The @ rules go at the top

All of the CSS rules starting with @ (@media, @font-face, @import) must be placed above any other CSS in the external style or embedded style sheet. In addition to making these rules easier to find, many of them won't work unless they're placed at the top.

Choose an organization scheme

You should choose a consistent organization pattern and stick to it. I'm not going to tell you *how* to organize your style sheets—that depends on what works for you—but here are a few ideas to consider:

- **Organize by selector type.** Start with HTML selectors, then IDs, and then classes.

- **Organize based on page structure.** Group rules based on their parent tags. This works even better with HTML5 because page structure is stronger. The downside occurs when the same rules need to be applied at different places in the page. You don't want redundant code, so it's best to separate those rules out into their own section.

- **Organize based on purpose.** Group rules based on which element you're applying a style to. Instead of being grouped according to where the element is in the page, the styles are grouped based on their content, module, functionality, or other specific use (such as headings, typography, ads, article, asides, layout grid, and so on.)

- **Organize alphabetically.** Literally list the selectors in alphabetical order. No, really. I've never used this method, but I've heard several developers swear by it. To me, it seems like a lot of work to maintain this organization scheme. Plus, what if you need to override a style later in the cascade, but it doesn't fit alphabetically?

You can use one of these methods, a combination of these methods, or a method you make up yourself. The key is to be consistent.

Code 15.2 Constant values such as colors and font stacks can be defined at the top of the page as a handy reference.

```
/*-------------------------------------------------------------------
## Color Glossary
dark gray:  rgb(51, 51, 85)
red:        rgb(255, 15, 34)
white:      rgb(235,235,355)
blue:       rgb(0, 0, 102)
## Font Glossary
header:     diavlo, "gill sans", helvetica, arial, sans-serif
body:       baskerville, georgia, times, "times new roman", serif
aside:      "gill sans", helvetica, arial, sans-serif
-----------------------------------------------------------------*/
```

Code 15.3 Section dividers used to organize the CSS file. Notice that they mimic the TOC.

```
/* HTML Selectors
-----------------------------------------------------------------*/
/**   HTML Selectors | Headers
-----------------------------------------------------------------*/
/* Content
-----------------------------------------------------------------*/
/** Content | Aside
-----------------------------------------------------------------*/
/*** Content | Aside | Right
-----------------------------------------------------------------*/
/*** Content | Aside | Left
-----------------------------------------------------------------*/
/** Content | Article
-----------------------------------------------------------------*/
```

Use specificity for hierarchy

Regardless of the overall organization scheme you choose, specificity (explained in Chapter 4) provides a natural organizational hierarchy for CSS rules (**Code 15.4**). Simply organizing your CSS rules using the selector specificity can make it a lot easier to find rules and track down problems.

Code 15.4 CSS rules ordered by specificity hierarchy. This makes them easier to follow.

```
article {,...}
article .intro {,...}
article .intro figure {,...}
article .intro figure figcaption {,...}
article .intro p {,...}
article .intro p em {,...}
article .intro p:firstline {,...}
```

Have a Style Sheet Strategy

Once your libraries, frameworks, and site-wide CSS are ready to go live, you need to pick the best strategy for deployment. It is always recommended that you place all your styles in one or more external style sheets, and then use either the `<link>` or `@import` code to apply them to a Web document.

At this juncture, you have two competing priorities:

- **Keep the file size as small as possible.** The larger the file size, the longer it takes to download. Of course, because it's text, your files have to be pretty large for this to be a problem, but it happens.

- **Keep the number of links and imports as low as possible.** The more links and imports you have to external CSS files, the more server calls you make, and the slower the page will load.

You can reduce file size by splitting style sheets into multiple external files and then linking only to the ones you need, but this means more links. You can have a single, all-inclusive CSS file, but such a file can grow quite large. Your job will be to balance these two issues. Here are a few methods for doing so.

The One for All method

The One for All method includes all your styles in a single master style sheet. With this method, creating well-organized and readable style sheets with a TOC is critical because you may be poring through hundreds or even thousands of lines of code **A**.

Pros—One download is faster than multiple downloads, and the file is then cached for use on other pages. In addition, with all of your code in one place, you don't have to worry about whether a page has access to the right styles.

Cons—This method may lead to large file sizes that can slow down the page loading time and take longer to render. Additionally, these files are harder to manage and edit.

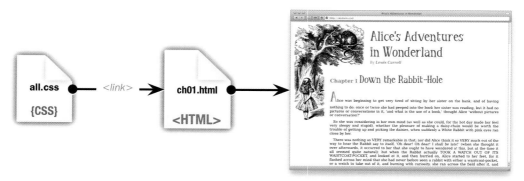

A The One for All method uses only a single gargantuan CSS file linked to the HTML document.

The Divide and Conquer method

The Divide and Conquer method uses multiple links to multiple style sheets on an as-needed basis per page. Start with a link to a file with global styles used by all pages, and then add links to styles used for that page only. For example, if you use a special carousel module only on the main page, it would not go into the global file, but would exist as a separate CSS file for the home page or as part of a CSS file of general components **B**.

Pros—Mix and match style sheets from your library to load only the styles you need and reduce bloated file sizes. Plus, as long as you keep your files organized, these are generally easier to edit.

Cons—Multiple files mean multiple server calls, which slows downloads. Plus, multiple files can be hard to keep up with, and their cascade order can conflict in unpredictable ways.

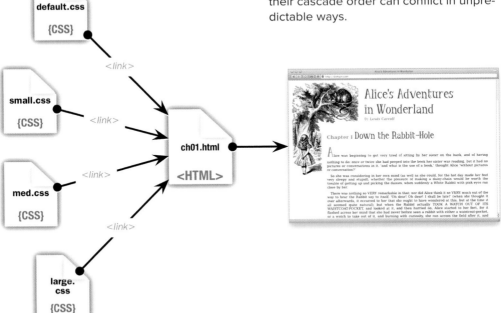

B The Divide and Conquer method splits the CSS into multiple files, which are then applied only if they are relevant to the page.

The Aggregate method

The Aggregate method uses **@import** to collect all the relevant CSS files from your library. The HTML document then has to link to only a single external file 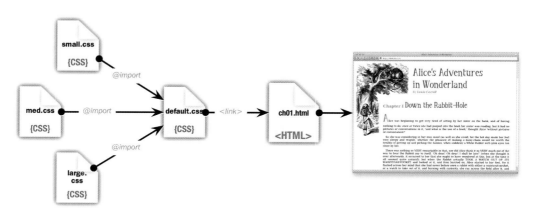

The Aggregate method uses **@import** to collect all the relevant CSS files from your library. The HTML document then has to link to only a single external file **C**.

Pros—Similar to the Divide and Conquer method, but by using only a single link, it's easier to add or remove styles as needed because they are in a single CSS file rather than spread out across multiple HTML files.

Cons—Similar to the Divide and Conquer method, but worse. This used to be a very popular CSS strategy until someone discovered that using **@import** often prevents external style sheets from loading simultaneously. Instead, they must load one after another, which slows things down. Additionally, since the linked parent style sheet has to load before the imported style sheets are seen by the browser, this method can lead to the page re-rendering as new styles become available.

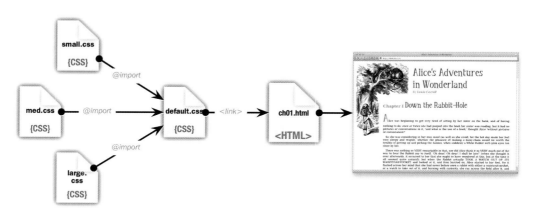

C The Aggregate method uses the @import rule to bundle the style sheets into a single file that is linked to the HTML document.

The Dynamic method

The Dynamic method relies not on your skills as a CSS coder, but on your skills writing server-side code. It is possible to write server scripts that take an aggregated CSS file full of **@imports** and combine them on the server into a single file for deployment **D**.

Pros—Combines the ease of use and lean file size of the Aggregate method with the speed of the One for All method.

Cons—Requires knowledge of server-side coding that is beyond the scope of this book. Talk to your server admin or developer for more details.

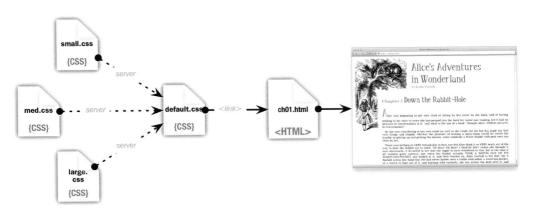

D The Dynamic method relies on the server to dynamically bundle the relevant CSS for an HTML document into a single CSS file.

Troubleshoot Your CSS Code

All too often, you carefully set up your style sheet rules, go to your browser, and see... *nothing*. Or the page is displayed as an ugly mishmash of content. Don't worry; this happens to everyone. Before you panic and throw your expensive laptop out the window, read through these suggestions.

Ask these questions

Many things could be preventing your style sheet rules from working properly; most of them are easily spotted. **A** points out some common problems you may encounter:

- **Are you missing any semicolons?** A missing semicolon at the end of a declaration will cause the entire rule to fail.

- **Did you remember to set the link relation?** If you leave out the `rel` property, many browsers will not load the external style sheet.

- **Did you open and close the declaration block with curly brackets?** If not, there's no telling what will happen.

- **Did you remember to close all your multiline comment tags?** If not, the rest of the CSS is treated as a comment. (See "Adding Comments to CSS" in Chapter 3.)

- **Does your selector contain typos?** If you forget the opening period or number sign (#) for classes and IDs, they won't work.

- **Did you mix up a class with an ID or vice versa?** I often think I've set up a selector as an ID, but it was actually a class.

- **Do the properties contain typos?** Typos in one property can cause the entire rule to fail.

- **Are the values you're using permitted for that property?** Using improper values may cause a definition to fail or behave unpredictably.

- **Does this property work on the browser you are testing on?** This is especially a problem if you are using new CSS3 properties. See Appendix A to make sure a property works on the browser you are using.

- **If your rules are in the head, did you use the `<style>` tag correctly?** Typos in the `<style>` tag mean that none of the definitions are used. In addition, if you set the media type, the styles will affect only the output to that medium. So setting the media type to print will prevent those styles from affecting content displayed on the screen. (See "Embedded: Adding Styles to a Web Page" in Chapter 3.)

- **If you are linking or importing style sheets, are you retrieving the correct file?** Check the exact path for the file. Also, remember that you should not include the `<style>` tag or any other non-CSS code in an external CSS file. (See "External: Adding Styles to a Web Site" in Chapter 3.)

- **Do you have multiple, conflicting rules for the same tag?** Check your cascade order. (See "Determining the Cascade Order" in Chapter 4.)

```
<html>
<head>
    <link src="myStyles.css" media="print">
    <style type="text/css media="screen">

        body { fant-size: 16px; }

        mystyle {
            cursor: pointer
            font-family: times new roman;
            font-size: bold; }

/*    This style should be used
      with paragraphs

        .copy { font-size: 12pz;

    <style>
</head>
<body>
    <p id="copy">
        Go Ask Alice…
    </p>
</body>
</head>
```

Ⓐ Errors are inevitable, but don't let them ruin your day. How many can you find? Flip the page to see the answers Ⓑ.

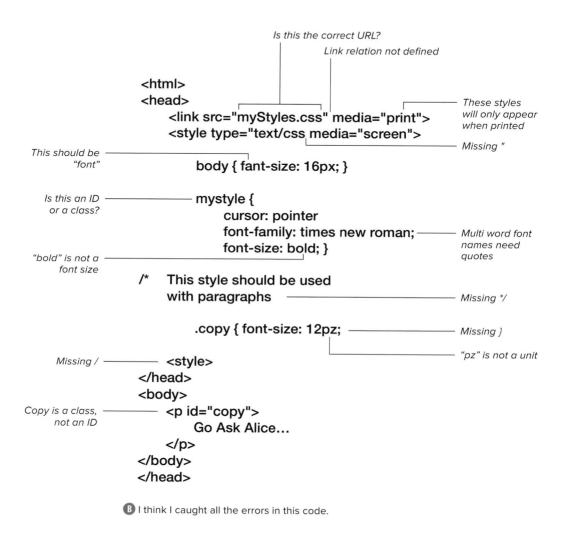

Is this the correct URL?

Link relation not defined

```
<html>
<head>
        <link src="myStyles.css" media="print">
        <style type="text/css media="screen">
    body { fant-size: 16px; }

    mystyle {
            cursor: pointer
            font-family: times new roman;
            font-size: bold; }

    /*    This style should be used
    with paragraphs

        .copy { font-size: 12pz;

        <style>
</head>
<body>
        <p id="copy">
            Go Ask Alice…
        </p>
</body>
</head>
```

These styles will only appear when printed

Missing "

This should be "font"

Is this an ID or a class?

Multi word font names need quotes

"bold" is not a font size

Missing */

Missing }

Missing /

"pz" is not a unit

Copy is a class, not an ID

B I think I caught all the errors in this code.

If all else fails, try these ideas

If you've looked for the preceding errors and still can't get your code to work, here are a few more things to try:

- **Make the declaration `!important`.** Often, your declarations will conflict with each other, and it may be hard to track down where the conflict is. Adding `!important` to the declaration (see "Making a Declaration !important" in Chapter 4) will ensure that if it is working, it is applied to the page.

- **Delete the rules and retype them.** When you can't see what's wrong, retyping code from scratch sometimes fixes the problem.

- **Test the same code on another browser and/or operating system.** It's possible that a property is buggy and doesn't work correctly in your browser. It's even possible that the browser doesn't allow that property to work with that tag.

- **Give up and walk away.** Just joking—although you might want to take a 15-minute break before looking at the problem again.

- **If nothing else works…** Try a different solution for your design.

View CSS in Firebug or Web Inspector

Most Web designers work in Firefox, Safari, or Chrome while they are developing because all three have excellent add-ons and built-in tools for analyzing and editing code. For Firefox, this functionality is provided by the Firebug add on, while both Safari and Chrome use the Web Inspector provided with Webkit.

Both tools allow on-the-fly editing of the CSS and HTML of the Web page you are viewing, which allows you to modify and debug your code on your local computer without affecting the live version. Although each tool has many unique features, both share several key capabilities for working with CSS:

- **Highlight elements.** As you roll over elements in the screen, they are highlighted in the HTML code or vice-versa.

- **View all rules applied to an element.** As elements are selected, the applied CSS code is displayed, showing declarations that have been overridden or crossed out.

- **Turn declarations on and off.** You can selectively enable and disable declarations to see how they affect the design.

- **Edit declaration properties and values.** In addition to switching declarations on and off, you can directly edit or add them to a rule.

- **View errors.** Display any HTML or CSS errors encountered.

Firebug for Firefox (Win/Mac)

The Firebug plug-in tool for Firefox has become the de facto standard for Web designers everywhere . You can get it from the Firefox add-ons Web site or directly from the Firebug Web site, *getfirebug.com*.

Getting started with Firebug

1. **Open the Firebug panel.** Navigate to the Web page you want to look at and then click the Firebug icon in the lower right of the browser window or choose View > Firebug.

continues on next page

Inspect   *HTML*   *CSS*

Ⓐ Firebug in Firefox.

2. **View the CSS.** You can view the CSS by itself by clicking the CSS tab, or view it side by side with the HTML by clicking the HTML tab. I generally work in side-by-side mode.

3. **Inspect an element.** Click the Inspect button and then click the element in the screen you want to inspect. As you hover over an element, its box will be outlined with color-coded margins and padding. Firebug also highlights the element in the HTML code and displays all of the CSS being applied. Declarations are crossed out if they have been overridden by other declarations and are not being applied. Click to select an element for editing.

4. **Turn off a declaration.** Hover to the left of the property name in the declaration, and a *not* symbol (⊘) appears. Click it to turn off the property, and click it again to turn on the property. In the viewport, you immediately see the effect of turning the property on and off.

5. **Edit a declaration.** Double-click the property name or value and you can type a new one. The effects of any changes will be visible almost immediately as you type.

6. **Add a new declaration.** Double-click the empty space to the right of the declaration you want to precede your new declaration, type the property name, press Tab, and then type the property value. Do *not* type the closing semicolon (;). Changes appear instantly as you type.

Web Inspector in Safari (Win/Mac) and Chrome (Win/Mac)

Both Safari and Chrome have this built-in Web developer tool, which allows you to quickly analyze and edit your CSS and HTML 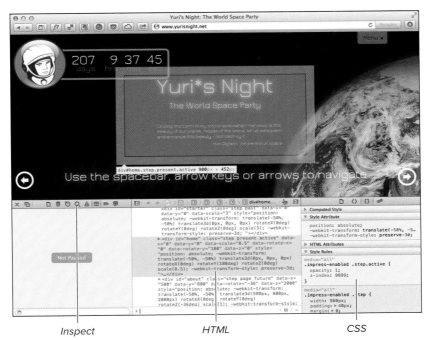. Both Safari and Chrome are available for Windows and Mac OS X:

www.apple.com/safari

www. google.com/chrome.

Getting Started with Web Inspector

1. **Turn on the Developer menu in Safari.** Open the Preferences panel for the browser, click the Advanced tab, and select "Developer menu in menu bar."

continues on next page

Inspect   *HTML*   *CSS*

B The Web Inspector in Safari. It looks pretty much the same in Chrome.

2. **Open the Web Inspector panel.** Navigate to the Web page you want to look at and in Safari choose Develop > Show Web Inspector, or in Chrome choose View > Developer > Developer Tools.

3. **View the CSS.** You can view the CSS side by side with the HTML by clicking the Elements tab.

4. **Inspect an element.** Click the Inspect icon (magnifying class) and then click the element in the screen you want to inspect. As you hover over an element, its box will be outlined, along with color-coded margins and padding. Firebug also highlights the element in the HTML code and displays all of the CSS being applied. Declarations are crossed out to indicate that they have been overridden by other declarations and are not being applied. Click to select an element for editing.

5. **Turn off a declaration.** Hover over the declarations in the CSS, and a check box will appear next to each on the right side. Deselect the check box to turn off the declaration. Select the check box to turn it on. In the viewport, you immediately see the effect of turning the declaration on and off.

6. **Edit a declaration.** Double-click the declaration you want to change and edit it as necessary. The effects of any changes will be visible almost immediately as you type.

7. **Add a new declaration.** Double-click the empty space to the right of the declaration you want to precede your new declaration, type the property name, and then type the property value. Do *not* type the closing semicolon (;). Press Return to make the changes appear.

TIP There is a "lite" version of Firebug available for Chrome and Safari. It's not as powerful, though, and I would recommend sticking with Web Inspector on those browsers.

TIP Keep in mind that if you reload the page at any point, any changes you have made will be lost.

A The W3C's Validator.

Validate Your CSS Code

The W3C provides a Web site called the CSS Validator **A** that lets you check your CSS code to confirm that it meets the requirements set in the W3C standards.

To use the W3C's CSS Validator:

1. To go to the W3C validator Web site, point your Web browser to jigsaw. w3.org/css-validator.

2. Choose the method to validate your CSS. You can enter a URL (by URI), enter the CSS code directly in a form (with a text area), or upload your files (by file upload). In this example, you'll submit a URL.

3. Enter the URL of your Web site or style sheet. I recommend entering the exact URL of the style sheet.

4. Wait. The validation takes only a few seconds. You're given a report of errors and other possible problems with your CSS.

TIP Although you don't need valid CSS for a browser to display your code, the validation process often helps locate code errors.

Minify Your CSS

Although creating readable CSS is great for editing and maintaining your code, all of those comments, spaces, and returns end up adding a lot of overhead to your file size. Additionally, although I'm sure you are a fine coder, there is always more room to sort and merge selectors for optimization.

If you want to cut down on your file size, before you deploy your site to the Web, create a *minified* version of your CSS code. Depending on the size of your CSS file, this can go far to reduce file size.

Don't delete the readable version. You need to keep that version around to make changes.

Minifying your own code is possible but can lead to numerous errors. Fortunately, several online tools are available to help you. My favorite is Minify CSS's CSS Compressor & Minifier **A**.

A The Minify CSS Compressor page at *www.minifycss.com/css-compressor*.

Code 15.5 My CSS code before being minified.

```
/*** box-properties.css ***/
body {
    margin: 0;
    padding: 0; }
header, section, nav, article, aside, figure,
→ figcaption, footer, hgroup {
    display: block; }
header, footer {
    clear: both;
    width: 100%; }
header {
    height: 135px; }
footer {
    height: 40px;
    padding: 30px 0 10px 0;
    text-align: center; }
h1 {
    width: 95%;
    max-width: 980px;
    min-width: 660px;
    margin: 0 20px 10px 5%;
    padding-top: 10px; }
hgroup h2 {
    margin: 30px; }
article h2 {
    width: 95%;
    margin-bottom: 60px; }article {
    width: 80%;
    max-width: 980px;
    min-width: 660px;
    margin: 150px 0 10px 0;
    border-top-right-radius: 20px;
    border-top: 10px transparent solid;
    border-right: 10px transparent solid;
    padding: 80px; }
article p {
    margin: 0; }
article h2 + p {
    margin-bottom: 1em;
    padding-bottom: 1em;
    -webkit-column-count: 2;
    -moz-column-count: 2;
    column-count: 2;
    -webkit-column-gap: 4em;
    -moz-column-gap: 4em;
    column-gap: 4em;
    -webkit-column-rule: 2px groove
    → rgba(0,0,0,.5);
```

Code 15.5 *continued*

```
    -moz-column-rule: 2px groove rgba(0,0,0,.5);
    column-rule: 2px groove rgba(0,0,0,.5); }
article h2 + p:first-letter {
    float: left;
    display: block;
    margin: .35em .2em .2em 0;
    padding: 0; }
aside {
    width: 200px;
    height: 400px;
    overflow: auto;
    border-radius: 20px/40px;
padding: 20px; }
footer nav a {
    margin: 0 1em; }
footer nav a:hover {
    outline: rgba(135,127,107,.65) 10px double;
}
figure {
    border: 6px double rgba(142, 137, 129,.5);
    clear: both; }
figure img {
    margin: 0; }
figure.cl-illo {
    border-radius: 10px; }
figure.bw-illo {
    border: 1em double rgba(142, 137, 129,.5);
    -webkit-border-image: url('../images/chrome/
    ⇢ border-02.png') 27 round;
    -moz-border-image: url('../images/chrome/
    ⇢ border-02.png') 27 round;
    -o-border-image: url('../images/chrome/
    ⇢ border-02.png') 27 round;
    border-image: url('../images/chrome/
    ⇢ border-02.png') 27 round; }
figcaption {
    border-top: 2px solid rgba(142, 137, 129,.5);
    padding: 10px; }
.floatleft {
    float:left;
    margin: 1em 2em 1em 0; }
.floatright {
    float:right;
    margin: 1em 0 1em 2em; }
.floatcenter {
    margin: 1em auto ; }
```

To minify your CSS:

1. **Visit Minify CSS.** Once you have finished your CSS code and are ready to go live on the Web, point your browser to www.minifycss.com/css-compressor.

2. **Load your CSS code.** You can either paste it directly into the form field or enter a URL from which to grab the CSS (**Code 15.5**). I pulled this code from Chapter 10.

3. **Choose your options.** Experiment to get the desired effect, but remember that your goal is to reduce your code file size as much as possible. You can also choose whether to output the code for you to copy or as a separate CSS file.

continues on next page

4. Process CSS. Click the Process CSS button under the field where you added your code. After a few seconds, a list of messages will appear showing the invalid properties discovered. Under that is your code to download or copy (**Code 15.6**).

If you are using CSS3, you can expect to see several invalid properties, since the Minifier does not include those yet.

5. TEST, TEST, TEST! Depending on how much you compressed your code, it may have changed a little or a lot. Regardless, it's different and may behave differently. If you encounter problems with the new CSS code, try minifying it again using different settings.

Code 15.6 The same CSS code after being minified.

```
body{margin:0;padding:0;}header,section,nav,
article,aside,figure,figcaption,footer,
hgroup{display:block;}header,footer{clear:
both;width:100%;}header{height:135px;}
footer{height:40px;padding:30px 0 10px;
text-align:center;}h1{margin:0 20px 10px
5%;max-width:980px;min-width:660px;padding-
top:10px;width:95%;}hgroup h2{margin:30px;}
article h2{margin-bottom:60px;width:95%;}
article{border-right:10px transparent
solid;border-top:10px transparent
solid;border-top-right-radius:20px;margin:
150px 0 10px;max-width:980px;min-width
:660px;padding:80px;width:80%;}article
h2 + p{-moz-column-count:2;-moz-column-
gap:4em;-moz-column-rule:2px groove
rgba(0,0,0,.5);-webkit-column-count:2;-webkit-
column-gap:4em;-webkit-column-rule:2px
groove rgba(0,0,0,.5);column-count:2;column-
gap:4em;column-rule:2px groove
rgba(0,0,0,.5);margin-bottom:1em;padding-
bottom:1em;}article h2 + p:first-letter{dis
play:block;float:left;margin:.35em .2em .2em
0;padding:0;}aside{border-radius:20px;height:
400px;overflow:auto;padding:20px;width:200px;}
footer nav a{margin:0 1em;}footer nav a:hov
er{outline:rgba(135,127,107,.65) 10px double;}
figure{border:6px double rgba(142,137,129,.5);
clear:both;}figure.cl-illo{border-radius:10px;}
figure.bw-illo{-moz-border-image:url(../images/
chrome/border-02.png) 27 round;-o-border-
image:url(../images/chrome/border-02.png)
27 round;-webkit-border-image:url(../images/
chrome/border-02.png) 27 round;border:1em
double rgba(142,137,129,.5);border-image:
url(../images/chrome/border-02.png) 27 round;}
figcaption{border-top:2px solid rgba(142,137,
129,.5);padding:10px;}.floatleft{float:left;
margin:1em 2em 1em 0;}.floatright{float:right;
margin:1em 0 1em 2em;}.floatcenter{margin:1em
auto;}article p,figure img{margin:0;}
```

33 CSS Best Practices

Throughout the pages of this book, I've offered numerous tips, recommendations, and suggestions. I've tried to follow my own advice in all of the code I'm presenting, but the necessities of creating useful examples had to be balanced against the needs of best practices for coding. So, to clear up any confusion, here are the 33 most important best practices for CSS, along with cross-references showing where you can find additional information.

1. **Always specify units for values except when the value is 0.** It's a simple equation:

   `0px = 0in = 0em = 0cm = 0% = 0mm = 0`

   Zero is always zero, and you don't need to define what kind of 0 it is.

   See "Values and Units Used in This Book" in the Introduction.

2. **Structure first, then presentation.** Some designers want to start designing pages without first placing the HTML structure, but this is like trying to put siding on a house that hasn't been framed yet.

   See "How Does HTML5 Structure Work?" in Chapter 2.

3. **Specify a doctype.** These days, using a DTD should go without saying, but an HTML document without a doctype is like a book without a cover. Not only do you not know what's in it, but the whole thing tends to fall apart.

   See "How Does HTML5 Structure Work?" in Chapter 2.

4. **All styles should be external.** To keep the Web site as easy to change as possible, the final styles should *always* be located in external files and *never* be embedded in the head or inline. Embedded or inline styles are acceptable during development but should all be moved into an external style sheet before deployment.

   See "External: Adding Styles to a Web Site" in Chapter 3.

5. **Keep the number of external style sheets to a minimum.** This may seem to contradict the previous statement, but every external style sheet is a call to the Web server, and every call slows down Web page loading. This is true whether you are using `<link>` or `@import`.

   See "External: Adding Styles to a Web Site" in Chapter 3.

6. **Place style links in the `<head>`, never in the `<body>`.** Styles placed in the `<body>` of an HTML document will not be applied to the page until *after* the Web page has displayed, causing the entire document to briefly flash as it re-renders the page with the styles. This is annoying and unattractive.

   See "External: Adding Styles to a Web Site" in Chapter 3.

7. **Use link to add styles to an HTML document and `@import` to add styles to other style sheets.** Older versions of Internet Explorer will load styles in the `<head>` as if they were in the `<body>`, causing the annoying flash as the page re-renders.

   See "External: Adding Styles to a Web Site" in Chapter 3.

8. **Include default styles for HTML elements.** Don't design by default. Use a CSS override to reset some values, but always define the default style for as many HTML elements as you will be using in your designs.

    See "(Re)defining HTML Tags" in Chapter 3.

9. **Use generic class names.** Classes are reused throughout a page, often combined with different elements, and are subject to change. If the name is based on a value, changing the value can make the class name confusing.

    See "Defining Reusable Classes" in Chapter 3.

10. **Use specific ID names.** IDs should be used only once per HTML document, so the name needs to specify what it is or what it's for.

    See "Defining Unique IDs" in Chapter 3.

11. **Add a unique class name or ID to the body tag of every page.** This gives every page its own unique identification, which you can then leverage to style the page separately from other pages.

    You can also add classes for the page's section or other designations that distinguish it in the site. This can help you reduce the number of external style sheets because it allows you to add styles for selective pages all in the same external file.

    See "Defining Reusable Classes" and "Defining Unique IDs" in Chapter 3.

12. Mix and match classes. You can apply multiple classes to a single element simply by placing the class names in the same class property in the tag, separated by spaces. This allows you to combine classes rather than creating new ones to meet a specific need.

See "Defining Reusable Classes" in Chapter 3.

13. Combine rules into selector lists. Elements that have the same CSS properties and values can be combined into a single CSS rule.

See "Grouping: Defining Elements That Are Using the Same Styles" in Chapter 3.

14. Use dynamic styles for form elements, buttons, and other interface elements. Many elements, such as form fields and form buttons, can have multiple dynamic states that can provide visual feedback for hover and also when a button is clicked or a form field is selected. Don't forget to style these, too.

See "Working with Pseudo-Classes" in Chapter 4.

15. Use `@media` rules and media queries to tailor the page to the device. Although not available to all browsers, media queries allow you to distinguish many mobile browsers, such as the iPhone, so that you can deliver a custom experience.

See "Querying the Media" in Chapter 4.

16. Favor specificity over classes and IDs, but only be as specific as necessary. Specificity allows you to selectively style an element *without* explicitly identifying it with a class or ID. Although classes and IDs can be useful, they will often limit the versatility of the page structure. Before adding a new class or ID to an element, see if you can use contextual styles.

On the other hand, don't make styles so specific that they apply only to very specific cases, when they may need to apply more broadly.

See "Defining Styles Based on Context" in Chapter 4.

17. **Avoid `!important`.** The `!important` value is a blunt weapon. It turns styles on and overrides the cascade order. This also means that it can be very tricky to override. If you do use `!important` during development, try to take it out before your site goes live.

See "Making a Declaration !important" in Chapter 4.

18. **Avoid unnecessary and repetitive repetition.** Style sheets can quickly become cluttered with redundant properties and values that do not actually change the value of whatever is already set. Remember that once a property value is set, it will cascade down to child elements.

For example, if you set the font size for the body, you will *never need to set it again* unless a specific element uses a different size. All too often I see the same font size set for element after element. Remember to check whether a style has already been set for a parent element before you set it.

See "Determining the Cascade Order" in Chapter 4.

19. **Use relative sizes for font size.** Although it is sometimes easier to use sizes such as pixels, using relative sizes such as ems allows you to scale text sizes on the page uniformly and keep better typographic rhythm.

See "Setting the Font Size" in Chapter 5.

20. **Prefer shorthand properties.** The shorthand properties, such as `font`, allow you to set multiple values with a single property. This not only cuts down on the amount of code, it also keeps similar property values together, making editing easier.

See "Setting Multiple Font Values at the Same Time" in Chapter 5.

21. **Use RGB for color.** You may see hex color values more often than RGB, but there is no really good reason to use one over the other from a code standpoint. Because RGB values are easier for mere mortals to understand *and* you can now set transparent colors using RGBA, I recommend always using RGB.

See "Choosing Color Values" in Chapter 7.

22. **Use background images or other styles for interface chrome.** The `<img>` tag should be used for images that are content: photographs, figures, or illustrations. Chrome constitutes the visual elements of the interface such as backgrounds, buttons, and other controls.

Instead of using the `<img>` tag to add these, interface chrome should be added using background images. This makes it easier to make changes or to completely rework the design without touching the HTML code.

See "Setting Background Images" in Chapter 7.

23. Use CSS sprites. Use sprites to add images to different dynamic states with only a single file that changes position to reveal each state. CSS sprites are faster to load than multiple images and do not flash as the states change.

See "Using CSS Sprites" in Chapter 13.

24. Use CSS for simple background gradients. Simple gradients are supported in most browsers now and can be used in backgrounds. Rather than slowing things down with images, use CSS gradients.

See "Creating Color Gradients" in Chapter 7.

25. Start with a clean slate. CSS resets allow you to set a level playing field, making it easier to design across multiple browsers.

See "Resetting Browser Default Styles" in Chapter 14.

26. Favor margin over padding. Due to problems with Internet Explorer and the box model, padding can cause problems with elements that have a defined width or height. If you have a choice, use margin.

See "Adjusting CSS for Internet Explorer" in Chapter 14.

27. Test your code in Firefox, Chrome, and/ or Safari while building, and then fix it for Internet Explorer. Although IE still has the lion's share of the browser market, it's easiest to build a site to Web standards, and then accommodate for IE's idiosyncrasies rather than the other way around.

See "Adjusting CSS for Internet Explorer" in Chapter 14.

28. Style all link states. Many designers will style only the default link state and maybe the hover state. However, you can also style visited and active states, which provide visual feedback to the user when clicking a link.

See "Styling Links vs. Navigation" in Chapter 13.

29. Use comments to keep notes and organize your code, especially for constant values. Notes are helpful for recording information about your design, especially in color or font values that you will be using consistently throughout your design. Notes can also be used to create section dividers in your code to help organize and make scanning for particular parts easier.

See "Create Readable Style Sheets" earlier in this chapter.

30. Use specificity to organize your code. Specificity is not just a great idea for styling; you can use it to create an outline-like format for your code, making it easier to scan and find related elements.

See "Create Readable Style Sheets" earlier in this chapter.

31. Favor `<link>` over `@import`. Although both can be used to bring style sheets into Web documents, tests have shown that most browsers will download linked style sheets faster than imported ones. This is true even if the `@import` is in an external style sheet because the parent external style sheet has to be loaded before its children are considered.

See "Have a Style Sheet Strategy" earlier in this chapter.

32. Minify your CSS before you launch.
Mean and lean code leads to faster download speeds, which always make for a better user experience. While you are developing your site, your code should be as readable as possible. But when you launch the site, you can remove all spaces, returns, and notes from your code.

See "Minify Your CSS" earlier in this chapter.

33. Use fonts for icons. With web fonts now a fact of life, we can rely on them for a variety of purposes that would have been unthinkable just a few years ago—most notably using them for icons instead of images. Images are limited by their sizes and styles, while fonts can be resized and restyled at will. This is especially important for responsive design, where sizes need to change depending on the display device in use.

See "Using Web Fonts" in Chapter 5.

CSS Quick Reference

Throughout this book, wherever new properties were introduced, I included a table showing the values for that property and the specific browser version in which support first appeared. But for quick reference, all you really care about is "does it work *now*?" or at least "does it work in browsers with major market share?" You also need to know in a hurry the default value, the types of elements that the property applies to, and whether its child elements will inherit its values. Well, look no further.

In This Appendix

The following tables include all of the CSS properties included in this book. However, to make it easier to scan for just those properties that will work, symbols indicate if a value is available for use (or not) by a particular browser:

- ■ **Available**—Supported in all versions of the browser in common usage.
- ◆ **Recently available**—Supported, but only in recent versions of the browser. Versions of the browser may still be in common use that do not support this value.
- ○ **Not available**—Not currently supported in any version of this browser.

Browsers legend

IE	Internet Explorer
FF	Firefox
S	Safari
C	Chrome
O	Opera

Table value legend

Applies to All—Property can be applied to any HTML tag.

Applies to Block—Property can be applied only to block-level tags.

Applies to Inline—Property can be applied only to inline tags.

Applies to list—Property can be applied only when the element is intrinsically a list element or has had the list display value applied to it.

Applies to positioned—Property can be applied only when the element has a positioning value specified.

Applies to table—Property can be applied only when the element is intrinsically a table element or has had the table display value applied to it.

Inherited—Yes—Styles are also applied to descendent elements.

Inherited—No—Styles are not applied to descendent elements.

Default Value:value—Values in bold are the default values for that property.

TABLE A.1 Basic Selectors

Type	Name	IE	FF	S	C	O
a	HTML	■	■	■	■	■
.class	Class	■	■	■	■	■
#id	ID	■	■	■	■	■
a b	Contextual	■	■	■	■	■
a * b	Universal	◆	■	■	■	■
a > b	Child	◆	■	■	■	■
a + b	Adjacent Sibling	◆	■	■	■	■
a ~ b	General Sibling	◆	■	■	■	■
[ATTR]	Attribute	◆	■	■	■	■

TABLE A.2 Pseudo-Classes

Name	IE	FF	S	C	O
:active	◆	■	■	■	■
:hover	■	■	■	■	■
:focus	◆	■	■	■	■
:link	■	■	■	■	■
:target	◆	■	■	■	■
:visited	■	■	■	■	■
:root	◆	■	■	■	■
:empty	◆	■	■	■	■
:only-child	◆	■	■	■	■
:only-of-type	◆	■	■	■	■
:first-child	◆	■	■	■	■
:nth-child(n)	◆	■	■	■	■
:nth-of-type(n)	◆	■	■	■	■
:nth-last-of-type(n)	◆	■	■	■	■
:last-child	◆	■	■	■	■
:first-of-type	◆	■	■	■	■
:last-of-type	◆	■	■	■	■
:lang()	◆	■	■	■	■
:not(s)	◆	■	■	■	■

TABLE A.3 Pseudo-Elements

Name	IE	FF	S	C	O
:first-letter, ::first-letter	■	■	■	■	■
:first-line, ::first-line	■	■	■	■	■
:after, ::after	◆	■	■	■	■
:before, ::before	◆	■	■	■	■

TABLE A.4 Font Properties

Name	Values	Applies To	Inherited	IE	FF	S	C	O
font	<font-style>	All	Yes	■	■	■	■	■
	<font-variant>			■	■	■	■	■
	<font-weight>			■	■	■	■	■
	<font-size>			■	■	■	■	■
	<font-height>			■	■	■	■	■
	<font-family>			■	■	■	■	■
	<visitor styles>			■	■	■	■	■
font-family	<family-name>	All	Yes	■	■	■	■	■
	serif			■	■	■	■	■
	sans-serif			■	■	■	■	■
	cursive			■	■	■	■	■
	fantasy			■	■	■	■	■
	monospace			■	■	■	■	■
font-size	<length>	All	Yes	■	■	■	■	■
	<percentage>			■	■	■	■	■
	smaller			■	■	■	■	■
	larger			■	■	■	■	■
	xx-small			■	■	■	■	■
	x-small			■	■	■	■	■
	small			■	■	■	■	■
	medium			■	■	■	■	■
	large			■	■	■	■	■
	x-large			■	■	■	■	■
	xx-large			■	■	■	■	■
font-size-adjust	**none**	All	No	○	■	○	○	○
	<number>			○	■	○	○	○
font-style	**normal**	All	Yes	■	■	■	■	■
	italic			■	■	■	■	■
	oblique			■	■	■	■	■
font-variant	**normal**	All	Yes	■	■	■	■	■
	small-caps			■	■	■	■	■
font-weight	**normal**	All	Yes	■	■	■	■	■
	bold			■	■	■	■	■
	lighter			■	■	■	■	■
	bolder			■	■	■	■	■
	100–900			■	■	■	■	■

TABLE A.5 Text Properties

Name	Values	Applies To	Inherited	IE	FF	S	C	O
letter-spacing	**normal**	All	Yes	■	■	■	■	■
	<length>			■	■	■	■	■
line-height	**normal**	Block	Yes	■	■	■	■	■
	<length>			■	■	■	■	■
	<percentage>			■	■	■	■	■
	<number>			■	■	■	■	■
text-align	**auto**	Block	Yes	■	■	■	■	■
	left			■	■	■	■	■
	right			■	■	■	■	■
	center			■	■	■	■	■
	justify			■	■	■	■	■
	inherit			■	■	■	■	■
text-decoration	**none**	All	Yes	■	■	■	■	■
	underline			■	■	■	■	■
	overline			■	■	■	■	■
	line-through			■	■	■	■	■
text-indent	**<length>**	Block	Yes	■	■	■	■	■
	<percentage>			■	■	■	■	■
text-shadow	**none**	All	Yes	◆	■	■	■	◆
	<color>			◆	■	■	■	◆
	<x-offset>			◆	■	■	■	◆
	<y-offset>			◆	■	■	■	◆
	<blur>			◆	■	■	■	◆
text-transform	**none**	All	Yes	■	■	■	■	■
	capitalize			■	■	■	■	■
	uppercase			■	■	■	■	■
	lowercase			■	■	■	■	■
vertical-align	**baseline**	Inline	No	■	■	■	■	■
	super			■	■	■	■	■
	sub			■	■	■	■	■
	<relative>			■	■	■	■	■
	<length>			■	■	■	■	■
	<percentage>			◆	■	■	■	■
white-space	**normal**	All	Yes	■	■	■	■	■
	pre			■	■	■	■	■
	nowrap			■	■	■	■	■
word-spacing	**normal**	All	Yes	■	■	■	■	■
	<length>			■	■	■	■	■

TABLE A.6 Color and Background Properties

Name	Values	Applies To	Inherited	IE	FF	S	C	O
background-attachment	**scroll**	Block	No	■	■	■	■	■
	fixed			■	■	■	■	■
	local			◆	○	■	■	◆
background-color	**inherit**	All	No	■	■	■	■	■
	<color>			■	■	■	■	■
background-image	**none**	All	No	■	■	■	■	■
	<url>			■	■	■	■	■
background-position	**top**	All	No	■	■	■	■	■
	left			■	■	■	■	■
	bottom			■	■	■	■	■
	right			■	■	■	■	■
	<length>			■	■	■	■	■
	<percentage>			■	■	■	■	■
background-repeat	**repeat**	All	No	■	■	■	■	■
	repeat-x			■	■	■	■	■
	repeat-y			■	■	■	■	■
	no-repeat			■	■	■	■	■
	space			◆	○	○	○	◆
	round			◆	○	○	○	◆
background-size *-moz-* *-webkit-* *-o-*	**auto**	All	No	◆	■	■	■	■
	<length>			◆	■	■	■	■
	<percentage>			◆	■	■	■	■
	cover			◆	■	■	◆	◆
	contain			◆	■	■	◆	◆
background-clip *-moz-* *-webkit-* *-o-*	**border-box**	All	No	◆	■	■	■	◆
	padding-box			◆	■	■	■	◆
	padding			◆	■	■	■	◆
	border			◆	■	■	■	◆
	content			◆	■	■	■	◆
background-origin *-moz-* *-webkit-*	**border-box**	All	No	◆	■	■	■	◆
	padding-box			◆	■	■	■	◆
	content-box			◆	■	■	■	◆
	padding			◆	■	■	■	◆
	border			◆	■	■	■	◆
	content			◆	■	■	■	◆
color	**inherit**	All	Yes	■	■	■	■	■
	<color>			■	■	■	■	■

TABLE A.7 List Properties

Name	Values	Applies To	Inherited	IE	FF	S	C	O
list-style	\<list-style-type\>	List	No	■	■	■	■	■
	\<list-style-position\>			■	■	■	■	■
	\<list-style-image\>			■	■	■	■	■
list-style-image	**none**	List	Yes	■	■	■	■	■
	inherit			■	■	■	■	■
	\<url\>			■	■	■	■	■
list-style-position	**inside**	List	Yes	■	■	■	■	■
	outside			■	■	■	■	■
	inherit			■	■	■	■	■
list-style-type	**none**	List	Yes	■	■	■	■	■
	inherit			■	■	■	■	■
	\<bullet-name\>			■	■	■	■	■

TABLE A.8 Table Properties

Name	Values	Applies To	Inherited	IE	FF	S	C	O
border-spacing	**\<length\>**	Table	Yes	■	■	■	■	■
	inherit			■	■	■	■	■
border-collapse	**separate**	Table	Yes	■	■	■	■	■
	collapse			■	■	■	■	■
	inherit			■	■	■	■	■
caption-side	**top**	Table	Yes	■	■	■	■	■
	bottom			■	■	■	■	■
	inherit			■	■	■	■	■
empty-cells	**show**	Table	Yes	■	■	■	■	■
	hide			■	■	■	■	■
	inherit			■	■	■	■	■
table-layout	**auto**	Table	No	■	■	■	■	■
	fixed			■	■	■	■	■
	inherit			■	■	■	■	■

TABLE A.9 User Interface and Generated Content Properties

Name	Values	Applies To	Inherited	IE	FF	S	C	O
content	**normal**	All	No	■	■	■	■	■
	none			■	■	■	■	■
	<string>			■	■	■	■	■
	<url>			■	■	■	■	■
	<counter>			■	■	■	■	■
	attr(<selector>)			■	■	■	■	■
	open-quote			■	■	■	■	■
	close-quote			■	■	■	■	■
	no-open-quote			■	■	■	■	■
	no-close-quote			■	■	■	■	■
	inherit			■	■	■	■	■
counter-increment	**none**	All	No	■	■	■	■	■
	<counter-name>			■	■	■	■	■
	<num>			■	■	■	■	■
	inherit			■	■	■	■	■
counter-reset	**none**	All	No	■	■	■	■	■
	<counter-name>			■	■	■	■	■
	<num>			■	■	■	■	■
	inherit			■	■	■	■	■
cursor	**auto**	All	Yes	■	■	■	■	■
	<url>			■	■	■	■	■
	<cursor-type-name>			■	■	■	■	■
	none			■	■	■	■	■
quotes	none	All	Yes	■	■	■	■	■
	<string>			■	■	■	■	■
	inherit			■	■	■	■	■

TABLE A.10 Box Properties

Name	Values	Applies To	Inherited	IE	FF	S	C	O
border	<border-width>	All	No	■	■	■	■	■
	<border-style>			■	■	■	■	■
	<border-color>			■	■	■	■	■
border-color	**transparent**	All	No	■	■	■	■	■
	<color>			■	■	■	■	■
	inherit			■	■	■	■	■
border-image *-moz- -webkit-*	**none**	All	No	○	■	■	■	■
	<url>			○	■	■	■	■
	<offsetnumber>			○	■	■	■	■
	round			○	■	■	■	■
	repeat			○	■	■	■	■
	stretch			○	■	■	■	■
border-radius	<length>	All	No	◆	■	■	■	■
	<percentage>			◆	■	■	■	■
border-style	**none**	All	No	■	■	■	■	■
	dotted			■	■	■	■	■
	dashed			■	■	■	■	■
	solid			■	■	■	■	■
	double			■	■	■	■	■
	groove			■	■	■	■	■
	ridge			■	■	■	■	■
	inset			■	■	■	■	■
	outset			■	■	■	■	■
	inherit			■	■	■	■	■
border-width	**<length>**	All	No	■	■	■	■	■
	thin			■	■	■	■	■
	medium			■	■	■	■	■
	thick			■	■	■	■	■
	inherit			■	■	■	■	■
clear	**none**	All	No	■	■	■	■	■
	left			■	■	■	■	■
	right			■	■	■	■	■
	both			■	■	■	■	■
	none			■	■	■	■	■

table continues on next page

TABLE A.10 **Box Properties** *continued*

Name	Values	Applies To	Inherited	IE	FF	S	C	O
display	**normal**	All	No	■	■	■	■	■
	block			■	■	■	■	■
	inline			■	■	■	■	■
	inline-block			■	■	■	■	■
	run-in			◆	■	■	■	■
	table			◆	■	■	■	■
	table-cell			◆	■	■	■	■
	table-footer-group			◆	■	■	■	■
	table-header-group			◆	■	■	■	■
	table-row			◆	■	■	■	■
	table-row-group			◆	■	■	■	■
	inline-table			◆	■	■	■	■
	none			■	■	■	■	■
	inherit			■	■	■	■	■
float	**none**	All	No	■	■	■	■	■
	left			■	■	■	■	■
	right			■	■	■	■	■
height	**auto**	Block	No	■	■	■	■	■
	<length>			■	■	■	■	■
	<percentage>			■	■	■	■	■
	inherit			■	■	■	■	■
margin	**<length>**	All	No	■	■	■	■	■
	auto			■	■	■	■	■
	<percentage>			■	■	■	■	■
max/min-height	**none**	Block	No	◆	■	■	■	■
	<length>			◆	■	■	■	■
	<percentage>			◆	■	■	■	■
	inherit			◆	■	■	■	■
max/min-width	**none**	Block	No	◆	■	■	■	■
	<length>			◆	■	■	■	■
	<percentage>			◆	■	■	■	■
	inherit			◆	■	■	■	■
outline	**<outline-width>**	All	No	◆	■	■	■	■
	<outline-style>			◆	■	■	■	■
	<outline-color>			◆	■	■	■	■

table continues on next page

Name	Values	Applies To	Inherited	IE	FF	S	C	O
outline-color	**transparent**	All	No	◆	■	■	■	■
	<color>			◆	■	■	■	■
	inherit			◆	■	■	■	■
outline-offset	**<length>**	All	No	○	■	■	■	■
	inherit			○	■	■	■	■
outline-style	**none**	All	No	◆	■	■	■	■
	dotted			◆	■	■	■	■
	dashed			◆	■	■	■	■
	solid			◆	■	■	■	■
	double			◆	■	■	■	■
	groove			◆	■	■	■	■
	ridge			◆	■	■	■	■
	inset			◆	■	■	■	■
	outset			◆	■	■	■	■
	inherit			◆	■	■	■	■
outline-width	**<length>**	All	No	◆	■	■	■	■
	thin			◆	■	■	■	■
	medium			◆	■	■	■	■
	thick			◆	■	■	■	■
	inherit			◆	■	■	■	■
overflow	**visible**	Block	No	■	■	■	■	■
	hidden			■	■	■	■	■
	scroll			■	■	■	■	■
	auto			■	■	■	■	■
overflow-x/y	**visible**	Block	No	■	■	■	■	■
	hidden			■	■	■	■	■
	scroll			■	■	■	■	■
	auto			■	■	■	■	■
padding	**<length>**	All	No	■	■	■	■	■
	<percentage>			■	■	■	■	■
width	**auto**	Block	No	■	■	■	■	■
	<length>			■	■	■	■	■
	<percentage>			■	■	■	■	■
	inherit			■	■	■	■	■

TABLE A.11 Visual Formatting Properties

Name	Values	Applies To	Inherited	IE	FF	S	C	O
bottom	auto	All	No	■	■	■	■	■
	<percentage>			■	■	■	■	■
	<length>			■	■	■	■	■
	inherit			◆	■	■	■	■
box-shadow *-moz- -webkit-*	none	All	No	◆	■	■	■	■
	inset			◆	■	■	■	■
	<x-offset>			◆	■	■	■	■
	<y-offset>			◆	■	■	■	■
	<blur>			◆	■	■	■	■
	<spread>			◆	■	■	■	■
	<color>			◆	■	■	■	■
clip	auto	Positioned	No	■	■	■	■	■
	rect(<top> <right> <bottom> <left>)			■	■	■	■	■
	inherit			■	■	■	■	■
left	auto	Positioned	No	■	■	■	■	■
	<percentage>			■	■	■	■	■
	<length>			■	■	■	■	■
	inherit			◆	■	■	■	■
opacity	<alphavalue>	All	No	◆	■	■	■	■
	inherit			◆	■	■	■	■
position	static	Positioned	No	■	■	■	■	■
	relative			■	■	■	■	■
	absolute			■	■	■	■	■
	fixed			◆	■	■	■	■
	inherit			◆	■	■	■	■
right	auto	Positioned	No	■	■	■	■	■
	<percentage>			■	■	■	■	■
	<length>			■	■	■	■	■
	inherit			◆	■	■	■	■
top	auto	Positioned	No	■	■	■	■	■
	<percentage>			■	■	■	■	■
	<length>			■	■	■	■	■
	inherit			◆	■	■	■	■
visibility	visible	Positioned	Yes	■	■	■	■	■
	hidden			■	■	■	■	■
	collapse			◆	■	■	■	■
z-index	auto	Positioned	No	■	■	■	■	■
	<num>			■	■	■	■	■
	inherit			■	■	■	■	■

TABLE A.12 Transform Properties

Name	Values	Applies To	Inherited	IE	FF	S	C	O
backface-visibility	**visible**	All	No	◆	◆	◆	■	○
-moz-	hidden			◆	◆	◆	■	○
-webkit-								
-o-								
-ms-								
perspective	**none**	All	No	◆	◆	◆	■	○
-moz-	<num>			◆	◆	◆	■	○
-webkit-								
-o-								
-ms-								
perspective-origin	<percentage>	All	No	◆	◆	◆	■	○
-moz-	<length>			◆	◆	◆	■	○
-webkit-	<keyword>			◆	◆	◆	■	○
-o-								
-ms-								
transform	matrix(<angle>)	All	No	◆	◆	◆	◆	◆
-moz-	matrix3d(<variations×16>,)			◆	◆	◆	◆	○
-webkit-	perspective(<num>)			◆	◆	◆	◆	○
-o-	rotate(<angle>)			◆	◆	◆	◆	◆
-ms-	rotateX(<angle>)			◆	◆	◆	◆	◆
	rotateY(<angle>)			◆	◆	◆	◆	◆
	rotateZ(<angle>)			◆	◆	◆	◆	○
	rotate3d(<num×3>,)			◆	◆	◆	◆	○
	scale(<num×2>,)			◆	◆	◆	◆	◆
	scaleX(<num>)			◆	◆	◆	◆	◆
	scaleY(<num>)			◆	◆	◆	◆	◆
	scaleZ(<length>)			◆	◆	◆	◆	○
	scale3d(num×3>,)			◆	◆	◆	◆	○
	skew(<angle×2>,)			◆	◆	◆	◆	◆
	skewX(<angle>)			◆	◆	◆	◆	◆
	skewY(<angle>)			◆	◆	◆	◆	◆
	translate(<length×2>,)			◆	◆	◆	◆	◆
	translateX(<angle>)			◆	◆	◆	◆	◆
	translateY(<angle>)			◆	◆	◆	◆	◆
	translateZ(<angle>)			◆	◆	◆	◆	○
	translate3d(<num×3>,)			◆	◆	◆	◆	○
transform-origin	<percentage>	All	No	◆	◆	◆	◆	◆
-moz-	<length>			◆	◆	◆	◆	◆
-webkit-	<keyword>			◆	◆	◆	◆	◆
-o-								
-ms-								
transform-style	**flat**	All	No	◆	◆	◆	◆	◆
-moz-, -webkit-, -o-, -ms-	preserve-3d			◆	◆	◆	◆	◆

TABLE A.13 Transition Properties

Name	Values	Applies To	Inherited	IE	FF	S	C	O
transition	<transition-property>	All	No	◆	◆	◆	◆	◆
-moz- *-webkit-* *-o-*	<transition-duration>			◆	◆	◆	◆	◆
	<transition-delay>			◆	◆	◆	◆	◆
transition-delay	**<time>**	All	No	◆	◆	◆	◆	◆
-moz- *-webkit-* *-o-*								
transition-duration	**<time>**	All	No	◆	◆	◆	◆	◆
-moz- *-webkit-* *-o-*								
transition-property	**none**	All	No	◆	◆	◆	◆	◆
-moz- *-webkit-* *-o-*	<CSSProperty>			◆	◆	◆	◆	◆
	all			◆	◆	◆	◆	◆
transition-timing-function	**linear**	All	No	◆	◆	◆	◆	◆
-moz- *-webkit-* *-o-*	ease			◆	◆	◆	◆	◆
	ease-in			◆	◆	◆	◆	◆
	ease-out			◆	◆	◆	◆	◆
	ease-in-out			◆	◆	◆	◆	◆
	cubic-bezier(<number×4>,)			◆	◆	◆	◆	◆

HTML and UTF Character Encoding

In Chapter 5, you used special HTML- and UTF-encoded characters. These are generally harder to find on your keyboard or may not be included in a particular font you are using. To ensure that they are properly represented, you should use the code presented in this appendix when adding the characters to your Web document.

TABLE A.1 HTML and UTF Character Encoding

HTML	Unicode	Glyph	Description
‘		'	left single quote
’		'	right single quote
‚		,	single low-9 quote
“		"	left double quote
”		"	right double quote
„		„	double low-9 quote
†		†	dagger
‡		‡	double dagger
‰		‰	per mill sign
‹		‹	single left-pointing angle quote
›		›	single right-pointing angle quote
♠		♠	black spade suit
♣		♣	black club suit
♥		♥	black heart suit
♦		♦	black diamond suit
‾		–	overline
←		←	left arrow
↑		↑	up arrow
→		→	right arrow
↓		↓	down arrow
™		™	trademark sign
				horizontal tab

	
		line feed

	 		space
	!	!	exclamation mark
"	"	"	double quotation mark
	#	#	number sign
	$	$	dollar sign
	%	%	percent sign
&	&	&	ampersand
	'	'	apostrophe
	(	(	left parenthesis
	)	)	right parenthesis

table continues on next page

TABLE A.1 HTML and UTF Character Encoding *continued*

HTML	Unicode	Glyph	Description
	&#42;	*	asterisk
	&#43;	+	plus sign
	&#44;	,	comma
	&#45;	-	hyphen
	&#46;	.	period
&frasl;	&#47;	/	slash
	0– 9	0–9	digits 0–9
	&#58;	:	colon
	&#59;	;	semicolon
&lt;	&#60;	<	less-than sign
	&#61;	=	equals sign
&gt;	&#62;	>	greater-than sign
	&#63;	?	question mark
	&#64;	@	at sign
	A– Z	A–Z	uppercase letters A–Z
	&#91;	[	left bracket
	&#92;	\	backslash
	&#93;	]	right bracket
	&#94;	^	caret
	&#95;	_	underscore
	&#96;	`	grave accent
	&#97 – z	a–z	lowercase letters a–z
	&#123;	{	left curly bracket
	|			vertical bar
	&#125;	}	right curly bracket
	&#126;	~	tilde
&ndash;	&#150;	–	en dash
&mdash;	&#151;	—	em dash
			nonbreaking space
&iexcl;	&#161;	¡	inverted exclamation
&cent;	&#162;	¢	cent sign
&pound;	&#163;	£	pound sterling
&curren;	&#164;	¤	general currency sign

table continues on next page

HTML	Unicode	Glyph	Description
¥	¥	¥	yen sign
&brkbar;	¦	¦	broken vertical bar
§	§	§	section sign
¨	¨	¨	umlaut
©	©	©	copyright
ª	ª	ª	feminine ordinal
«	«	«	left angle quote
¬	¬	¬	not sign
­	­		soft hyphen
®	®	®	registered trademark
¯	¯	¯	macron accent
°	°	°	degree sign
±	±	±	plus or minus
²	²	²	superscript two
³	³	³	superscript three
´	´	´	acute accent
µ	µ	µ	micro sign
¶	¶	¶	paragraph sign
·	·	·	middle dot
¸	¸	¸	cedilla
¹	¹	¹	superscript one
º	º	º	masculine ordinal
»	»	»	right angle quote
¼	¼	¼	one-fourth
½	½	½	one-half
¾	¾	¾	three-fourths
¿	¿	¿	inverted question mark
À	À	À	uppercase A, grave accent
Á	Á	Á	uppercase A, acute accent
Â	Â	Â	uppercase A, circumflex accent
Ã	Ã	Ã	uppercase A, tilde
Ä	Ä	Ä	uppercase A, umlaut
Å	Å	Å	uppercase A, ring

table continues on next page

HTML	Unicode	Glyph	Description
Æ	Æ	Æ	uppercase AE
Ç	Ç	Ç	uppercase C, cedilla
È	È	È	uppercase E, grave accent
É	É	É	uppercase E, acute accent
Ê	Ê	Ê	uppercase E, circumflex accent
Ë	Ë	Ë	uppercase E, umlaut
Ì	Ì	Ì	uppercase I, grave accent
Í	Í	Í	uppercase I, acute accent
Î	Î	Î	uppercase I, circumflex accent
Ï	Ï	Ï	uppercase I, umlaut
Ð	Ð	Ð	uppercase Eth, Icelandic
Ñ	Ñ	Ñ	uppercase N, tilde
Ò	Ò	Ò	uppercase O, grave accent
Ó	Ó	Ó	uppercase O, acute accent
Ô	Ô	Ô	uppercase O, circumflex accent
Õ	Õ	Õ	uppercase O, tilde
Ö	Ö	Ö	uppercase O, umlaut
×	×	×	multiplication sign
Ø	Ø	Ø	uppercase O, slash
Ù	Ù	Ù	uppercase U, grave accent
Ú	Ú	Ú	uppercase U, acute accent
Û	Û	Û	uppercase U, circumflex accent
Ü	Ü	Ü	uppercase U, umlaut
Ý	Ý	Ý	uppercase Y, acute accent
Þ	Þ	Þ	uppercase THORN, Icelandic
ß	ß	ß	lowercase sharps, German
à	à	à	lowercase a, grave accent
á	á	á	lowercase a, acute accent
â	â	â	lowercase a, circumflex accent
ã	ã	ã	lowercase a, tilde
ä	ä	ä	lowercase a, umlaut
å	å	å	lowercase a, ring
æ	æ	æ	lowercase ae

table continues on next page

TABLE A.1 **HTML and UTF Character Encoding** *continued*

HTML	Unicode	Glyph	Description
ç	ç	ç	lowercase c, cedilla
è	è	è	lowercase e, grave accent
é	é	é	lowercase e, acute accent
ê	ê	ê	lowercase e, circumflex accent
ë	ë	ë	lowercase e, umlaut
ì	ì	ì	lowercase i, grave accent
í	í	í	lowercase i, acute accent
î	î	î	lowercase i, circumflex accent
ï	ï	ï	lowercase i, umlaut
ð	ð	ð	lowercase eth, Icelandic
ñ	ñ	ñ	lowercase n, tilde
ò	ò	ò	lowercase o, grave accent
ó	ó	ó	lowercase o, acute accent
ô	ô	ô	lowercase o, circumflex accent
õ	õ	õ	lowercase o, tilde
ö	ö	ö	lowercase o, umlaut
÷	÷	÷	division sign
ø	ø	ø	lowercase o, slash
ù	ù	ù	lowercase u, grave accent
ú	ú	ú	lowercase u, acute accent
û	û	û	lowercase u, circumflex accent
ü	ü	ü	lowercase u, umlaut
ý	ý	ý	lowercase y, acute accent
þ	þ	þ	lowercase thorn, Icelandic
ÿ	ÿ	ÿ	lowercase y, umlaut

Index

brightness, using color wheel to choose, 198
browser extensions, CSS3, 12–13
browsers
    default margin issues, 267
    default styles, 20, 358–362
    defining style sheets, 118
    displaying documents, 286
    evolution of CSS, 6–7
    how CSS works, 4–5
    inherited styles, 20
    mouse pointer appearance and, 238
    responsive design for multiple. *See* responsive
        Web design
    symbols indicating values available for use by.
        See quick reference
    teaching to count, 242–243
    using HTML5, 29
    Web font formats for, 134–135
    Web font support, 134
    z-index order determined by, 295
bullets, 223–227

C

cache, font file, 139
Canvas element, new in HTML5, 27
capitalize value, **text-transform**, 164–165
caption keyword, mimicking visitor's font
    style, 152
caption-side property, tables, 233–234
cascade order
    !important declaration and, 117–118
    best practices, 403
    determining, 119–121
    grouped selectors and, 66
    troubleshooting CSS code, 386
    typeface overrides and, 132
case, setting text, 164–165
characters
    encoding HTML, 129
    encoding HTML and UTL, 423–428
    specifying character set, 126
child elements
    box model, 250
    of element's box, 250
    family tree, 70
    floating elements in window, 263
    in nested tags, 250
    pseudo-classes for styling, 90–91
    setting position of, 293
child selectors, 76–77, 346
choke, setting shadows, 302
Chrome, 393
circle shape value, radial gradients, 193
class selectors
    CSS rules, 9
    defining, 53–56
    elements styled by, 36
    troubleshooting CSS code, 386

classes
    defining reusable, 53–56
    generic names for, 401
    mixing and matching, 402
    setting up float, 264
clear property, 264
clearfix class, 335
clip property
    setting background images, 205–206, 210
    text-overflow, 261
    visibility area, 298–299
clipping, defined, 288
colon (:), CSS declarations, 39
color
    best practices, 404–405
    emotional associations of color, 196
    gradients. *See* gradients, color
    links, 86–87
    new in CSS3, 14
    for readable style sheets, 378–379
    shadows, 302
    text drop shadows, 166–167
    transitioning CSS properties, 320–324
color palette, 196, 200
color properties
    accessibility for visually impaired, 201
    choosing color palette, 196–201
    choosing color values, 185–190
    creating color gradients, 191–195
    getting started, 184
    other ways to add color, 190
    overview of, 183
    putting it all together, 217–218
    quick reference, 414
color property, 106, 202
Color Scheme Designer tool, 200
color stop, 192, 194
color values
    alpha values for transparency, 190
    backgrounds, 204
    borders, 270–271
    for color keywords, 185–187
    color wheel, 198
    HSL, 189
    multiple background images, 213
    overview of, 185
    RGB, 188–189
    shadows, 303
    text, 202
color wheel
    basics, 198–200
    online tool for advanced, 200
color-index property, media queries, 106
Colour Contrast Check tool, 203
ColRD: Palette Creator tool, 200
column-count property, 278
column-gap property, 279
column-rule property, 279
columns. *See* multicolumn layouts

combinatory selectors, 71
comments
    adding to CSS, 67–68
    best practices, 406
    grouping selectors with, 64–66
    section headers as, 378–379
    setting up conditional styles for IE, 364–365
compact property, 254
complementary color-combination scheme, 199
compound color-combination scheme, 199
compression, CSS code, 396–398
condensed fonts, 150
conditional styles, Internet Explorer
    fixing box model for older versions, 338
    overview of, 363–365
    responsive Web design, 353, 370–373
content. *See also* generated content properties
    adding using CSS, 240–241
    background color, 196–197
    controlling overflow, 259–260
    defining background image, 208, 211
    of element's box, 250
    new features in CSS3, 15
    progressive enhancement and, 355
    setting how box sizes, 258
    styling for print, 114
content property, 240, 242–243, 250–251
content-box value, **box-sizing**, 258
contextual selectors, 70
contextual styles
    descendants, 71–75
    only children, 76–77
    overview of, 71
    siblings, 78–81
converting licensed fonts, 140
copy, color(s) for, 197
counter lists, multiple, 242–243
couplet values, RGB hex, 188
CSS (Cascading Style Sheets), overview
    browser extensions, 12–13
    defined, 1
    evolution of, 6–7
    HTML and, 8
    libraries and frameworks, 376
    rule parts, 11
    styles, 2
    types of rules, 9–10
    understanding, 3–5
    what's new in CSS3, 14–15
    word processor styles vs., 3
CSS basics
    basic selectors, 36
    comments, 67–68
    embedded styles, 40–42
    external styles, 43–49
    grouping, 64–66
    HTML tags, 50–52
    inline styles, 37–39
    overview of, 35

reusable classes, 53–56
unique IDs, 57–60
universal styles, 61–63
CSS resets
    Eric Meyer's, 362
    overriding browser default styles with, 358–359
    with universal selectors, 63
    using universal selector for simple, 360
    what you should reset, 359
    Yahoo's Reset CSS, 361
CSS sprites
    adding CSS image rollovers to Web page, 342–344
    best practices using RGB for, 405
    creating using background images, 211
    origin of, 344
    overview of, 342
CSS Validator, 395
CSS1 (CSS Level 1), 7
CSS2 (CSS Level 2), 7
CSS2.1 (CSS Level 2.1), 118
CSS3 (CSS Level 3), 7, 14–15, 29
CSS3 Gradient Generator, 195
CSS4 (CSS Level 4), working draft, 15
CUR images, 239
curly brackets { }, CSS rules
    class selectors, 53
    embedded styles, 41
    external CSS file, 45
    HTML tags, 50–52
    troubleshooting CSS code, 386
currentcolor keyword, 188, 204
cursive fonts, 128
cursors, mouse pointer appearance, 238–239

D

debugging CSS, 118
decimal values, color, 185–187, 189
decimals, setting bullet style, 223
declarations
    colons in, 39
    CSS rules and, 11
    grouped selectors receiving same, 64–66
    HTML tags and, 38–39, 52
    making **!important**, 117–118
    quotation marks in, 39
    reusable classes and, 54
    troubleshooting CSS code, 386, 389
    unique IDs and, 58
    universal styles and, 61
    viewing CSS, 392, 394
default styles, browser, 20, 358–362
DeGraeve's Color Palette Generator tool, 200
<del> tag, text strikethrough vs., 180
dependent class selector, 36, 54
dependent ID selector, 36, 60
descendants, 70–71, 115–116

design and interface techniques
creating CSS drop-down menu, 345–346
creating multicolumn layouts with `float`,
330–333
fixing box model for older versions of IE,
337–338
fixing `float` problem, 334–336
getting started, 328–330
putting it all together, 347–348
styling links vs. navigation, 339–341
using CSS sprites, 342–344
dingbats, 129
display area, browser, 287
`display` property, 252–254, 297
`<div>` tag, 27, 56, 332
Divide and Conquer method, style sheet
strategy, 383
doctype (<!DOCTYPE>)
browser modes set by, 363
HTML document structure, 19, 30–31, 399
for markup languages, 29
reasons to include, 32–33
document type definition (DTD), 337–338
documents
basic HTML, 30–31
browser windows displaying, 286
editing in HTML5, 27
parts of, 286–287
structure of HTML, 20
double quotation marks ("..."), declaration lists, 39
drag-and-drop, 27
drop shadows, 166–168, 302–303
drop-down menus, CSS, 345–346
DTD (document type definition), 337–338
Dynamic method, style sheet strategy, 385
dynamic pseudo-classes, 82–83, 88–89,
320–324
dynamic styles, 402

E

editing declarations, 392, 394
element edge, 287
element family tree, 70
elements, HTML
applying CSS properties to specific, 23
block-level, 22
controlling overflow, 259–261
displaying, 252–254
floating in window, 262–264
including default styles for, 401
inspecting, 392–394
not setting style for particular, 94–95
setting border, 269–270
setting margins of, 265–267
setting outline, 268
setting padding, 276–277
setting positions, 290–291
setting width and height, 255–258, 287
types of, 21–23

understanding box of, 250–251
visual formatting properties. *See* visual
formatting properties
`ellipsis`, `text-overflow` property, 261
elliptical corners, borders, 273
elliptical shape value, radial gradients, 193
`<em>` tag, 20, 72–81, 144–145, 160, 174
Emastic CSS framework, 376
Embedded OpenType (EOT) Web font format,
134–135, 137–138, 140
embedded style sheets
adding, 40–42
making declaration `!important`, 117–118
not placing in final code, 42
using @media rule to specify styles, 112
emboss text, text shadows, 168
emotional associations, color, 196
`empty-cells` property, 232
encoding
HTML and UTL character, 423–428
HTML character entities, 129
End User License Agreements (EULA), Web fonts,
140
EOT (Embedded OpenType) Web font format,
134–135, 137–138, 140
EULA (End User License Agreements), Web fonts,
140
evolution, of CSS, 6–7
expanded fonts, 150
extensions, CSS browser
creating color gradients, 191
defined, 12
importance of coding with, 326
external CSS files
adding styles to Web sites, 43–49
defining CSS rules in, 52, 57
external style sheets
best practices, 400
making declaration `!important`, 117–118
placing all styles in, 381
progressive enhancement and, 355
using @media rule to specify styles, 112

F

fantasy fonts, 128
`<figcaption>` tag, HTML5, 28
`<figure>` tag, HTML5, 28
fire effect text, text shadows, 168
Firebug, 390–392, 394
`:first-child` pseudo-class, 90–91
`:first-letter` pseudo-element, 96–99
`:first-line` pseudo-element, 96–99
`:first-of-type` pseudo-class, 90–91
fixed design, multicolumn layout, 332–333
fixed method, `table-layout`, 228
fixed positioning, 290–291
Flash, 20
`float` property, 262–264, 330–336
`:focus` pseudo-class, 88–89

Intuit CSS framework, 376
iPhone, 107–110
ISO 8859-1 character set, 126
italicized text, 147–148, 340

J

JavaScript, 8, 32–33
justified text, 173

K

kerning, 160, 181
keywords
    color, 185–187
    linear gradients, 191
    overflowing content, 260
    radial gradients, 193
    shadow, 302–303
    transformation origin, 315

L

`:lang()` pseudo-class, 92–93
language, styling for specific, 92–93
large.css, 368–369
`:last-child` pseudo-class, 90–91
`:last-of-type` pseudo-class, 90–91
layouts
    multicolumn, 278–279, 330–333
    Web design. *See* responsive Web design
leading, adjusting, 162–163
`left` keyword, 263–264
legal issues, Web fonts, 140
legibility, and font size, 144
length value
    adjusting leading, 162–163
    background images, 208–209
    borders, 270, 272
    clipping visibility area, 299
    defined, 311
    element width or height, 256
    indenting paragraphs, 176
    letter spacing, 159
    margins, 266
    multicolumn text layout, 278
    multiple background images, 215
    padding, 276
    positioned elements, 292
    shadows, 302–303
    spacing table cells, 229
    text drop shadows, 166
    transformations, 311
    transitions, 320–324
    word spacing, 161
letterforms. *See* fonts
letterpress text, text shadows, 168
letters
    adjusting space between, 159–160
    bullet style for, 223
`letter-spacing` property, 159–160

libraries and frameworks, CSS, 376
licensed fonts, 140–143
lightness, HSL values, 189–190, 198
line height, CSS resets for, 359
linear gradients, 191–192, 195
`line-height` property, 153, 162–163
line-through, text, 179
link pseudo-classes
    adding transitions between states, 320–324
    importance of order, 89
    overview of, 82–83
    styling links, 84–87
link states
    add CSS image rollovers to Web page, 344
    contrasting link appearances, 86
    styling all, 406
`<link>` tag
    best practices, 381, 400
    conditional styles for IE, 364
    connecting external CSS and HTML files, 43, 45
    favoring over @import, 406
    linking to style sheets with, 46–47
    media queries, 108–111
    specifying styles with @media rule, 112
    WFSBs using, 142
links
    color for, 197
    contrasting appearances for, 84–87
    to external CSS file, 43, 46–47
    minimizing, 47
    navigation vs. styling, 406
    states, 82
    to style sheet, 46
    styling, 84–87
    styling documents in <head>, 400
    styling navigation, 339–341
    text shadows for, 167
    troubleshooting CSS code, 386
list properties
    bullets, 223–225
    getting started, 220–222
    multiple list styles, 226–227
    quick reference, 415
`list-item` value, `display`, 253
lists
    background color for, 197
    sequentially numbered, 242–243
`list-style` shorthand property, 226–227
`list-style-image` property, 224, 226
`list-style-position` property, 225, 227
`list-style-type` property, 223, 227
Little Trouble Girl font, 139
local versions, Web font service bureau, 143
logical operators, conditional styles for IE, 364
LoVe HAte mnemonic, pseudo-element order, 89
lowercase text, 164

S

Safari, 393
sans-serif fonts, 127
saturation, HSL values, 189–190, 198
Scalable Vector Graphics (SVG) Web fonts, 20,
    135, 139
scale(), **scaleX()**, or **scale(Y)** value, 2D
    transforms, 314–315
scale3d() value, 3D transforms, 319
scaleZ() value, 3D transforms, 319
scientific notation, 175
scroll, 205, 208, 215
scroll keyword, **overflow**, 260
search engines, **content** property and, 241
section headers, readable style sheets, 378–379
<section> tag, 28–29, 336
selective styling
    !important declaration, 117–118
    @media rule, 112–113
    based on context. *See* contextual styles
    based on tag attributes, 100–103
    cascade order, 119–121
    element family tree, 70
    inheritance of styles, 115–116
    media queries, 104–111
    overview of, 69
    for print, 114
    with pseudo-classes. *See* pseudo-classes
    with pseudo-elements, 96–99
selectors
    attribute, 100
    basic CSS, 36
    combinatory, 71
    grouping, 64–66
    HTML. *See* HTML selectors
    organizing style sheets by types of, 378
    pseudo-class, 83
    pseudo-element, 96
    quick reference to, 410
    styling elements to exclude certain, 94–95
    troubleshooting CSS code, 386
semicolons (;)
    character entities beginning with, 129
    defining styles directly in HTML tag, 38
    locating in **!important** declaration, 118
    separating multiple declarations, 11
    troubleshooting CSS code, 386
separate value, **border-collapse**, 230–231
serif fonts, 127
SGML (Standard Generalized Markup
    Language), 19
shadows
    adding text drop, 166–170
    setting element's, 302–303
shape value, radial gradients, 193
shorthand properties
    !important, 404
    background, 212–216

    best practice to use, 404
    font, 152–154, 163
    list-style, 226–227
    matrix(), 314
    matrix3d(), 319
    overriding value set by, 154
    transition, 322–324
sibling selector, 78–79
siblings, family tree, 70
single quotation marks ('...'), 39
size, file
    best practices, 381
    drawbacks of single master style sheet, 382
    reducing, 381
    setting font-stack and, 132
size property, background images,
    205–206, 209
size values, radial gradients, 193
skew(), **skewX()**, or **skew(Y)** value, 2D
    transforms, 314
slash (/), comments, 67
small-caps, 151
small-caption: keyword, 152
small.css, 366–367, 370–372
smart quotes, 39
spacing
    horizontal text alignment, 171–173
    between table cells, 229
<span> tag, 56
specificity
    best practices, 402–403, 406
    cascade order determined by, 121
    hierarchy of CSS rules, 380
stacking order, 288, 294–295
Standard Generalized Markup Language
    (SGML), 19
states
    adding transitions between element, 320–324
    link, 82, 84
    styling navigation and link, 339–341
    using CSS sprites, 342–344
static positioning, 288, 290–291
status-bar: keyword, 152
stretched images, borders, 275
strict mode, browsers, 363
strikethrough, text, 180
<strong> tag
    aligning text vertically, 174
    defining font size, 145
    as nested tag, 70
    redefining in CSS, 8, 50–52
    styling descendants, 72–75
    styling siblings, 78–81
structural elements
    CSS rules, 11
    new features in HTML5, 27–28
    placing before designing, 399
    using, 29
structural pseudo-classes, 82–83

transition properties
    3D transformations, 316–319
    adding transitions between element states, 320–324
    getting started, 308–310
    new features in CSS3, 14
    overview of, 307
    putting it all together, 325–326
    quick reference, 422
transition property, 322–324
transition-delay values, 323–324
transition-duration values, 323–324
transition-property value, 323–324
transition-timing-function values, 323–324
translate(), **translateX()**, or **translate(Y)** value, 2D transforms, 314
translate3d() value, 3D transforms, 319
translateZ() value, 3D transforms, 319
transparency
    creating border with, 304
    setting alpha values for color, 190
    styling for print by avoiding color, 114
transparent keyword, 204, 213
triad color-combination scheme, 199
troubleshooting CSS code, 386–389
TrueType (TTF) Web font, 134, 138, 140
TTF (TrueType) Web font, 134, 138, 140
type families. *See* font families
typeface overrides, 132
typography
    affecting how text appears, 157
    understanding on Web, 125
    using Web fonts for. *See* Web fonts

U

undecorating text, 179–180
underlines
    differentiating hypertext from text, 340
    text decorations, 179–180
    using **border-bottom** for text, 359
understudy fonts, 131, 133, 146
universal selector
    adding default transitions to, 324
    CSS resets using, 360, 362
    CSS rules, 10
    defining universal styles, 61–63
    elements styled by, 36
    styling descendants universally, 74–75
unvisited links, setting appearance, 86–87
uppercase, setting text case, 164–165
URL
    adding multiple background images, 214
    changing mouse pointer appearance, 239
    defining background image, 206
    defining own graphic bullets, 224
    setting border image, 275

user interface
    designing. *See* design and interface techniques
    inline styles, 39
user interface properties
    getting started, 236–237
    mouse pointer appearance, 238–239
    overview of, 235
    putting it all together, 246
    quick reference, 416
UTF-8 (8-bit Unicode Transformation Format) character set, 126, 423–428

V

validation, CSS code, 395
values
    2D transform, 311, 313–315
    3D transform, 318–319
    clip, 298–299
    color, 185–190
    content, 241
    CSS browser extensions working with, 13
    cursor, 238–239
    defining styles based on tag attributes, 100–103
    defining styles in HTML tag, 38
    display type, 252–254
    font-stretch, 150
    grouped selector changing, 66
    indenting paragraphs, 176
    letter-spacing, 159–160
    linear gradient, 191
    line-height, 162–163
    media type, 104
    multiple font, 152–154
    placing at top of CSS code in comments, 67–68
    position, 292–293
    radial gradient, 192
    specifying units for, 399
    structural elements of CSS rules, 11
    text decorations, 179–180
    text transform, 164–165
    transformations, 311, 316
    transitions, 323–324
    troubleshooting CSS code, 386
    vertical text alignment, 174–175
    word-spacing, 161
vertical alignment
    centering numbers in blocks, 336
    CSS resets for text, 359
    text, 174–175
vertical-align property, 174–175
viewport
    browser, 286
    responsive design with media queries, 370–372